VICTORIAN LITERATURE

Modern Essays in Criticism

Edited by AUSTIN WRIGHT

Carnegie Institute of Technology

A GALAXY BOOK

New York   OXFORD UNIVERSITY PRESS   1961

© 1961 by Oxford University Press, Inc.

Library of Congress Catalogue Card Number: 61-5078

Fourth printing, 1965

Printed in the United States of America

PREFACE

IN the last thirty years or so, English literature of the Victorian period has received increasingly widespread and respectful study. The Victorian age, extremely long and extremely complex, marked by the writings of some of the major figures in English literature and by an unprecedented flood of printed matter of all sorts, is a vast storehouse of literary materials which have caught and held the attention of countless scholars of our era on both sides of the Atlantic. Sufficiently far removed in time from the Victorians to be able to view them objectively, critics of the last three decades have thoughtfully reconsidered and re-appraised them in an effort to place them in proper perspective. Victorian literature enjoys as a result a much loftier status than was accorded to it in the early years of the present century.

To select material for a small book from the mass of recent criticism of the Victorians is an arduous and perplexing task. In this volume are twenty-eight essays, the oldest written in 1928, more than half dating from the 1950's. Four articles, which are placed first, are general in nature or concern groups of authors; the remaining twenty-four, on twenty-two individual writers, are arranged alphabetically with respect to the names of the authors treated. The essays vary widely in scope and purpose: some concern the whole of a writer's output, others only a single work; some are devoted largely to style, some to ideas, some to sources. It is hoped that as a whole they provide the student and the general reader with a useful sampling of critical approaches to the three principal genres of Victorian literature—novel, poetry, and non-fictional prose.

It was of course inevitable—and regrettable—that only a fraction of the rich material at hand could be chosen for inclusion. With certain exceptions, there is no more than a single article on any one Victorian, and in many instances this rule required elimination of numerous valuable essays from consideration. Moreover, a number of important studies peculiarly appropriate for the volume could not be considered

iii

because of their length. And there was not space for an essay on every Victorian figure who deserves treatment in such a volume.

Many of my colleagues in the field of Victorian studies kindly responded to my requests for recommendations of articles to be reprinted. It would be gratifying to me to name them here, but since I alone am responsible for decisions as to what was finally included, I have reluctantly decided to forego that action.

Except for some minor revisions relative to the use of quotation marks and italics, and the relegation of footnotes to the end of each article, the essays are reproduced in their original form.

My warm thanks are extended to the authors and publishers whose co-operation made the production of this volume possible. Identification of source and statement of permission to reprint are given individually with each essay.

AUSTIN WRIGHT

Carnegie Institute of Technology
September 1960

CONTENTS

CONTENTS

VICTORIAN LITERATURE

Modern Essays in Criticism

JEROME HAMILTON BUCKLEY

"Victorianism"

> Oh, so, when modern things are thrust
> By death below the coffin lid,
> Our liberal sons will spurn our dust
> And wonder what it was we did.
> —TENNYSON

BY the time of Prince Albert's death in 1861, many of the Manchester liberals had come to regard the monarchy as merely the relic of an unprogressive age which had not yet learned the advantages of a complete *laissez faire*. Five years later, when Victoria had long since retired from public life, John Bright addressed a great rally of British reformers, some of whom were prepared to demand the queen's abdication. As suggested president of the new republic, Bright was earnestly confident of his cause. Still, he felt it only right during the course of his remarks to repudiate the libels that his more zealous followers had passed upon their widowed sovereign. But the mere mention of Victoria's name brought an immediate and not altogether expected response: of one accord the republican audience arose to sing with fervent heart and voice,

> God save our gracious Queen,
> Long live our noble Queen,
> God save the Queen![1]

Victoria indeed outlived most of Bright's republicans by many years. She lived long—long enough to see her name indissolubly linked to a remarkable century's culture. Yet if "Victoria" had once been able to awaken a distinct and uniform impression in the minds of one assembly, the age which bears her name has since been subject to diverse and divided judgment. Already by the 1890's "Victorian" had become a favorite derogatory epithet to a generation which, ironically enough, was spending lavishly of its pounds and poetry to celebrate Victoria's Diamond Jubilee. And into the twentieth century "Victorianism," defined ambiguously if at all, persisted, a shield for the conservative and a target for the modernist.

Any cultural period suffers distortion from a generalized indictment, however speciously formulated. But the outlines of the Victorian era blur beyond recognition in the confusion of contradictory charges. The Victorians, we are told, were "a poor, blind, complacent people"; [2] yet they were torn by doubt, spiritually bewildered,[3] lost in a troubled universe. They were crass materialists, wholly absorbed in the present, quite unconcerned "with abstract verities and eternal values"; [4] but they were also excessively religious, lamentably idealistic, nostalgic for the past,[5] and ready to forego present delights for the vision of a world beyond. Despite their slavish "conformity," [6] their purblind respect for convention, they were, we learn, "rugged individualists," given to "doing as one likes," [7] heedless of culture, careless of a great tradition; they were iconoclasts who worshiped the idols of authority. They were, besides, at once sentimental humanitarians and hard-boiled proponents of free enterprise. Politically, they were governed by narrow insular prejudice, but swayed by dark imperialistic designs. Intellectually and emotionally, they believed in progress, denied original sin, and affirmed the death of the Devil; yet by temperament they were patently Manichaeans to whom living was a desperate struggle between the force of good and the power of darkness.[8] While they professed "manliness," they yielded to feminine standards; if they emancipated woman from age-old bondage, they also robbed her of a vital place in society.[9] Though they were sexually inhibited [10] and even failed to consider the existence of physical love, they begat incredibly large families and flaunted in their verses a morbidly over-developed erotic sensibility.[11] Their art constitutes a shameless record of both hypocrisy and ingenuousness. And their literature remains too purposeful, propagandistic, didactic, with too palpable a design upon the reader; yet it is clearly so romantic, aesthetic, "escapist," that it carries to posterity but a tale of little meaning.

Since most of such charges represent personal reaction rather than objective analysis, the terms "Victorian" and "Victorianism" have acquired the vaguest of emotional connotations. They have become what Ruskin chose to call "masked words droning and skulking about us." While the social historian [12] of the Victorian age who is able to withhold opinion is forever aware of intrinsic complexities, the critic intent upon cultural evaluation is constantly betrayed into premature judgment. And it is the aggregate of these judgments that obscures definition. Many are agreed that in Victorianism inheres a single tragic flaw which vitiates all its sounder impulses. But to one it is a moral hypocrisy,[13] to another a deliberate sentimentalism,[14] to a third a social snobbery.[15] An eminent debunker [16] laments the total failure of the critical faculty. And a sensitive student of abnormal psychology detects in all Victorian life "a manifestation of the anal complex [17] operating upon the group psyche." Yet all the subtleties of oversimplification merely confuse; "Victorianism" remains obscure; we approach no nearer the Victorian essence.

But whatever its central defect, the age, we gather, must in some hidden way have been deeply pernicious. Apparently so persuaded, not a few essayists have attempted to salvage their favorite Victorian authors from the contamination of an unfortunate background. Lewis Carroll has been recently depicted as a frustrated professor attacking "those jungles of nonsense which were merely the daily life" of cultured adults "in the now legendary reign of Victoria"; and his biographer advises us that we may safely "call the *Alice* books art, and the entire Victorian age a neurosis." [18] From a similar point of view, the Brownings may be commended for having reared their son Pen with intelligence and sympathy, for "neither Robert nor Elizabeth Browning were in any way typical Victorian parents." [19] Even Tennyson, who is somewhat more difficult to dissociate from his milieu, finds an apologist who contends that the Laureate, having resisted the "rigid dogma" of his time, may speak to an inquiring modernity, "in spite of all his Victorianism." [20]

It has been possible to recognize the manifold dissatisfactions and rebellions of Carlyle, Dickens, Ruskin, Morris, Samuel Butler, and at the same time to insist that "the note of revolt is not characteristic of the Victorian Age." [21] By definition, the cultural leader must advance beyond his less gifted contemporaries in grasping the problem of his time, but he can scarcely be considered a leader at all if he stands entirely out of relation to those who lag behind. It is, therefore, by no means clear how reasonably we may dogmatize about the acquiescence of the Victorian era, when many of its most representative and influential writers appear restive or refractory. At any rate, we are hardly to be convinced by criticism like that of the British scholar who, writing in the year of the Munich appeasement, condemns Victorian smugness, with the conviction that Englishmen of 1938 have "scarcely a trace of complacency left." [22]

Whether or not, then, their entire age was spiritually apathetic, the most articulate Victorians were, like wakeful minds in any generation, quite prepared to assail omnipresent stupidity and vicious self-satisfaction. Often, to reinforce their assault on the forts of folly, they resorted to the same sort of oversimplified indictment that has since been turned against them. Almost always, they were able to muster their attack with a vigor of statement compared to which latter-day polemics pale into gentle censure. John Morley, for instance, could ally impassioned eloquence to reasoned principle in his denunciation of Victorian England as "a community where political forms, from the monarchy down to the popular chamber, are mainly hollow shams disguising the coarse supremacy of wealth, where religion is mainly official and political, and is ever ready to dissever itself alike from the spirit of justice, the spirit of charity, and the spirit of truth, and where literature does not as a rule permit itself to discuss serious subjects frankly and worthily—a community, in short, where the great aim of all classes and orders with power is by dint of rigorous silence, fast shutting of the eyes, and stern stopping of the ears, somehow to keep the social pyramid on its apex, with the fatal result of preserving for England its glorious fame as a paradise for the well-to-do, a purgatory for the able, and a hell for the poor." [23]

If Morley, by reason of his relationship to the positivist radicals of the seventies, seems too clearly biased a witness, we may turn to a comparatively calm early Victorian chronicler who makes no claim to peculiar insight. Reporting with statistical exactitude on the industrial advance of his generation, George Richardson Porter paused to caution a complacent reader against undue optimism. "It must be owned," he wrote, "that our multiplied abodes of want, of wretchedness, and of crime—our town populations huddled together in ill-ventilated and undrained courts and cellars—our numerous workhouses filled to overflowing with the children of want—and our prisons (scarcely less numerous) overloaded with the votaries of crime, do indeed but too sadly and too strongly attest that all is not as it should be with us as regards this most important branch of human progress." [24] Beside strictures so disillusioned and so vehement, twentieth-century anti-Victorianism seems imaginatively stale and rhetorically flabby. The Victorians are still their own severest critics, possessed of an

6

amazing capacity for detachment, a singular command of invective, and, as we shall see, an unequaled talent for parody. "Victorianism" was undoubtedly, at least in part, a monster created by rebellious spirits and bequeathed to a posterity which all too frequently is content to regard the spirits as the monster's children.

Violent and vituperative as it frequently was, Victorian self-criticism found direction in the implicit sense that the faults it assailed were remediable by individual and collective reform. For the Victorians were quite unable to view their long era as a static entity, a unique whole to be described by a single sweeping formula. The doctrine of organic development was so thoroughly diffused throughout nineteenth-century science and philosophy that no serious thinker could escape its implications. Whether or not the thoughts of men were widening with the process of the suns, there were everywhere evidences of continual growth and decay. Wistfully Frederic Harrison looked to the joys of a vanished past; early Victorian life, he felt sure, must have been pleasanter than existence in the seventies, for certainly Dickens and Thackeray "tell us of a livelier, jollier age than that recorded in *Middlemarch* and *Fors Clavigera*." [25] In a more sanguine mood, Walter Besant chronicled the incalculable changes between the accession of Victoria and the Golden Jubilee. He lingered over quaint customs long outmoded, as if contemplating the strangeness of a remote antiquity; for in 1887 he could find scant similarity to early Victorian tastes, no parallel, for instance, to the rules of etiquette acceptable fifty years before:

Never ask a lady any questions about anything whatever.

If you have drunk wine with every one at the table and wish for more, wait till the cloth is removed.

Never permit the sanctity of the drawing-room to be violated by a boot. [26]

If many changes were wrought by deliberate reformers fighting old prejudices, many also, like the shift in standards of deportment, resulted from the gradual operation of hidden social forces.

All in all, the Victorian period achieved little of the stability we have learned to associate with a semimythical neoclassic culture. It moved from form to form, and nothing stood. Almost every Victorian thesis produced its own antithesis, as a ceaseless dialectic worked out its designs. Throughout the period there were vast differences between rural and urban society; the fields of the agrarian South were, as Mrs. Gaskell suggested, a far cry from the smoky cities of the industrial North. And between the towns themselves sharp distinctions could be drawn; the London of Oscar Wilde had little in common with the Birmingham of Joseph Chamberlain. Besides, the "climate of opinion" varied from year to year, from decade to decade; the seventies was perhaps as distant from the eighties as we imagine the twenties of our own century remote from the thirties. The Victorian age as a whole was forced to adapt itself to new values as old traditions crumbled; and the term "Victorian" is, therefore, egregiously abused when invoked to describe attitudes that the Victorians inherited, modified, or discarded.

Viewed in its long perspective, nineteenth-century culture appears entirely relative to the manifold developments of a changing society. Yet within the Victorian period itself, "Victorianism" may well have been a necessary postulate, a distinct absolute deduced from a vague composite of social and aesthetic values which creative thinkers felt compelled to dismiss, in order to clear the way for radical innovation. And to the Edwardians the fiction may have served an essential purpose in assisting towards fresh objectives, until such a time as those objectives were attained and the generation of Virginia Woolf and James Joyce might devise the myth of "Edwardianism." Ultimately the debunking of things Victorian became an amusing pastime rather than a meaningful criticism; the distortion of a past culture represented little more than the evasion of a present problem. Havelock Ellis, who in 1890 had attacked all that seemed to him false within the Victorian world, lived to find "the gesture that was once a vital reaction to real things" becoming at last "a stale and empty trick." [27]

Now that half a century has elapsed since Victoria's death, facile repudiation of the Victorian era seems, in truth, quite as outmoded as the attitudes we can no longer recapture. But the sentimentalization that in some quarters has replaced it is scarcely more constructive. The interests of modern design are not appreciably furthered by the self-conscious revival of baroque styles or the rediscovery of brica-brac which has acquired the charm of the antique. We can understand the significant backgrounds of contemporary thought only by transcending indiscriminate praise or blame. Collective guilt, we have learned, is never easy to determine; and value-judgments are best confined to specific creeds and individual works of art.

Working inductively, distrustful of "masked words" and slanted evidence, the historian might discover the sources of the precise concepts upon which less objective interpreters have based their general indictment. The idea of progress, for instance, an idea which admittedly had considerable currency during the Victorian period, might be related to a broader cultural context. It might be seen as an outgrowth of Cartesian philosophy, receiving its major extension among the *philosophes* of eighteenth-century France, passing with variations through the anarchism of Godwin and the poetry of Shelley towards the socialism of Saint-Simon and the positivism of Comte, until with Herbert Spencer came the assumption that progress and evolution moved consistently in the same direction. Or within the age alone, it might be linked to the Victorian's awareness of his very real social advance. The notion of perfectibility would seem to have some immediate sanction at a time when men were devising a system of education on a broad democratic basis, establishing the rights of free speech and trade unionism, progressively extending the franchise, reshaping their entire legal code, and discovering the principles of a medical science by which the sum of human suffering might be immeasurably reduced.

It might then be debated whether the idea of progress was not as much an incentive to further reform as a cause of stupefying satisfaction with the advances already achieved. Yet a cursory review of Victorian opinion indicates that the idea, whatever its effect upon those who embraced it, was much less widely accepted than we have been led to believe. Huxley, who was at least as articulate as Spencer, insisted that evolutionary change not seldom ran counter to ethical improvement. And Tennyson, whose early visions of the future have too readily convicted his generation of blind optimism, attained by 1886 a thoroughly disillusioned view of the "glooming alleys" where "Progress halts on palsied feet" and a sense of the disaster involved in the failure of social adaptation to keep pace with scientific discovery; if Tennyson held to a modified faith in evolution, he recognized the possibility of regression:

> Forward then, but still remember how the course of time will swerve,
> Crook and turn upon itself in many a backward-streaming curve.[28]

The Victorian temper is thus not to be adequately gauged in terms of a concept which flourished long before 1837 and was subject to important qualification from 1850 onwards.

Many of the specific values associated with the anomaly known as "Victorianism" have, like the idea of progress, partial basis in objective evidence; and the inconsistency of the generalizations itself testifies to the bewildering complexity of the era. It is almost impossible to reduce a culture so various to a common denominator; and conflict, indeed, may emerge as the only unity in a great diversity. Yet it is not difficult to find certain doctrines perhaps opposing each other but recurring with an insistency which suggests the breadth of their influence. Probably the most prominent of these, in the early Victorian period at any rate, are Evangelical religion and Benthamite philosophy, both pre-Victorian in origin and both vigorously questioned throughout the nineteenth century. To the one has been ascribed the sententious hypocrisy of Mr. Podsnap; to the other, the uncompromising factualism of Mr. Gradgrind. But apart from their baneful effects, which are to some extent problematical, each encouraged a sense of social responsibility which did much to mitigate the miseries of an expanding industrialism; each contributed, even to its bitterest enemies, something of its earnestness and fixity of vision.

If hardheaded Benthamism was ultimately undermined by the reservations and subtleties of the greatest utilitarian, its zeal for practical reform infected many who found Mill's hedonistic paradox more ingenious than convincing. And if Evangelical restraints and dogmas slowly dissolved under the scrutiny of critical intelligence, the old thirst for righteousness animated so reluctant a heretic as George Eliot, so willful an agnostic as John Morley. Whether actuated by self-interest or Christian principle, moral duty remained for most a categorical imperative. With all the assurance of his brother's orthodoxy, F. W. Newman the freethinker could insist that "all social action, all national cohesion, all reverence for law, all sanctity in rule, is founded upon man's moral conscience." [29] For a few social purpose seemed at one time effectively to coalesce with ethical premise in the short-lived Religion of Humanity. But even to fervent atheists like Charles Bradlaugh the demand for moral sanction and the claims of social justice seemed inescapable. Craving adjustment amid the peril of change, representative Victorians, at least until the seventies, sought either in the radiance of God or in the dim consciousness of man some spiritual absolute by which to interpret and control their material advance; whatever misdirections they may frequently have followed, their impulse was in essence deeply religious. [30]

Prince Albert, we are told, was much concerned with art, though unfortunately he felt it to lie "somewhere between religion and hygiene." [31] Now, if for "hygiene" we might substitute "the general health of the body politic," Prince Albert's view of art would differ little from the first principles of any considerable mid-Victorian aesthetician. The "morality of art"—its religious content—lay in its relationship to the full experience and its power to speak to mankind in the language of universal emotion. For it was the artist's first duty to communicate, and the substance of his message was necessarily of social and, therefore, moral significance. To Ruskin it was clear that the student of art gained the deepest insight into the totality of human affairs. And to Arnold it seemed natural that the critic of books should be first and last a critic of society. The "moral aesthetic" was by no means a Victorian invention; it rested on the major premises of almost every classical aesthetic theory. Yet it bore special relevance to Victorian needs. Confronted with the unprecedented developments of nineteenth-century culture, an emerging middle class with the meagerest intellectual traditions behind it strove desperately to achieve standards of judgment. The early Victorian poet, sometimes no more certain than his contemporaries, was expected to furnish instruction as well as amusement. He could fulfill his vital function in society only by passing dramatic commentary upon the conflicts of his time. Often like Tennyson he had first to relinquish a personal prejudice for a more disinterested aesthetic. But usually he came in the end to feel his renunciation morally—and socially—essential. At all events, out of his sacrifice was born a considerable didactic literature.

In its many-sided concern with manners and morals, the Victorian era was not unlike the Elizabethan age, when conduct-books, pamphlets, plays, sermons, poems explored the problems of degree in an expanding economy. Both periods brought to the present a deep sense of the national past, based upon high scholarship and eager research. Both shared the excitement of vital education. Far from sinking beneath the weight of its "moral," their art at its best followed new experience beyond the bounds of thought. In the years after 1850 novelists and poets exploited the forgotten "local color" of every English county to produce a kind of nineteenth-century *Poly-Olbion*.[32] Like the Elizabethans, the Victorians embarked on their own voyages of discovery. To the far corners of the unknown traveled "manly" adventurers—Layard to buried Nineveh, Livingstone to the dark heart of Africa, Richard Burton to Brazil and Tanganyika and the Great Salt Lake in a valiant effort to live his unexpurgated Arabian nights.

But whether at home or abroad, many a Victorian captured the almost Elizabethan exuberance that led Hurrell Froude to exclaim on the launching of the Oxford Movement in 1833: "What fun it is living in such times as these! How could one now go back to the times of old Tory humbug!"[33] A tireless emotional energy carried Carlyle through continents of passionate prose, just as a physical stamina impelled the somewhat calmer Leslie Stephen to tramp the fifty miles from Cambridge to London on a hot day.[34] Like the Elizabethans, the high Victorians valued a manifold competence; Ruskin like Bacon took all knowledge to be his province, and whether or not, as Whistler suggested, he failed to master his specific subject, he left his mark on many others. Not without some reason, then, did John Addington Symonds conclude that "the English Renaissance of the sixteenth century became renascent in the nineteenth."[35]

Yet it will not do to press the parallel too far. Symonds himself detected in the Victorian period, whatever its buoyancy and promise, elements of "world fatigue" which were, he felt, quite alien to the Elizabethan temper. Certainly the desperate unbelief that permeates so much of Arnold's verse and wracks so little of his prose arises from distinctly Victorian cultural conditions, a sad contemplation of withering faith and an unprecedented fear of encroaching materialism. The paralysis of doubt that is said to have gripped Arnold's generation is far removed from the divided aims of a disillusioned Hamlet. Even if, as seems likely, both conflicts have been overstated, the very real crosscurrents of Victorian assent and denial are scarcely "Elizabethan" in source or direction.

Victorian society was forever subject to tensions which militated against complete spontaneity and singleness of purpose. It experienced in various forms the self-consciousness that is at once the strange disease of modern life and the genesis of analytic science. It learned to fear its own ardors, to distrust the falsehood of extremes. Whenever artist or philosopher was betrayed by the intensity of his conviction, Victorian parody served to restore a lost perspective; laughter prodded eccentric genius into an awareness of common reality. Despite the resounding clash of individual wills, there was until late in Victoria's reign a desire for cultural synthesis urgent enough to inspire from even the most rebellious many a concession to an established social morality. It was often as if the discords were hushed by a half-heard imperious command, "Hark, the dominant's persistence till it must be answered to!" Again and again the poet dreamed of a remote harmony which might catch up diverse themes into a larger pattern, a meaningful Victorian counterpoint. Tennyson prayed for his whole generation a prayer which might be echoed by Victorians of vastly different intellectual persuasion:

Let knowledge grow from more to more,
But more of reverence in us dwell;
That mind and soul according well,
May make one music as before.

For all his sharp censure of Victorian culture, even John Morley came to feel that the prayer had been at times richly fulfilled; in the best effort of his age he saw "mind and soul according well." In 1921, nearly fifty years after the first appearance of his essay *On Compromise*, he added a few words by way of epilogue, a Victorian's final answer to a skeptical posterity. "Whatever we may say of Europe between Waterloo and Sedan," he wrote, "in our country at least it was an epoch of hearts uplifted with hope, and brains active with sober and manly reason for the common good. Some ages are marked as sentimental, others stand conspicuous as rational. The Victorian age was happier than most in the flow of both these currents into a common stream of vigorous and effective talent. New truths were welcomed in free minds, and free minds make brave men." Though later critics might charge the Victorians with divorcing intellect and feeling, the liaison was in fact well sustained into the 1870's, and the process of separation was, as we shall see, prolonged and painful. By 1884, when Ruskin sensed a great "storm cloud of the nineteenth century" blotting out the sun and breaking an old "harmony," English culture, heedless of his mid-Victorian warnings, was entering upon a new phase of its development.

NOTES

1. For the anecdote, see Frank Hardie, *The Political Influence of Queen Victoria* (London, 1935), p. 206.
2. The charge is stated ironically by Arnold Bennett (*The Old Wives' Tale*, chap. I), but is seriously repeated in various forms; cf. H. H. Asquith, *Some Aspects of the Victorian Age* (Oxford, 1918), p. 6, or an incidental remark by an art critic in the *New Yorker*, Jan. 26, 1946, p. 58.
3. Cf. H. V. Routh, "The true sign of the times was spiritual isolation" (*Towards the Twentieth Century*, New York, 1937, p. ix); or see W. C. Frierson, *The English Novel in Transition* (Norman, Okla., 1942), p. 36.
4. H. J. and Hugh Massingham, eds., *The Great Victorians* (Garden City, 1932), p. 11; or, for a more extravagant judgment, see E. B. Burgum, "Victorianism," *Sewanee Review*, XXXVI (1928), 282, 286.
5. Cf. Routh, *Towards the Twentieth Century*, p. 45.

6. Cf. Osbert Sitwell, *Sober Truth* (London, 1930), p. 22, or A. C. Ward, *Twentieth-Century Literature* (New York, 1940), pp. 2–3.

7. Arnold's charge freely echoed by the neo-humanists, who often dismiss Arnold himself along with his lost generation.

8. Contrast Routh, *Towards the Twentieth Century*, p. 74, with William Gaunt, *The Aesthetic Adventure* (New York, 1945), p. 237.

9. Cf. Edith Batho and Bonamy Dobrée, *The Victorians and After* (London, 1938), p. 81; contrast G. M. Trevelyan, *English Social History* (New York, 1942), p. 521: "The last thirty years of Victoria's reign . . . the real period of the 'emancipation of women' in England."

10. Cf. Batho and Dobrée, *The Victorians and After* p. 37, or Florence B. Lennon, *Victoria through the Looking-Glass* (New York, 1945), *passim*.

11. See Mario Praz, *The Romantic Agony* (London, 1933).

12. Observe the wise cautions of Trevelyan, *English Social History*, p. 509, and of G. M. Young, *Victorian England* (London, 1936), p. 150.

13. See Bonamy Dobrée, "Addison," *Essays in Biography* (London, 1925), p. 206. Addison seems to Dobrée sufficiently hypocritical to merit the title "the first Victorian."

14. Lascelles Abercrombie, for instance, in a generally judicious estimate of Tennyson, speaks of "that false emphasis of feeling which is the peculiar vice of the Victorian age"; see *Revaluations* (London, 1931), p. 63.

15. See O. F. Christie, *The Transition from Aristocracy* (London, 1927), p. 108; here the historian indulges in generalization.

16. Lytton Strachey, still the liveliest of the iconoclasts; see esp. "A Victorian Critic" (Arnold), *Characters and Commentaries* (New York, 1933).

17. See Anna Kavan (author of the distinguished fiction, *Asylum Piece*), "Back to Victoria," *Horizon*, XIII (1946), 65.

18. See Lennon, *Victoria through the Looking-Glass*, p. 5.

19. Isabel C. Clarke, *Elizabeth Barrett Browning* (London, 1929), p. 241.

20. See William H. Swift, "Tennyson in the Twentieth Century," *Search Quarterly*, III (1933), 343; cf. also C. H. O. Scaife, *The Poetry of Alfred Tennyson* (London, 1930), p. 96.

21. See Asquith, *Aspects of Victorian Age*, p. 13.

22. Batho and Dobrée, *Victorians and After*, p. 36.

23. See Morley, *Critical Miscellanies* (London, 1923), pp. 74–75.

24. G. R. Porter, *The Progress of the Nation* (London, 1851), p. 631.

25. See Harrison, *Autobiographic Memoirs*, 2 vols. (London, 1911), II, 313.

26. Quoted by Walter Besant, *Fifty Years Ago* (New York, n.d.), p. 124.

27. Havelock Ellis, *The New Spirit* (1890), preface to the 1926 edition (Boston, 1926), p. xii.

28. Tennyson, "Locksley Hall Sixty Years After" (1886).

29. F. W. Newman, *Causes of Atheism* (Ramsgate, 1871), p. 12.

30. Cf. R. C. K. Ensor, *England, 1870–1914* (Oxford, 1936), p. 137.

31. See Clive Bell, "Victorian Taste," in R. S. Lambert, ed., *Art in England* (Pelican Books, 1938), p. 45.

32. A comparison suggested by Oliver Elton, *A Survey of English Literature, 1780–1880*, 4 vols. (New York, 1920), III, 3.

33. Quoted by John Henry Overton, *The Church in England*, 2 vols. (London, 1897), II, 324–325.

34. See F. W. Knickerbocker, *Free Minds* (Cambridge: Harvard University Press, 1943), p. 29.

35. See Symonds, *Essays Speculative and Suggestive*, 2 vols. (London 1890), II, 274.

LIONEL STEVENSON

The Pertinacious Victorian Poets[1]

THE English literature of the Victorian period seems to be emerging at last from the cloud of contempt that has overshadowed it for the past generation. All types of literature endured their share of that disdain, but upon poetry it was heaped without mitigation. Although the writers of expository prose were stigmatized for inconsistency of thinking, for hypocritical morality, for ornate rhetoric, it had to be admitted that they struggled obstinately with many basic problems of the modern world and that their opinions largely determined our contemporary standards and even our political experiments. The novelists were accused of sentimentality, melodrama, prudishness, didacticism, and external characterization; but there was no denying the fact that somehow they had created a multitude of human beings who insisted on inhabiting the reader's memory like living acquaintances, in spite of their reprehensible lack of all Freudian symptoms. The poets, however, incurred the full brunt of all the same indictments, without the qualifying allowances that partially sheltered their prose brethren.

Now that a century has passed since the heyday of Victorianism, it is the prose writers who have a head start in the parade toward respectability. Readers are discovering with amazement that Carlyle and Ruskin, Mill and Arnold, said many of the things that the present age thinks it is discovering for the first time, and said them not only more powerfully than our pundits do, but also with recommendations that have tonic virtue for an exhausted world. And in the post-Kafka age of the novel, with symbolic universality or mythopœic implication

From *University of Toronto Quarterly*, XXI (1952), 232–45. Reprinted by permission of the publisher and the author. Minor revisions and additions were made by Professor Stevenson in 1960.

freed from the fetters of photographic realism, Victorian fiction also is revealing unsuspected depths. A modern book on Dickens, for instance, announces that "Blake and Dickens are the two writers who hold the key to the nature of our cultural crisis today." [2]

A similar rehabilitation may be expected for the Victorian poets, but the portents of it are still few. One reason, probably, is that in their own era the Victorian poets were glorified by so many devout enthusiasts that the modern reader with critical intelligence hesitates to express himself in their favour. The long shelf of books on such subjects as "The Message of *In Memoriam*" and "Browning as a Philosophic and Religious Teacher" gave the impression that moralizing was the sole purpose and justification of their work, and furthermore that it had been expounded so exhaustively by these adherents that no further analysis of any sort need be undertaken.

The current attitude was revealed in a volume entitled *The Reinterpretation of Victorian Literature* (1950), produced under the auspices of the Modern Language Association of America. The dozen authorities who contributed to it were presumably the best informed and most loyal devotees of Victorianism among the scholars of this country. Nevertheless, the book is likely to perpetuate the layman's conviction that the Victorians were long-winded philosophizers. The various essays deal ably with a number of the significant ideas that pervade Victorian literature, but there is a minimum of attention to any of its artistic qualities, and such comments as can be found deal almost exclusively with the techniques of prose. When any of the poets are mentioned at all, it is as incidental evidence of some theory or attitude that is more significantly displayed by the prose writers.

This disregard for the Victorian poets as artists is particularly astonishing at a time when the most aggressive school of criticism is emphasizing the images, the patterns, and the verbal nuances of poetry. In their use of the whole antecedent range of poetic forms and themes, the Victorians were far more eclectic than any other poetic group has ever been. They borrowed from all ages, but they were not slavish imitators. Experimenting with a full consciousness of poetic artistry, they widened the scope of English poetry, both in subject-matter and in technique, to an unparalleled extent. And the fact that traditional themes and allusions richly embellish their poetry can scarcely be regarded as a defect at a time when the dominant school of modern poetry demands recognition of allusions as a primary condition of poetic enjoyment.

As soon as one begins to investigate the critical studies of Victorian poetry that have been published, their inadequacy is apparent. Some of the most valid current techniques of poetic analysis are those which deal with vocabulary, with the grouping and recurrence of archetypal images, and with the process of absorption by which poets combine elements from diversified sources. For minute observation of individual style, an invaluable aid is the study of a poet's revisions of his own work. It has long been recognized with what skill Tennyson rewrote and improved many of the poems which first appeared in 1832, and that a comparison of the earlier versions with those published ten years later can show his maturing mastery of melody and image. But beyond this obvious investigation no further study was made until recently, when some of the numerous unpublished manuscripts were examined. For instance, as some readers have already suspected, it is now proved that Tennyson planned a long reflective poem about his political and social beliefs—a companion piece to the religious disquisition in *In Memoriam*. Not only did he print three fragments of this uncompleted poem, the mysteriously untitled "Love thou thy Land," "You ask me why," and "Of old sat Freedom," but he also, over many years, incorporated segments of it into several of his major poems on public issues, such as the "Ode on the Death of the Duke of Wellington."

The original manuscript of "Tithonus" has also been uncovered. This poem, which is now considered one of the best of Tennyson's classical monologues, was withheld from publication for a quarter of a century, and was allowed to get into print only because the poet's friend Thackeray was importuning him for a contribution to his new magazine. A comparison of the original version with the published text adds much evidence of Tennyson's scrupulous sense of connotation and verbal melody.[3]

For few other Victorian poets has even this degree of textual study been undertaken. Several of the best-known poems by Dante Gabriel Rossetti were extensively reworked after their first publication; indeed, "The Blessed Damozel" went through two separate revisions. Although Paull F. Baum has made admirable analyses of this poem, "The House of Life," and others, on the basis of their successive drafts, much remains to be done in defining the mysterious fascination of Rossetti's work. Matthew Arnold was another persistent reviser of his poems even after they got into print; and the preliminary drafts of some of them have been published by Chauncey B. Tinker and Howard F. Lowry in their excellent book, *The Poetry of Matthew Arnold*. But the two Victorians with the most utterly individual styles,

Browning and Swinburne, have been subjected to practically no analysis. In public or private collections there must be a good deal of manuscript material, such as the first draft of Swinburne's "Hertha" that Miss Fannie E. Ratchford published in 1924.[4] A study of their methods of revision could provide clues to the way in which each developed his personal poetic idiom.

We may now turn from purely stylistic questions to another of the major interests of modern criticism, the sources and associative relationships of images and symbols. A noteworthy article, entitled "Tennyson as a Modern Poet," has been published by Professor Arthur J. Carr, of the University of Michigan, who has served as an editor of the *avant-garde* magazine *Accent*. He states the thesis of his article thus:

> . . . he is our true precursor. He shows and hides, as if in embryo, a master theme of Joyce's *Ulysses*—the accentuated and moody self-consciousness and the sense of loss that mark Stephen Dedalus. He forecasts Yeats's interest in the private myth. He apprehended in advance of Aldous Huxley the uses of mysticism to castigate materialistic culture. And in *Maud,* at least, he prepared the way for the verse of Eliot's "Preludes" and "Prufrock." At some crucial points Tennyson is a modern poet, and there are compelling reasons why we should try to comprehend him.[5]

In the course of his essay, Professor Carr touches briefly on a number of Tennyson's principal poems. The only intensive research into the poet's symbolism has been that which Professor William D. Paden published in his volume, *Tennyson in Egypt*. Dealing solely with the poems of his adolescence, which were almost all discarded from later editions of his work, this study reveals much about the background of reading which fired the youthful poet's imagination, and therefore it could serve as a foundation for a similar inquiry into the unconscious resources from which Tennyson drew his later and greater poems. His own description of "a kind of waking trance I have frequently had quite up from my boyhood when I have been all alone" suggests that the subconscious (or supra-conscious) played as strong a part in his creative processes as in those of Coleridge and others who have been exhaustively analyzed. In a paper published elsewhere, I tried to interpret one of Tennyson's recurring symbols, the imprisoned maiden.[6] Another paper, by Professor E. D. H. Johnson, has dealt with the flower imagery in *Maud*.[7] But much of greater importance remains to be sought.

The most maligned of Tennyson's long poems is *The Princess*. Its mingling of satire and seriousness, its presentation of modern social comedy in the guise of medieval romance, its "chimeras, crotchets, Christmas solecisms" (as the poet himself termed them), which struck earlier critics as merely an incongruous *mélange des genres*, ought to appeal to a more sophisticated age that approves several simultaneous levels of signification. The ideological topic, of course, was strictly contemporary, and Tennyson undoubtedly drew many details from his own environment. It has been suggested that the character of Princess Ida was modelled upon his friend Lady Duff-Gordon, the strong-minded yet charming controversialist who was an inspiration also to Thackeray and George Meredith. A fantasy of this type, however, is bound to have much of the *pastiche*, with overtones of allusion enhancing its effect of elegant make-believe.

Several passages distinctly echo well-known lines of *Twelfth Night*, which was another comedy of a lady who wilfully turned her back on normal sexual impulses, and whose emotional defences were undermined through the presence of a transvestite intruder. The young prince, in the disguise of a girl student, ventures to plead with Princess Ida to reconsider her rejection of her suitor:

> "Again?" she cried, "are you ambassadresses
> From him to me? We give you, being strange,
> A licence; speak, and let the topic die."
> I stammer'd that I knew him—could have wish'd—
> "Our king expects—was there no precontract?
> There is no truer-hearted—ah, you seem
> All he prefigured, and he could not see
> The bird of passage flying south but long'd
> To follow: surely, if your Highness keep
> Your purport, you will shock him ev'n to death. . . ."

When the Princess expresses only an aloof pity for her adorer, an appeal is aimed toward a more vulnerable point:

> "Ere half be done, perchance your life may fail . . .
> might I dread that you,
> With only Fame for spouse and your great deeds
> For issue, yet may live in vain, and miss,
> Meanwhile, what every woman counts her due,
> Love, children, happiness?"

The whole conversation parallels the one which occurs in *Twelfth Night* when Olivia, having decided that "we'll once more hear Orsino's embassy," gives audience to the page-boy who is Viola in disguise:

Viola: 'Tis beauty truly blent, whose red and white
Nature's own sweet and cunning hand laid on:
Lady, you are the cruellest she alive,
If you will lead these graces to the grave
And leave the world no copy.

Olivia: . . . Were you sent hither to praise me?

Viola: I see you what you are, you are too proud;
But, if you were the devil, you are fair.
My lord and master loves you; O, such love
Could but be recompensed, though you were crowned
The nonpareil of beauty!

Olivia: How does he love me?

Viola: With adorations, fertile tears,
With groans that thunder love, with sighs of fire. . . .
If I did love you in my master's flame,
With such a suffering, such a deadly life,
In your denial I would find no sense. . . .

Still closer is the verbal parallel elsewhere, when Lady Psyche finds
that her baby has been adopted by the Princess after the mother's
expulsion:

> "But I will go and sit beside the doors,
> And make a wild petition night and day,
> Until they hate to hear me like a wind
> Wailing forever, till they open to me
> And lay my little blossom at my feet. . . ."

This, of course, is bound to recall Viola's lines:

> Make me a willow cabin at your gate
> And call upon my soul within the house;
> Write loyal cantons of contemned love,
> And sing them loud even in the dead of night;
> Halloo your name to the reverberate hills,
> And make the babbling gossip of the air
> Cry out Olivia!

While the central situation and some of the actual phrases of *The
Princess* thus link it with a Shakespearean comedy, the general setting
is more definitely associated with several romances of chivalry. Although Tennyson was already meditating an epic on the legends of
King Arthur at the time when he wrote *The Princess,* no critic seems
to have discussed the Arthurian element in this poem. Much of the
story can be paralleled in a group of romances centring upon Morgan
le Fay, King Arthur's sister. Under the name of Morcades, she was

described as ruling over the Chastel des Puceles with five hundred ladies and damsels. In the Middle English romance of Sir Percival, the name of her domain is translated as "Maydenlande." In several of the romances, she was besieged by a pagan king because she had rejected him as a suitor. In another story she gave birth to an illegitimate child and had him smuggled out of the castle. More familiar versions of the story depict her and her ladies as inhabiting the Isle of Avilion and healing wounded warriors with the aid of magic arts. All these elements appear in Tennyson's poem: Princess Ida rules over a manless paradise with six hundred maiden inmates; she is besieged by a neighbouring king because she has refused to be betrothed to his son; a complicating factor within the college is the presence of a young child; and at the end of the story the princess and her ladies emerge to nurse the hero and his comrades back to health. Thus Tennyson selects and adapts mythological material to provide symbols for his theory about the conflict of the sexes.

When we turn our attention to Browning, the highly idiosyncratic quality of his symbols is indicated by the fact that C. Willard Smith has devoted a whole book to the restricted topic of *Browning's Star Imagery*. Even more baffling is the question of the imaginative stimuli responsible for the poet's choice of topics and details for his dramatic monologues. The need for investigation of the problem has been obscured by the fact that many of his best-known poems are overtly based upon historical personalities or scenes. But this really increases the complexity of the process, because the dense texture of the poems results from an intermingling of suggestions from other sources. Browning was not so scientifically minded as to select a topic merely for the purpose of reconstructing some historical phenomenon, no matter how vividly. There was as much immediate personal incentive as in a Keats ode or a Wordsworth sonnet.

Obviously enough, of course, "Fra Lippo Lippi" was largely a defence of Browning's poetic methods against critical sneers; and similarly "Pacchiarotto and How He Worked in Distemper" contained oblique allusions to individuals of the poet's own time. Just as definitely, though perhaps less consciously, "The Statue and the Bust" was not written to condemn a Florentine duke for failing to elope with Count Ricciardi's incarcerated wife, but to justify Robert Browning for having eloped with Mr. Barrett's incarcerated daughter. I suspect, therefore, that any other poem of Browning, if it carries conviction as an emotional utterance, may have been inspired by some occurrence within his own experience. For example, I suggest that "A Grammarian's Funeral" is not only a tribute to the scholarly devotion of the first Renaissance philologists, but just as much a memorial to Hugh Stuart Boyd, the classical scholar who was Elizabeth Barrett's chief instructor in Greek and for whom she expressed her enthusiasm in "Wine of Cyprus." Boyd became blind at the age of forty-seven, but continued energetically with his researches; one of his later treatises was "An Essay on the Greek Article." When he died in 1848, at the age of sixty-seven, Mrs. Browning wrote three sonnets in his memory; and "A Grammarian's Funeral" appeared in Browning's next volume of miscellaneous poems. In a letter many years later he referred sympathetically to "the poor, old blind, forsaken man's death." [8]

As to less personal derivation of his themes, a revealing insight is provided by Donald Smalley's publication of Browning's Essay on Chatterton. This book is less important as an addition to the brief canon of Browning's published prose than it is for the introduction, in which Professor Smalley shows how Browning's elaborate theory about Chatterton's self-deception came to be transmuted into the portrayal of a Moslem fanatic in The Return of the Druses, the play that he was writing at almost the same time. It will not be unreasonable, therefore, to propose unacknowledged origins for some of Browning's other works.

One of his poems, to be sure, has been subjected to an extensive analysis of its associative complex; but this is because it so conspicuously differs from the normal Browning type. "Childe Roland to the Dark Tower Came" is a vivid piece of fantastic description, without the usual focus upon characterization; and Browning admitted that the poem "came upon me as a kind of dream. I had to write it, then and there." In 1925 Harold Golder published an article that subjected this poem to the same sort of scrutiny that Lowes was applying to The Ancient Mariner and Kubla Khan.[9] The principal sources of imagery as adduced by Golder were the fairy tale of Jack the Giant Killer, Palmerin of England, certain adventures of St. George in The Seven Champions of Christendom, and, for specific details, The Faerie Queene, Don Belianis of Greece, Orlando Furioso, and other works. Soon afterwards William C. DeVane added another important and totally different source—a grotesque landscape described in Gérard de Lairesse's neo-classical treatise on The Art of Painting.[10] Yet these and other commentators seem to be going out of their way to ignore a familiar Arthurian episode that Browning must certainly have known, and which has several identical details and also has the same feeling of horror and suspense as the Browning poem.

In Malory's "Tale of Sir Gareth of Orkney" the newly dubbed young knight has to traverse "a black launde" and "a pass that is called the Pass Perilous," and must face many terrors, including the knowledge that numerous other and more renowned champions have failed in the same quest. At last he reaches the castle of the Red Knight of the Red Laundes: "and also there was fast by a sycamore tree, and there hung an horn, the greatest that ever they saw, of an elephant's bone; and this Knight of the Red Laundes had hanged it up there, and if there came any errant-knight, he must blow that horn, and then will he make him ready and come to him to do battle. . . . And herewith he [Gareth] spurred his horse straight to the sycamore tree, and blew so the horn eagerly that all the siege and the castle rang thereof." Malory makes the whole experience thoroughly materialistic, with the hero defeating a series of actual enemies throughout the journey, and with the failure of his predecessors visibly displayed: "There hung full goodly armed knights by the neck, and their shields about their necks with their swords, and gilt spurs upon their heels, and so there hung nigh a forty knights shamefully with full rich arms." Furthermore, Gareth has a companion, the scornful Lady Linet, and it is her constant taunting that magnifies his perils. Characteristically, Browning shifts the whole conflict into the subjective realm, by making Childe Roland ride alone, with only fragmentary memories and vague dreads to be outfaced.

It is natural that an English poem of chivalry should contain Arthurian echoes; but it must be observed that Browning's eponymous hero is not from the matter of Britain but from the matter of France, and one episode has recognizable roots in the story of Charlemagne's paladin. Sir Gareth was not the only knight who defiantly blew a horn at a moment of grim crisis. When the original Roland's rearguard contingent was surrounded at the pass of Roncevaux, he was too proud to blow his ivory horn to summon back the main army to rescue them; but after his force was cut to pieces his last heroic gesture was to sound the horn so that the message should reach Charlemagne, thirty leagues away.

If one fairly short poem of Browning's can yield such a wide range of suggestions, his other work may safely be assumed to contain discoverable traces of the process which the poet himself described in his analogy of "the ring and the book." Yet a glance at the notes in any standard college text will show that the editors have been content to dilate upon the known historical facts for the poems that possess avowed prototypes, and to pass the others with a mere comment that they are fictitious. Of "My Last Duchess," one text-book remarks, "the speaker is an imaginary Duke of Ferrara." [11] Of "The Bishop Orders His Tomb at St. Praxed's Church," another editor says, "the Bishop is an imaginary personage." [12] True as far as they go, these statements ought to arouse immediate curiosity as to how the personages became so vivid in the imagination of a writer with Browning's passion for historical accuracy.

Many readers have felt some sort of kinship between these two poems, as though they were companion pictures of Italian Renaissance egoism; and one scholar has proposed a common origin for both of them. John D. Rea, in an article published in 1932,[13] traced the two poems to Vespasio Gonzaga, Duke of Sabbioneta, whose biography was written by Irenio Affó in the eighteenth century. Like Browning's Duke, this one was a patron of artists, and he had three wives, the first of whom he suspected of infidelity. She abruptly disappeared, and a surviving letter of the Duke's explained that "she died suddenly of apoplexy . . . without being able to speak a word." Like Browning's Bishop, this Duke of Sabbioneta, while lying in his last illness, dictated a will in which he instructed his daughter to lay out 1,500 scudi for a magnificent tomb, using the stone that he had brought from Rome for the purpose, and to spend a further 2,500 scudi in embellishing the church in which he was to be buried.

Mr. Rea's suggestion is plausible, and provides objective evidence for the feeling that the two poems were somehow linked in their conception. Many questions, however, remain. Why did Browning head "My Last Duchess" with the sub-title "Ferrara"? Why did he tell an inquirer that "the commands were that she should be put to death, *or he might have had her shut up in a convent*" (my italics)? Why was the death-bed egotism of the Duke of Sabbioneta transferred to a wealthy, greedy, sensual churchman? Louis S. Friedlander established the connection with Ferrara by suggesting the career of Duke Alfonso II.[14] In my opinion, Browning's Duke is a composite of several members of the Este family, including both Duke Alfonso and his father, Ercole II.[15] This sustains the link with the Bishop through the character of Ercole's brother, Cardinal Ippolito d'Este the Younger. Duke Ercole, one of the most lavish in the line of dukes who accumulated the magnificent art collection at Ferrara, married eighteen-year-old Princess Renée of France for purely dynastic reasons, and then became infuriated because she insisted upon giving sanctuary to French Protestant refugees. He took her children from her, put her in prison, and finally forced her to recant her Calvinist sympathies. As for his brother, the Cardinal was notorious for his stinginess (he gave Ariosto no reward in return for his dedication of *Orlando Furioso*); he was defeated as a candidate for the Papacy because of his scandalously worldly conduct; and he is best remembered for the building of the gorgeous Villa d'Este at Tivoli. We begin to get a glimpse of Browning's creative methods when we see him thus selecting details from several separate models and combining them under the guise of fictitious characters so that he can intensify one particular impression and thus epitomize a historical era in a single episode.

Apart from these historical antecedents, "My Last Duchess" reveals also an interesting literary reminiscence. The Victorian poets were addicted to providing what they considered to be psychologically valid versions of stories previously enshrined in conventional sentiment. Sometimes the revision was explicitly identified with the original, as in Tennyson's "Ulysses" and Browning's "The Glove"; more often the connection was tacit, and perhaps unconscious. In this sense, "My Last Duchess" seems to be a rectification of Shakespeare's romantic portrayal of Leontes in *The Winter's Tale*.

Like Browning's Duke, Leontes was egotistically suspicious of his innocent wife's virtue. He raged to see her and Polixenes "making practis'd smiles, as in a looking-glass," even though Polixenes was the visitor whom he had pressed to remain; similarly the Duke was infuriated when his wife smiled and blushed at the compliments of the friar whom he had brought in to paint her portrait. Leontes did not mention his jealousy, but planned the murder of his friend and (when this failed) imprisoned his wife, brought her to trial, and threatened her with death; the Duke did not "stoop" to chide his wife for her indiscretion, but "gave commands" which presumably caused her death.

The resemblance between the play and the poem would not be noticeable were there not the famous "statue scene" in the last act. Sixteen years a widower, Leontes is being urged by his courtiers to remarry. Paulina interposes to say, "give me the office to choose you a queen—she shall not be so young as was your former." She later takes Leontes to her house to see a statue of his late wife, "a piece many years in doing, and now newly performed by that rare Italian master, Julio Romano; . . . he so near to Hermione hath done Hermione that they say one would speak to her and stand in hope of answer." Leontes says:

> Your gallery
> Have we pass'd through, not without much content
> In many singularities, but we saw not
> That which my daughter came to look upon,
> The statue of her mother.

Paulina explains that because of the rare verisimilitude of the portrait she keeps it "lonely, apart," and she then draws a curtain and displays the so-called statue. "Behold! and say 'tis well," she says triumphantly.

> I like your silence; it the more shows off
> Your wonder.

All this exactly parallels the situation in Browning's poem except that the roles of the widower and the marriage envoy are reversed; in the poem it is the Duke who leads the visitor through the rarities of his collection and then uncovers "my last Duchess . . . Looking as though she were alive. I call That piece a wonder now," while the marriage envoy gazes in silent amazement.

"My Last Duchess," then, condensed a central situation of *The Winter's Tale* into fifty-six lines; but it also ironically controverted the theme. Shakespeare had transformed Leontes in a single moment from a monster of unreasonable jealousy and sadistic pride into an inconsolable penitent; Browning showed the Duke of Ferrara complacently boasting of his arrogance and preparing to re-enact the circumstances with a new victim.

One other well-known monologue of Browning's may also be cited, as it gives an even better example of the way that commentators seem wilfully blind to any hint that the poet himself offered. "The Laboratory" carries the sub-title "Ancien Régime," which of course specifically connotes the Versailles court during the century or so immediately preceding the French Revolution. Nevertheless, the textbook editors struggle diligently to ignore the clue. One says, "It is impossible to say whether the period is the sixteenth, the seventeenth, or the eighteenth century." [16] Another tells us: "The sub-title indicates that the poem was set in France, possibly in the later sixteenth century, under the regency of Catherine de' Medici." [17] A third goes still further back in history: "The subtitle leads us to believe that the time is that of the Middle Ages, when poison was the common method employed of doing away with those who were in the way." [18] And a fourth even implies that Browning did not know what his own phrase meant: "The poem gives an incident characteristic of Italy in the sixteenth and seventeenth centuries, but Browning apparently intends *Ancien Régime* to mean France before the Revolution." [19] Even our leading contemporary authority on Browning, William C. DeVane, said flatly in his *Browning Handbook:* "No source has been found for *The Laboratory,* and I should not expect to find one." [20]

And yet all the while the identification reposed in a single word used by one of the first explicators of Browning's poems, who assumed that his readers knew enough of French history to grasp the significance of his reference. Arthur Symons, in his *Introduction to the Study of Browning,* termed the young woman who visited the laboratory "a Brinvilliers." [21] One has only to read the career of that coquettish and murderous marquise, in the heyday of the court of Louis XIV, to find that practically every detail of Browning's poem has its parallel in her exploits. The Marquise, like Browning's heroine, was "a little woman with very soft blue eyes, and said to be of marvellous beauty. Ste. Croix [her lover] and Mme de Brinvilliers got their knowledge from Christopher Glaser, a Swiss chemist, author of a treatise on chemistry and discoverer of potassium sulphate. The lovers wrote of their poisons as 'Glaser's recipes.' . . . The tale that Ste. Croix was suffocated through the breaking of a glass mask while he was preparing some poisonous substances . . . according to Funck Brentano has no foundation in fact." [22] Another authority tells us that "the Marquise de Brinvilliers found sexual satisfaction in the agonies of her victims." [23]

It is easy to see, however, how the special techniques of the dramatic monologue obliged the poet to evolve a fictitious personage instead of portraying the real one. Mme de Brinvilliers was motivated mainly by greed; she planned and carried out the poisonings in conjunction with her lover; and she conducted her campaign of death for six years before being discovered. By changing the motive to jealousy and conceit, by making the murderess concoct the scheme alone, and by merely forecasting a series of further crimes when she realizes "what a wild crowd of invisible pleasures" reside in the chemist's phials, Browning greatly increased both the emotional intensity and the artistic unity of the story.

This same poem may be used also to illustrate an earlier topic of the present discussion, the poet's devices of form and phrase. The opinion of many critics is summarized by DeVane when he says that the poem "exhibits Browning's delight in catching the atmosphere of a time and place in small compass." [24] But no one has done much to show that the "atmosphere of time and place" is reproduced by the technique as skilfully as by the contents. The fluent couplets provide a remarkably good equivalent for the alexandrines of French classical drama, and a specific resemblance to one of the most famous depictions of pitiless revenge can be seen when a stanza of "The Laboratory" is compared with a passage in Racine's *Andromaque:*

> Not that I bid you spare her the pain!
> Let death be felt and the proof remain;
> Brand, burn up, bite into its grace—
> He is sure to remember her dying face.

Here is Racine's Hermione gloating:

> Quel plaisir de venger moi-même mon injure,
> De retirer mon bras teint du sang du parjure,
> Et, pour rendre sa peine et mes plaisirs plus grands,
> De cacher ma rivale à ses regards mourants! (IV, iv)

As well as recalling French classical tragedy, "The Laboratory" also recalls a well-known poem by a later French classicist, who succumbed to romanticism—"La Toilette de Constance," by Casimir Delavigne. Except for its final stanza, Delavigne's poem is a dramatic monologue, and in it a petted and coquettish girl reveals her invincible selfishness while she makes ready to attend a brilliant party where she will meet a former lover. Her manner toward her maid is exactly similar to the lady's attitude toward the chemist in Browning's poem, and the refrain lines,

> Je vais au bal ce soir
> Chez l'ambassadeur de France,

are paralleled by Browning's reiteration of "go where men wait and dance at the King's."

By citing a few examples of the connotations and complex overtones discoverable in poems by Tennyson and Browning, I hope to have demonstrated what I can only term the pertinacity of the Victorian poets. They refuse to be dismissed as pretentious moralizers or sentimental embroiderers. The modern admirers of Tennyson have dwelt upon his genuine presentation of psychopathic melancholy and frustration. Browning might be given similar credit for his repeated portrayals of vicious criminals. With a stubborn determination to keep poetry alive in an era when it was threatened not only by the rivalry of well-written prose but also by the current dominance of scientific and materialistic values, the Victorians studied all elements of their art and assiduously sought to improve what they had written. Their creative imagination embodied itself in significant symbols which were shaped through a mingling of personal emotion with traditional themes. For half a century the critics have insisted on considering them only as sociologists or metaphysicians and then condemning them for alleged inadequacy in that role. Let us begin to do them justice by regarding them as artists.

NOTES

1. This paper was delivered before the Philological Association of the Pacific Coast on November 25, 1950, as the presidential address.

2. Jack Lindsay, *Charles Dickens: A Biographical and Critical Study* (New York, 1950), 5.

3. Mary Joan Donahue, "Tennyson's *Hail, Briton!* and *Tithon* in the Heath Manuscript," *PMLA*, LXIV, 1949, 385-416.

4. Fannie E. Ratchford, "The First Draft of Swinburne's *Hertha,*" *Modern Language Notes*, XXXIX, 1924, 22-6.

5. Arthur J. Carr, "Tennyson as a Modern Poet," *University of Toronto Quarterly*, XIX, 1950, 361. [The article is reprinted in the present volume, pp. 311-33.]

6. Lionel Stevenson, "The 'High-born Maiden' Symbol in Tennyson," *PMLA*, LXIII, 1948, 234-43. See also C. de L. Ryals, "The 'Fatal Woman' Symbol in Tennyson," *ibid.*, LXXIV, 1959, 438-43.

7. E. D. H. Johnson, "The Lily and the Rose: Symbolic Meaning in Tennyson's *Maud,*" *ibid.*, LXIV, 1949, 1222-7.

8. *Letters of Robert Browning*, ed. Thurman L. Hood (New Haven, 1933), 76.

9. Harold Golder, "Browning's *Childe Roland,*" *PMLA*, XXXIX, 1924, 963-87. Although *The Road to Xanadu* was not yet published, Golder indicated in a footnote that he was acquainted with it.

10. William C. DeVane, "The Landscape of Browning's *Childe Roland,*" *ibid.*, XL, 1925, 426-32.

11. J. Stephens, E. H. Beck, R. H. Snow, eds., *Victorian and Later English Poets* (New York, 1937), 1198.

12. E. K. Brown, ed., *Victorian Poetry* (New York, 1942), 791.

13. John D. Rea, "My Last Duchess," *Studies in Philology*, XXIX, 1932, 120-2.

14. Louis S. Friedlander, "Ferrara and 'My Last Duchess,' " *ibid.*, XXXIII, 1936, 656-84.

15. Other parallels with the poem are to be found in the career of Duke Nicholas III (1384-1441). See my article, " 'My Last Duchess' and *Parisina,*" *Modern Language Notes*, LXXIV, 1959, 489-92.

16. Brown, *Victorian Poetry*, 791.

17. Stephens, Beck, and Snow, *Victorian and Later English Poets*, 1195-6.

18. W. H. Rogers, ed., *The Best of Browning* (New York 1942), 510.

19. J. W. Bowyer and J. L. Brooks, eds., *The Victorian Age: Prose, Poetry, and Drama* (New York, 1938), 1072.

20. William C. DeVane, *A Browning Handbook* (New York, 1935), 154. In his revised edition (1955) DeVane modified his statement and incorporated some of the points made in this paragraph.

21. Arthur Symons, *An Introduction to the Study of Browning* (London, 1886), 75.

22. A. and M. Wynter Blyth, *Poisons: Their Effects and Detection*, 5th ed. (New York, 1920), 11–12.

23. Montague Summers, *Essays in Petto* (London, 1928), 94.

24. William C. DeVane, ed., *The Shorter Poems of Robert Browning* (New York, 1942), 341.

CURTIS DAHL

The Victorian Wasteland

In recent years much has been written about the "wasteland" poets
of the early twentieth century. But it should not be forgotten that
the Victorians also used wasteland imagery with great effectiveness to
express their melancholy moods. Thomas Hardy, for instance, in his
somber majestic heath represents the vast and unchanging reality
around man that inescapably shapes his destiny. Oscar Wilde starkly
paints the waste courtyard of Reading Gaol and sees in its bareness
the bitter irony of the love that kills. William Morris depicts sodden
hopelessness in the dreary landscape of *The Haystack in the Floods*
and the emptiness of all experience in *The Hollow Land*. The turbid
longings and passionate regrets in the strange house Wuthering
Heights echo in the accents of Heathcliff across Emily Brontë's barren
moors. Arthur Hugh Clough in the lyric *Say Not the Struggle Nought
Availeth* compares life to a battle on smoky ground beside tired
waves and hopes bravely for the rising of the sun. The best examples
of Victorian wasteland poetry, however, are to be found in poems by
Tennyson, Browning, Arnold, Swinburne, and Thomson. In an analysis of the meaning with which each of these poets invests his wasteland, comparisons to the early or "wasteland" poems (not the later
poems) of T. S. Eliot are inevitable.

I

In Tennyson's *The Holy Grail*, the eighth of the *Idylls of the King*,
the dry and rocky "land of sand and thorns" through which Percivale
rides in search of the Grail represents the difficult road which a man

From *College English*, XVI (1955), 341–47. Reprinted by permission of
the National Council of Teachers of English, and the author.

searching for an other-worldly ideal must traverse. The mortal world seems dry and thorny to those who have a thirst too spiritual for its waters to quench. Dust swirls up from the wasteland, and lightnings without rain strike. But the road is not one that all men must travel. It is a way consciously chosen by knights in opposition to Arthur's wishes. For all ordinary men, even for ordinary knights of the Table Round, it is a lonely and barren path. Only the saintly Galahad's perfect purity gives him the vision that transforms the simple chapel where he and Percivale pray into the resting place of the Holy Grail. He has a sacred calling that draws him toward the Holy City over bridges that vanish for Percivale. The wasteland for him is not as for the others a place of drought and thirst. But even Percivale, though he is pure enough to glimpse the Grail's radiance, finds it a lonely and waterless tract. He is left in the dry thorns, while other even less dedicated knights find only death in the black swamp. Their bones whiten the edge. It is only the exceptionally godlike who can pierce through the wasteland to reach the Holy City or even catch a gleam of the light of salvation. For most men the attempt, as Arthur predicts, leads to failure or death.

Thus Tennyson through Arthur warns ordinary men to avoid the spiritual wasteland that lies before men who search for mystic salvation outside the duties of the mortal world. Too intense, too unworldly idealism, too complete spirituality will turn ordinary life, as it does for Percivale (and indeed also for the hypocritical St. Simeon), to dust. For Arthur and for Tennyson the realities of life on earth are not waste, are not dry and bare. They only appear so to men whose eyes are dazzled by a divine radiance too bright for earth. Some few men are Galahads who should follow the quest; but most men are Lancelots who despite their sins should help to build the kingdom of God on earth, to serve mankind rather than follow an ideal of religion apart from the practicalities of ordinary living. To see human life as a desert, as Percivale does, is wrong. This view is obviously in sharp contrast with T. S. Eliot's implication in *The Waste Land* (which also makes use of the Grail legend) that every man should seek in the waste the rose of salvation watered by the streams of grace. For Eliot the death of the Fisher King can alone bring fertility to the wasteland; for Tennyson, King Arthur, who represents the earthly ideal, must live in order that life may bloom. For both poets there is a desert in the garden and a garden in the desert, but Tennyson would make the desert blossom like the rose by causing men to live and work in the mortal world, while Eliot sees fertility for the wasteland only in the death-bringing search for the grail or the sacramental death of the Fisher King.

In contrast, the "dark strait of barren land" where the final battle in the mist takes place in *The Passing of Arthur,* represents in part Tennyson's vision of a world in which ideals seem to have failed. Arthur's great kingdom has apparently come to naught; even his last knight Sir Bedivere is in the final scene almost unfaithful. God still seems to speak through nature, "in the shining of the stars" and the "flowering of His fields," but man's destiny is a dark barren land of mist and uncertainty, blasphemy and strife. The wasteland symbolizes, as it does also for Clough and for Arnold, the intellectual and spiritual battlefields of Tennyson's time. Nothing can be seen clearly; one knows not who is on one's side; and when the bitter wind comes at evening, all is desolate. Even religion and faith, symbolized by the ruined chapel and broken cross, are in decay.

At first this wasteland appears as barren as that of any modern poet. Yet it is a wasteland in which heroism and victory, even though in a cause apparently lost, are possible. Arthur has won his present battle: Modred lies dead before him. And because one last knight is faithful to him, Arthur can live to come again and reclaim the wasteland in some future age. Tennyson does not, as Eliot might, have Arthur find redemption in the ruined chapel. The dying king is carried away from the chapel toward a body of water much larger than that in the holy font, a body of living water in nature itself. Salvation for Tennyson springs from a broader change than that brought about by any merely sacramental or personal cleansing. Tennyson reads hope of God's protean love even in the dreary panorama of a battlefield seemingly waste. After the clouds of doubt have blown away, God's stars shine.

II

In Browning's *Childe Roland to the Dark Tower Came,* the significance of the wasteland, the "stubbed ground" and "stark black dearth" and "fell cirque," is related to the theme of going forward bravely at any cost, even death. Just as in *Prospice* there is one last battle to be fought before the victory of death can be attained, so at the end of his search Childe Roland has a final test. To be loyal to his quest he must traverse the barren waste that lies in the shadow of the valley of death. Like the rotted oaks in *The Holy Grail,* like the broken pillar in Eliot's *The Hollow Men,* everything here speaks of what has been and is now no longer. This land has not always been desert.

The stubbed ground was "once a wood"; the horrid engine once had a use; the horse now blind probably belonged formerly to some other questing knight. The changing of the former natural beauty to a wasteland seems the work of a moody fool, as haphazard as Caliban's slaying the twenty-first crab. Thus the lowness, the "mute despair," the treacherous and "suicidal" qualities of this land represent those unexplained shiftings of good to evil which confront all men as they pass through life.

Childe Roland to the Dark Tower Came is not, however, a gloomy poem. Browning is not focussing his attention on the wasteland any more than in *How They Brought the Good News* he is principally interested in the route from Ghent to Aix. The scrubby, blotchy land through which he rides and the mysterious tower itself are merely trials to test his strength. The one question is whether Childe Roland is fit for the supreme strife. He abhors the land from the depths of his soul; he senses its evilness and thinks that the river may have been "a bath for the fiend's glowing hoof." But every black eddy of the stream, every staring bone of the horse, every cockleburr and thistle of the land is there for the purpose of bringing out the best in him. Because he keeps his courage to the end, because like the Grammarian he triumphs over his wasteland, every horrid aspect of it becomes a thing of good and glory for him. The wasteland leads to the divine land of promise.

In contrast to Eliot's, Browning's wasteland is one that can be conquered by man's unaided courage. No sacrament of purgation, no specifically religious rite of atonement is needed, nor can the suffering and victory be vicarious. Here the rats of decay can be killed by a knight's spear. Instead of being a land dry in its lack of spiritual insight, this is a tract into which only those with clear eyes and a definite purpose enter. Roland does not wander in the waste because he knows no ford into richer country; he is dedicated from the start to seek out the Dark Tower. At the close of the poem he may seem to fail, but in enduring to the end he has truly conquered. And though the divine spark in him is his individual courage, because like Percivale he is a member of a pledged Band his victory has more than only individual significance. Eliot's Magi, after a long hard journey through hostile lands, feel in the end only bitter discontent and a sense of alienation from their fellows. Roland, however, in the "fell cirque" before the blind tower experiences a sense of glorious fellowship with Cuthbert and Giles and the other knights who have fought, successfully or unsuccessfully, before him. With their voices in his ears and with the slug horn sounding, he approaches the end. For Browning the wasteland is a field of victory.

III

Matthew Arnold's wasteland is not usually a place of victory but a dry unproductive present age between two more noble eras, "one dead / The other powerless to be born." In *Rugby Chapel*, however, two kinds of wasteland appear. One is the land of eddying dust, comparable to that of *The Hollow Men*, where most men aimlessly mill. But Arnold in the poem is much more interested in those stronger men whose tragedy is not lack of ideals but unrealized ideals. To represent their struggle he uses, like Eliot, the image of a harsh journey through mountains—

> The road winding among mountains
> Which are mountains of rock without water.

Unlike Eliot, however, Arnold postulates a "clear-purposed goal," a City of God certainly known and accepted though ignored by most men. He believes in a sure ideal at the bound of the waste, not a ruined Jerusalem or Athens or Alexandria with falling towers. Arnold's hope lies in social order and unity, and his City of God may be on earth rather than in heaven. Arnold believes, furthermore, in heroes especially endowed with the strength and courage to lead the straggling line of mankind through the mountains. Indeed, the wasteland may perhaps have been created in part to give opportunity to such human yet divinely inspired leadership. While Eliot sees salvation and rebirth in the mystic rose or in rain from heaven, Arnold finds it in social action in obedience to great human leaders. Eliot seems to show no certain faith in anything except salvation for the individual. His men wander in the wasteland one by one; each must himself seek divine grace. Thus for Eliot the wasteland is a place of almost passive endurance. For Arnold it is a path of active, almost military struggle. In one there is only dry rock; in the other there are cataracts and avalanches and a lonely inn among the clouds, where a "gaunt and taciturn host" welcomes the weary.

Dover Beach is more characteristic of the bulk of Arnold's poetry. On the "naked shingles" of the darkling strand Arnold feels himself isolated from the intellectual and moral standards of those around him. Like a child reared in an old abbey garden, like Mycerinus retired to his secluded castle, Arnold sees from afar the banners passing and sighs for lost palaces beneath the sea. The great ages of the past are gone; those of the future have not yet come; and the present is a darkling plain on which ignorant armies clash by night. Arnold does not, like Tennyson, identify himself with one of the combatants or imply that the struggle, however confused, is a noble one. Like the Greek in mournful awe before the fallen Runic stone, like the Carthusian monk in a world that has forgotten faith, he stands aloof and merely comments on "the strange disease of modern life" with its "sick hurry" and "divided aims." He is saddened by what he sees, but he knows that only in clarity and detachment of vision does hope lie.

Is this wasteland not comparable to MacLeish's in *The Too-Late Born?* The modern poet, though come too late to take part in the battle, has at least heard the echoes of the mighty horn of Roland in the passages of Spain. Yet, though warriors like Roland existed in the past, they have fought only to suffer defeat. While Arnold finds the ebbed sea of faith still sadly tossing the pebbles on the beach, and the battle on the plain still in progress, MacLeish some seventy years later knows that whatever was heroic in the past was defeated in the past. He finds only

> The dead against the dead and on the silent ground
> The silent slain.

In the modern poet there is little of Arnold's belief that an age of expansion will follow one of concentration, that the hard dry earth of the wasteland holds seeds from past eras that with cultivation can blossom again.

IV

Though in his pantheistic poem *On the Downs* Swinburne sees the barren stretches of the downs as imbued with the same life that is within us and therefore as understandable phases of a living whole, a more characteristic use of wasteland imagery is to be found in *A Forsaken Garden.* In the deserted garden overlooking the sea the flower beds are "blossomless," the walks bare, the seed plots dry and thorny. The roses that once grew there and the nightingale that once sang there have disappeared. The only lasting forces are those of change and destruction: the sea-wind still blowing over the dry garden, the sea still eating at the base of the cliff until the wasteland itself topple into the waves. Love, like the roses, will perish; the lovers who once walked in the garden have gone to the grave. Existence is thus a wasteland, "a round where life seems barren as death," and in death itself there is no hope. The only alleviation of despair is the prospect that the never-ceasing billows of purposeless change will at last bring the peace of complete oblivion. Then death itself will lie dead.

Thus in *A Forsaken Garden*, as in the *Hymn to Proserpine*, *The Last Oracle*, and many parts of the trilogy on Mary Stuart, Swinburne is lamenting the decay of a past of beauty and passion in comparison to which the present seems barren. The chaplets of Apollo and Venus, the laurels of Ronsard and the Pléiade, the roses in the forsaken garden have withered; only their thorns are left. That these flowers may have been blossoms of lust and sadism only increases Swinburne's regret for them; the deepest vice to him seems infinitely preferable to insensitive, over-moral philistinism. It is, indeed, probably the triumph of Christian virtue over pagan sensuality and aestheticism that causes the wasteland. Swinburne does not believe that a return to pagan beauty can ever be achieved; the roses can never bloom again. But he receives a kind of negative comfort in his confidence that time eventually will destroy even the wasteland of Christian ethics. Proserpine, goddess of eternal death, gathers all things to herself; the blossoms of the sea will continue to bloom when the forsaken garden has disappeared far beneath its waves.

Swinburne's scale of values is clarified when it is compared to the almost directly contradictory scale of Eliot. The rose, symbol for Eliot of Christian salvation, is for Swinburne the symbol of the raptures of pagan vice. Eliot's wasteland is dry because Christian ideals have not penetrated to it, Swinburne's because Christian ethics have devastated it. Eliot finds in the wasteland too many Sweeneys controlled by their coarse sexual appetites; Swinburne sees life a wasteland largely because the beauty of sexual passion has been suppressed. Like Eliot, Swinburne finds the inner essential truth of existence hidden seed—like in the dry ground of a waste garden. However, the truth he finds is not the saving grace of Christianity; instead it is merely the empty comfort that all things are inevitably swept away by the tides of fate. This very insistence on the foreordained destruction of even the thorns of life by the blind surging forces of change gives a dignity to Swinburne's wasteland that much of the modern wasteland lacks. For instance, there is a passion in Mary Stuart's revolt against the land of Knox that is nowhere echoed by Eliot's Magi, who on their return find that they too have become strangers in their own land. Mary has faith at least in her own twisted standards, in the delight of cruel love, and in the consciousness of her deadly power, but the Magi, though they have seen the miracle, are still unsatisfied. Sexual desire itself in Swinburne has a certain nobility since it leads to beauty and courage even when it is adulterous or masochistic. It does not end in the sordid amours of *The Fire Sermon* or the shallow hesitation of Prufrock. The eternal sea swirling at the beetling cliff beneath the forsaken garden has majesty and power. For the Victorians great forces are in the world, even though they may be forces for evil. These call forth violent protest or vehement adulation. The modern wasteland, on the contrary, is often a place of doubt and hesitation. With Swinburne, for instance, we course the barren but beautiful moors of Northumberland riding vigorously against the sea-born wind. With Eliot we dance around the prickly pear at five o'clock in the morning.

v

Through the huge, dark, silent, partly ruined metropolis that in *The City of Dreadful Night* James Thomson describes as lying in a "trackless wilderness" between the "waste marches" of a river and "moorland dark" and "stony ridges," he expresses an unrelieved and hopeless pessimism far deeper even than the sometimes posed gloominess of Swinburne. In Thomson's great city, the edges of which disappear into the illimitable darkness, there is not even the comfort of inevitable oblivion. In this city faith has been poisoned, love stabbed, and hope starved. If God exists, he is malignant; if not, we are ruled eternally by purposeless, unthinking Chance. Even death is no refuge, for hell itself denies entrance to the hopeless. Mighty ruins around the city hint a better past, but we cannot return to it. We belong nowhere.

In many respects Thomson's wasteland is like that of the twentieth century poets. The pall of dark despair over the city is paralleled in Eliot's *Ash Wednesday* and by the "brown fog of a winter noon" over the "unreal city" of London in *The Waste Land*. Like Eliot's Hollow Men we wander in darkness between heaven and hell. But there is a difference. Though dreary, life in the City of Dreadful Night is never so small and coarse or so cheaply sinister as that pictured by Eliot's *Preludes* or *Gerontion*. The dark river that winds by Thomson's towers of despair is not a Thames filled with dead dogs and orange peels. It is a calm and mighty and deep river. It flows from the depths of the human soul into a boundless ocean of meaningless misery. It is water that allays no thirst but of which every man must drink. Thomson reaches nearly the ultimate in despair. Of modern poets perhaps only E. A. Robinson equals his futilitarian power. But just as Eliot in his attacks on modern life always implies values he would like to see restored, even Robinson in *Credo* feels the vague "coming glory of the Light." Furthermore, Richard Cory going home one fine summer's day, Ben Jonson chatting about his friend from Stratford, and Mr. Flood holding his party on the hill display a stoical, sometimes almost humorous acceptance of the apparent nothingness of life that differs from Thomson's intense protest. Thomson does not wander calmly through his wasteland. He feels its terrors to the full, sees fiends in every somber shadow, and pours out through his imagery a passionate and personal anguish. Though he searches for light, though he intensely questions all he meets, he finds only dreadful night. His sole comfort is that he need not even to himself keep up the pretense of courage, for though he is one of the inhabitants of a great city, no one cares about him.

Writers in all centuries have compared their worlds to wastelands. Ezekiel writes of the Valley of Dry Bones. Vergil's Aeneas traverses the misty plains of the dark underworld. Dante's "indifferent" wander aimlessly in shadows. Milton pictures Christ tempted in the wilderness, while Shakespeare portrays Lear storm-wracked on a bleak and desolate heath. Bunyan's Pilgrim trudges a dark path through the blasted Valley of the Shadow of Death. Each age has invested the wasteland image with its own meaning. The wasteland of the Victorian poets is on the whole more dignified, more static in significance, more restrained in regard to sex, more specifically social rather than individual, and more nostalgic toward the past than that of most twentieth century poets. Nevertheless, the dry rocks and wasted vegetation of the cactus land were as vital and meaningful symbols to the generation of Arnold and Tennyson as they are to that of Eliot and MacLeish. The wasteland, often thought to be a modern discovery, had been thoroughly explored by the Victorians before the twentieth century was born.

LORD DAVID CECIL

◆

Early Victorian Novelists:
As They Look to the Reader

THEY crowd the shelves of every gentleman's library. *Editions de luxe,*
heavy with gilding and the best rag paper, standard reprints clothed
in an honorable and linen simplicity, dim behind glass doors, or sallow
with exposure to dust and daylight, the serried lines confront one,
Dickens, Thackeray, Trollope, George Eliot, lawful and undisputed
monarchs of literature. At least so they were; else how should they have
attained their majestic position on the shelves, rubbing shoulders on
equal terms, as it were, with Milton and Gibbon and Boswell's *Life
of Johnson?* But no author's reputation is certain for fifty years at
least after his death. Will these novelists keep their high place? The
experience of the last few years might lead one to doubt it.

For one thing people do not read most of them as they used. As
often as not when one tries to open the glass bookcase the lock sticks,
stiff with disuse. And those that have read them have not all done it in
a respectful spirit. The learned and Olympian kind of critic speaks of
them less often than of French or Russian novelists; while the bright
young people of the literary world, if they mention them at all, do so
with boredom and contempt and disgust.

All this is partly due to the fact that these writers have been under
the cloud that inevitably obscures the heroes of an age just passed. To
appreciate the art of another period one must, to a certain extent,
enter into its spirit, accept its conventions, adopt "a willing suspension
of disbelief" in its values. For if we have no sympathy for what it is

From *Early Victorian Novelists: Essays in Revaluation* by Lord David Cecil,
Copyright 1935. Used by special permission of the publishers, The Bobbs-
Merrill Company, Inc. (Indianapolis) and Constable and Company Limited
(London), and the author.

trying to say, we shall not be able to judge if it says it well. But by some mysterious law of human taste it is almost impossible to enter into the spirit of the age that comes just before one's own. The clothes in the pictures of one's great-grandmother in youth, look charming and picturesque; those in pictures of one's mother look merely grotesque; so grotesque, indeed, that it is impossible to discriminate between them. And similarly the mental fashions of the last generation seem so absurd to the next one that it cannot estimate their comparative merits at all.

Pope could not admire any Caroline, the Romantics could not admire Pope, and the Edwardians could not admire the Victorians. It was not that they disagreed with their ideals more than with those of other ages. They complained a great deal, it is true, of the Victorian ideal of domesticity; but they did not disapprove of it any more than they did of the Elizabethan ideal of virginity. And this they never complained of at all. Critics rebuked Tennyson for representing Lancelot as an English gentleman of 1860, but were only interested when Shakespeare represented Troilus as an English gentleman of 1590. The last age, like a relation, is too close for a man to be able to view it with the detachment necessary for criticism. Why this should be is not clear. Can it have a Freudian explanation, some huge mass Oedipus complex against the father's generation? Perhaps the psychologists could explain it for us. How pleasant if they should divert their attention for a moment from the dingy problems of the individual subconsciousness!

Any way, inevitable reactions have their inevitable ends. After a few years a period passes from shadow into the sunless impartial daylight of history, its books to be surveyed in perspective with the rest of literature, to be judged as personally or as little personally as those of the Greeks and Hebrews. That which has permanent value emerges, that which only appealed to a transitory phase of taste is finally obscured. Now the first thin rays of the dawn have begun to strike the nineteenth century. Tennyson is admired again: it is Conrad not Carlyle whom the lively Rhadamanthuses of our weekly reviews are condemning to everlasting oblivion. At length it should be possible to arrive at some estimate of the novelists; to get that detached general view of them that we need in order to come to any sort of final verdict. We now realize that the fact that they may be Victorian is no more a cause for praise or blame than the fact that Chaucer is medieval. If we like them it is not because they express "the best aspirations of our great age"; if we dislike them it is not because we think, if indeed we have ever been so foolish, that they do not show "a truly modern mind" or "values unacceptable to a post-war generation"—nauseous jargon of the 1920's. Let us unlock the glass door and pull down the books and see what they look like.

Well, they do not look at all the same as they used. The first thing that strikes one is that there is no Victorian Novel in the sense of a school with common conventions and traditions conterminous with the reign of Queen Victoria. There is one sort of novel before George Eliot and another after her. On the other hand the earlier sort is not peculiar to the Victorian age. Our grandfathers, naturally enough, were chiefly struck by the differences between their own contemporaries and the writers preceding them. And, of course, there is a large difference in moral point of view and some smaller differences in subject: for every great writer in his turn extended the range of subject matter. But from the literary point of view, the point of view of form, the differences are much less than the likenesses. Between 1750 and 1860 the broad conception of what a novel should be did not change. *Tom Jones, Roderick Random, Waverley, Nicholas Nickleby* are constructed on the same lines, composed within the same convention.

For, and this is the second feature that strikes us as we turn afresh the dusty pages, up till George Eliot the English novel is very definitely one school. Not a conscious school, with consciously common style and subject matter, like the fifteenth-century Italian painters, or the Elizabethan lyrical poets. The novel, the expression of the individual's view of the world, is always predominantly individualistic; the English, the wilful, eccentric self-confident English, are the most individualistic of mankind, and the nineteenth century is the most individualistic of periods. *Laisser faire* ruled the roost as triumphantly in the realm of art as in those of economics. No generalization that one makes about these writers will be equally true of all. But of all, except Emily Brontë, certain generalizations are true. The main outline of their novels is the same. Their stories consist of a large variety of character and incident clustering round the figure of a hero, bound together loosely or less loosely by an intrigue and ending with wedding bells. Compared with the French, for instance, or the Russians, they seem an independent national growth with its own conventions, its own idiosyncrasies; strong in the same way, in the same way weak.

And here we come to the third outstanding fact about them. They are an extraordinary mixture of strength and weakness. There is no denying that the greatest English novelists are often downright bad;

and in their greatest novels. At any moment and without a word of warning the reader may fall like a stone from a high flight of inspiration into a bog of ineptitude. There is hardly a book of Dickens which is not deformed by false sentiment, flashy melodrama, wooden characters; as often as not the hero is one of them; Thackeray's heroes are not much better; while whole passages of Charlotte Brontë could be incorporated without any effect of incongruity of style or sentiment in any penny novelette about pure maidens and purple passions.

Their faults of form are as bad as the faults of matter. It is very rare for a Victorian novelist before George Eliot to conceive the story as an organic whole of which every incident and character forms a contributory and integral part. Dickens chooses a conventional plot, generally a highly unlikely one, then crams it as by physical violence on to a setting and character with which it has no organic connection; so that the main interest of the book lies in characters and scenes irrelevant to the story. In *Shirley* Charlotte Brontë suddenly changes the center of the interest from Caroline to Shirley herself, half-way through the book. Thackeray had more idea of maintaining unity of interest; but his grasp on the development of the plot is very slack; in *Pendennis* and *The Newcomes* it drifts along in a succession of episodes to be cut short or extended as the author's caprice dictates. And both he and Trollope think nothing of having two or three plots devoid of any essential connection, flowing on in happy parallel independence at the same time.

But over and above the actual faults of these books one is struck by their limitations. They miss out so much of life, and so much of the important parts of it. They avoid—have we not heard it from the infuriated lips of a hundred earnest young students?—any detailed treatment of the animal side of human nature. To those whose austere task it is to study the masterpieces of contemporary fiction this may seem a recommendation: and it is true that aesthetically it is not nearly so disastrous an inhibition as that which modern novelists seem to feel against the pathetic and heroic emotions. But a picture of human life which gives us hardly anything of its primary passion, or of those classes and types of people whose chief concern it is, must be a scrappy affair. The male novelists—the women seem more robust about emotion—shrink from passion even in its respectable manifestations. It is often a major motive in their plots as it has been in all plots since stories first began; but they pat the beast gingerly with fingers protected by a thick glove of sentimental reverence, and then hastily pass on.

But sex is not the only important omission from their books. We find little about the broader, more impersonal objects that occupy mankind; his relation to thought, to art, to public affairs. And though Dickens and Thackeray like to sprinkle their emotional scenes with a few drops of undenominational piety, to play a little soft music on the organ, as it were, to give solemnity to a death-bed, religion is never the chief preoccupation of their characters as it is that of Alyosha Karamazov. This limitation of subject matter limits in its turn their range of characters. Their most successful creations, Mr. Micawber, Becky Sharp, Mrs. Proudie, Madam Beck, are all what actors call "character parts," marked individual types whose interest lies in their comic or picturesque idiosyncrasy of speech and manner rather than in their relation to any general problems or interests of human nature. They are of the family of the Aguechecks and Dame Quicklys; there are no Hamlets among them, no intellectuals, statesmen or artists. For those deeper issues of human life which are the main interests of such characters do not form any part of the Victorian subject matter.

And as a result they hardly ever stir those profounder feelings to which the very greatest art appeals. The great Russians were to make the novel rouse the same emotions as tragedy or epic. Except for Emily Brontë, the Victorian novelists did not. And her emotional quality, for all its splendor, is too remote from the normal experience of mankind to bring her into the circle of great tragedians. Anna Karenina is a tragic figure as Othello is a tragic figure; Heathcliff is rather the demon lover of a border ballad.

And yet in spite of all these sins of omission and commission, to re-read these books is not to be disappointed. For their defects are more than counterbalanced by their extraordinary merits, merits all the more dazzling to us from the fact that they are so noticeably absent from the novels of our contemporaries. Apart from anything else, they tell the story so well. And though this may not be the highest merit of the novelist, it is, in some sort, the first; for it satisfies the primary object for which novels were first written. Mankind, like a child, wanted to be told a story. It is noticeable that people still give Dickens and Thackeray to children; and this is not, as some critics seem to suggest, because they are infantile, but because they make the story immediately and easily interesting. Improbable though the plot may be, it keeps one on tenterhooks so that one cannot put down the book at the end of a chapter, but must look over the next leaf to see what is going to happen. The most ardent admirer has never turned the next leaf of *Ulysses* in order to see what was going to happen. Nor, even from a higher point of view, is the power to tell a story unimportant. For unless his interest is thoroughly engaged, how can a reader warm to that heightened, softened, acceptant condition of mind in which alone he is receptive of aesthetic impression? We turn once more to *Ulysses,* and repeat, how indeed!

And though from one aspect these novelists' range is limited, from another it is very large; much larger than that of most writers to-day. *Vanity Fair, Martin Chuzzlewit,* are not, like most modern novels, concentrated wholly on the fortunes of that handful of individuals who are its chief characters; they are also panoramas of whole societies. Now, as we read their pages, we are rubbing shoulders with kings and statesmen at Waterloo or Brussels, now huddling in an emigrant ship across the Atlantic, listening now to sharpers exchanging their plans across the sordid table of a gin palace, to schoolboys stridently teasing, to the genteel malice of a provincial drawing-room, to footmen relaxing over their beer; now we share the murmured confidences of two girls as the candle burns blue on the dressing-table and the ball-dress rustles from smooth shoulders to the floor. A hundred different types and classes, persons and nationalities, jostle one another across the shadow screen of our imagination. The Victorian novelists may miss the heights and depths, but they cast their net very wide.

And their range of subject is not larger than their range of mood. Modern novelists are all specialists, experts. There are the serious writers who wish to make a contribution to literature, Mr. Galsworthy, say, Mr. Aldous Huxley, Mrs. Woolf. And they in their turn can be subdivided: Mr. Galsworthy, the sociological realist, intent to diagnose society; Mr. Huxley, the philosopher, to whom fiction is a vehicle by which to convey his considered—and discouraging—ideas about life; Mrs. Woolf, the artist, who uses human life as a carpet-maker uses his colored skeins to weave a ravishing design. Then there are the frivolous writers, Mr. P. G. Wodehouse, Mrs. Agatha Christie, who write without thought of posterity, to entertain the reader of the moment, Mr. Wodehouse by laughs, Mrs. Christie by thrills. But the Victorians, the irresponsible Victorians, do not bother to sort themselves into any such categories. They write equally for the train journey and for all time; they crowd realism and fantasy, thrills and theories, knockabout farce and effects of pure aesthetic beauty, cheek by jowl on the same page; they are Mr. Galsworthy and Mr. Huxley and Mrs. Woolf, Mrs. Christie and Mr. Wodehouse, all in one. A book like *David Copperfield* is a sort of vast schoolboy hamper of fiction: with sweets and sandwiches, pots of jam with their greased paper caps, cream and nuts and glossy apples, all packed together in a heterogeneous deliciousness. And as a result it fills and stimulates the reader as the filtered vitamin B of contemporary genius hardly ever does. For it appeals to so many more of his sympathies: before familiarity has dulled his responsiveness to one set of stimuli it has evoked another.

But it is not their range or their power to tell a story that makes these novels so impressive. You can have an excellently told story dealing with half the people and passions under heaven which is only in a minor sense a work of art at all. And where the Victorians succeed so sensationally is precisely on their artistic side, in that quality which distinguishes a work of art from a work of thought or a work of practical use. Not that they are conscious artists like Mr. George Moore, for instance, solely and laboriously concerned to present their works in accordance with the strictest aesthetic canons. If they were, their books would not be so badly constructed. But art is not so exclusively the question of presentation and arrangement that some of our more pretentious critics seem to think; art is not the same as craft. If it were, Fletcher would be a greater dramatist than Webster, Goldsmith a greater poet than Blake. No, the specific mark of a work of art is that it is a "creation," a new, individual and living entity, owing something of its character, no doubt, to its subject and more to the personality of its creator, yet differing from and independent of either. Without this independent vitality the most accomplished portrait remains a photograph, the most intimate history a record. Nor can any "craft," however skillful, create a work of art till the raw material of experience on which it is working has been first transmuted to the stuff of which art is made. And the distinguishing, essential qualification of the artist is what for want of a better name is called "creative imagination"; the power, that is, which generates that union of artist and material in which alone the child of artistic life is born.

It is this quality of creative imagination which our novelists possess in such a supreme degree. It is their distinguishing characteristic; it is also the characteristic in which their successors are so markedly inferior to them. The material of the novelist is the world of human beings and their relations to one another. These he apprehends and selects in such a way as to create a new world, founded it is true on the real one, and, it may be, elucidating certain aspects of it, but with an independent energy and idiosyncrasy of its own. The modern realist tends just to reproduce the real world. He traces the life of an adolescent girl in a provincial town, or the stream of consciousness of an unsuccessful sculptor, or whatever his drab subject may be, with the detailed accuracy of a Dutch little master or a government blue-book. But that is all he does. His imagination never gets to work on the facts; the act of creation is never performed. So that the books have no independent vitality; they exist only in relation to their models, and can communicate no sense of reality to someone to whom these models mean nothing. They are photographs, not pictures.

Now the great Victorian novels are all pictures. Sometimes they are fanciful and romantic, connected with reality only by a frail thread; more often they, too, stick close to the facts of actual existence. But these facts are never merely reproduced, they are always fired and colored by a new and electric individuality. The act of creation is always performed. A street in London described by Dickens is very like a street in London; but it is still more like a street in Dickens. For Dickens has used the real world to create his own world, to add a country to the geography of the imagination. And so have Trollope and Thackeray and Charlotte Brontë and the rest of them. To read a paragraph of any of their books is to feel blowing into one's mental lungs unmistakably and invigoratingly a new and living air, the air of Dickensland, Thackerayland, Brontëland. For these authors possess in a supreme degree the quality of creative imagination.

It shows itself in the setting of their stories. Each has his characteristic, unforgettable scenery: Dickens' London, hazed with fog, livid with gaslight, with its shabby, clamorous, cheerful streets, its cozy and its squalid interiors, its stagnant waterside; and the different London of Thackeray: the west end of London on a summer afternoon, with its clubs and parks and pot-houses, mellow, modish and a little dusty, full of bustle and idleness; and Mrs. Gaskell's countryside, so pastoral and sequestered and domesticated: and the elemental moorland of the Brontës.

It shows itself in their actual conception of incident. Mr. Lockwood's first haunted night in the little room in Wuthering Heights, Lucy Snowe's drugged roaming through midnight Villette, garish with carnival, Bill Sikes, trapped in that sordid island by the river, Esmond come home after ten years' absence to the cathedral where Lady Castlewood's face gleams pale in the candleshine and the handful of worshipers mutter the weekly evensong: these stir the heart and stick in the memory, not because they are especially true to life, nor because of the characters—the picture remains in our minds when the very names involved in it are long forgotten—but because in themselves they are dramatic and picturesque. As a picture is an "invention" of line and color, so are these, brilliant "inventions" of scene and action.

Imagination shows itself still more in their humor. Indeed the very fact that they have humor shows that they are creative; for humor is not a record of facts but a comment on them. To make a joke of something means, by definition, to make something new of it; not just to leave it where it is. The masterpieces of contemporary fiction, one may note, have little humor: there are few jokes in *Sons and Lovers*, *Portrait of the Artist as a Young Man*. But in *Vanity Fair* and *David Copperfield* and *Barchester Towers* there are hundreds. All the great Victorian novelists are humorists. And humorists each in a style of his own. Mr. Micawber, Captain Costigan, Mrs. Proudie, Miss Matty Jenkins, Paul Emanuel, are all comic in different ways.

But, of course, the most important expression of the creative imagination lies in the most important part of any novel, in the characters. The Victorians are all able to make their characters live. They do not always do it, they are as unequal about this as they are about everything else. And even when they do the result is often, from the realist's point of view, preposterous. What real human being ever acted like Mr. Rochester or talked like Mr. F.'s aunt? But Mr. Rochester and Mr. F.'s aunt are none the less alive for that. We should recognize them if they came into the room, we could imagine how they would behave if we were not there to see; their words and gestures and tricks of speech are their own and no one else's. Nor are the normal average characters, Johnny Eames or Molly Gibson, less individual. They are not types. If they do something characteristic one's first feeling is not "How like a girl, how like a young man!" but "How like Molly Gibson, how like Johnny Eames!" Within the limits the Victorians' range of character might seem inexhaustible. Their books linger in the memory, not as stories or theses, but as crowds; crowds of breathing, crying, laughing, living people. As long as they live, the books that house them will never die.

This extraordinary mixture of strength and weakness, then, is the second startling characteristic of the English novel. It is the striking characteristic of most English literature. The Elizabethan dramatists, the Caroline lyric poets, are as sensationally bad at one time as they are sensationally good at another. But in the Victorian novel a natural predisposition was intensified by two circumstances. For one thing the form was so new. We have seen that the broad conception of the novel form held by Dickens and Thackeray was still the same as that held by Fielding and Smollett, the creators of the novel; so that the Victorian novel is still the novel in its first stage. Nor had it yet achieved its present lofty position in the hierarchy of letters. The novel is now a dominating literary form. The leading writers of the last thirty years, Mr. Wells, say, or Mr. Lawrence, express themselves and their theories through the novel, as the leading spirits in the Elizabethan age expressed themselves through poetry and drama. No one would call the more serious works of these authors light reading. But on its first appearance the novel—and this is the second circumstance about it making for inequality—was regarded as, of its nature, light reading. As late as 1880 well-brought-up children were taught not to read novels before luncheon; Herbert Spencer maintained that no novels but those of George Eliot were of sufficiently serious value to be in the London Library. The Victorian reader idled away an evening over a novel when he did not feel up to tackling history or poetry. Now we might go to the cinema; the novel then was, *in some degree*, regarded in the same way as the cinema is now, as a frivolity, a relaxation, an entertainment.

This meant it had to be written with a special regard to the taste of its audience. All entertainments are, compared with the more serious forms of art. He who lives to please must please to live. The Victorian novelists lived to please that great middle class which, between 1750 and 1850, gradually became the predominating force in England.

They were remarkable people—how else indeed could they have done what they did?—with their insatiable appetite for life, their huge capacity for laughter and tears, their passionate conviction on every subject under heaven, full of inspiration and enterprise and eccentricity and determination. At the same time they were conceited, didactic and obstinate. And, like all people who have had to make their own way in the world, they had no traditions of taste and thought and conduct; if their achievements were sometimes cosmic, their outlook was often parochial. They were not men of the world; they did not value the things of the mind for themselves: they were the great English Philistines. Nor were they broadened by the fact that the predominant religious temper of their day was set by the narrow creed and relentless morality of the Evangelicals.

These circumstances inevitably accentuated any tendency to in-equality in the novel. Because it was in its first stage, it was bound to be technically faulty. It had not yet evolved its own laws; it was still bound to the conventions of the comic stage and heroic romance from which it took its origin, with their artificial intrigues and stock situations and forced happy endings. Because it was looked on as light reading its readers did not expect a high standard of craft, nor mind if it had occasional lapses; especially as they themselves had no traditions of taste by which to estimate it. On the other hand they strongly objected to spending their hours of light reading on themes that were distressing or an intellectual strain. They did not read a novel for the same reason that they read *Hamlet;* they did not want it to be like *Hamlet.* While their moral views made any frank or detailed treatment of the physical side of life simply and finally impossible.

It is to be noted that here the Victorians show a definite decline from earlier novelists. The growing strength of the middle classes made them less cultivated and more puritanical than their predecessors. Technically, for instance, Scott is as defective as any of them, but he looked at life from the standpoint of a far more civilized tradition. He understands a man of another period like Dryden as triumphantly as Thackeray fails to understand a man of another period like Swift; he can write on France with the educated appreciation of a man of the world, while Dickens writes on Italy with the disapproving self-complacency of a provincial schoolmaster. And though Scott was a man of orthodox moral views, with a strong natural distaste to speak-ing of what he felt to be indelicate, if he has to, he does it straight-forwardly and without fuss. Effie Deans' lapse from virtue is referred to without any of that atmosphere of drawing the blinds and lowering the voice and getting out the pocket handkerchief, in which Dickens has seen fit to enshroud the similar fate of little Em'ly. More-over, Effie is ultimately permitted to marry a baronet and live out the remainder of her life in comparative peace; while poor Em'ly is shipped off to Australia to spend her remaining days there, single and in low spirits. For a crime so heinous as hers, poetic justice could with decency demand no lesser punishment.

But if the peculiar circumstances of their age encouraged the Victorians' peculiar faults, they are equally responsible for most of their peculiar merits. It was because the novelist had to entertain that he learned to tell the story so well. If it did not engage the reader's attention he would not trouble to finish it; and because he had to entertain, not a literary coterie but the general reading public, the novelist learned to cover a wide range of subject and mood; a range further extended by the fact that the public, though not seriously interested in art, was seriously interested in life and held strongly moral views about it. He had to be Mr. Galsworthy, Mr. Huxley, Mrs. Woolf, Mrs. Christie and Mr. Wodehouse in one, for his readers would not have been satisfied with so narrow a field of experience as each of these authors separately appeals to.

His special circumstances cannot be held equally responsible for his greatest merit, for his imagination. The seed of inspiration falleth where it listeth. But it can be said that circumstances provided it with a fertile field. Youth is no less the period of creative inspiration in schools of writing than in individual writers. Moreover the writer who lives to please needs to be an artist in a way that the writer who lives to instruct does not. For his work must have intrinsic attractions apart from the importance of anything he has to say. We enjoy *David Copperfield*, not because it is full of ideas about life like *Point Counterpoint*, or gives us a great deal of information about the professional classes in early twentieth-century England like *The Forsyte Saga*, but because it is a delightful object in itself, like a Schubert air or a Sung vase.

What, then, is our final impression of these novels? We have opened the glass bookcases and dragged the books down and read them. Shall we return them to their honorable places, tested and worthy peers of Milton and Boswell; are they the undisputed masterpieces of fiction that their contemporaries thought them? Not altogether. I have compared them to the Elizabethan drama. And with intention. For they have a great deal in common; each the first, irresistible outcome of a new and major channel of literary expression, vital and imaginative in the highest degree, but inevitably stained by immaturity and inefficiency and ignorance. So that with a few wonderful exceptions, *Vanity Fair* and *Wuthering Heights*, their books are aggregations of brilliant passages rather than coherent wholes. And for this reason they are not among the very greatest novels, they do not attain that minute, final circle of the paradise of fiction, the circle of *War and Peace* and *Fathers and Children* and *Emma*.

But though they are not the very greatest, they are great. For their merits are of so superlative a kind, forged in the central heat of the creative imagination, rich in the essential precious stuff from which the art of the novel is made. Here again they are like the Elizabethans; and to be truly appreciated must be approached in the same spirit.

One must make up one's mind to their imperfections; to condemn them for improbable plots or conventional endings is as foolish as to condemn *Dr. Faustus* or *The Duchess of Malfi* for the same reason. On the other hand one must accustom one's eye to discern and concentrate on their splendid merits. Of course, there will always be readers for whom these will not afford sufficient compensation; readers who do not set a supreme value on the purely aesthetic qualities. All the eloquence of Lamb could not reconcile Mr. William Archer and Mr. Bernard Shaw to Webster; and no doubt those puritanical Philistines of our own day who read a story first of all to find "a reflection of the contemporary consciousness" or "a serious attempt to express significant values" will always think Dickens and Trollope frivolous and infantile. But those who do care for art as such will discover a satisfaction in them that all the conscientious craftsmanship and accurate observation and technical experiment of today hardly ever provide. Nor is it a satisfaction which is likely to grow less in future generations. For the achievements of the art of letters, the fall of a phrase, a man or a moment made vivid in a few scrawls of ink, can survive, fresh with all the glowing tints of youth, when towered temples and embattled cities have become no more than sunshine and silence and a chip of stone in the sand.

F. L. LUCAS

—◆—

Matthew Arnold

Je ne puis approver que ceux qui cherchent en gémissant.
—PASCAL

"YOUR Middle-Class man thinks it the highest pitch of development of civilization when his letters are carried twelve times a day from Islington to Camberwell and from Camberwell to Islington, and if railway trains run to and fro between them every quarter of an hour. He thinks it is nothing that the trains only carry him from an illiberal, dismal life at Islington to an illiberal, dismal life at Camberwell." Here rings out a new note of rebellion amid the complacent peace of the Victorians. The man who wrote that had not been, like Browning, a happy little boy in this same Camberwell, already gratifying his taste for the grotesque by keeping queer pets, and preserved by the most indulgent of parents from the rigours of a public school; nor again, like Tennyson, a gloomy little boy growing up in a Lincolnshire rectory under a father so melancholy that the child would lie sometimes on the graves in Somersby Churchyard, sobbing to be dead; Matthew Arnold was very differently educated in the monastic culture of Rugby under his father the great Doctor, the editor of Thucydides and the author of six volumes of sermons. That boyhood stamped him for life. To the end, like his father, he kept this mixture of literature and dogma; to the end, like Milton, he remained half Greek and half Hebrew, half poet and half prophet. This Biblical element in Arnold made him, like Tennyson and Browning, too prone to preach: but he remains a contrast to them in other ways. He was more cultivated, both by nature and by nurture. His manner was exquisite; maddening, some

From *Ten Victorian Poets* (Cambridge at the University Press, 1940), 39–53. Reprinted by permission of the Cambridge University Press.

thought. "Damn this fop!" cried his opponents in controversy, "can nobody annoy him?" George Sand likened him in youth to "a young Milton on his travels." "I should not dare," said Crabb Robinson, "to be intimate with so clever a young man." And at the close of one of his Oxford lectures, the Master of Jesus was heard murmuring: "The angel ended." In consequence Arnold never shrieks like Tennyson in parts of *Maud,* nor bellows like Browning in *Pacchiarotto.* He had also a clearer mind, more intellectual honesty, more sense of practical reality—as we might expect in a poet whose more active temper turned him also into a critic, a religious controversialist, and an inspector of Nonconformist schools from Yarmouth to Pembroke and from Yorkshire to the Thames, having his children born in lodging-houses and living himself on buns hastily eaten in class-rooms before astonished schoolchildren. "Not here, O Apollo, were haunts meet for thee."

And so, though Arnold remains in many ways a typical Victorian, a poet struggling with a preacher, he is, I think, less tiresome in his pulpit than Tennyson or Browning. If his greater fastidiousness, his stronger sense of truth, his practical activities prevented him from writing so much poetry, they prevented him also from writing so much bad poetry. And there is a further important difference: Arnold is poignantly conscious of the conflict in himself. It tears him, and he sees it, and it becomes in our eyes all the more painful, but also the more moving—not a muddle, but a battle; not. stupid, but tragic. For Arnold was indeed at war with himself; the artist in him with the moralist, the Greek poet with the Hebrew prophet, the lover of Byron and passion and the beauty of the South with the disciple of Wordsworth and knowledge and the sternness of the North. For some, Arnold is a pedant and a prig: really, he was something much more human and more unhappy. It was no saint of marble, nor yet of plaster, who wrote *The New Sirens,* and heard so clearly the music, the passion, the persuasion in their voices as they called to him, "with blown tresses and with beckoning hands"—

> "Come", you say, "opinion trembles,
> Judgement shifts, convictions go:
> Life dries up, the heart dissembles;
> Only what we feel, we know.
> Hath your wisdom known emotions?
> Will it weep our burning tears?
> Hath it drunk of our love-potions
> Crowning moments with the weight of years?"

He makes, in answer, his refusal; but it is not made without a pang—

> Yes—I muse—and if the dawning
> Into daylight never grew—
> If the glistering wings of morning
> On the dry noon shook their dew—
> If the fits of joy were longer—
> Or the day were sooner done—
> Or, perhaps, if Hope were stronger—
> No weak nursling of an earthly sun . . .
> Pluck, pluck, cypress, O pale maidens,
> Dusk the hall with yew.

Nor was this conflict in Arnold a mere storm in an ink-pot, an agony in an armchair: it was fought out also in Arnold's real life. We know no details. He wished that no biographer should ever disturb his dust; he wished in vain, of course; but the evidence remains often scanty. He has, however, traced for us himself, in that series of lyrics called *Switzerland,* the shadowy outline of the struggle between his love for a French girl he met there, Marguerite, and his sense that her past with others made impossible a future for him and her together. Here too in the end he tears himself free—

> Me let no half-effac'd memories cumber!
> Fled, fled at once, be all vestige of thee—
> Deep be the darkness, and still be the slumber—
> Dead be the past and its phantoms to me!
>
> Then, when we meet, and thy look strays towards me,
> Scanning my face and the changes wrought there—
> *Who,* let me say, *is this Stranger regards me,*
> *With the grey eyes, and the lovely brown hair?*

Just as his own Margaret in *The Forsaken Merman* breaks away from the unconsecrated love that she leaves lonely for ever beneath the waves, so between Marguerite and himself Arnold set "the unplumb'd salt, estranging sea." He loved again; he married; and, to make marriage possible, he gave himself up to sit in class-rooms while Nonconformist School-masters lectured before him on indiarubber and the Gunpowder Plot. He had conquered; but he remembered.

> Calm's not life's crown, though calm is well.

He still heard out of the distance of the past that voice loved once so well—

Say, has some wet bird-haunted English lawn
Lent it the music of its birds at dawn?

He told himself tales of long-parted lovers joined again in the sunset of their days, of Iseult tossing through the surf of the Atlantic once more to Tristram's arms. He felt desperately the loneliness of all human life, the need for some hand to touch in the darkness of its desolation, whether Marguerite's or another's—

> Ah, love, let us be true
> To one another! For the world which seems
> To lie before us like a land of dreams,
> So various, so beautiful, so new,
> Hath really neither joy, nor love, nor light,
> Nor certitude, nor peace, nor help for pain;
> And we are here as on a darkling plain
> Swept with confused alarms of struggle and flight,
> Where ignorant armies clash by night.

But to that supreme cry of Arnold's loneliness, the Stoic in him made answer, that the battle in the darkness must none the less be fought on to its lonely end.

> We cannot kindle when we will
> The fire that in the heart resides;
> The spirit bloweth and is still,
> In mystery our soul abides:
> But tasks in hours of insight will'd
> Can be through hours of gloom fulfill'd.

Loneliness, indeed, is not only the doom of man, it is the price of man's greatness—

> Alone the sun arises, and alone
> Spring the great streams.

And after the battle—what victory, what reward, here and beyond? None, is Arnold's answer—unless it be a little calm, perhaps, before the dreamless calm of all eternity.

> Charge once more, and then be dumb!
> Let the victors when they come,
> When the forts of folly fall,
> Find thy body by the wall.

There is surely something more spirited here than Tennyson's vague gropings for "the larger hope"; something less self-important than

Browning's greeting the unseen with a cheer, which seems to me too like putting a paper-hat on the Sphinx.

Arnold may have been a little too sure which, exactly, the Forts of Folly were. That clash of ignorant armies in the gloom was surely a truer, as well as a finer, image of human life with all its blind perplexities. But it is impossible not to respect the man's sincerity. *In Memoriam* is often more beautiful; but beside it the poetry of Arnold, at its best, seems to rise like a mountain-peak, cold and clear in the grey peace of evening, above the musical but bewildered murmurings of a twilit forest. Indeed, as a summary of the essential things in Arnold, I often remember Stevenson's lines on the Highlands of Galloway—

> Hills of the sheep, and homes of the ancient, vanished races,
>   And winds austere and pure.

There the "hills of the sheep" may stand for the influence on Arnold of Wordsworth and the poetry of Westmorland; the "homes of the ancient, vanished races" for that other influence of Greece and Palestine; and the "winds austere and pure" for the breath of Arnold's own spirit.

But although this long struggle in Arnold makes him a more moving figure, the final victory of the Stoic side of him makes him also a little bleak. A larger, healthier nature would, one feels, have reconciled this inner conflict; the victory of ascetic self-discipline involves a defeat of other elements in human nature just as important. Renan says somewhere of Arnold's master, Marcus Aurelius, that he lacked one vital thing—the kiss of a fairy at his birth. Arnold had not been left unkissed; but, no doubt with the able assistance of his father the Headmaster of Rugby, he studied only too successfully at times to forget it. He feels that the world of Nature seems "to bear rather than rejoice"; and we feel the same of him. He does lack gaiety, lightness of touch, the ironic acceptance of a world past our mending, the smile of Montaigne, the laugh of Voltaire, the "feather-pate of folly" that bears the falling sky. It is not really sensible to be always so sadly wise. In real life, indeed, Arnold could smile very charmingly, even at his own expense; "my wife," he would say, "has all my graces and none of my airs"; and he was delighted when on his American tour he found himself compared by a Chicago newspaper to "an elderly macaw pecking at a trellis of grapes." But as a poet, I think, he suffered from this over-austere philosophy of his. It is not, indeed, its sadness that matters. The greatest poetry in the world is largely the saddest; and *The Times* has seldom surpassed its comment on Arnold's *Empedocles*— "He is disgusted with the world; a state of mind with which we have no sympathy whatever." But Arnold's puritanism did damage his verse by giving it a strain of dispirited monotony, just as it certainly warped his criticism. When we listen to him denouncing the letters of Keats, and the circle of Shelley, and the character of Burns, and the lack of character in Coleridge, and the seduction-theme of *Faust*, and the "disrespectability" of Heine, and the "hunger, rebellion, and rage" of poor Charlotte Brontë, we realize with a gasp what a Victorian this satirist of Victorianism could be, what a Philistine this scourge of the Philistines himself always remained. There was justice as well as wit in Swinburne's jest about "David the son of Goliath"; and Chaucer, whom Arnold blamed as having too little "high seriousness," might easily have answered with a smile that his critic had too much. Arnold recognized two main elements in poetry— natural magic and moral profundity; but with his fetish about poetry being "criticism of life" he too often in practice sacrificed the magic to the morals.

This asceticism shows itself even in his style; even here he tended to prefer sackcloth to satin. Sometimes he attained a very happy mean between the two; *Sohrab and Rustum* is a fine thing in this simple grandeur of its style as in other ways; and that great cry of the fallen Sohrab might well be Arnold's own—

> Truth sits upon the lips of dying men,
> And falsehood, while I lived, was far from mine.

But too often his bareness becomes threadbare, and his contempt for the graces too like that of an early Christian hermit sitting in a cell with no furniture but a platter and a pipkin. How could he write things like these?—

> Agamemnon's unhappy,
> Matricidal, world-fam'd,
> Seven-cubit-statur'd son;

or again—

> Sculptors like Phidias,
> Raphaels in shoals,
> Poets like Shakespeare—
> Beautiful souls.

Whole pieces like *Balder* and *Merope* wear the same gaunt, white-washed, work-house air. And yet there are also moments when Arnold grows suddenly rich, and turns from building in corrugated iron, to marble and porphyry. In *The Scholar Gipsy* and *Thyrsis*, those two laments for a dead age and a dead friend, he allows himself a new magnificence, of language and metre alike; rather as some stern St. Benedict might grant to death what he refused to life and permit a splendour of gold and velvet to glitter on a brother's funeral-rites. Then Arnold at last becomes as lovely as sincere, and the disenchantment of old age itself vanishes before the spell of perfect words.

> Yes, thou art gone! And round me too the night
>   In ever-nearing circle weaves her shade.
>   I see her veil draw soft across the day,
> I feel her slowly chilling breath invade
>   The cheek grown thin, the brown hair sprent with grey;
>   I feel her finger light
> Laid pausefully upon life's headlong train;
>   The foot less prompt to meet the morning dew,
>   The heart less bounding at emotion new,
> And hope, once crushed, less quick to spring again.

There, in that lament for the lost Thyrsis, Arnold, it seems to me, truly and finally found himself. At last he was content, following Keats, to be, for moments at least, simply beautiful. To-day his religious discussions are dead. We smile wonderingly at his attempt to convert the Church of England from a personal God to "a stream of things not ourselves, a stream of Tendency making for Righteousness"—it remains so clear that such a stream, whether or no it made for Righteousness, was not made for worship. His criticism, again, is still respected; but it dates. It is by his poetry that Arnold lives to-day; a poetry often as bare and rugged as a Greek mountain, but in its gentler moods recalling those quiet English waters that flow past Laleham Churchyard where he lies. In the words of Sir William Watson—

> And nigh to where his bones abide,
> The Thames with its unruffled tide
> Seems like his genius typified,
>   Its strength, its grace,
> Its lucid gleam, its sober pride,
>   Its tranquil pace.

A forgotten poet of an earlier age saw likewise in the Thames the symbol of these same qualities; and when we remember that Denham stands, with Waller, at the opening of our neo-classic age, there is a special fitness in applying to Arnold, our last great neo-classic, the famous couplet on that river in Denham's poem, *Cooper's Hill*—

> Though deep, yet clear: though gentle, yet not dull:
> Strong without rage: without o'erflowing, full.

But, after all, we need not go to other poets for rivers; Arnold has himself fashioned the noblest symbol of his own life in that picture, not of the Thames, but the Oxus, which leads us so magnificently away from the night-hung battlefield where Rustum mourns for ever above the son he slew—

> But the majestic River floated on,
> Out of the mist and hum of that low land,
> Into the frosty starlight, and there mov'd,
> Rejoicing, through the hush'd Chorasmian waste,
> Under the solitary moon: he flow'd
> Right for the Polar Star, past Orgunjè,
> Brimming, and bright, and large: then sands begin
> To hem his watery march, and dam his streams,
> And split his currents; that for many a league
> The shorn and parcell'd Oxus strains along
> Through beds of sand and matted rushy isles—
> Oxus, forgetting the bright speed he had
> In his high mountain cradle in Pamere,
> A foil'd circuitous wanderer—till at last
> The long'd-for dash of waves is heard, and wide
> His luminous home of waters opens, bright
> And tranquil, from whose floor the new-bath'd stars
> Emerge, and shine upon the Aral Sea.

WALTER JACKSON BATE

Matthew Arnold

No English or American critic since Coleridge has had a more extensive influence than Matthew Arnold. For his influence has operated in
at least three ways. He was, in one sense, something of a spokesman
for nineteenth-century poetic taste. Secondly, through Arnold, more
cosmopolitan ideas became readily accessible to English-speaking
critics and readers; after becoming current, these have passed unobtrusively into much of the criticism of the past forty years, including
that which now looks back on Arnold himself as either academically
ineffectual or else as an evil spirit representing "romantic" tastes in
style. Lastly, much of the modern defence of the central educational
value of literature rests—where the defence is impressive—on classical
premises resurrected and popularized, however vaguely and sketchily,
by Arnold.

Arnold's position is therefore much more complex than it appears to
be at first sight. One especially needs to prevent his role as a spokesman for nineteenth-century literary taste from assuming undue importance. It is indeed true that the influence of Arnold, during the later
years of the nineteenth and the first two decades of the twentieth
centuries, helped to standardize the poetic taste of the period. But
this is largely because Anglo-American writers and critics chose only
some of his opinions and tastes to echo and extend. This influence
illustrates the more strictly Victorian side of Arnold. This is the
Arnold who is now often said to have "re-examined" English poetry
in the light of merely nineteenth-century standards, as T. S. Eliot has
been said to "re-examine" it later by other standards. It is the Arnold
who looked down on the eighteenth century as an "age of prose,"

From *Criticism: The Major Texts*, edited by Walter Jackson Bate, copyright,
1952, by Harcourt, Brace and Company, Inc.

who spoke of using isolated lines of poetry as "touchstones," and who valued a vaguely declamatory "poetry of statement," lightly graced by what he called "magic." But the only basis Arnold himself offers for such a confined interpretation is found in scattered remarks, and in one particular essay, "The Study of Poetry," originally written not as a central credo or discussion of aims but only to serve as an introduction—for general readers not too well acquainted with poetry—to the popular collection, Ward's *English Poets* (1880).

Arnold's main significance as a critic lies elsewhere: in his constant support of the dignity of critical thinking; his attempt to lift the view of the English-speaking reader toward a wider, more cosmopolitan range; his reapplication of classical criteria; and, above all, his courageous attempt, in an increasingly hostile environment, to reassert the traditional value of literature. Through him, English criticism, which had subsided into mediocrity after Coleridge and Hazlitt, became reanimated and broadened. It became aware of the alert critical intelligence at work in mid-nineteenth-century France, and was reminded once again of the wide aims of classical theory. As a result, Anglo-American criticism of the twentieth century took on a new range and sophistication. Through Irving Babbitt and Paul Elmer More, some of Arnold's ideas were systematized into the "New Humanism," which turned militantly upon both the romantic art and the scientific naturalism of the nineteenth century. Following Arnold, such critics looked back to some classical values but, unlike Arnold, they interpreted them with a quite unclassical dogmatism and openly didactic bias. Critics of a very different sort from the "New Humanists" took stands which, though some of them were not aware of it, had first been made possible for modern English and American criticism by Arnold. More formalistically minded critics, in England and especially America, drew suggestions from both classical and nineteenth-century French critical sources. Without Arnold, either directly or through such disciples as Irving Babbitt, their attention to such sources might not have spread so rapidly. Arnold's frequently voiced charge that the English are not critically minded became one of the clichés of modern criticism. And despite his strong antagonism to Arnold, the chief critical writer since World War I, T. S. Eliot, found himself—as he took the place of Arnold—following the procedure if by no means the opinions of his predecessor, and employing a prose style strikingly similar in its conscious, urbane simplicity and its occasional irony. Arnold's notable "Function of Criticism at the Present Time" is paralleled by Eliot's briefer "Function of Criticism," in which Arnold's censure of the Englishman's extreme individualism and antipathy to criticism is repeated by Eliot. Arnold's examination of particular poets —and by no means from just a "nineteenth-century" point of view—is matched by Eliot's examinations of other poets in the light of different stylistic values. Finally, although here the differences between the men are at their widest, Arnold's excursions into more general fields, as in *Culture and Anarchy* (1869), also anticipate similar excursions by Eliot in his *Idea of a Christian Society* and *Notes Toward a Definition of Culture*. The respective conceptions of culture involved in these works offer one of the quickest means of contrasting these two critics.

II

Our concern, however, is not to suggest the rather labyrinthine by-ways of Arnold's influence so much as to indicate briefly the central concern of his critical writing, and the more significant ways in which he ramified and applied it. This central premise is his conception of *culture*, which is most clearly and persuasively defined in his essay, "Sweetness and Light," from *Culture and Anarchy*. Culture, to begin with, is an *activity* of mind. It is not, that is, a body of memorized information, but a quality that characterizes an actual way of living, thinking, and feeling—a quality that consists "in *becoming* something rather than in *having* something, in an inward condition of the mind and spirit, not in an outward set of circumstances." It is the ability, in short, to react in accordance with what is true and valuable. Hence it is necessary to have every aspect of that mind as eager and open as possible in order to be able to descry, as effectively as one can, what *is* true and valuable. This eagerness Arnold termed *curiosity*, or the energetic "desire after the things of the mind simply for their own sakes and for the pleasure of seeing them as they are." To "see things as they are" demands openness as well as eagerness of mind. "Disinterestedness"—the rare ability to rise above sect or clique, the desire to see things in their true nature as distinct from an eager interest to prove a preconceived or indoctrinated idea—"disinterested-ness" and "flexibility" are also fundamental characteristics of culture. They are among the primary virtues that should characterize criticism, too. For the ideal that guides criticism is naturally that of culture in the broadest sense. Otherwise criticism would have little real purpose or dignity, and would simply be one more unessential way of passing the time.

It is to Arnold's credit that he himself, as a practicing critic, was unusually "disinterested." He was not a propagandist for any particu-

64

lar school of Victorian poetry. He did not feel compelled to exalt the nineteenth century as one of the great poetic ages merely because he happened to live in it, nor did he disparage it for the same reason. He was far from being provincially nationalistic. His conception of culture was not confined by the standards or boundaries of any one group. In this respect he differs from some of his more recent detractors who extol critical "disinterestedness" in a theoretical way, but who have approached literature from the point of view of fixed economic, political, historical, or religious interests, or else in terms of restricted stylistic values even more intolerant and exclusive than those which had led Arnold to dismiss eighteenth-century poetry. In fact, Arnold has often been censured precisely because of his disinterestedness. His religious and social attitudes especially have been disparaged for this reason. The former have been considered "flabby" because they were not based on a particular theology, and the latter have been regarded as "aristocratic" and "aloof" because he did not expound a specific political creed. But disinterestedness is always liable to be censured as intellectual flabbiness by critics who are dominated by compelling and rigid preconceptions acquired through accident or despair. In his political and economic outlook, far from being "aristocratic" in the ordinary sense of the term, Arnold prophetically believed that the proletariat would come to control the England of the future, and for that reason he courageously felt that no time should be lost in enlightening and educating it as much as possible. He seems ultimately, however, to have desired a state socialism of sorts, one characteristic of which was that it should be completely classless. Far from being class-minded, therefore, he sensibly felt that the hope of the world was not to be found in either the aristocracy (the "Barbarians"), the prosperous commercial class (the "Philistines"), or the "populace," as they then were. Rather, "culture seeks to do away with classes" and with all artificial forms of "inequality"—an inequality that "materializes the upper class, vulgarizes the middle class, brutalizes the lower class."

III

But it is not enough to "see things as they are," however clearly and flexibly. Human perfection implies that one is really fulfilling knowledge by feeling actively and conducting oneself accordingly. This, as David Perkins has shown in his interpretation of Arnold's classical premises, is the central assumption in Arnold's critical thought. In order to integrate the "total man," emotion must be aroused, brought into play, and then illuminated and led by intelligence. The end, as Mr. Perkins says, is a "union of all the facets of human response in moving towards the same object." "There would be no quarrel between desire and intelligence. For desire would follow, carry out, and complete intelligence by intensifying rational awareness. Value judgments, moreover, would then be felt as an emotion, applied instantaneously, and, in a new experience, would immediately inform our emotional reactions." Hence the Greek belief in the power of art to "awaken and develop one's total capacity for reacting," and Arnold's "own confidence in the humanities, especially poetry, as the most effective means of informing and developing . . . the 'whole man'—that is, man as a total process of desiring, feeling, and thinking. . . . " The central premise, in other words, is simply this: that if the end of human culture is the open sensitivity, the integrated and informed feeling and conduct of the "total man," then, as a matter of sheer common sense, the various pursuits of man should naturally be evaluated and *ranked* to the degree that they lead to this end. On this basis, therefore—on the basis of the Greek ideal of *Eros*, the ideal that in the most complete and active way "good should be forever present to us"—Arnold, in "Literature and Science," followed the great classical justification of the liberal and humane arts, but in a more flexible, less rigorously didactic way than did Sir Philip Sidney. Literature especially, because of the broad range of human life that it can exploit and interpret, can serve as the vital transmitter of experience, inciting the emotional interests of man, instilling knowledge imperceptibly but securely, enlarging the sweep of one's mental and imaginative horizon, and developing sympathetic openness. In doing so, it not only educates in the immediate sense, through the particular insights and experiences that it offers and infiltrates into one's feeling. But it also educates in an *ultimate* sense, through heightening, developing, and organizing the individual as a living, reacting creature. It thus ministers to that *sincerity*, to that final *honesty* of character, in which the mind and the heart are one—in which the heart follows and completes the dictates of the mind, and knowledge, rendered habitual and instinctive, is genuinely felt and acted upon through an enlarged, clearer, more vital state of being. Arnold's criticism is best understood when viewed in the light of this ideal. It not only sustains him in his most valuable and influential role: that of an *apologist* for literature, who tried to reassert essential ends at a time when Western thought—in criticism as in almost everything else —was becoming increasingly absorbed in means for their own sake.

But this conception of what is the most valuable function of poetry also underlies the qualities for which Arnold looked in poetry—concreteness, moral import and range, "magic" or suggestiveness of style, and unity of impact—and provides the criteria by which he consistently attempts to evaluate particular poets and works.

IV

Literature—or "poetry" in the broadest sense of the term—is uniquely capable of furthering the enlightened activity of mind that Arnold calls culture, first because of the range and diversity of its subject matter, and, second, because it communicates in a formative and effective way through offering what is itself a living experience, rather than through abstract analysis and description. Poetry, broadly interpreted, is "nothing less," said Arnold, "than the most perfect speech of man." Poetry, that is to say, is the use of language in the most effective, reaching, and suggestively adequate way possible. It emerges when, through verbal expression, man "comes nearest to being able to utter the truth." The range of poetry—taking poetry as a whole rather than thinking of it in terms of any one specific poem—is thus as broad as what human speech itself can cover or suggest. The diversity of experience treated in the various forms of poetry—the drama, the lyric, philosophical verse, the epic, satire—is a concrete indication. Poetry can thus *include* the results, the intellectual insights and conclusions, of science or indeed of any branch of knowledge. Unlike specific sciences, it is not restricted in its subject matter; and it is likely that "the student of humane letters only" will be less "incomplete" than "the student of the natural sciences only."

But aside from the range, variety, and importance of what it can take as its subject, the high and liberal value of poetry especially results through the form in which it can interpret and transmit experience. To begin with, poetry does not merely chronicle specific details. It interprets details in the light of ideals, of aspirations, of knowledge, and of moral evaluation. On the other hand, poetry is rooted in the *concrete:* it is not a branch of theoretical ethics. Poetry joins together both the idea and the concrete. By serving simultaneously as the "interpretess of the natural world" and as the "interpretess of the moral world"—by feeling and conceiving the concrete, that is, in terms of human values—poetry is thus analogous to human experience itself. For in our actual lives, Arnold insists, we are constantly seeing and feeling things in the light of what we regard as their desirability or value: as we experience things, the concrete is not divorced from the idea, from the interpreting and evaluating of it —it is not divorced if we are having a genuine *experience* rather than being confused and bewildered. We are not, indeed, undergoing a meaningful experience if we think and evaluate purely on an abstract plane, isolated from our daily concerns, and then live, perceive, and react on a concrete plane without any relevance to anything we have ever conceived or believe to be valuable. It is in this sense, then, and not with a naïve didactic implication, that poetry can be said to be able to deal with the most fundamental and pressing of all problems —"the question, *how to live.*" To this extent, poetry is "moral" in its function. For "the question, *how to live,*" as Arnold said in his essay on Wordsworth, "is itself a moral idea; and it is the question which most interests every man, and with which, in some way or other, he is perpetually occupied. A large sense is of course to be given to the term *moral.* Whatever bears upon the question, 'how to live,' comes under it." The greatness of English poetry at its best resides in the vigorous imaginative power with which it has related moral ideas to concrete life.

Hence, in estimating and distinguishing the value of particular poems or particular poets, Arnold is led to regard "the noble and profound application of ideas to life" as "the most essential part of poetic greatness." Accordingly, poetry must first of all work within and through the concrete. Arnold's censure of abstract didactic poetry, such as we find in Wordsworth's *Excursion* or in much eighteenth-century verse, and his lack of sympathy with neoclassic poetic style generally, are based on his belief that they lack a sufficient concrete anchorage. His remarks on his own verse-play, *Empedocles on Etna,* indicate a similar viewpoint: it is not a living drama evolving inevitably from a concrete situation. Secondly, the presence of relevant and significant "ideas" is naturally to be expected in poetry of substantial worth. Especially if other elements are—so far as they can be separately noted—more or less equal, then the more significant the ideas and the more pertinent they are to human life, the better the poem. Keats's *Isabella,* for example, may have occasional vivid lines or phrases; but it cannot for that reason, as Keats himself would probably have admitted, take high rank as a poem. But of course neither the concreteness nor the intellectual significance of the "ideas" can be evaluated separately. The unique achievement of "literary genius is a work of *synthesis*"—of joining together these two elements. It is the "noble and profound *application* of ideas to life."

The success of a poem, therefore, depends on the success with which such a combining or synthesizing is attained. This is quite in agreement with the general modern stress on organic unity in style. Where Arnold would differ from more abstractly esthetic critics, however, is in also emphasizing that the synthesis cannot be evaluated in a vacuum; it cannot be evaluated apart from what is *being synthesized*. The "antique symmetry" of Greek style, for example, is meaningful and genuine because it emerges from "fit details strictly combined, in view of a large general result 'nobly conceived." The more significant the elements and ideas being brought together into the organic unity, the greater the synthesis needed to contain, balance, and reconcile them. *King Lear* and Keats's ode, *To Autumn*, may both be successful examples of a centralizing of various elements into a unified esthetic form or totality. But what is being synthesized in *King Lear* is more vividly applicable to a wider range of human experience: it is at once more universal and more energetically vital; and the synthesis of it into the form it attains is therefore the more powerful, extensive, and valuable. It offers, in short, a more "noble and profound application of ideas to life." Hence Arnold's reservations about nineteenth-century poetry in the Preface to the *Poems* (1853). The great and permanent themes of poetry were being replaced, he felt, both by a subjective concern of the poet with his own feelings for their own sake and also by an increasing technical interest in the "part" rather than the "whole"—in "expression," in language, imagery, or versification. His viewpoint is prophetically applicable to twentieth- as well as nineteenth-century poetry. It is altogether to the credit of Arnold's broad classical premise that, through the perspective it offers, such differences as exist between nineteenth- and twentieth-century poetry do not appear as diametrical opposites but may be seen as in some respects very much alike, or else as different sides of the same coin.

Poetry, then, like every other human pursuit, should be evaluated in the light of man's most basic concern: the active attainment of culture, in the broadest sense, and the total and integrated perfecting of himself and his potentialities as an aware, responsive, and active creature. It is in simultaneously tapping the intellectual, imaginative, and emotional resources of man, and in bringing them to bear on its objects in a unified, harmonious way, that poetry secures its most formative and salutary effect. It brings us into a sympathetic and rounded "contact with the essential nature of these objects," so that we are "no longer bewildered and oppressed by them" but, by assimilating the realization of them into our habitual feelings, become more "in harmony with them; and this feeling calms and satisfies as no other can." Through "magic" of style, we are incited to participate actively and imaginatively in the experience of the poem. In this living identification, we re-create and feel within ourselves the emerging resolution and unity of form that leads out, guides, and gives meaning to its various parts, thus permitting them to fulfill themselves by dawning into "a large general result nobly conceived." Such an experience, continued and gradually broadened in scope, directly subserves the ideal of human culture itself, in which the various aspects of the human character are integrated, sustaining and completing each other by themselves co-operating toward "a large general result nobly conceived."

NOTES

Arnold's *Works* (15 vols., 1903–04), though not complete, is the most comprehensive edition. Selections from the criticism include those of G. K. Chesterton (1906), H. G. Rawlinson (1924), D. C. Somervell (1924), and the Viking Portable *Matthew Arnold* (ed. Lionel Trilling, 1949). Books dealing with Arnold include A. P. Kelso, *Matthew Arnold on Continental Life and Literature* (Oxford, 1914); Stuart Sherman, *Matthew Arnold: How to Know Him* (1917); and especially Lionel Trilling, *Matthew Arnold* (1939). Among articles, see T. S. Osmond, "Arnold and Homer," *Essays and Studies, English Assoc.*, III (1912), 71–91; F. L. Wickelgren, "Arnold's Literary Relations with France," *Modern Language Review*, XXXIII (1938), 200–14; and especially David Perkins, "Arnold and the Function of Literature," in the *Journal of English Literary History*, XVIII (1951), 287–309, to which I am strongly indebted for suggested material and interpretations offered in this introduction.

ROBERT B. HEILMAN

Charlotte Brontë's "New" Gothic

IN that characteristic flight from cliché that may plunge him into the
recherché the critic might well start from *The Professor* and discover
in it much more than is implied by the usual dismissal of it as Charlotte Brontë's poorest work. He might speculate about Charlotte's
singular choice of a male narrator—the value of it, or even the need
of it, for her. For through William Crimsworth she lives in Héger,
making love to herself as Frances Henri: in this there is a kind of
ravenousness, inturning, splitting, and doubling back of feeling.
Through Crimsworth she experiences a sudden, vivid, often graceless
mastery. But these notes on the possible psychology of the author are
critically useful only as a way into the strange tremors of feeling
that are present in a formally defective story. Pelet identifies "a
fathomless spring of sensibility in thy breast, Crimsworth." If Crimsworth is not a successful character, he is the channel of emotional
surges that splash over a conventional tale of love: the author's disquieting presence in the character lends a nervous, off-center vitality.
The pathos of liberty is all but excessive (as it is later in Shirley
Keeldar and Lucy Snowe): Crimsworth sneers, ". . . I sprang from
my bed with other slaves," and rejoices, "Liberty I clasped in my
arms . . . her smile and embrace revived my life." The Puritan
sentiment (to be exploited partially in Jane Eyre and heavily in Lucy
Snowe) becomes tense, rhetorical, fiercely censorious; the self-righteousness punitive and even faintly paranoid. Through the frenetically
Protestant Crimsworth and his flair for rebuke Charlotte notes the

From *From Jane Austen to Joseph Conrad,* edited by Robert C. Rathburn
and Martin Steinmann, Jr. (pp. 118–32). University of Minnesota Press.
Copyright 1958, University of Minnesota. Reprinted by permission of the
publisher and the author.

little sensualities of girl students ("parting her lips, as full as those of a hot-blooded Maroon") and the coquettish yet urgent sexuality of Zoraide Reuter perversely responding to Crimsworth's ostensible yet not total unresponsiveness to her: "When she stole about me with the soft step of a slave, I felt at once barbarous and sensual as a pasha."

Charlotte looks beyond familiar surfaces. In Yorke Hunsden she notes the "incompatibilities of the 'physique' with the 'morale.'" The explosive Byronic castigator has lineaments "small, and even feminine" and "now the mien of a morose bull, and anon that of an arch and mischievous girl." In this version of the popular archetype, "rough exterior but heart of gold," Charlotte brilliantly finds a paradoxical union of love and hate; she sees generosity of spirit sometimes appearing directly but most often translated into antithetical terms that also accommodate opposite motives—into god-like self-indulgence in truth-telling; almost Mephistophelian cynicism; sadism and even murderousness in words.

Charlotte's story is conventional; formally she is for "reason" and "real life"; but her characters keep escaping to glorify "feeling" and "Imagination." Feeling is there in the story—evading repression, in author or in character; ranging from nervous excitement to emotional absorption; often tense and peremptory; sexuality, hate, irrational impulse, grasped, given life, not merely named and pigeonholed. This is Charlotte's version of Gothic: in her later novels an extraordinary thing. In that incredibly eccentric history, *The Gothic Quest*, Montague Summers asserts that the "Gothic novel of sensibility . . . draws its emotionalism and psychology . . . from the work of Samuel Richardson." When this line of descent continues in the Brontës, the vital feeling moves toward an intensity, a freedom, and even an abandon virtually non-existent in historical Gothic and rarely approached in Richardson. From Angria on, Charlotte's women vibrate with passions that the fictional conventions only partly constrict or gloss over—in the center an almost violent devotedness that has in it at once a fire of independence, a spiritual energy, a vivid sexual responsiveness, and, along with this, self-righteousness, a sense of power, sometimes self-pity and envious competitiveness. To an extent the heroines are "unheroined," unsweetened. Into them there has come a new sense of the dark side of feeling and personality.

The Professor ventures a little into the psychic darkness on which *Villette* draws heavily. One night Crimsworth, a victim of hypochondria, hears a voice saying, "In the midst of life we are in death," and he feels "a horror of great darkness." In his boyhood this same "sorceress" drew him "to the very brink of a black, sullen river" and managed to "lure me to her vaulted home of horrors." Charlotte draws on sex images that recall the note of sexuality subtly present in other episodes: ". . . I had entertained her at bed and board . . . she lay with me, . . . taking me entirely to her death-cold bosom, and holding me with arms of bone." The climax is: "I repulsed her as one would a dreaded and ghastly concubine coming to embitter a husband's heart toward his young bride; . . ." This is Gothic, yet there is an integrity of feeling that greatly deepens the convention.

From childhood terrors to all those mysteriously threatening sights, sounds, and injurious acts that reveal the presence of some malevolent force and that anticipate the holocaust at Thornfield, the traditional Gothic in *Jane Eyre* has often been noted, and as often disparaged. It need not be argued that Charlotte Brontë did not reach the heights while using hand-me-down devices, though a tendency to work through the conventions of fictional art was a strong element in her make-up. This is true of all her novels, but it is no more true than her counter-tendency to modify, most interestingly, these conventions. In both *Villette* and *Jane Eyre* Gothic is used but characteristically is undercut.

Jane Eyre hears a "tragic . . . preternatural . . . laugh," but this is at "high noon" and there is "no circumstance of ghostliness"; Grace Poole, the supposed laugher, is a plain person, than whom no "apparition less romantic or less ghostly could . . . be conceived"; Charlotte apologizes ironically to the "romantic reader" for telling "the plain truth" that Grace generally bears a "pot of porter." Charlotte almost habitually revises "old Gothic," the relatively crude mechanisms of fear, with an infusion of the anti-Gothic. When Mrs. Rochester first tried to destroy Rochester by fire, Jane "baptized" Rochester's bed and heard Rochester "fulminating strange anathemas at finding himself lying in a pool of water." The introduction of comedy as a palliative of straight Gothic occurs on a large scale when almost seventy-five pages are given to the visit of the Ingram-Eshton party to mysterious Thornfield; here Charlotte, as often in her novels, falls into the manner of the Jane Austen whom she despised. When Mrs. Rochester breaks loose again and attacks Mason, the presence of guests lets Charlotte play the nocturnal alarum for at least a touch of comedy: Rochester orders the frantic women not to "pull me down or strangle me"; and "the two dowagers, in vast white wrappers, were bearing down on him like ships in full sail."

The symbolic also modifies the Gothic, for it demands of the reader a more mature and complicated response than the relatively simple thrill or momentary intensity of feeling sought by primitive Gothic. When mad Mrs. Rochester, seen only as "the foul German spectre—the Vampyre," spreads terror at night, that is one thing; when, with the malicious insight that is the paradox of her madness, she tears the wedding veil in two and thus symbolically destroys the planned marriage, that is another thing, far less elementary as art. The midnight blaze that ruins Thornfield becomes more than a shock when it is seen also as the fire of purgation; the grim, almost road-less forest surrounding Ferndean is more than a harrowing stage-set when it is also felt as a symbol of Rochester's closed-in life.

The point is that in various ways Charlotte manages to make the patently Gothic more than a stereotype. But more important is that she instinctively finds new ways to achieve the ends served by old Gothic—the discovery and release of new patterns of feeling, the intensification of feeling. Though only partly unconventional, Jane is nevertheless so portrayed as to evoke new feelings rather than merely exercise old ones. As a girl she is lonely, "passionate," "strange," "like nobody there"; she feels superior, rejects poverty, talks back preco-ciously, tells truths bluntly, enjoys "the strangest sense of freedom," tastes "vengeance"; she experiences a nervous shock which is said to have a lifelong effect, and the doctor says "nerves not in a good state"; she can be "reckless and feverish," "bitter and truculent"; at Thornfield she is restless, given to "bright visions," letting "imagina-tion" picture an existence full of "life, fire, feeling." Thus Charlotte leads away from standardized characterization toward new levels of human reality, and hence from stock responses toward a new kind of passionate engagement.

Charlotte moves toward depth in various ways that have an imme-diate impact like that of Gothic. Jane's strange, fearful symbolic dreams are not mere thrillers but reflect the tensions of the engage-ment period, the stress of the wedding-day debate with Rochester, and the longing for Rochester after she has left him. The final Thorn-field dream, with its vivid image of a hand coming through a cloud in place of the expected moon, is in the surrealistic vein that appears most sharply in the extraordinary pictures that Jane draws at Thorn-field: here Charlotte is plumbing the psyche, not inventing a weird décor. Likewise in the telepathy scene, which Charlotte, unlike Defoe in dealing with a similar episode, does her utmost to actualize: "The feeling was not like an electric shock; but it was quite as sharp, as strange, as startling: . . . that inward sensation . . . with all its unspeakable strangeness . . . like an inspiration . . . wondrous shock of feeling. . . ." In her flair for the surreal, in her plunging into feeling that is without status in the ordinary world of the novel, Charlotte discovers a new dimension of Gothic.

She does this most thoroughly in her portrayal of characters and of the relations between them. If in Rochester we see only an Angrian-Byronic hero and a Charlotte wish-fulfillment figure (the two identifications which to some readers seem entirely to place him), we miss what is more significant, the exploration of personality that opens up new areas of feeling in intersexual relationships. Beyond the "grim," the "harsh," the eccentric, the almost histrionically cynical that superficially distinguish Rochester from conventional heroes, there is something almost Lawrentian: Rochester is "neither tall nor graceful"; his eyes can be "dark, irate, and piercing"; his strong features "took my feelings from my own power and fettered them in his." Without using the vocabulary common to us, Charlotte is presenting maleness and physicality, to which Jane responds directly. She is "assimilated" to him by "something in my brain and heart, in my blood and nerves"; she "must love" and "could not unlove" him; the thought of parting from him is "agony." Rochester's oblique amatory maneuvers become almost punitive in the Walter-to-Griselda style and once reduce her to sobbing "convulsively"; at times the love-game borders on a power-game. Jane, who prefers "rudeness" to "flattery," is an instinctive evoker of passion: she learns "the pleasure of vexing and soothing him by turns" and pursues a "system" of working him up "to considerable irritation" and coolly leaving him; when, as a result, his caresses become grimaces, pinches, and tweaks, she records that, sometimes at least, she "decidedly preferred these fierce favors." She reports, "I crushed his hand . . . red with the passionate pressure"; she "could not . . . see God for his creature," and in her devotion Rochester senses "an earnest, religious energy."

Charlotte's remolding of stock feeling reaches a height when she sympathetically portrays Rochester's efforts to make Jane his mistress; here the stereotyped seducer becomes a kind of lost nobleman of passion, and of specifically physical passion: "Every atom of your flesh is as dear to me as my own. . . ." The intensity of the pressure which he puts upon her is matched, not by the fear and revulsion of the popular heroine, but by a responsiveness which she barely masters: "The crisis was perilous; but not without its charm . . ." She is "tortured by a sense of remorse at thus hurting his feelings"; at the moment of decision "a hand of fiery iron grasped my vitals . . . blackness, burning! . . . my intolerable duty"; she leaves in "despair"; and after she has left, "I longed to be his; I panted to return . . ."—and for the victory of principle "I abhorred myself . . . I was hateful in my own eyes." This extraordinary openness to feeling, this escape from the bondage of the trite, continues in the Rivers relationship, which is a structural parallel to the Rochester affair: as in Rochester the old sex villain is seen in a new perspective, so in Rivers the clerical hero is radically refashioned; and Jane's almost accepting a would-be husband is given the aesthetic status of a regrettable yielding to a seducer. Without a remarkable liberation from conventional feeling Charlotte could not fathom the complexity of Rivers— the earnest and dutiful clergyman distraught by a profound inner turmoil of conflicting "drives": sexuality, restlessness, hardness, pride, ambition ("fever in his vitals," "inexorable as death"); the hypnotic, almost inhuman potency of his influence on Jane, who feels "a freezing spell," "an awful charm," an "iron shroud"; the relentlessness, almost the unscrupulousness, of his wooing, the resultant fierce struggle (like that with Rochester), Jane's brilliantly perceptive accusation, ". . . you almost hate me . . . you would kill me. You are killing me now"; and yet her mysterious near-surrender: "I was tempted to cease struggling with him—to rush down the torrent of his will into the gulf of his existence, and there lose my own."

Aside from partial sterilization of banal Gothic by dry factuality and humor, Charlotte goes on to make a much more important—indeed, a radical—revision of the mode: in *Jane Eyre* and in the other novels, as we shall see, that discovery of passion, that rehabilitation of the extra-rational, which is the historical office of Gothic, is no longer oriented in marvelous circumstance but moves deeply into the lesser known realities of human life. This change I describe as the change from "old Gothic" to "new Gothic." The kind of appeal is the same; the fictional method is utterly different.

When Charlotte went on from *Jane Eyre* to *Shirley*, she produced a book that for the student of the Gothic theme is interesting precisely because on the face of things it would be expected to be a barren field. It is the result of Charlotte's one deliberate venture from private intensities into public extensities: Orders in Council, the Luddites, technological unemployment in 1811 and 1812, a social portraiture which develops Charlotte's largest cast of characters. Yet Charlotte cannot keep it a social novel. Unlike Warren, who in the somewhat similar *Night Rider* chose to reflect the historical economic crisis in the private crisis of the hero, Miss Brontë loses interest in the public and slides over into the private.

The formal irregularities of *Shirley*—the stop-and-start, zig-zag movement, plunging periodically into different perspectives—light up the divergent impulses in Charlotte herself: the desire to make a story from observed outer life, and the inability to escape from inner urgencies that with centrifugal force unwind outward into story almost autonomously. Passion alters plan: the story of industrial crisis is repeatedly swarmed over by the love stories. But the ultimate complication is that Charlotte's duality of impulse is reflected not only in the narrative material but in two different ways of telling each part of the story. On the one hand she tells a rather conventional, open, predictable tale; on the other she lets go with a highly charged private sentiency that may subvert the former or at least surround it with an atmosphere of unfamiliarity or positive strangeness: the Gothic impulse.

For Charlotte it is typically the "pattern" versus the "strange." She describes "two pattern young ladies, in pattern attire, with pattern deportment"—a "respectable society" in which "Shirley had the air of a black swan, or a white crow. . . ." When, in singing, Shirley "poured round the passion, force," the young ladies thought this "strange" and concluded: "What was *strange* must be *wrong; . . .*" True, Charlotte's characters live within the established "patterns" of life; but their impulse is to vitalize forms with unpatterned feeling, and Charlotte's to give play to unpatterned feeling in all its forms. She detects the warrior in the Reverend Matthew Helstone; reports that Malone the curate "had energy enough in hate"; describes Shirley weeping without apparent reason; recounts Mrs. Yorke's paranoid "brooding, eternal, immitigable suspicion of all men, things, creeds, and parties"; portrays Hiram Yorke as scornful, stubborn, intolerant of superiors, independent, truculent, benevolent toward inferiors, his virtues surrounding an aggressive *amour propre*.

Shirley is given a vehement, sweeping, uninhibited criticalness of mind; in her highly articulate formulations of incisive thought is released a furious rush of emotional energy. Within the framework of moral principles her ideas and feelings are untrammeled. She vigorously debunks clichés against charity, but against the mob she will defend her property "like a tigress"; to Yorke's face she does a corrosive analysis of his personality; she attacks Milton in a fiery sweeping paean to Eve, the "mother" of "Titans"; in an almost explosive defense of love she attacks ignorant, chilly, refined, embarrassed people who "blaspheme living fire, seraph-brought from a divine altar"; when she insists that she must "*love*" before she marries, her "worldly" Uncle Sympson retorts, "Preposterous stuff!—indecorous—unwomanly!"

Beside the adults who in ways are precocious are the precocious children—the Yorkes who have their parents' free-swinging, uninhibited style of talk; Henry Sympson, having for his older cousin Shirley an attachment that borders on sexual feeling; and most of all Martin Yorke, aged fifteen, to whose excited pursuit of Caroline, almost irrelevant to plot or theme, Charlotte devotes two and a half zestful chapters. Martin is willing to help Caroline see Robert Moore, "her confounded sweetheart," to be near her himself, and he plans to claim a reward "displeasing to Moore"; he thinks of her physical beauties. Once he gets between Robert and Caroline at good-bye time; "he half carried Caroline down the stairs," "wrapped her shawl round her," and wanted to claim a kiss. At the same time he feels "power over her," he wants her to coax him, and he would like "to put her in a passion—to make her cry." Charlotte subtly conveys the sexuality of his quest—a rare feat in the nineteenth-century novel.

In Robert Moore, the unpopular mill-owner, Charlotte finds less social rightness or wrongness than his strength, his masculine appeal; her sympathy, so to speak, is for the underside of his personality. It "agreed with Moore's temperament . . . to be generally hated"; "he liked a silent, sombre, unsafe solitude"; against the vandals his "hate is still running in such a strong current" that he has none left for other objects; he shows "a terrible half" of himself in pursuing rioters with "indefatigable, . . . relentless assiduity"; this "excitement" pleases him; sadistically he likes to "force" magistrates to "betray a certain fear." He is the great lover of the story; he almost breaks Caroline's heart before he marries her, and he even has a subtle impact on Shirley, teasingly communicated, though officially denied, by Charlotte. What Caroline yields to is his "secret power," which affects her "like a spell." Here again Charlotte records, as directly as she can, simple sexual attractiveness. From the problem novel she veers off into "new Gothic"; in old Gothic, her hero would have been a villain.

True to convention, the love stories end happily. But special feelings, a new pathos of love, come through. Louis Moore demands in a woman something "to endure, . . . to reprimand"; love must involve "prickly peril," "a sting now and then"; for him the "young lioness or leopardess" is better than the lamb. There is that peculiarly tense vivacity of talk between lovers (the Jane-Rochester style), who discover a heightened, at times stagey, yet highly communicative rhetoric, drawing now on fantasy, now on moral conviction, verging now on titillating revelation, now on battle; a crafty game of love, flirting with an undefined risk, betraying a withheld avowal, savoring the approach to consummation, as if the erotic energy which in another social order might find a physical outlet were forcing itself into an electric language that is decorous but intimately exploratory. Between Louis Moore, who has "a thirst for freedom," and Shirley, to whom finding love is the Quest for the Bridle (for "a *master* [whom it is] impossible not to love, and very possible to fear"), there is an almost disturbingly taut struggle, a fierce intensification of the dual between Mirabel and Millamant, complex feelings translated into wit, sheer debate, abusiveness of manner, and a variety of skirmishings; Louis, the lover, adopting the stance of power and consciously playing to fright; the pursuit of an elusive prey ending in a virtual parody of "one calling, Child!/And I replied, My Lord"; over all of this a singular air of strained excitement, of the working of underlying emotional forces that at the climax leads to a new frenetic intensification of style in Louis's notebook:

> "Will you let me breathe, and not bewilder me? You must not smile at present. The world swims and changes round me. The sun is a dizzying scarlet blaze, the sky a violet vortex whirling over me."
> I am a strong man, but I staggered as I spoke. All creation was exaggerated: colour grew more vivid: motion more rapid; life itself more vital. I hardly saw her for a moment; but I heard her voice—pitilessly sweet. . . . Blent with torment, I experienced rapture.

Nor does Charlotte's flair for "unpatterned feeling" stop here: Shirley, the forceful leader who has already been called "a gentleman" and "captain," languishes under the found bridle of the masterful lover, whom she treats chillily and subjects to "exquisitely provoking" postponements of marriage; he calls her a "pantheress" who "gnaws her chain"; she tells him, "I don't know myself," as if engagement had opened to her eyes a previously undetected facet of her nature. Though "these freaks" continue, she is "fettered" at last; but not before the reader is radically stirred by the felt mysteries of personality. Before Charlotte, no love story tapped such strange depths, no consummation was so like a defeat.

Here Charlotte is probing psychic disturbance and is on the edge of psychosomatic illness. The theme draws her repeatedly. When Caroline thinks Robert doesn't love her, she suffers a long physical decline, described with painful fullness. She "wasted," had a "broken spirit," suffered "intolerable despair," felt the "utter sickness of longing and disappointment," at night found "my mind darker than my hiding-place," had "melancholy dreams," became "what is called nervous," had "fears I never used to have," "an inexpressible weight on my mind," and "strange sufferings," believed at times "that God had turned His face from her" and sank "into the gulf of religious despair." Charlotte divines this: "People never die of love or grief alone; though some die of inherent maladies which the tortures of those passions prematurely force into destructive action." Caroline lingers in illness, has fancies "inscrutable to ordinary attendants," has a hallucination of talking to Robert in the garden. Shirley, having been bitten by a dog which she believes to be mad, becomes seriously ill; psychosomatic illness springs directly from Charlotte's special sensitivity to the neurotic potential in human nature. A complementary awareness, that of the impact of the physical on the psychic, appears when she observes the "terrible depression," the "inexpressible—dark, barren, impotent" state of mind of Robert when he is recovering from a gunshot wound.

To give so much space to a lesser work is justifiable only because some of its contents are of high historico-critical significance. Though *Shirley* is not pulled together formally as well as *Jane Eyre* or even the more sprawling *Villette*, and though the characters are as wholes less fully realized, still it accommodates the widest ranging of an extraordinarily free sensibility. Constantly, in many different directions, it is in flight from the ordinary rational surface of things against which old Gothic was the first rebel in fiction; it abundantly contains and evokes, to adapt Charlotte's own metaphor, "unpatterned feeling." It turns up unexpected elements in personality: resentfulness, malice, love of power; precocities and perversities of response; the multiple tensions of love between highly individualized lovers; psychic disturbances. And in accepting a dark magnetic energy as a central virtue in personality, Charlotte simply reverses the status of men who were the villains in the sentimental and old Gothic modes.

Of the four novels, *Villette* is most heavily saturated with Gothic—with certain of its traditional manifestations (old Gothic), with the undercutting of these that is for Charlotte no less instinctive than the use of them (anti-Gothic), and with an original, intense exploration of feeling that increases the range and depth of fiction (new Gothic).

As in *Jane Eyre*, Charlotte can be skillful in anti-Gothic. When

Madame Beck, pussyfooting in espionage, "materializes" in shocking suddenness, Lucy is made matter-of-fact or indignant rather than thrilled with fright. "No ghost stood beside me . . ." is her characteristic response to a Beck surprise. Once the spy, having "stolen" upon her victims, betrays her unseen presence by a sneeze: Gothic yields to farce. Technically more complex is Charlotte's use of the legend of the nun supposedly buried alive and of the appearances of a visitant taken to be the ghost of the nun: Charlotte coolly distances herself from this by having Lucy dismiss the legend as "romantic rubbish" and by explaining the apparitions as the playful inventions of a giddy lover. True, she keeps the secret long enough to get a few old Gothic thrills from the "ghost," but what she is really up to is using the apparitions in an entirely new way; that is, for responses that lie beyond the simplicities of terror.

First, the apparitions are explained as a product of Lucy's own psychic state, the product, Dr. John suggests, of "long-continued mental conflict." In the history of Gothic this is an important spot, for here we first see the shift from stock explanations and responses to the inner human reality: fiction is slowly discovering the psychic depths known to drama for centuries.

Then, when Lucy next sees the nun, she responds in a way that lies entirely outside fictional convention: "I neither fled nor shrieked . . . I spoke . . . I stretched out my hand, for I meant to touch her." Not that Lucy is not afraid, but that she is testing herself—an immense change from the expectable elementary response: the *frisson* disappears before the complexer action that betokens a maturing of personality.

Finally, Paul and Lucy both see the spectre and are thus brought closer together: they have had what they call "impressions," and through sharing the ghost they assume a shared sensibility. Paul says, "I was conscious of rapport between you and myself." The rapport is real, though the proof of it is false; the irony of this is a subtle sophistication of Gothic.

The responsiveness, the sensitivity, is the thing; many passages place "feeling" above "seeing" as an avenue of knowledge. Reason must be respected, for it is "vindictive," but at times imagination must be yielded to, like a sexual passion at once feared and desired. There is the summer night when the sedative given by Madame Beck has a strange effect:

> Imagination was roused from her rest, and she came forth impetuous and venturous. With scorn she looked on Matter, her mate—

"Rise!" she said; "Sluggard! this night I will have *my* will; nor shalt thou prevail."

"Look forth and view the night!" was her cry; and when I lifted the heavy blind from the casement close at hand—with her own royal gesture, she showed me a moon supreme, in an element deep and splendid.

. . . She lured me to leave this den and follow her forth into dew, coolness, and glory.

There follows the most magnificent of all Charlotte's nocturnes: that vision of the "moonlit, midnight park," the brilliance of the fete, the strange charm of places and people, recounted in a rhythmical, enchanted style (the "Kubla Khan" mode) which at first reading gives the air of a dream mistaken for reality to what is in fact reality made like a dream. This is a surrealistic, trance-like episode which makes available to fiction a vast new territory and idiom. The surrealistic is, despite Montague Summers, one of the new phases of Gothic, which in its role of liberator of feeling characteristically explores the non-naturalistic: to come up, as here, with a profounder nature, or a nature freshly, even disturbingly, seen.

The surrealism of Lucy's evening is possible only to a special sensitivity, and it is really the creation of this sensitivity, in part pathological, that is at the apex of Charlotte's Gothic. In *The Professor* the tensions in the author's contemplation of her own experience come into play; in *Shirley* various undercurrents of personality push up into the social surfaces of life; in *Jane Eyre* moral feeling is subjected to the remolding pressures of a newly vivid consciousness of the diverse impulses of sexuality; and in *Villette* the feeling responses to existence are pursued into sufferings that edge over into disorder. The psychology of rejection and alienation, first applied to Polly, becomes the key to Lucy, who, finding no catharsis for a sense of desolation, generates a serious inner turmoil. She suffers from "a terrible oppression" and then from "anxiety lying in wait on enjoyment, like a tiger crouched in a jungle . . . his fierce heart panted close against mine; . . . I knew he waited only for sun-down to bound ravenous from his ambush." Depression is fed by the conflict between a loveless routine of life and her longings, which she tried to put down like "Jael to Sisera, driving a nail through their temples"; but this only "transiently stunned" them and "at intervals [they] would turn on the nail with a rebellious wrench: then did the temples bleed, and the brain thrill to its core."

These strains prepare us for the high point in Charlotte's new

Gothic—the study of Lucy's emotional collapse and near breakdown when vacation comes and she is left alone at the school with "a poor deformed and imbecile pupil." "My heart almost died within me; . . . My spirits had long been gradually sinking; now that the prop of employment was withdrawn, they went down fast." After three weeks, storms bring on "a deadlier paralysis"; and "my nervous system could hardly support" the daily strain. She wanders in the street: "A goad thrust me on, a fever forbade me to rest; . . ." She observes a "growing illusion" and says, ". . . my nerves are getting overstretched; . . ." She feels that "a malady is growing upon" her mind, and she asks herself, "How shall I keep well?" Then come "a peculiarly agonizing depression"; a nine-days storm: "a strange fever of the nerves and blood"; continuing insomnia, broken only by a terrifying nightmare of alienation. She flees the house, and then comes the climactic event of her going to a church and despite the intensity of her Protestant spirit entering the confessional to find relief.

From now on, overtly or implicitly, hypochondria and anxiety keep coming into the story—the enemies from whose grip Lucy must gradually free herself. At a concert she spotted the King as a fellow-victim of "that strangest spectre, Hypochondria," for on his face she saw its marks, whose meaning, "if I did not *know*, at least I *felt*, . . ." When, after her return to Beck's on a rainy night, things are not going well, a letter from Dr. John is "the ransom from my terror," and its loss drives her almost to frenzy. She describes night as "an unkindly time" when she has strange fancies, doubts, the "horror of calamity." She is aware of her "easily-deranged temperament." Beyond this area of her own self-understanding we see conflicts finding dramatic expression in her almost wild acceptance of Rachel's passionate acting of Phèdre ("a spectacle low, horrible, immoral"), which counterbalances her vehement condemnation of a fleshy nude by Rubens (one of the "materialists"). Paul identifies her, in a figure whose innocence for him is betrayed by the deep, if not wholly conscious, understanding that leads Charlotte to write it: "a young she wild creature, new caught, untamed, viewing with a mixture of fire and fear the first entrance of the breaker in."

There is not room to trace Lucy's recovery, especially in the important phase, the love affair with Paul which is related to our theme by compelling, as do the Jane-Rochester and Louis Moore-Shirley relationships in quite different ways, a radical revision of the feelings exacted by stereotyped romance. What is finally noteworthy is that Charlotte, having chosen in Lucy a heroine with the least durable emotional equipment, with the most conspicuous neurotic element in her temperament, goes on through the history of Lucy's emotional maturing to surmount the need for romantic fulfillment and to develop the aesthetic courage for a final disaster—the only one in her four novels.

Some years ago Edmund Wilson complained of writers of Gothic who "fail to lay hold on the terrors that lie deep in the human soul and that cause man to fear himself" and proposed an anthology of horror stories that probe "psychological caverns" and find "disquieting obsessions." This is precisely the direction in which Charlotte Brontë moved, especially in Lucy Snowe and somewhat also in Caroline Helstone and Shirley Keeldar; this was one aspect of her following human emotions where they took her, into many depths and intensities that as yet hardly had a place in the novel. This was the finest achievement of Gothic.

Gothic is variously defined. In a recent book review Leslie Fiedler implies that Gothic is shoddy mystery-mongering, whereas F. Cudworth Flint defines the Gothic tradition, which he considers "nearly central in American literature," as "a literary exploration of the avenues to death." For Montague Summers, on the other hand, Gothic was the essence of romanticism, and romanticism was the literary expression of supernaturalism. Both these latter definitions, though they are impractically inclusive, have suggestive value. For originally Gothic was one of a number of aesthetic developments which served to breach the "classical" and "rational" order of life and to make possible a kind of response, and a response to a kind of thing, that among the knowing had long been taboo. In the novel it was the function of Gothic to open horizons beyond social patterns, rational decisions, and institutionally approved emotions; in a word, to enlarge the sense of reality and its impact on the human being. It became then a great liberator of feeling. It acknowledged the nonrational—in the world of things and events, occasionally in the realm of the transcendental, ultimately and most persistently in the depths of the human being. (Richardson might have started this, but his sense of inner forces was so overlaid by the moralistic that his followers all ran after him only when he ran the wrong way.) The first Gothic writers took the easy way: the excitement of mysterious scene and happening, which I call old Gothic. Of this Charlotte Brontë made some direct use, while at the same time tending toward humorous modifications (anti-Gothic); but what really counts is its indirect usefulness to her: it released her from the patterns of the novel of society and therefore permitted the flowering of her real talent—the talent for finding and giving dramatic form to impulses and feelings which, because of their depth or mysteriousness or intensity or ambiguity, or of their ignoring or transcending everyday norms of propriety or reason, increase wonderfully the sense of reality in the novel. To note the emergence of this "new Gothic" in Charlotte Brontë is not, I think, to pursue an old mode into dusty corners but rather to identify historically the distinguishing, and distinguished, element in her work.

MELVIN R. WATSON

———◆———

Tempest in the Soul: The Theme and Structure
of *Wuthering Heights*

I

IN THE century since its publication, *Wuthering Heights*, like the
plays of Shakespeare with which it has often been compared, has been
the subject of many diverse criticisms and interpretations. Almost no
one has been audacious enough to deny its power and its unique
place in the development of English fiction, but few have made an
unprejudiced attempt to understand what Emily Brontë strove for
in her one full-length study of human nature—its impulses and its
desires, its loves and its hates, its disasters and its triumphs, its defeats and its victories. Because of its strange, elemental fierceness and
barbarity, its stormy setting, divorced from the world as we know it,
its seemingly crude, inartistic structure, and its superhuman emotions,
Wuthering Heights is not an easy book to discuss. Yet if it is the
masterpiece that it is admitted to be, it must present a valid interpretation of life in people who are believable, however seldom their
prototypes may appear in the world as we know it; it must concern
itself with a theme which we can all understand; and it must show
a power of architectonics, however unconventional or imperfect from
the inexperience of the architect that power might be.

Certainly *Wuthering Heights* is different, primarily, perhaps, because its author was an individualist who spurned the easy road of
convention. Not for her was the typical Victorian novel with its study
of normal men and women in the ordinary pursuits of life. Considered

Reprinted from *Nineteenth-Century Fiction,* Vol. 4 (1949), No. 2, pp. 87–
100, published by the University of California Press. Reprinted by permission of the publisher and the author.

as a novel of that kind, it is a miserable failure, badly organized and badly told, with two heroes—Edgar Linton and Hareton Earnshaw—neither of whom is strong or prominent enough to carry the story, and with a villain who overrides the action and is at last triumphantly united with the heroine who has died midway through the book. The plan then becomes incontrovertibly confusing, the point of view too blatantly awkward, the presence of two generations unnecessary, and the conclusion a travesty of poetic justice.

Nor are other possibilities any more feasible as a complete explanation of what Emily Brontë was doing. Although revenge plays a large part in the story, it cannot be considered merely a revenge tragedy analogous to the dramas of Kyd, Chapman, or Marston. The dissolution of the revenge motif in the last chapters and the supreme happiness of Heathcliff as he prepares for his reunion with Catherine rule out such an explanation. To consider this merely the account of Heathcliff's and Catherine's love is equally fantastic. Love there is of a superhuman strength, and thwarted love it is which motivates much—but not all—of Heathcliff's hatred; but if this is a love story and nothing more, the importance of Hindley, Hareton, Cathy, and Linton is misplaced, the entire last half is ill-proportioned, and the ending is off key. If, on the other hand, we assume that *Wuthering Heights* is nothing more than a Gothic romance, we automatically exclude it as a serious study of any human problem.

One last possibility must be considered. In his detailed and provocative essay on Emily Brontë, Lord David Cecil contends that what we have is an allegory setting forth her conception of the universe, a universe built up from two opposing forces—storm and calm,—and that the theme is the re-establishment of the cosmic order which has been disturbed by faulty external actions, by an improper mixture of the two forces in the marriages of Catherine and Edgar, and of Isabella and Heathcliff, which produce children of love and hate respectively, and by the introduction of an extraneous element in the person of Heathcliff. Two principal weaknesses of this interpretation suggest themselves. *Wuthering Heights* is not, I believe, a metaphysical dissertation in which the Heights and Thrushcross Grange are a microcosm and their inhabitants only allegorical puppets whose wooden actions serve to envision a Brontëan universe. Doubtless, Emily Brontë had her own unconventional views of the world, which inevitably became a part of the fabric of *Wuthering Heights,* but surely she was attempting something more concrete, more closely related to human experience than this. But, more important, such an analysis relegates

Heathcliff to a position of less prominence than he occupies. Heathcliff *is* the story. He not only acts and suffers, but causes others to act and suffer; his strength permeates the story; his power for good and for evil shocks and surprises the reader; his deeds and his reactions from the ghastly beginning to the pastoral close make a coherent whole out of what might have been a chaotic heap.

Wuthering Heights, then, is a psychological study of an elemental man whose soul is torn between love and hate. He is a creature about whose past nothing is known. A dark, dirty beggar, he was picked up on the Liverpool streets by Mr. Earnshaw and brought to the secluded part of the world known as the moors, where he has ample space to work out his destiny. Only the elemental passions of love and hate receive any development in the elemental environment by which he was molded. His strength of will and steadfastness of purpose he brought with him to the moors, but there they were prevented by external events from following their natural course. There he was hardened by his physical surroundings, toughened and embittered by the harsh treatment of Hindley, disillusioned by what he considered the treachery of Catherine, on whom he had poured love out of his boundless store. Then he resolves to even scores by crushing everyone who has stood in his way, everyone who has helped to thwart his happiness, the specter of which haunts him for seventeen long years during which he works out the venom which has accumulated in his soul. As soon as part of the venom is removed and the day of happiness begins to dawn, he no longer has the will to keep up his torturing.

This is a daring theme, subject to much misinterpretation, for during most of the action Heathcliff performs like a villain or like a hero who has consciously chosen evil for his companion. When completely understood, however, he is neither an Iago for whom evil is a divinity nor a Macbeth who consciously chooses evil because of his overpowering ambition, but rather a Hamlet without Hamlet's fatal irresolution. Like Hamlet, he was precipitated into a world in which he saw cruelty and unfaithfulness operating. His dilemma was not Hamlet's, for he has no father to avenge or mother to protect, but in a way he has evil thrust upon him if he is to survive among harsh surroundings. And Heathcliff was not one to hesitate when faced with an alternative, however tragic the consequences might be.

Though Heathcliff is not perhaps more sinned against than sinning, his actions are produced by the distortion of his natural personality. This distortion had already begun when Mr. Earnshaw brought him into Wuthering Heights, a "dirty, ragged, black-haired child." Already he was inured to hardship and blows; already he uncomplainingly accepted suffering, as when he had the measles, and ill treatment from Hindley if he got what he wanted. From the very first he showed great courage, steadfastness, and love. But with Mr. Earnshaw's death Hindley has the power to degrade Heathcliff to the status of a servant. A weak, vindictive character, as cruel as Heathcliff without Heathcliff's strength, Hindley prepares for his own destruction by his inhumanity to Heathcliff and the other inhabitants of the Heights. Though Heathcliff was forced down to an animal level, he took a silent delight in watching his persecutor sinking also into a life of debauchery. Nor was he alone, for he had Cathy, on whom he poured his devotion and love. They were inseparable. On the moors by day or in the chimney corner by night, they chatted and dreamed whenever Heathcliff was not busy with the chores. But the visit to Thrushcross Grange introduced Cathy to another world to which she opened her arms, and that world contained Edgar Linton. Edgar held a superficial attraction for Cathy which Heathcliff could never understand and which he feared, for, having possessed Cathy for some years, he feared losing even part of her attention. The final blow, a blow which turns Heathcliff from sullen acquiescence to tragic determination, comes when Cathy confesses to Ellen her infatuation with Edgar and her resolve to marry him so that she and Heathcliff can escape from the repressive world of Wuthering Heights. Not once did she think of giving up Heathcliff, but Heathcliff inadvertently overhears only the first part of the conversation. Cathy has deserted him for a mess of pottage, for fine clothes and refined manners; she is ashamed of his rough exterior, of his lack of polish; she would be degraded to marry him as he is. Heathcliff doesn't stay to hear Cathy confess her oneness with him:

> If all else perished, and *he* remained, *I* should still continue to be; and if all else remained, and he were annihilated, the universe would turn to a mighty stranger: I should not seem a part of it. My love for Linton is like the foliage in the woods: time will change it, I'm well aware, as winter changes the trees. My love for Heathcliff resembles the eternal rocks beneath: a source of little visible delight, but necessary. Nelly, I *am* Heathcliff. He's always, always in my mind: not as a pleasure, any more than I am always a pleasure to myself, but as my own being.

His mind is made up. If love alone is insufficient to hold Cathy, he will secure the necessary money and polish; if his only happiness is to be snatched from him, he will turn to hate; and now not only Hindley will be the object of his wrath, but Edgar also. As long as he had Cathy, his worldly condition, his suffering, was as nothing; without her, all is chaff to be trampled underfoot.

For three years, during which he vanishes from sight, he prepares himself, the poison in his system increasing all the time until love is submerged in a sea of hate which he must drain off before love can reassert itself. Union with Cathy is his one desire. Since physical union is made impossible by her death—not that it was ever important,—the union must be spiritual, but the world and the people of the world must be subjugated before such happiness can be achieved. The course is set, the wind is strong, the bark is sturdy, the journey long. For seventeen years Heathcliff wreaks his vengeance on Hindley, Edgar, and Isabella and on their children Hareton, young Cathy, and Linton. The account of the trip is not pretty. Even in the love scenes before the elder Cathy's death there is a savage passion which strikes terror to the heart of the beholder, unlike any other scenes in the course of English fiction; and before the masochistic treatment of Isabella, Hareton, young Cathy, and Linton we cringe. Here is a man haunted by a ghost of happiness for which he must exorcise his soul, a soul filled with accumulated hatred. That he ceases his reign of terror before Hareton and young Cathy have been completely broken is due not to any loss of spiritual strength but to the realization that the end of the voyage is near, that the tempest is subsiding, and that reunion with Cathy is about to be consummated. In Heathcliff one looks in vain for Christian morals or virtues; his is a primitive, pagan soul; yet love conquers even a Heathcliff in the end—after his soul has been purged of the hate in and with which he has lived for decades. The evil that he does springs not from a love of evil itself, but from the thwarting of the natural processes of love.

In the development of this theme everyone, even Catherine, is subordinated to Heathcliff, as important as many of them are in molding Heathcliff's character, in serving as contrasts to him, or in receiving the force of his hatred. Mr. Earnshaw introduces him to the Heights but exits too early to be more than a puppet, except as he favors Heathcliff over Hindley and thus encourages the waif's willful ways and prepares for the tragedy that is to follow. Hindley reverses his father's actions. He has inherited all the cruelty of the moors without any of their saving strength; he vents his accumulated wrath on Heathcliff but treads himself the primrose path of dalliance. His habits of drinking and gambling make him a clay pigeon when Heathcliff has prepared himself for revenge. He is a despicable character whose downfall calls forth no sympathizing tear. Edgar Linton, on the other hand, contrasts with Heathcliff in another way. In another novel he might have been a conventional Victorian hero; he is presentable and well-mannered, sincere but somewhat smug, honest but thoroughly conventional, good-looking but pallid, devoted to Catherine but incapable of understanding or possessing her. His moral sense the Victorian reader could comprehend and sympathize with. In *Wuthering Heights*, however, he is an anomaly, owning Catherine without possessing her, resenting Heathcliff but lacking the power to thwart him. Though he lives under the shadow of the volcano, he suffers only as he sees those whom he loves—Isabella, Cathy, and Linton—submerged by the lava of hate. And Edgar is as helpless as the peasants who lived near Vesuvius. Isabella, as weak as Catherine is strong, as conventional as Catherine is unconventional, as superficially attracted to Heathcliff as Catherine was to Edgar, allows Heathcliff to make his first inroads on Thrushcross Grange. An emotional, giddy girl who had no knowledge of men or their motives, she felt only the physical attraction of a dark, handsome, well-dressed newcomer to her small circle of acquaintances. Too late she discovered that she was to be only a tool, used briefly and then cast aside to be worn away by rust. Though completely convincing in her role, she is significant only as the device which enables Heathcliff to gain control of Thrushcross Grange.

Catherine alone stands as a near equal to Heathcliff. Beautiful, selfish, willful, she strides through the first part of *Wuthering Heights* like the queen that she is. She understands Heathcliff because she is like him. She could control him, but she forfeits that power by her marriage to Edgar. One of the greater ironies of the book is this: that by her action intended primarily to help Heathcliff she partly alienates herself from him and blows to flame the fire of hatred which produces an eruption lasting seventeen years. She failed to think her decisions through. When she makes her fatal confession to Ellen, not once does she consider the effect of her choice on Heathcliff. She assumes that she can continue to rule both Edgar and Heathcliff as she has done in the past, but she reckons without his pride. Catherine, however, was no hypocrite; she loved both Edgar and Heathcliff—in entirely different ways; she was faithful to her marriage vows, but they could not prevent her feeling a spiritual kinship with Heathcliff. The love scene in chapter xv, overpowering as it is, contains nothing gross, nothing merely physical. It is symbolic of a union which the two cannot resist, for it expresses a likeness of the two souls. But Catherine had deserted him and brings upon herself the curses of heaven and hell that she shall wander as a ghost until he has subjugated the world and attained spiritual union with her. During the last half of the book, Catherine is present only as a spirit, an influence which continually goads Heathcliff like the Furies of old. In the final analysis it is her *spirit*, not Catherine herself, that is important for the novel as a whole.

The presence of the second generation caused many early commentators to stumble, for they failed to recognize that Hareton, young Cathy, and Linton are essential to the theme. Time is necessary for Heathcliff to eradicate the hate from his soul in order that love can reassert itself; furthermore, in order to gain the wealth and power which, he feels, separated him from Catherine, he must possess not only Wuthering Heights but Thrushcross Grange as well. This he can accomplish only through the marriage of Cathy and Linton. His relation to Hareton is peculiar. Though he once ironically saved him from death when Hindley in a drunken fit let him fall over the banisters, he takes a savage delight in degrading him as he was once degraded by Hindley. Hareton is saved by the absence of hatred in his heart, and the fondness between him and young Cathy blossoms in time to prevent his becoming just an animal. The love which develops out of and in spite of the hate which surrounds them—but develops as that hate is subsiding—provides the calm and symbolic ending of the book.

II

The structure of *Wuthering Heights* is as different and unconventional as the theme. How could it be otherwise? New wine should not be poured into old bottles. Though there are superficial awkwardnesses and old-fashioned conventions in the point of view, this seems to be the inevitable way of telling such a story. The structure provides yet another analogy with Elizabethan drama, for it is consciously organized like a five-act tragedy, with breaks always indicated at the appropriate points. The method of telling the story, "in terms of autobiography thrice involved," as William Dean Howells said, is necessary for this structure. Mr. Lockwood, the relative nonentity who records the story as told to him by Ellen Dean, lives in the community only a few months before Heathcliff dies; yet representing, as he does, normal humanity, and experiencing enough of the confusion of Wuthering Heights to make him believe anything about these creatures, and being the audience before whom their past is unfolded, a past which is broken into segments by Ellen's or Mr. Lockwood's interruptions, he lends credibility to the events and serves as a curtain marking off the divisions of the story.

The Prologue (chapters i-iii), like that of a Greek tragedy, sets the tone and character of the book. Here, through a perfectly detached spectator, an ordinary person from the outside world, we are catapulted into the story at a point just before the denouement. Lockwood observes the primitive quality of the life at Wuthering Heights, the brutality and the coldness evident on every hand, both inside and out; he witnesses the inhumanity and the hatred of Heathcliff; he experiences the ghastly night in Catherine's old bedchamber, with Cathy's spirit crying for entrance—or was it a dream? He is as confused, as shocked, and as mystified as any reader could be; naturally he is curious to discover more about these strange inhabitants of this peculiar establishment. This beginning is not accidental; it is the triumph of an artistic spirit that realized the difficulties inherent in her material. If the strange behavior of her characters was to be made believable, she must storm the citadel with the first assault; she must make Lockwood's reactions coincide with the reader's and cause both to suspend their disbelief until they have discovered the background for the present situation. Ellen Dean, fortunately, is able to satisfy all his curiosity.

Though this minor-character point of view seems the only possible one for this story, certain disadvantages loom before us. Ellen is at moments plot-ridden. The climactic last scene between Cathy and Heathcliff is arranged by Ellen, and she is the direct cause of young Cathy's and Linton's getting so friendly; yet we feel that here Ellen is merely the agent of fate; these things would have happened whether or not Ellen had intervened. Certain time-honored but slightly unnatural conventions, also, are used. Ellen gets part of the story in a letter from Isabella—hardly a person to correspond with a servant; she secures needed information about the situation at Wuthering Heights by gossiping with Zillah, the new servant there; but, more significant, she acquires mental reactions and attitudes from the confessions to her, such as Catherine's in chapter ix, Heathcliff's in chapter xxi, and Edgar's in chapter xxv. Except for the first, these are really soliloquies in the Elizabethan sense and should be accepted as such. Finally, to have Ellen Dean as narrator, we must accept the fact that a servant can be in many places where she would not ordinarily be and hear many things that she would not ordinarily hear: for example, the last scene between Cathy and Heathcliff in chapter xv, or Heathcliff's description of what he did on Catherine's burial day and of his looking at her corpse after many years, in chapter xxix. But the advantages gained by having the story told by an eyewitness are weighty enough to balance all these disadvantages. Dramatic intensity is secured by seeing the story unfold with all the freshness and vigor with which Ellen saw it. Ellen relates the story with breaks to set off the divisions as it actually happened. She has no favorites; though she may at moments betray partialities, she makes no consistent attempt to whitewash any of the characters or events. And she lends further credibility to the story by recounting only what she has seen or heard.

Act I, including chapters iv-vii, introduces the first generation, provides the initial complications in Hindley's treatment of Heathcliff, and the effect on Cathy of her visit to the Grange, and ends with Heathcliff's defiance of Hindley: "I'm trying to settle how I shall pay Hindley back. I don't care how long I wait, if I can only do it at last. I hope he will not die before I do!" Mrs. Dean interrupts herself to remind Lockwood that she should stop, but is persuaded to continue her tale.

The next section, containing only two chapters, includes the birth of the first member of the second generation, Hareton, develops Cathy's relation with Edgar Linton, and climbs to a minor climax when Heathcliff inadvertently hears Cathy declare that she has accepted Edgar's proposal of marriage. The last few pages of the act hurry over three years, at the end of which Cathy and Edgar are married. Here Ellen Dean stops because of the lateness of the hour.

After Lockwood has recovered from a four weeks' illness brought on by his first visit to Wuthering Heights, he demands more of "the history of Mr. Heathcliff." Ellen responds with Act III, leading up in its five chapters to the main climax of the novel. From the first meeting of Cathy and Heathcliff after her marriage to the arrangement for their last scene a few hours before her death, this act runs the gamut of emotional intensity. Heathcliff finishes the ruin of Hindley by catering to his taste for drink and gambling and secures mortgages on Wuthering Heights; he elopes with Isabella after she has thrown herself at his feet; he physically chastises Edgar for daring to interfere in his talks with Catherine; he alternates between passionate love and fierce hatred in his attitude toward Catherine and helps produce in her a fever from which she dies. Instead of ending this act with the climactic scene between Cathy and Heathcliff from which she never recovers, Emily Brontë only prepares for it, but presents the climax itself at the beginning of the next act. Again her technique seems right, for not only does this break give the reader a chance to catch his breath, but it makes of Act IV a more symmetrical structure.

The interruption at the end of chapter xiv is the last one until Mrs. Dean has brought the story up to date at the close of chapter xxx. In the week intervening between the close of chapter xiv and the beginning of chapter xv, Mrs. Dean has told Mr. Lockwood the rest of the story, which he has determined to continue in her own words. Since the structural breaks in Act IV and the beginning of Act V are not so important as the others, there is no necessity for inventing interruptions. Casual comments are enough to mark the breaks now, of which there are three, one at the beginning of chapter xviii ("continued Mrs. Dean") to indicate the last part of Act IV, and another in the opening line of chapter xxv ("said Mrs. Dean") to indicate the start of Act V. The other break, slightly more prominent than these, sets off the climactic scene, the birth of young Cathy, and the death of Catherine from the rest of this section and occurs in the middle of chapter xvi. These events, though a bridge between the rising and the falling actions, were to be clearly marked off from the less dramatic events of this act: the birth of Linton after Isabella's escape from Wuthering Heights, the mention of her death some years later, the death of Hindley—these occupy the middle of the act,—and the development of the second generation, which fills up the last "scene" of the act.

By the close of the first "scene" of Act V, Nelly Dean has brought Lockwood up to date. The machinations of Heathcliff have accomplished the marriage of young Cathy and Linton, and with the death of Edgar, and then of Linton, Heathcliff has come into possession of Thrushcross Grange. Lockwood's visit to Wuthering Heights after his recovery, described in chapter xxxi and forming the second part of this last act, prepares the reader for the final resolution of the drama. Several crucial months have elapsed since the memorable night spent in Catherine's former bedchamber, months during which the inhabitants of the Heights have changed. Heathcliff now wonders about the wisdom of his treatment of Hareton, for when he looks for Hindley in his face, he sees only Catherine. Hareton is making gigantic efforts to pull himself up by his bootstraps by learning to read in order to impress Cathy. Cathy, though still bitter and morose from her harsh treatment, and changed less than the other two, totters on the verge of a readjustment. Wisely, this scene has been inserted to make the reformation in the last chapters easier to accept.

When Lockwood saw Wuthering Heights for the first time, he was impressed in this manner:

> Pure, bracing ventilation they must have up there at all times, indeed; one may guess the power of the north wind blowing over the edge, by the excessive slant of a few stunted firs at the end of the house; and by a range of gaunt thorns all stretching their limbs one way, as if craving alms of the sun. Happily, the architect had foresight to build it strong; the narrow windows are deeply set in the wall, and the corners defended with large jutting stones.

The locked gate, the padlocked door, and the fierce dogs added to his sense of awe. On his last visit, after a nine months' absence from the moors, he was struck by a different atmosphere:

> Before I arrived in sight of it, all that remained of day was a beamless amber light along the west: but I could see every pebble on the path, and every blade of grass, by that splendid moon. I had neither to climb the gate nor to knock—it yielded to my hand. That is an improvement, I thought. And I noticed another, by the aid of my nostrils; a fragrance of stocks and wallflowers wafted on the air from amongst the homely fruit-trees.

The explanation for the difference both in external and internal atmosphere is supplied by Nelly Dean as she once again brings Lockwood up to date, detailing the increasing friendship and then love between Cathy and Hareton and the dissolution and final death of Heathcliff as the possibility of permanent reunion with his Cathy makes his face glow with a ghastly happiness. To escape the lovers, Lockwood vanishes through the kitchen door; and as he later meditates on the quietness of the kirk where Edgar, Cathy, and Heathcliff lie buried side by side, the story whispers itself out.

As careful as she was in constructing the story, so meticulous was Emily Brontë in maintaining unity of place and tone. The reader never leaves the moors, once he has arrived there with Mr. Lockwood. He travels between Wuthering Heights and Thrushcross Grange; he sees the graves on the hillside and catches an occasional glimpse of Peniston Crag; he knows where the road to Gimmerton branches off from the road with which he is well acquainted, but never does he follow that road to the outer world. When Mr. Earnshaw travels to Liverpool, when Heathcliff disappears, when Isabella escapes, when Edgar goes to get Isabella's son, the reader remains on the moors, awaiting their return or news of their death. Wuthering Heights, Thrushcross Grange, and the rippling moors between—these are the physical bounds of the story. And so with the tone. No comic scenes or characters lighten the dramatic intensity of the action. Even Joseph is more ironic than comic, and Mr. Lockwood's occasional facetious comments are outside the action and have no influence upon it. Though incapable of understanding the book, Charlotte Brontë sensed the power attained through this unity: "Its power fills me with renewed admiration; but yet I am oppressed; the reader is scarcely ever permitted a taste of unalloyed pleasure; every beam of sunshine is poured down through black bars of threatening cloud; every page is surcharged with a sort of moral electricity."

Wuthering Heights is not the "work of immature genius," "awkwardly and illogically constructed," a study of "unnatural passion"; nor is it, I believe, the "one perfect work of art amid all the vast varied canvases of Victorian fiction." In theme and structure, however. it is the product of a mature artist who knew what effects she wished to achieve and possessed the ability to carry her scheme through to a logical and satisfying conclusion. Her theme of the relationship between love and hate is universal in its significance; her structure, if not unique in English fiction, is the ideal one for this story which could not be confined within the relatively narrow bounds of the drama.

WILLIAM O. RAYMOND

---◆---

The Infinite Moment

THOUGH it is now sixty years since the death of Robert Browning, the time is yet unripe for a definitive estimate of his place amongst English men of letters. During his lifetime he experienced, perhaps to a greater extent than any of his contemporaries, the vicissitudes of a poet's lot. A long period of depreciation, in which his poetry was a byword for difficulty and obscurity, was followed by a sudden access of fame. From the time of the publication of *The Ring and the Book* in 1868–69 until his death in 1889, his niche beside Tennyson as one of the two master poets of the Victorian era was secure. Criticism was succeeded by panegyric, reaching its acme in the adulation of the Browning Society and its mushroom offshoots in England and America.

In the sixty years that have passed since Browning's death, his poetic reputation has varied as widely as in his lifetime. The pendulum of critical opinion has again swung violently from one extreme to the other. In particular, Browning has suffered, along with Tennyson, from the general reaction inimical to Victorianism and all its works which has characterized the opening decades of the twentieth century. There are signs that the nadir has been reached, and that a juster and truer appreciation of the Victorian epoch is at hand. But we are still in the wake of that inevitable shift of literary evaluation which marks the transition from one generation to the next. The baiting of Victorianism continues to be a favourite sport of modern writers; and prevailing currents of present-day historical and aesthetic criticism run counter to some of the cherished ideals and

From *The Infinite Moment and Other Essays in Robert Browning* (Toronto: University of Toronto Press, 1950), 3–18. Reprinted by permission of the publisher.

standards in life and art of our Victorian forerunners. Part of this censure is wholesome, part is regrettable, but the winnowing of our Victorian inheritance by the fan of time is as yet incomplete.

A tentative estimate, within brief compass, of Browning's place in English letters must strive for centrality of view. In reckoning with a poet of such far-ranging interests, it is important to insist that he be appraised first of all as an artist. However beguiling the bypaths of his work in literature may be, it is essential to keep steadily in sight the beaten highway, lit by the flash of his genius, where his powers are exhibited at full stretch.

Yet such an emphasis should not be inconsistent with a recognition of the composite nature of Browning's contribution to English poetry. In certain ways he is both an intellectual and a moralist, and the philosophical, ethical, and theological aspects of his writings are fruitful subjects of inquiry. Much has been said concerning the confinement of these elements of his work within a set Victorian mould. But in dealing with a mind of a rare order and a poet of genius, stress should be laid upon those gleams of intuition which break through the conventional Victorian framework with keen insight into the heart of life and the problems of man's destiny. Such a reverie as that of Pope Innocent XII, in *The Ring and the Book,* is no mere collection of theological platitudes. It is a definitive summing-up of Browning's philosophy of life, and a high watermark of metaphysical thought in nineteenth-century poetry, enriched by acute religious perception.

Nevertheless, it is inevitable that a study of the didactic interests of Browning often leads to the periphery rather than to the centre of his poetry. Within their sphere, prodigious mental energy or moral fervour tends to obscure the poet. There is in him a conflict between imagination and intellect, only resolved in the poems of happiest vein, written between 1840 and 1870, beginning with *Pippa Passes* and ending with *The Ring and the Book.* For the understanding of his view of life, the deep-seated opposition between faith and reason pivotal to his thought, his ethical outlook, his conception of the relation between God and man and of man's place in the universe, a consideration of the earlier and later poems lying outside his golden period of imaginative vision is indispensable. Nor can the depths of Browning's analysis of character be plumbed without a knowledge of those stages of his work which abound in subtle probing of impulse and motive, the incidents in the development of the soul underlying outward action.

In order to comprehend these varying interests, a student must toil through the labyrinth of *Sordello*, "a bewildering potpourri of poetry, psychology, love, romance, humanitarianism, philosophy, fiction, and history." [1] He must wrestle with poems which in the aggregate, at any rate, tax his patience and mental faculties even more than that "Giant Despair" of English letters. Some of the later writings of Browning, while they contain lines and passages of sheer poetic beauty, are jungles of involved argument. The mind reels amid the elusive, ever shifting sophistries of *Fifine at the Fair* and *Aristophanes' Apology*, or is repelled by the sordidness of *Red Cotton Night-Cap Country*. Though the poet tells us that a delectable ortolan is sandwiched between the plain bread of *Ferishtah's Fancies*, the appetite of the average reader is hardly reconciled to the crust he must crunch before reaching the toothsome bird.

Even the wit and dexterity of Browning's numerous studies in casuistry scarcely atone for their redundancy. We are dizzied by their juggling and wearied by their tortuousness. *Mr. Sludge, "the Medium," Bishop Blougram's Apology*, and *Prince Hohenstiel-Schwangau* are overweighted with ratiocination. The hair-splitting arguments of the lawyers in *The Ring and the Book* make gnarly and tiresome reading, and their crabbed forensic quibbles are only slightly enlivened by quaint Latin puns illustrating the humour of pedants. Whatever tribute is due to Browning's ingenuity in constructing these cumbersome leviathans of verse, the most ardent devotee of the poet, when caught in their toils, must compare his state of mind to that of Milton's spirits in torment, who "found no end in wandering mazes lost."

Happily for Browning's enduring fame as an artist, he has written a large body of fine poetry in which he was able to exorcise his intellectual devil. He cast it from him, even as the hero of one of his poems, in rollicking mockery of arid scholasticism, tossed the bulky tome of Sibrandus Schafnaburgensis into the crevice of a garden tree. "Plague take all your pedants, say I!" It is a pleasure to turn from the "grey argument" of tracts of his verse to the magic of such poetry as is garnered in *Dramatic Romances* and *Men and Women*. Here imagination has not been supplanted by dialectic; and passion and intuition are enlisted in the depicting of character and situation with swift and brilliant portraiture. The sweep and vivacity of Browning's humanism are a perpetual source of delight. As a humanist he is of the lineage of Chaucer and Shakespeare, a poet of whose work it may be said, "here is God's plenty." Above all other Victorian writers, he has that spaciousness of mind we are wont to link with the Elizabethans. Spiritually a disciple of the Renaissance, he is akin to that

great age in his zest of life, *élan* of temperament, overflowing curiosity regarding the ways and works of man. His creative genius has
many facets and in richness and versatility is unsurpassed in nineteenth-century English literature. How far flung is his poetic net and
what treasure trove he brings to land! Strange fish sometimes, but all

> Live whelks, each lip's beard dripping fresh,
> As if they still the water's lisp heard
> Through foam the rock-weeds thresh.

I intend to centre my estimate of Browning on his artistic quality.
This, in itself, has various aspects, and many of them must be left
untouched. His dramatic gift, its capacity and limitation, is a fascinating theme, but it has been exhaustively written on from various points
of view. The style and diction of his verse have been the subject of
a number of technical treatises. I have in mind, rather, to dwell on
what may be called the elemental spirit of Browning's art. This choice
is in part due to a wish to take issue with what I conceive to be the
general drift of Browning criticism at present. If I interpret this
rightly, its quarrel is with the whole tone and temper of the poet's
work, not with this or that specific weakness.

An initial definition is, therefore, necessary. What is the basic element which inhabits and glints through the body of Browning's verse
as its pervasive and animating soul? Can we in reading his numerous
poems, so diverse in theme and setting, "loose their subtle spirit" in
a cruce, like the Arab sage of *In a Gondola?*

Writing to Elizabeth Barrett in 1845,[2] Browning spoke of his poetry
as momentary escapes of a bright and alive inner power and (in a
figure of speech) compared it to flashes of light he had seen at sea
leaping out at intervals from a narrow chink in a Mediterranean
pharos. The vehemence and impulsiveness of Browning's verse have
been universally recognized. Both the form and the content of his
poetry are vividly impressionistic. His favourite medium is the dramatic monologue, which in his best work is the distillation of a crucial
moment of human experience. Light is focused at one point in a white
heat of concentration and intensity. In the revelation of the significance of the precipitous moment, vivacity and turbulence are outstanding attributes of his poetic diction and spirit.

Yet the general recognition of the flair or impetuosity of Browning's
poetry has by no means been accompanied by unanimity of opinion
concerning its merit. Differing judgments of this essential quality have
led to a battle of controversy, dividing the poet's admirers and de-

tractors into hostile camps. Before singling it out for praise, it is, therefore, well to glance at some of the criticism it has provoked. "Cockney Sublime, Cockney Energy," was FitzGerald's jaundiced comment.[3] In our own day, Mr. Santayana, in an essay "The Poetry of Barbarism," has scored the work of Browning as that of "a thought and an art inchoate and ill-digested, of a volcanic eruption that tosses itself quite blindly and ineffectually into the sky." [4] Santayana likens Browning to Whitman, and in this comparison has been followed by T. S. Eliot.

The germ of that approach to Browning's writings which emphasizes their so-called barbaric, Gothic, ultra-romantic elements, may be found back in 1864, in Bagehot's "Wordsworth, Tennyson, and Browning, or, Pure, Ornate, and Grotesque Art in English Poetry." It is a conception that was taken up and enlarged upon by Chesterton in his arresting but untrustworthy biography of the poet. Of late it has been made a formidable weapon of attack in the hands of a school of aesthetic thought which extols classical standards and is deeply distrustful of romanticism. F. L. Lucas has given recent expression to this neo-classicist credo in *The Decline and Fall of the Romantic Ideal*. Our appraisal of it will depend on whether we regard romanticism as abnormal and pathological, or as rooted in an experience of life as normative and intrinsic as that on which the classic tradition is based. It is important to recognize that criticism of Browning as voiced by Irving Babbitt, Santayana, F. L. Lucas, and T. S. Eliot is an offshoot of a general neo-classicist position.

Viewed as a whole, the modern indictment of the energy of Browning's poetry seems a weighty one. At present, the moral, intellectual, and aesthetic aspects of his outlook on life are all suspect. To Santayana, the poet's vagrancy of impulse is indicative of the barbarity of his genius, the essence of which lies in the fact that to him "life is an adventure, not a discipline; that the exercise of energy is the absolute good, irrespective of motives or of consequences." [5] To Babbitt, Browning's unrestrained emotion is an example of those centrifugal and neurotic tendencies that, from the standpoint of neo-classicism, are regarded as evidence of a decadent romanticism. Passion and sensation, we are told, run riot in his poetry, and there is an utter lack of classical decorum, balance, and repose. To Mr. Lucas, there is a trace of a bouncing vulgarity in Browning's energetic verse, which smacks too much of the hearty hail-fellow-well-met manner of a Philistine. Metaphorically speaking, the unfastidious poet slaps his readers on the back. His "stamping and shouting," the jarring dissonances of his verse, "his hastily scribbled poems as fuzzy and prickly and tangled as a furzebush"[6] are at once excesses of his temperament and an undisciplined romanticism. Such comments are reminiscent of an earlier criticism that all of Browning's poetry is summed up in the line, "*Bang-whang-whang* goes the drum, *tootle-te-tootle* the fife."[7]

Although, in justice to Mr. Lucas, it should be noted that he does recognize the vitality of Browning's dramatic portrayal of human life, the general tenor of his criticism seems to me indicative of a mental twist which inhibits him from depicting the great men of letters of the Victorian age with disinterested objectivity. It is the fate of every generation to have its idols shattered by the hammer blows of the succeeding generation. Since the publication of Lytton Strachey's life of Queen Victoria, there have been many acute and witty *exposés* of the foibles, conventions, and conservatisms of the Victorian era. Yet what so many twentieth-century critics lack is a perception of the dignity, poise, and stability of that era, an ethos contributing to the endowment of its principal personages with nobility of character. To ignore these basic elements in Victorianism in delineating its great men is to view the age through a subtly distorted mirror in which every figure is out of focus.

Every man, it has been said, has the defect of his quality, and it might be added, every poet in his art has the defect of his quality. Browning's energy and vitality at times din the ear and become strident and overpowering. Though "barbarism" is not supposed to be a mid-Victorian vice, there is something unbridled in his rush of passion and the militant romanticism of his verse. He can write metallic poems and rhyming exercises. When he is lost in the Cretan labyrinth of his longer poems, his style is as crabbed and involved as his subject-matter.

But the error and insufficiency of the criticism I have been reviewing seems to be that it fastens exclusively on the negative rather than on the positive aspect of the poet's elemental attribute. For it is precisely the dash or verve of his poetry which constitutes its perennial originality and attractiveness. It is a strain running like an *elixir vitae* through his verse in its golden era, giving it headiness and flavour. We are reminded of the violent rush of a mountain torrent frothing and seething amongst rocks and fretting its channel, but compensating for its lack of smooth rhythmical flow by the spin and dance, the spray and sparkle of its waters. "Passion's too fierce to be in fetters bound." From the critical censure of Browning's energy and impulsiveness we turn away, as our eye falls, perchance, with renewed delight on the opening lines of *Pippa Passes:*

> Day!
> Faster and more fast,
> O'er night's brim, day boils at last:
> Boils, pure gold, o'er the cloud-cup's brim
> Where spurting and suppressed it lay. . . .

The relation between the form and the content of the poetry of Browning is often a tension rather than a harmony. All poetry, he once wrote to Ruskin, is the problem of "putting the infinite within the finite." [8] It would carry us too far afield to show how the antithesis of infinite and finite is perpetually in his thought. But it is clear that the crux of the struggle in his life as an artist was the difficulty of bodying forth the content of his imagination and intellect in adequate poetic forms. In *Sordello,* which in many ways is a confessional document, there is a vivid account of the hero's attempt to forge a new language, in an Italian dialect, capable of expressing the novelty of his thoughts and perceptions. The analogy between this and Browning's wrestling with language is unmistakable. Like Sordello, he was striving to make his diction a suitable vehicle for the new type of analytic poetry he was writing. The arduousness of the process is realistically described:

> He left imagining, to try the stuff
> That held the imaged thing, and, let it writhe
> Never so fiercely, scarce allowed a tithe
> To reach the light—his Language. (II. 570–73)

Sordello, from the point of view of style, is a gigantic experiment in artistic technique. It is apprentice work of a faulty kind, yet through its convolutions the poet was feeling his way towards his true manner.

And when, after the murkiness of *Sordello,* the art of Browning begins to clear nobly in *Pippa Passes,* discovers its true bent in *Dramatic Lyrics* and *Dramatic Romances,* and reaches its meridian in *Men and Women,* the triumph of his style is all the more impressive because it has been hardly won. In the dramatic monologue of medium length, he found the poetic instrument he had vainly sought in *Sordello.* His metres and diction instinctively adapt themselves to impressionistic vignettes of picturesque situations and crucial moments in the lives of men and women, often enriched by pregnant historical or artistic backgrounds. Tension of style remains, but it is a close-packed, sensitive tension that is responsive to the subtle and varied play of highly charged thought and emotion. The tempo of Browning's diction in his great dramatic monologues is rapid to the point of abruptness. The metres have the beat of a driving energy. The music of his verse is uneven rather than smooth flowing, involving frequent suspensions and resolutions.

Le style c'est l'homme; and the racy, colloquial style of Browning in the best of his dramatic monologues is a revelation of his intrinsic quality. He has used a greater variety of metres than any other modern poet, but his verse is never rigidly set in a conventional mould. In reading Tennyson's lines,

> All in the blue unclouded weather
> Thick-jewell'd shone the saddle-leather,

we realize that the imagery is enclosed in a sedate metrical framework. But when Browning writes,

> To mine, it serves for the old June weather
> Blue above lane and wall,

there is a natural felicity in the utterance which shakes itself free from formal trappings.

Within its own province, there is a finality in the organic structure, the Sophia and Technê of Greek art; where communication is so wedded to inspiration, form to content, that, as Browning has pointed out in *Old Pictures in Florence,* it achieves perfection in the sphere of the finite. But romantic art, as an emanation of the spirit of man in one of the two basic moments of his experience, has a genius of its own. It may lack the radiance of classic art, that clarity and harmony representative of "the depth and not the tumult of the soul." Yet there is a place on the altars of literature for the Dionysiac fire of romantic art: Dionysiac fire at times, but, when it burns as a purer flame, the light of the Holy Grail. Poetry must in certain moods reveal the tension of the spirit straining at the leash of form, and infinite passion shattering the web of finite expression:

> Thoughts hardly to be packed
> Into a narrow act,
> Fancies that broke through language and escaped.

Therefore, despite the frown of the classicist, a lover of Browning's poetry may take pleasure in its romantic beauty and in the free rein given to passion and sensation. He may enjoy its impressionistic glooms and glances, its live and nervous diction responsive to the "moment one and infinite" of electrically charged emotion. He may feel the justification of a content that overweighs the form, and a tension that is like the pent-up energy of a storm-cloud:

> There are flashes struck from midnights,
> There are fire-flames noondays kindle. . . .

A few examples of the flair and verve of Browning's verse may be cited at random from the poems composed between 1840 and 1870.

The sensuousness of Browning's imagery is vivid and often opulent, but never cloying or languorous. He has too much energy ever to indulge in the sleepy sensuousness of Spenser. Frequently his imagery is associated with a wealth and exotic splendour of colour. In *Popularity*, his eye revels in the Tyrian blue or purple dye extracted from a secretion in the shell of the murex, and he combines this colour with the lustre of gold in two dazzling pictures. The dye, he tells us, is

> Enough to furnish Solomon
> Such hangings for his cedar-house,
> That, when gold-robed he took the throne
> In that abyss of blue, the Spouse
> Might swear his presence shone
>
> Most like the centre-spike of gold
> Which burns deep in the blue-bell's womb,
> What time, with ardours manifold,
> The bee goes singing to her groom,
> Drunken and overbold.

Images of light, sound, and motion are conjoined in the triumphant close of *Rabbi Ben Ezra*, where the philosophic argument of the Jewish sage takes imaginative wings:

> Look not thou down but up!
> To uses of a cup,
> The festal board, lamp's flash and trumpet's peal,
> The new wine's foaming flow,
> The Master's lips a-glow!
> Thou, heaven's consummate cup, what need'st thou
>   with earth's wheel? (ll. 175–80)

Abt Vogler is fine example of a sustained piece of imagery, representing a crescendo of feeling evoked by music. In other poems, imagery flares forth at the peak of an emotional mood like a beacon of passion. How the lines kindle in *The Statue and the Bust* when the cowardly and procrastinating lovers are contrasted with the militant saints of God!

> Only they see not God, I know,
> Nor all that chivalry of his,
> The soldier-saints who, row on row,
> Burn upward each to his point of bliss. . . . (II. 220–23)

Browning's descriptions of nature are as impressionistic as his vistas of human life, and reveal to an equal degree his elemental property. There is occasional tranquillity in his landscapes, but as a rule this is the brief hush that follows or precedes a moment of highly wrought emotional tension. As the lovers in *By the Fire-side* wait for the flash of revelation that is to fuse their lives in one, the the brooding quietness of evening o'erhangs woodland and mountain.

> Oh moment, one and infinite!
> The water slips o'er stock and stone;
> The West is tender, hardly bright:
> How grey at once is the evening grown—
> One star, its chrysolite! (II. 181–85)

But Browning's typical delineation of nature is in keeping with the high tide of dramatic passion that surges through his poetry. In *Pippa Passes*, the lightning seems to search for the guilty lovers, Sebald and Ottima, like the bared sword of divine justice.

> Buried in woods we lay, you recollect;
> Swift ran the searching tempest overhead;
> And ever and anon some bright white shaft
> Burned thro' the pine-tree roof, here burned and
>   there,
> As if God's messenger thro' the close wood screen
> Plunged and replunged his weapon at a venture,
> Feeling for guilty thee and me: then broke
> The thunder like a whole sea overhead. . . . (I. 190–97)

In *The Ring and the Book*, the Pope's one hope for the salvation of Guido is visualized through a similar piece of fiery landscape painting.

> I stood at Naples once, a night so dark
> I could have scarce conjectured there was earth
> Anywhere, sky or sea or world at all:
> But the night's black was burst through by a blaze—

> Thunder struck blow on blow, earth groaned and bore,
> Through her whole length of mountain visible:
> There lay the city thick and plain with spires,
> And, like a ghost disshrouded, white the sea.
> So may the truth be flashed out by one blow,
> And Guido see, one instant, and be saved. (X. 219–28)

Browning's delight in brilliant and intense colour blends with his love of Italian scenery. In *De Gustibus*, he prefers a Mediterranean vista, "the great opaque blue breadth of sea without a break," to the pastoral lanes and coppices of England. He takes particular pleasure in the semi-tropical bounty of nature in June in these lines of *Pippa Passes*:

> Well for those who live through June!
> Great noontides, thunder-storms, all glaring pomps
> That triumph at the heels of June the god
> Leading his revel through our leafy world. (III. 153–56)

The freshness and animation of the poet's landscapes are as typical as their emotional thrust. He pictures Florence as seen in spring "through the live translucent bath of air," when "river and bridge and street and square" are as clear "as the sights in a magic crystal ball." The common phenomenon of the breaking of ice in a pond gives birth, in *The Flight of the Duchess*, to the following exquisite description:

> Well, early in autumn, at first winter-warning,
> When the stag had to break with his foot, of a morning,
> A drinking-hole out of the fresh tender ice
> That covered the pond till the sun, in a trice,
> Loosening it, let out a ripple of gold,
> And another and another, and faster and faster,
> Till, dimpling to blindness, the wide water
>   rolled. . . . (II. 216–22)

Il fait vivre ses phrases. It is, as I have striven to show, the incomparable gusto of Browning's poetry that is its essential quality. And this gusto is not the outpouring in art of the hearty exuberance of a Philistine, or the pietistic enthusiasm of an irresponsible optimist. It is rather—if one may apply to it words used by Arthur Symons in connection with the humour of *The Pied Piper of Hamelin* and *Confessions*—"the jolly laughter of an unaffected nature, the effervescence of a sparkling and overflowing brain." [9] It has its roots in a sound physical constitution, a fine fibre of intellect, and a glow of life which, to cite Elizabeth Barrett's tribute, "shows a heart within blood-tinctured, of a veined humanity." [10]

Undoubtedly, Browning's superb physical health is an element of this gusto. In *Saul*, David sings of "our manhood's prime vigour," the play of muscle and sinew, "the leaping from rock up to rock," and "the plunge in a pool's living water." Idealist though the poet is, there is a genial and aromatic flavour of mother earth in his writings, and he draws sustenance from her which races through his veins like the sap of trees in spring. "Oh, good gigantic smile o' the brown old earth!" he exclaims in *James Lee's Wife*. This touch with earth is reflected in his unique chronicling of insect life, that form of animal existence which is in most intimate conjunction with the soil. The prodigal and spawning energy of nature, riotous with life, is whimsically portrayed in *Sibrandus Schafnaburgensis*. The worm, slug, eft, water-beetle, and newt, invading the covers of a ponderous volume, are symbolic of sheer animal frolic, mocking dry-as-dust pedantry and the dead bones of a musty scholasticism:

> All that life and fun and romping,
> All that frisking and twisting and coupling,
> While slowly our poor friend's leaves were swamping
> And clasps were cracking and covers suppling!

Allied with this love of energy in the physical world is Browning's keen perception of the grotesque. For the grotesque is a bold and peremptory shattering of conventional moulds. As Chesterton has said: "The element of the grotesque in art, like the element of the grotesque in nature, means, in the main, energy, the energy which takes its own forms and goes its own way." [11]

But the *élan* of the poet's art has more subtle and spiritual springs in his intellectual and emotional gifts. These gifts have their extravagances. The suppleness of Browning's mind and his temperamental impetuosity often lead him to strain at the curb of form. Yet the turns and twists of his verse, his metrical liberties, his unexpected and at times somersaulting rhymes, are usually the bubbling-up of irrepressible high spirits, chafing at the yoke of aught that is tame or conventional. It should be noted that he only gives rein to an "outrageous gallop of rhymes" in poems having a certain raciness or bohemianism of content, such as *The Flight of the Duchess, Old Pictures in Florence,* or *Pacchiarotto.* When set in their proper perspective and viewed in relation to the whole body of his poetry, these outward flourishes of style, even when pushed to the verge of idiosyncrasy, are not to be condemned sweepingly as barbaric wilfulness. They are often the frothings of a superabundant vitality, a tang of life like that of Fra Lippo Lippi, shattering the moulds of artistic decorum in a spirit of Puckish impishness.

> A laugh, a cry, the business of the world. . . .
> And my whole soul revolves, the cup runs over,
> The world and life's too big to pass for a dream,
> And I do these wild things in sheer despite,
> And play the fooleries you catch me at,
> In pure rage! (II. 247–54)

Though we must look to the future for an impartial evaluation of Victorian literature, it is evident that Browning, with the possible exception of Carlyle, had a more robust and sinewy mind than any of his contemporaries. He is a great humanist; and however deeply and broadly he quarries in the mine of the thoughts and emotions of men and women, the vein never runs thin, though it may lead at times through tortuous tunnels. The horizons of an intellect of such power and fertility are vast; and linked with this amplitude is the gift of communicating the joy and tingle of his contact with life. In this respect he allies himself with Chaucer, Fielding, and Scott. Like theirs his interest in humanity is unflagging, and while he does not maintain their objectivity of representation, he probes deeper than any of his forerunners into the inner springs of character.

As we travel imaginatively with Browning in many climes and ages, a panorama full of light and colour is unrolled. On a spacious canvas, through an astonishing variety of circumstance, he mirrors the subtle and ceaseless play of impulse and motive flaming up in moments of highly wrought passion into the crux of action,

> When a soul declares itself—to wit,
> By its fruit, the thing it does! [12]

In speaking of the poems of Browning that culminate with *The Ring and the Book*, Mr. Osbert Burdett has said: "If it be still urged that the poetry of Browning loses for want of repose, the reply is that, in these poems, we do not miss it but are carried by the poet while we read into his own world of vigorous healthy imagination, a world so rich, vivid, and finely fashioned that it is one of the most original and dramatic possessions of our literature." [13]

While individual judgments are always relative, it is a test of quality when we can return in later years with unabated pleasure to the work of a poet loved in youth, and "obey the voice at eve, obeyed at prime." Browning measures up to this test, because the volume of his poetry is "the precious life-blood of a master spirit." Into its pages, through the alchemy of genius, the elixir of a generous personality has been distilled. In a large human sense, the best of Browning's work does not date—always a touchstone of worth.

In the most famous passage of *The Advancement of Learning*, Bacon says of poetry: "And, therefore it was ever thought to have some participation of divineness, because it doth raise and erect the mind, by submitting the shows of things to the desires of the mind." The classicist may complain that Browning bullies "the shows of things" into submission. Despite his recognition of "the value and significance of flesh," he does at times wrest the body of art, its sensuous elements, in order to

> Make new hopes shine through the flesh they fray,
> New fears aggrandize the rags and tatters:
> To bring the invisible full into play!
> Let the visible go to the dogs—what matters? [14]

Yet it is the informing presence of a discursive, fully charged mind that is an unfailing source of enjoyment to the sympathetic reader of his poetry. Like Donne, whom in many ways Browning strikingly resembles, he might have spoken of "the sinewy thread my brain lets fall." In this fibre of thought, interwoven with ardour of temperament, lies the genesis of his verve and originality—that flash of life which I have singled out as the essential quality of his poetry.

NOTES

1. William Clyde DeVane, *A Browning Handbook* (New York, 1935), p. 79.

2. *The Letters of Robert Browning and Elizabeth Barrett Barrett, 1845–1846* (London, 1899), I, 17.

3. A. M. Terhune, *The Life of Edward FitzGerald* (New Haven, 1947), p. 254.

4. From *Interpretations of Poetry and Religion* (New York, 1900), p. 189.

5. *Ibid.*, p. 206.

6. F. L. Lucas, *Ten Victorian Poets* (Cambridge, 1948), pp. 36; 23.

7. Cf. Browning's letter to Isabella Blagden, cited in *Letters of Robert Browning*, collected by Thomas J. Wise and ed. by Thurman L. Hood

(New Haven, 1933), p. 82. See also F. R. G. Duckworth, *Browning: Background and Conflict* (London, 1931), p. 121.

8. *The Works of John Ruskin*, ed. by E. T. Cook and Alexander Wedderburn, XXXVI (London, 1909), xxxiv.

9. *An Introduction to the Study of Browning* (London, 1916), p. 27.

10. *Lady Geraldine's Courtship*, stanza 41.

11. G. K. Chesterton, *Robert Browning* (New York, 1903), p. 149.

12. *By the Fire-side*, ll. 244-45.

13. *The Brownings* (London, 1928), p. 338.

14. *Old Pictures in Florence*, ll. 149-52.

◆

Thomas Carlyle: The Rembrandt of English Prose

I

In the year 1834 a tall, gaunt, middle-aged Scotsman of peasant origin drove with his wife, in a hackney coach loaded with their modest belongings, across London to Chelsea. As they passed through Belgrave Square a canary the lady carried with her burst into a lively trill of song, which the care-worn couple tried to take as a happy bird-omen for an adventure that was to be so momentous for themselves—and for the world also, though they didn't know it. In the little house in Cheyne Row which was their destination they remained until they died, and the house is now a museum and memorial of their lives.

Carlyle's history before this descent on London is well known. Born in 1795 (the year of Keats's birth), he was destined, as the cleverest son of a Scottish peasant family, for the ministry; and to Edinburgh the boy trudged to prepare himself for that career. He soon abandoned it, however, for literature, and attained, after some years of bitter poverty, a modest success which enabled him to marry, somewhat above his position, that brilliant mocking-bird of genius whom he was to love and quarrel with till her death. His earlier literary attempts, though scholarly and well-written, showed no signs of that mingled fire and gloom which were to make his later writings famous. In the eyes of the great Jeffrey, however, they found favour; Carlyle's contributions to the *Edinburgh Review* were welcomed, and

From *Reperusals and Re-Collections* by Logan Pearsall Smith [1936]. Reprinted by permission of Harcourt, Brace and Company, Inc., and Constable and Company Limited.

Jeffrey declared that he showed great promise of becoming an elegant and accomplished writer.

Then Carlyle did what Jeffrey and literary Edinburgh regarded as a mad and almost wicked thing. He retired to the desert, taking his delicate wife to live in a tiny house which she had inherited, far away on a hill-top amid the moors of Dumfriesshire—perhaps the dreariest and bleakest spot in the British Islands. What drove him thither was a determination to become something more than a mere elegant writer for the reviews. He had tried, but failed, to obtain a professorship or other position of independence; and poverty and solitude he was prepared to face. But beneath this determination was a confused consciousness of something germinating and growing within him which oppressed his mind; an accumulating weight of meaning, some great thought which he must deliver to the world or be for ever wretched. For the greater part of six years, from the age of thirty-three till he was almost forty, he remained in this rock-bound seclusion, brooding on his message, and experimenting in many ways to utter his unutterable thought. In the articles he wrote and published his prose began to gleam and darken with strange lights and shadows, which horrified his friends in Edinburgh, who honestly believed that he was going mad.

But the old Goethe and the young Emerson heard from afar a new and poignant note in English literature; Goethe wrote him letters of precious encouragement, and Emerson journeyed from America and paid one August day what Carlyle called an "angel's visit" to the desolate pair at Craigenputtock.

II

How shall we diagnose this prolonged crisis in Carlyle's life? Was the troubled voice within him the moan of his indigestion, the voice, as he himself ironically described it, from the interior of his liver, or an outcry from some other physical maladjustment which he was destined to transmute—as genius can—into a source of power? Or was it, as some have held, a linguistic crisis in the career of an artist who had not yet found his medium of expression; a flood, seeking to burst forth, of splendid words and imaginative phrases; a confused accumulation on his palette of the pigments in which alone he could portray his vision of the world?

To this descendant of stern Scottish Calvinists the crisis could seem nothing but a moral crisis. The world stood in dire need of a Prophet he felt, not an artist; and in doubt and fear the thought grew

114

upon him that he was perhaps this destined Prophet; that Fate had called upon him to deliver to mankind a message of tremendous import. What had driven him into the rocky solitudes was, he believed, the great Mystery of Existence, the dire need to face the Sphinx-like riddle of the Universe; to wrestle with it for an answer; to be answered or perish! "The idea of the Universe," he notes in his journal, "struggles dark and painful in me, which I must deliver out of me or be wretched." The dark enigma of human life, the strangeness of man's position, standing amid the Immensities and Eternities alone on his little platform of existence, and facing the Universe which in awful majesty looms before him, a Universe with which his fundamental relation is deeper than all other relations, since the discovery of what is the right way of life depends upon his attitude to these powers of which he knows almost nothing—Carlyle's sense of the drama of this sublime situation lies at the core of all his meaning. If indeed we note in his writings those passages in which the words and rhythms are most resonant, and the accent falls with the strongest emphasis, we shall find they are the expression of the cosmic wonder and terror which formed the darkly flaming background of all his thoughts. The Universe of force and fire in which man finds himself is certainly a phenomenon which may well fill him with amazement; and that amazement has grown ever greater, the more he has learned of the strangeness of its constitution. Most men, however, are little troubled by that sense of their relation to it which was the master obsession of Carlyle's mind; the Universe, he wrote to Goethe from his lonely hill-top, was growing daily to him more mysterious, more august; and against this curtain of the *flammantia moenia mundi* he was afterwards to depict his grandest portraits, attributing, often with little warrant, to their figures vast imaginative thoughts that were more his than theirs. To Dr. Johnson, he wrote, the fact of this Universe was "wonderful, unspeakable, divine-infernal": upon Mahomet the great mystery of existence glared in also, with its terrors, with its splendours. "What am I," he makes the Prophet wonder in his desert wanderings, "what *is* this unfathomable Thing I live in, which men name Universe? What is Life? What is Death?" "The grim rocks," Carlyle wrote, "of Mount Hara, of Mount Sinai, the stern sandy solitudes answered not. The great Heaven rolling silent overhead, with its blue-glancing stars, answered not. There was no answer."

Yet Carlyle believed that there was an answer, desperately believed that in the thunders from Sinai and the voice from the whirlwind he had heard the answer. He made, like Pascal, the great *saltus* of faith, as Professor Grierson calls it, that identification of the divine authority and the human conscience, that desperate belief that Goodness and Justice are at the heart of things, however appalling and mysterious their workings may appear. But although he believed that some "new and deeper view of the world" had arisen in him, his doctrine, when he formulated it, was in essence the stern Calvinism of his peasant ancestors, shorn indeed of its theological dogmas, but still darkly oppressive. With this doctrine and a richly coloured and resonant vocabulary in which to proclaim it, he descended from his hilltop like a fiery meteor, fallen from another planet, to denounce the materialism and Baal-worship of his age, and to prophesy to London of the Woe to come.

His reception was encouraging, but somewhat disconcerting as well. To be stoned by the world is a fate for which prophets are prepared; but what if the world welcomes and applauds them, and insists on crowning their brows with inappropriate roses? This was before very long Carlyle's experience. The world of fashion, which had crowded round the pulpit of that other prophet, Edward Irving—Carlyle's dearest friend and once dearer to his wife—who had also come from Annandale to London to preach damnation to it (and had damned himself, his friends believed, in the process), now flocked to Carlyle's lectures and read his pamphlets; and the more he lashed them with his marvelous vocabulary of denunciation, the louder grew their acclamations. For a moment Carlyle's head grew giddy; for a moment he dreamed of a great resounding lecture-tour in America, in which he should proclaim, as with a lion's voice, to that continent the divine constitution of the Universe; that it was God's creation and not—"No, a thousand times no!"—that of some Upholsterer. But before long he came to loathe "the detestable mixture of prophecy and play-actorism" which he called public lecturing, and he abandoned it as soon as he could afford to do so. He had always before his eyes the really dreadful fate of his poor friend Irving, who had been ruined by his "swim-gloat" of London popularity, and the fate too of his two other fellow-Scotsmen, Burns and Walter Scott, the one ruined and the other made bankrupt by the world.

III

Carlyle lived for nearly fifty years in the honourable simplicity of his Chelsea home. He was regardless of wealth, and refused the honours and titles which were offered to him. He continued to be a voice crying in the wilderness; but so thrilling, so splendid was his voice, that the world would come to listen to it, and sometimes entice him away to their enchanted precincts. A prophet loves influence, a talker must have his audience; and in the great world Carlyle found an audience with the leisure to listen to and appreciate his splendid declamation. "They keep Carlyle," Emerson wrote, "as a sort of portable cathedral-bell, which they like to produce in companies where he is unknown, and set a-swinging, to the surprise and consternation of all persons." Was he being corrupted by the World? the visiting idealists from New England sadly asked each other; had this denouncer of flunkery become himself a flunkey? Was this exposer of shams a sham himself? Carlyle never became a flunkey; he said what he thought, he did what he liked, and made no concessions to the world of any kind. That he had been changed by the world's enchantment into what seemed like a sham-prophet, a Jeremiah with castanets, winking at his audience over the footlights, was the more well-grounded suspicion of these earnest observers. One of them, however, the elder Henry James, saw deeper into the matter; Carlyle was, he said, in essence not a moralist at all, but an artist; picturesqueness in man and nature was what he cared for above all things; he was, in fact, a painter who valued the good and evil of the world as a painter does his pigments, for the opportunities they give for the display of his pictorial powers.

Now that this verdict has come to be generally accepted: now that posterity has come to fix its attention, not on the moralist in Carlyle, but on the great unconscious artist beneath his prophet's garb: now that his incomparable gift of expression—a gift which Matthew Arnold compared to that of Shakespeare—the rich accumulation in the gloom of his great imagination of darkly gleaming words and images, in the chiaroscuro of which he placed his scenes and portraits: now that this, and not his moral message, is what delights his readers, it is of interest to find a phrase to describe the ultimate quality of his pictorial vision. Such a formula or phrase, such a taper to light up and help us to explore Carlyle's murky volumes, is supplied to us by his fellow-countryman, Professor Grierson, in the words borrowed from him as the title of this essay. When Carlyle's best critics have written best about him, when James Russell Lowell, for instance, writes of scenes in his history which are seized on in an instant of intense illumination amid the surrounding darkness; when Leslie Stephen defines him as a painter who sacrifices everything to obtain the strongest contrasts of light and shade, and describes those passages of history in which Carlyle shows himself an unequalled master, "those little islands of light in the midst of the darkening gloom of the past, on which you distinguished the actors of some old drama actually alive and moving"—do not these descriptions read like descriptions of Rembrandt's scenes of Bible history, with their shadows and glooms and strange illuminations? Carlyle possessed indeed the intense vision of the great Dutchman, and a mastery like his of the art of etching, and in a phrase or two could burn in upon our imagination some tiny, illimitable landscape, the figure of some grotesque old man or woman, some dim-lit interior of a peasant's cottage. Carlyle possessed also Rembrandt's broad touch—his free, rapid handling, his mastery of dramatic action, his sense of character, and his gift for character-portrayal. From his great canvases, as from Rembrandt's, strange old faces look at us with all the sadness and mystery of existence in their disdainful, weary eyes: Southey's eyes "filled with gloomy bewilderment and incurable sorrow," Coleridge's eyes "as full of sorrow as of inspiration," and in the eyes of the saintly old Chalmers "a serene sadness as if evening and star-crowned night were coming on."

Thus Carlyle brushes in his great word-pictures with a palette full, like that of Rembrandt, with mingled shades and colours. But from his theology, his cosmic musings, he derived elements beyond the handling of any mere painter's brush, by means of which he could depict his figures enveloped in a quasi-metaphysical atmosphere of mingled light and darkness. This sense of the mystery of existence, exasperated as it was by insomnia and ill-health, led him to create a new kind of shudder, a nightmarish, somnambulistic sensation, for which he found or invented (and he was a great creator of new words) a vocabulary for its expression, thus shedding on many of the scenes in his own life, or in the lives of other people, a spectral mist, out of which grotesque faces gaze on us with awful eyes in silence. The word *spectre* was indeed just the word he needed to express the kind of ghostly astonishment with which he contemplated existence; we find it frequently in his pages, and he formed, in his wild, free way, many derivatives and composites which are first found, for the most part only found, in his writings; *spectracally, spectracalities, spectralisms, spectre-chimeras,* man as a *spectre-fighting* animal, and Carlyle himself "a spectre moving amid spectres," engaged in a dream-like struggle with that cloud-capt, fire-breathing spectre, the modern Democracy which he hated. The Shakespearean compound, "cloud-capt," was an echo of his earliest experiences in the art of words, when, as a schoolboy at Annan, one market-day, an itinerant Italian "crying images" displayed for sale a plaster cast of what a woman in the crowd called "Shankspeare," and while she read beneath the bust the lines from *The Tempest* about "the cloud-capt towers, the gorgeous palaces," the little peasant boy listened entranced to the concluding words

> We are such stuff
> As dreams are made on, and our little life
> Is rounded with a sleep.

These lines, thus heard in early youth, echoed in Carlyle's mind all his life, and as an old man of eighty he declared that they were the finest that had ever been written.[1]

IV

This life-long, almost physical sensation of the spectracality and dream-like nature of life was enriched also from another set of morbidly acute sensations. Carlyle's exacerbated sense of hearing made him acutely sensitive to sound; and perhaps no writer since the Hebrew prophets made such constant use of audible sensations in the phrases and metaphors of his writing. His great prose-poem on the French Revolution is not only a great gallery of scenes and portraits depicted in the smoke and glare of that volcanic outburst, but it is a great tone-poem as well, a rushing vociferous piece of orchestral music, resonant with trumpets and battle-cries, with salvoes of artillery and wild peals of tocsin-bells ringing from all steeples. Carlyle's response to the experience of life or history was indeed more like that of a painter or a musician than that of a thinker, and was more capable of expression in the language of visual or audible sensations than in the logical speech of scientific thought or reason. Ah! he wrote in one of his letters, could he but play on a violin or trombone, he could then express the inexpressible meaning, the preternatural feeling, in him—and that would be his speech!

And yet Carlyle, full as he felt himself of music, had no sense at all for the music of poetry. He tried to write poetry, tried it again and again, worked hard at it, but his verse was really grotesque in its badness. The lines he sang in his discordant voice to Jane Welsh during his courtship of that young lady:

> The gay saloon 'twas thine to tread,
> Its stateliest scenes adorning,

can only be equalled in their bathos by his translation of Mignon's lovely song in *Wilhelm Meister*:

Kennst du das Land? . . . Dahin, Dahin
Möcht 'ich mit dir, O mein Geliebter, ziehn—

Know'st thou that land so transcendently fair?
Oh, would, my Beloved, that we could go there.

Like Sir Thomas Browne, and Jeremy Taylor, he was a poet in his prose, but he was more prosaic than they in his poetry. But, like these seventeenth-century writers, his prose had much of the splendour and music which makes English imaginative prose so magnificent an organ of expression. This mastery was, however, a late acquirement and as has been said already, his early work shows no evidence of it.

v

It almost always happens that in the writings of a great author we find some vivid sensations of his early years to which he often returns, and which, as he grows more and more the master of his style, he describes with a power that becomes ever greater. For Carlyle these sensations were derived from the scenes in which he passed his boyhood, and above all from that great view of the Solway and the surrounding mountains which spread before him as he trudged the six-mile road from Ecclefechan, where he was born, to Annan, where he went as a schoolboy, and whither, at the age of nineteen, he returned as a schoolmaster. This magnificent Solway region, with its sands and quicksands and the roar of the great tides as they rush upon them, has been one of the two parts of Scotland, Ruskin says, in which the highest intellectual, moral and poetic powers of the Scottish race have been developed. Burns was born at no great distance, and over this region Scott, in two of his greatest novels, has shed the purple cloud of his imagination. Carlyle returns again and again in memory to this landscape, would often revisit it, and always the "great roar of the Solway," the everlasting ocean voices, "prophesying of Eternity, coming hither from Eternity," sounded like an unearthly music in his ears, more unearthly than he could say. At each visit to this region its spectral quality grows upon him: "Tartarus itself," he wrote in 1837, "and the pale Kingdoms of Dis could not have been more preter-natural"; and later he wrote in his *Reminiscences:* "Words cannot utter the wild and ghastly expressiveness of that scene to me; it seemed as if Hades itself and the gloomy realms of death and eternity were looking out on me through those poor old familiar objects; as if no miracle could be more miraculous than this same bit of space and bit of Time spread out before me."

The mountains of Annandale, grim-bright in stormy weather, with hail-storms, "black, brief, spring tempests," rushing fiercely down their valleys and blotting out the sunshine—in these alternations of sun and storm, he seemed to find a symbol of what was the essential meaning to him of his own existence. Again and again he evokes these mountains in his writings, and ever with greater expressiveness as his mastery of language increases. This enrichment of his powers can be well illustrated by putting side by side two of his mountain descriptions, the first written at the age of twenty-nine in a love-letter to Jane Welsh, and another, twelve years after their marriage, to his friend Thomas Erskine:

April 15, 1824. I am often very calm and quiet. I delight to see these old mountains, lying in the clear sleep of twilight, stirless as death, pure as disembodied spirits. . . . They are my own mountains! Skiddaw and Helvellyn, with their snowy cowls, among their thousand azure brethren are more to me than St. Gothard and Mont Blanc; Hartfell and Whitecombe raise their bald and everlasting heads into my native sky; and far beyond them, as I often picture, in their bright home, are Jane and her mother, sometimes thinking of me.

April 3, 1848. Dear Mr. Erskine. I see nobody: I do not even read much. The old hills and rivers, the old earth with her star firmaments and burial-vaults, carry on a mysterious, unfathomable dialogue with me. It is eight years since I have seen a spring, and in such a mood I never saw one. It seems all new and original to me—beautiful, almost solemn. Whose great laboratory is that? The hills stand snow-powdered, pale, bright. The black hailstorm awakens in them, rushes down like a black swift ocean tide, valley answering valley; and again the sun blinks out, and the poor sower is casting his grain into the furrow, hopeful he that the Zodiacs and far Heavenly Horologes have not faltered; that there will be yet another summer added for us and another harvest.

There are critics who maintain that prose is merely the sincere expression of thought and feeling, and these may find the first passage, written in all the sincerity of a lover, is better prose than the second, addressed to an elderly lawyer; but to others it may seem that the second passage in Carlyle's late-acquired manner is superior in expressiveness and style. It is a matter of taste; but for those whose taste for magnificence in prose makes them prefer the later example, it will be of interest to quote a longer passage of this Rembrantesque way of writing:

Perhaps few narratives in History or Mythology are more significant than that Moslem one, of Moses and the Dwellers by the Dead Sea. A tribe of men dwelt on the shores of that same Asphaltic Lake; and having forgotten, as we are all too prone to do, the inner facts of Nature, and taken up with the falsities and outer semblances of it, were fallen into sad conditions,—verging indeed towards a certain far deeper Lake. Whereupon it pleased kind Heaven to send them the Prophet Moses, with an instructive word of warning, out of which might have sprung "remedial measures" not a few. But no: the men of the Dead Sea discovered, as the valet-species always does in heroes or prophets, no comeliness in Moses; listened with real tedium to Moses, with light grinning, or with splenetic sniffs and sneers, affecting even to yawn; and signified, in short, that they found him a humbug, and even a bore. Such was the candid theory these men of the Asphalt Lake formed to themselves of Moses. That probably he was a humbug, that certainly he was a bore.

Moses withdrew; but Nature and her rigorous veracities did not withdraw. The men of the Dead Sea, when we next went to visit them, were all changed into Apes, sitting on the trees there, grinning now in the most unaffected manner; gibbering and chattering very genuine nonsense; finding the whole Universe now a most indisputable Humbug! The Universe has *become* a Humbug to these Apes, who thought it one. There they sit and chatter, to this hour; only, I believe, every Sabbath there returns to them a bewildered half-consciousness, half-reminiscence; and they sit, with their wizened smoke-dried visages, and such an air of supreme tragicality as Apes may; looking out through those blinking smoke-bleared eyes of theirs, into the wonderfulest universal smoky Twilight and undecipherable disordered Dusk of Things; wholly an Uncertainty, Unintelligibility, they and it; and for commentary thereon, here and there an unmusical chatter or mew:—truest, tragicalest Humbug conceivable by the mind of man or ape! They made no use of their souls; and so have lost them. Their worship on the Sabbath now is to roost there, with unmusical screeches, and half-remember that they had souls.

To illustrate once more the development of Carlyle's style, let us contrast an early description of Coleridge's talk, with the famous passage in the *Life of Sterling*.

In 1824, on his first visit to London, he wrote:

Coleridge is a steam-engine of a hundred horses' power, with the boiler burst. His talk is resplendent with imagery and shows of thought; you listen as to an oracle, and find yourself no jot the wiser. He is without beginning or middle or end. . . . A round, fat, oily, yet impatient little man, his mind seems totally beyond his own control;

he speaks incessantly not thinking or remembering, but combining all these processes into one.[2]

He writes later:

> The good man, he was now getting old, towards sixty perhaps.. . . . A heavy-laden, high-aspiring and surely much-suffering man. His voice, naturally soft and good, had contracted itself into a plaintive snuffle and singsong; he spoke as if preaching,—you would have said, preaching earnestly and also hopelessly the weightiest things. I still recollect his "object" and "subject," terms of continual recurrence in the Kantean province; and how he sang and snuffled them into "om-m-mject" and "sum-m-mject," with a kind of solemn shake or quiver, as he rolled along.[3]

VI

The difference between Carlyle's early prose, and the richness and resonance of his late style, is due partly to the immense vocabulary he had acquired, with its "depth of fathomless adjective," and the most far-fetched phrases of remote allusion, but, above all, as a needed corrective for this elevation his use of idiom and spoken speech. "I think he has seen, as no other in our time," his best critic, Emerson, wrote of him, "how inexhaustible a mine is the language of Conversation. He does not use the *written* dialect of the time, in which scholars, pamphleteers and the clergy write, nor the Parliamentary dialect, in which the lawyer, the statesman, and the better newspapers write, but draws strength and mother-wit out of a poetic use of the spoken vocabulary, so that his paragraphs are all a sort of splendid conversation."

This distinction which Emerson makes between the written and the spoken dialect is of capital importance in our appreciation of Carlyle's prose. Almost all our authors make use of the written dialect of their time, and rich and beautiful it is as they often use it; but this written dialect has a tendency to desiccation, is always on the way to becoming a dead language; and marvellous is the effect, like that of a fresh breeze from a window suddenly opened into a musty room, of the accents and syncopations and free syntax of the spoken voice. "The good man, he was now getting old, towards sixty perhaps"—no such living phrase speaks to us in Carlyle's early writings. Literature in many of its aspects is, as Stevenson said, "no other than the shadow of good talk"; and this shadow or echo of good talk gives life, not only to the prose of dialogue and of drama—as with Plato or with Shakespeare—but there are essayists who, like Dryden and Charles Lamb, have endowed as by a miracle their pens with the gift of living speech. Certainly Carlyle's slowly acquired mastery of this most difficult of the arts of writing is his most remarkable achievement; and his later writings are all, as Emerson said, a sort of conversation—that splendid conversation of his which was one of the amazements of the age he lived in. For nearly fifty years he poured forth a splendid monologue, a Niagara of talk, a rhapsody of denunciation, vituperation, of scoffs and jeers, of pathos and self-mockery and harsh laughter, with overtones in it of pathos and soft music, mingled with Rabelaisian touches which made his hearers shake with laughter. This marvellous monologue, delivered in the plangent singsong of his broad Scottish accent, produced a splendour of expression which, as one listener said, could hardly be faced with steady eyes. Sometimes the "haggard, moon-struck age" he lived in was the object of his fury; or he would turn on England, now become a "dim owlery and habitation of doleful creatures," of Higginbothams and Rigmaroles, and galvanic Puseyisms and dances of the sheeted Dead, all rushing on together to the Bottomless Abyss. And then the fierce old "calamity-howler" would turn on some American visitor present, to denounce, with wicked delight, the democratic hope and "nigger-delirium" of their country, chanting the praises of slavery, of whips and hand-cuffs and brass-collars, in words that made their hair stand on end. "New spiritual Pythons, plenty of them; enormous Megatherions, as ugly as were ever born of mud, loom huge and hideous out of the twilight Future on America," he chanted, in terms more true than they could guess, at these terrified "sky-blue" idealists and mild "potato-philosophers" from New England. And then the great lamenting voice would begin the burden of his own woes, the woes of a wretched, mourning, heavily laden creature, "impoverished, bilious, bug-bitten, and bedevilled," and sunk deep in the mud-oceans that raged from without and within. The chaos that reigned in Cheyne Row, the dust and dismay of house-cleaning, the smell of paint, the horror of veal-soup, and the perpetual ear-torment that agonized his ears, the screech of railway whistles at night, "like the screech of ten thousand cats, and every cat of them as big as a cathedral," piano-thumpings next door, the voices of screaming parrots and demon fowls, the howling of dogs, and a "dim tremendous sound of organ grinders advancing from the distance," were his frequent themes. Mrs. Carlyle had a fiery temper and a bitter tongue as well; and beneath the real devotion of this couple resentments smouldered, jealousies, disappointments, and unavowed frustrations, that would sometimes burst out in flame and uproar.

VII

Now that silence has fallen on that dwelling, what remains of the din of the great battle that so vociferously these two waged against the world and fate, against the anarchy within and without their walls? Is there nothing left as Carlyle wrote of a famous feline con-- flict in Kilkenny, but "a peaceable annihilation—a neighbourhood de- livered from despair"? Much remains; and the delivered neighbour- hood did well when it celebrated the upheaval of that memorable crater amid its quiet streets. The great lava-flood of molten words that once flowed from that now extinct volcano has cooled into im- mense expanses of varied reading—into many volumes at least of good letters that delight the world.

Both Carlyle and Jane Welsh were incomparable letter-writers; which surpassed the other is a matter of controversy among their admirers, and many give the palm to Jane Welsh rather than to her husband. To others, the reading of Carlyle's letters, with their humour, pathos and splendid phrasing, is an even richer experience; and one fine critic, Henry James, the novelist, has put on record his boundless admiration for Carlyle as a letter-writer—as perhaps the very greatest of the masters of that art. Carlyle's vivid power of expression enables us to accompany his sonorous personality through a long period of the nineteenth century; and the incomparable keenness of the vision of his all-devouring eye etches for us in lightning flashes, or depicts in finished portraits, the great figures of his age. And as the dust of oblivion falls more thickly on that age, and the focus of interest and illumination shifts, posterity may come to gaze upon the nineteenth century through the windows of this house in Chelsea, as we now look back on the eighteenth century through those of Dr. Johnson, whom Carlyle with his prejudices, his intolerances, his tenderness, and the affection beneath his rugged sternness, resembles in many ways. Cer- tainly it is Carlyle's letters, and perhaps above all those in the volumes of his correspondence with Emerson—one of the noblest and most beautiful records of human friendship—that will attract most readers: his letters, and the extracts from his journal which Froude prints in that brave and brilliant biography, which almost deserves to rank with Boswell's in outspokenness and vividness of character-portrayal. And with these will come Carlyle's autobiographical *Reminiscences,* and his half-autobiographical *Life of Sterling,* both of which, written from the deep wells of sorrow, reverence and affection in him, are so full of Rembrantesque pictures and shadowy recollections of the past.

The taste for most of Carlyle's historical writings and all his prophetic denunciations is a more special taste; but to those addicted to draughts of this most potent spirit, the intoxication it produces is one for which the craving constantly recurs. Always for them, even in the fairest weather, a thunderstorm broods over Chelsea, and sooner or later will sweep down upon them. Once again that dark genie will burst from his jinn-bottle and fill the skies; and although they may have recovered their standards of good taste and reason, it is with a foreboding of horror that they gaze at the volumes of this outrageous old Enchanter which they know that they are fated to read again.

VIII

Carlyle was an earthborn spirit, a Titan, groaning under the Etna of his dark obsessions; his attempts to scale those heavens of serene contemplation to which Goethe and Emerson attained were always defeated; always he fell back into his mud-element with outcries of despair. In him, as in Rembrandt, the sense of beauty was deficient, and the lovely light of reason shone but dimly and fitfully on his mind. "His power of expression," Jowett said of him, "outran his real intelligence, and constantly determined his opinion." But it is for his expression, not for his opinions, that many set so high a value on his writings—for that splendour and music, of which, since the seventeenth century, Carlyle was one of the greatest masters. Carlyle's failure to impose his narrow, rigoristic, moralistic, joyless Annandale view of the world upon the world, added an element of tragedy to his deeply tragic sense of life. He suffered also the deeper tragedy of those who attempt to deify the Universe; who personify it as a God to find that they have made a Devil of it. Their cosmic piety plunges them into such abysses of moral contradiction that it becomes, as many believe it became with Carlyle, a mask of atheism and dark despair.

Carlyle was a "sick giant," as Emerson said of him; and "if genius were cheap," Emerson added, "we might do without Carlyle, but in the existing population, he cannot be spared." With this final verdict of his life-long friend, let us take leave of him as we see him walking with David Masson in the park one evening, under his extraordinary tall, broad-brimmed hat, which gave him the air of an old magician, and gazing up at the stars that were growing brighter as the daylight faded. He spoke of the infinite beauty and harmony of the Universe; but soon the old prophetic fury seized him; he began to denounce the irreverent, mocking spirit of the age. Too much jest, too much irony and laughter, too much sniggering at things! And then, as if remembering his own wild satirical torch-dancings, he paused, and giving a shrug of self-disgust: "Ah," he exclaimed, "I have given too much in to that myself!"; and the proud, melancholy old man walked on, lost in his life-long dialogue under the earnest stars with Death, Judgment and Eternity.

NOTES

1. In the same year William Allingham notes in his diary that one day Carlyle told him how, just after he had got out of his bath that morning and was drying his old body, the strange problem of his existence roused in him a kind of fury or exaltation, and he exclaimed: "What the Devil then am I? After all these eighty years I know nothing at all about it."

2. *Thomas Carlyle,* Moncure D. Conway, 1881, p. 195.

3. *Life of John Sterling,* Chap. VIII, p. 65.

CLYDE K. HYDER

Wilkie Collins and *The Woman in White*

INSCRIBED on a tombstone in Kensal Green Cemetery are the following words: "In memory of Wilkie Collins, author of 'The Woman in White' and other works of fiction." This inscription, written (as his will shows) by Collins himself, pays tribute to the book which probably stands highest among his works in the esteem of his readers.

No other name is marked on that stone, but with Collins lies buried Caroline Elizabeth Graves,[1] who died in June, 1895, at 24 Newman Street, aged sixty-one, apparently the widow of a George Robert Graves.[2] After Mrs. Graves's death Collins's grave was for a time under the care of Martha Rudd.[3] These two women, Mrs. Graves and Martha Rudd, had shared Collins's bequest. To Mrs. Graves, Collins left his "gold studs and gold sleeve links" and some furniture, £200, and one moiety of the income from his estate; to Martha Rudd his watch and chain, £200, and a moiety of the income from his estate.[4] After the death of Mrs. Graves, her share of the income was to pass to "her daughter," Elizabeth Harriet. In the record of her marriage (dated early in 1878) Elizabeth Harriet, called "Harriette Elizabeth Laura Graves," gave her age as 24, so that obviously she was born about 1854. The heroine of *The Woman in White* may, therefore, have been named after her. One cannot be entirely certain about her exact relationship to Collins: was she more than a foster daughter?[5] After the death of Martha Rudd, her moiety of the estate was to go to the three children whom Collins acknowledges as his own: Marian, born at 33 Balsover Street, Portland Place, July 4, 1869; Harriet Constance, born in the same place on May 14, 1871; William Charles, born at 10 Taunton Place, on December 25, 1874. Martha Rudd and

From *Publications of the Modern Language Association*, LIV (1939), 297–303. Reprinted by permission of the publisher and the author.

her children, at least for some time after Collins's death, passed under the name of Dawson.[6]

In a biography of his father, the artist Millais, who was a friend of Wilkie Collins, John G. Millais declares that a scene in *The Woman in White*—the scene which Charles Dickens considered one of the two most dramatic descriptions he could recall [7]—was based on experience.[8] According to Millais, as his father and Wilkie and Charles Collins were walking one night, they saw a beautiful young woman dressed in white approach, hesitate as if in distress, and walk on, to be followed by Wilkie Collins. Collins later told his companions that the young woman, from a good family, had fallen into the power of an unscrupulous man who had subjected her to threats and "mesmeric influences" of an alarming nature. Kate Dickens, who married Charles Collins, Wilkie's brother, is said to have believed that it was the fugitive in white who afterwards lived with Collins.[9] If this belief was correct, the young woman was Caroline Elizabeth Graves, whose name is listed in London directories under the same address as Collins's. It is noteworthy, if not especially significant, that *The Fallen Leaves,* one of Collins's most daring books (and one which incurred considerable censure because of the Socialist hero's befriending and finally marrying a girl of the streets), was dedicated "To Caroline." [10]

Though Millais's attempt to connect fact and fiction should be regarded with some skepticism, Collins's emotional experience may have affected his writing. More than once he introduces a character whose allegiance in love is divided.[11] The facts about his private life, hardly more than hinted at in print, must have been known in some circles. Not long after his death, when some friends proposed a memorial in his honor, in St. Paul's, the Dean and the Chapter reported adversely, stating that other than literary considerations had to be taken into account.[12]

It is no secret that Collins was fond of reading records of criminal cases,[13] especially those written in French, and more than one commentator has mentioned casually that Collins derived from such a source suggestions for *The Woman in White*.[14] The exact source, which seemingly has not been pointed out, was the celebrated case of Madame de Douhault, which Collins found discussed fully in Maurice Méjan's *Recueil des Causes Célèbres* . . . (second edition, Paris, 1808, etc.),[15] a book in his own library.

The relevant parts of this famous case may be briefly outlined: Adélaïde-Marie-Rogres-Lusignan de Champignelles (1741–1817) was married in 1764 to the Marquis de Douhault, and became a widow in 1787. Her father died in 1784. Madame de Douhault's brother, M. de Champignelles, obtained as much of his father's estate as he could, including some of the inheritance rightfully belonging to his mother and his sister. Of the mother's hardships under altered circumstances, another sister, abbess of Montargis, had some knowledge, and urged her sister Madame de Douhault to recover for their mother some share of the paternal bequest. Madame de Douhault thereupon planned a trip to Paris and announced her plan both to her sister and to Madame de Polignac, a correspondent. During a visit to some friends she expressed misgivings about the proposed journey, but her friends succeeded in calming her temporarily. Near the end of December, 1787, she left Chazelet, accompanied by a coachman, a chambermaid, and a servant. She stopped at Orléans, where she usually lodged at the house of M. Dulude (or du Lude), a nephew and an heir. On this occasion Dulude refused to receive her and induced her to go to the house of M. de la Roncière, a relative, whose mother had died suddenly eight days before at her son's house, about four leagues distant from Orléans. On January 15, 1788, on the eve of departing for Paris, Madame de la Roncière invited Madame de Douhault to go for a drive along the banks of the Loire. Soon after taking a pinch of snuff given her by Madame de la Roncière, Madame de Douhault suffered a violent headache which obliged her to return. Directly she fell into a deep slumber and was put to bed.

Madame de Douhault remembered all these events clearly, but what happened subsequently at Orléans was as indistinct as the events in an evil dream. She believed that she slept for several days; she woke to find herself in the Salpêtrière, under the name of Blainville. The supposed Madame de Douhault being dead, her estate was liquidated by M. de Champignelles and her heirs.

The correspondence of Madame de Douhault was for a time intercepted, but in June, 1789, by means of a woman whose favor she had won she succeeded in sending a letter to Madame de Polignac, and through Madame de Polignac's agency regained her liberty.

> Une surveillante reçut l'ordre de lui remettre ses habits, dont l'indication était écrite sur un papier, et Madame de Douhault reprit son déshabillé blanc, le linge et les poches qu'elle avait en entrant à la Salpêtrière.

Madame de Polignac and her friends recognized Madame de Douhault; in fact, nobody at Versailles questioned her identity. When she went to the château at Champignelles, she was recognized by her own former domestics as well as by other people. The elaborate system of intrigue and defamation and the ingenious machinations by which Madame de Douhault's brother sought to discredit her attempt to regain her rightful status need not be reviewed here.[16] The case dragged on for years. To her cause the son of a former member of her household, an advocate named Delorme, with whom Madame de Douhault lived for a time, in vain devoted his talent and his fortune.[17]

Obviously Collins took from the story of Madame de Douhault the idea for Count Fosco's plot, to rob Laura of her property by destroying her identity. Fosco and Sir Percival carry out the plan by burying Anne Catherick, Laura's half-sister, as Laura, and substituting Laura for Anne at the asylum from which Anne had escaped—details which Collins added to make his narrative more logical. Laura's instinctive dread of spending a night at her aunt's house in London, on her journey towards Cumberland, may correspond to Madame de Douhault's misgivings, though a novelist's foreshadowing needs no such explanation. Laura's imperfect memory of the events which preceded her trip to the asylum is possibly a bit more reminiscent of the French case. Finally, one wonders whether Madame de Douhault's "déshabillé blanc" did not suggest the detail from which the novel derives its title,[18] in spite of Millais's story. To be sure, women in white are strangers neither to fiction nor to legend.[19]

The use of a legal case may have influenced the form of the narrative.[20] In the first chapter of *The Woman in White* Collins explains: "The story here presented will be told by more than one pen, as the story of an offence against the laws is told in Court by more than one person. . . ." Thus a section of the story is related by the character whose testimony seems most pertinent; at the same time this character, like the speakers in *The Ring and the Book*, reveals a good deal of himself. An early reviewer pointed out that since each witness tells only what he knows, his ignorance piques the reader's curiosity.[21]

In his introductory remarks to *Basil* Collins called the novel and the play "twin-sisters in the family of Fiction," the one "a drama narrated" and the other "a drama acted." In a dramatic novel like *The Woman in White* every incident is necessarily planned with care. One inconsistency of time in the first edition, subsequently corrected, did escape the author.[22] In a dramatic novel, too, fatalism is often prominent. Dreams, a favorite subject with an author himself susceptible to weird dreams, foreshadow important events: The letter warning Laura against marriage with Sir Percival (Chapter XI of the first part) contains an account of an ominous dream. Before departing on the journey that ended at the asylum, Laura has bad dreams. More important is the dream of Marian Halcombe (Chapter VI in the second epoch) in which she sees Walter Hartright escaping pestilence, shipwreck, and other perils; the dream ends with the prophetic vision of Hartright at a tomb—as events are to prove, the tomb of Anne Catherick. And Anne Catherick herself enters the story like a figure in a vision:

> There, in the middle of the broad, bright highroad—there, as if it had that moment sprung out of the earth or dropped from the heaven— stood the figure of a solitary Woman, dressed from head to foot in white garments, her face bent in grave inquiry on mine, her hand pointing to the dark cloud over London, as I faced her.

And thus she disappears:

> So the ghostly figure which has haunted these pages, as it haunted my life, goes down into the impenetrable gloom. Like a shadow she first came to me in the loneliness of the night. Like a shadow she passes away in the loneliness of the dead.

The plot having been conceived, certain characters were essential. As Collins once explained,[23] a victim can hardly exist without a villain, and because the crime was too ingenious for an English villain, the author chose a foreigner. Since Collins had visited Italy in his boyhood, his choice of an Italian was natural. Moreover, Italy was the home of such organizations as "The Brotherhood." Fosco's tool, Sir Percival, was necessarily a "weak shabby villain."

To Count Fosco, justly regarded as Collins's greatest achievement in characterization, Collins gave a Falstaffian physique, because, he said, of the popular notion that a fat man could hardly be villainous. He accounted for Fosco's pets thus: "I knew a man who loved canaries, and I had known boys who loved white mice, and I thought the mice running about Fosco while he meditated on his schemes would have a fine effect." Fosco's devotion to his pets, like Long John Silver's fondness for his parrot, is a humanizing touch. To be sure, there are harsher qualities behind the Count's kindness: "The Count lit a cigarette, went back to the flowers in the window, and puffed little jets of smoke at the leaves, in a state of the deepest anxiety about killing the insects." Collins attributed to Fosco some of his own tastes and interests—for example, knowledge of the arts, fondness for Italian opera and good cooking, cosmopolitanism, criticism of English ways. His kind of humor is an apt vehicle for Fosco's egoistic gusto and self-assertive banter. Collins's admiration for Napoleon led him to attribute to Fosco the physical appearance of that dramatic character. There is something grandiose, too, in Fosco's *savoir-faire*, his skill in intrigue, his virtuosity in deception, his knowledge of human nature. So convincing is the portrait that one foreigner considered himself the pattern for Fosco, as Collins relates:

> He naturally insisted on receiving satisfaction for this insult, leaving the choice of swords or pistols to me as the challenged person. Information, on which he could rely, had assured him that I meditated a journey to Paris early in the ensuing week. A hostile meeting might, under such circumstances, be easily arranged. His letter ended with these terrible words: "J'attendrai Monsieur Vilkie [*sic*] avec deux temoins à la gare." Arriving at Paris, I looked for my honorable opponent. But one formidable person presented himself whom I could have wounded with pleasure—the despot who insisted on examining my luggage.[24]

Marian Halcombe writes of Fosco: "The one weak point in that man's iron character is the horrible admiration he feels for *me*." Fosco says of Marian:

> With that woman for my friend I would snap these fingers of mine at the world. . . . This grand creature—I drink her health in my sugar-and-water—this grand creature, who stands in the strength of her love and her courage, firm as a rock, between us two and that poor, flimsy, pretty blonde wife of yours—this magnificent woman, whom I admire with all my soul. . . .

Readers have always shared Fosco's admiration. *The Woman in White* inspired several letters from bachelors who expressed their wish to marry the original of Marian.[25] Next to Fosco she is Collins's most memorable character.

In comparison with Fosco and Marian, Laura and Walter do seem rather colorless—virtuous enough but less interesting than some minor figures: Professor Pesca, Italian teacher of languages, as eccentric as Gabriele Rossetti (at one time perhaps the best-known teacher of Italian in London; and, by the way, a member of the *Carbonari* in his youth, as Pesca was of "The Brotherhood"), important at the beginning and towards the end of the novel; Mr. Gilmore, whose professional and individual oddities are well sketched; Philip Fairlie, a delightfully self-centered hypochondriac (doubtless partly inspired by the author's occasional irritations and drawn *con amore*)—"nothing but a bundle of nerves dressed up to look like a man." Nor can one forget Mrs. Catherick, atoning for an unconventional past by a respectability which rejoices at the clergyman's bow. The Dickensian touch, slight in most of these characters, is more marked in one or two of the servants.

When all is said, it is as a story that *The Woman in White* has most interest. It was the story-tellers—Scott and Cooper and Dumas—that Collins cared for most among novelists; and he usually chose to write in an unadorned style, relishing most such prose as that of Byron's letters. Since Collins himself belongs among the great story-tellers rather than among the great novelists, *The Woman in White* well opens with this thrilling sentence: "This is the *story* [26] of what a Woman's patience can endure, and what a Man's resolution can achieve."

NOTES

1. Private information.
2. Entry of death at Somerset House.
3. Private information.
4. Wilkie Collins's will.
5. An unpublished letter written by Collins in 1880 appears to mention "Mama." Hall Caine, on the other hand, *My Story* (New York, 1909), p. 333, speaks of Collins's "affectionate adopted daughter."
6. The entry of the son's birth gives his name as William Charles Collins Dawson, the mother's name as Martha Dawson, formerly Rudd, the father's name as William Dawson, and the father's profession as Barrister at Law (Collins had received legal training at Lincoln's Inn). "Martha Dawson" was the informant.
7. *The Recollections of Sir Henry Dickens, K. C.* (London, 1934), p. 54.
8. The passage by Millais is quoted in S. M. Ellis's *Wilkie Collins, Le Fanu and Others* (London, 1931), p. 27.
9. S. M. Ellis, *op. cit.*, p. 28.
10. In a letter to Louise Chandler Moulton, dated June 22, 1880, Collins speaks of his plan for continuing the story begun in *The Fallen Leaves*—a plan never to be carried out: "The married life—in the second part—will be essentially a happy life, in itself. But the outer influence of the world which surrounds this husband and wife—the world whose unchristian prejudices they have set at defiance—will slowly undermine their happiness and will, I fear, make the close of the story a sad one."
11. As in *The Evil Genius* and "Brother Griffith's Story of a Plot in Private Life," in *The Queen of Hearts*.
12. *The Critic*, April 12, 1890, p. 182.
13. Some of the "Cases Worth Looking at," in *My Miscellanies*, were

drawn from J. Peuchet's *Mémoires tirés des Archives de la Police de Paris* (Paris, 1838).

14. See, for example, Hall Caine's *My Story* (New York, 1909), p. 329.

15. The chief details may be found in III, 5 ff., "Affaire de Madame de Douhault"; VI, 5–92, "Suite de l'Affaire de Madame de Douhault."

16. A brief resumé of the case may be found in Larousse's *Grand Dictionnaire universel du XIXe Siècle* (Paris, 1870), VI, 1157.

17. In an address to the Emperor in later years, Madame de Douhault is made to say: "J'ai soixante ans, j'existe au milieu de trente millions d'individus; et tous les rapports qui me liaient à la societé sont brisés! Je ne suis civilement ni fille, ni épouse, ni Française, ni étrangère!" She finally died in wretched circumstances.

18. The choice of title was difficult. Collins explains that he smoked an entire case of cigars before finding a suitable title. Chewing the end of his last cigar, he looked at the North Foreland Lighthouse and thus addressed the building: "You are ugly and stiff and awkward . . . as stiff and as weird as my white woman. White woman!—woman in white! The title, by Jove!" The story is told in an article in *The World*, Dec. 26, 1877, pp. 4–6.

19. For a discussion of the White Lady of Avenel, a character in Scott's *Monastery*, and several legendary white ladies, see Coleman O. Parsons, "Association of the White Lady with Wells," *Folk-Lore*, XLIV (September, 1933), 295–305.

20. According to *The World* (*loc. cit.*), Collins had been asked to take up a case of wrongful imprisonment in an asylum. His short story "Fatal Fortune" deals with such a theme, which also interested Charles Reade. See *Readiana* (London, 1883), pp. 113–126.

21. *The Times,* October 30, 1860, p. 6.

22. *The Times, loc. cit.,* pointed out that Collins was "a whole fortnight out of his reckoning. . . . We could easily show that Lady Glyde could not have left Blackwater Park before the 9th or 10th of August." The fact that Dickens and the readers of *All the Year Around* did not observe the error, *The Times* adds, is a tribute to Collins's narrative skill. Collins acknowledged the error in a letter to his publisher, commenting, however, that "Shakespeare has made worse mistakes—that is one comfort, and readers are not critics who test an emotional book by . . . rules of arithmetic, which is a second consolation. Nevertheless we will set it right the first opportunity. . . ." The letter is quoted in Edward Marston's *After Work* (London, 1904), p. 85.

23. *The World, loc. cit.*

24. From "Reminiscences of a Story-Teller," *The Universal Review,* I, 182–192.

25. *The World, loc. cit.*

26. The italics are mine.

EDGAR JOHNSON

The World of Dombeyism

THE period of *Dombey and Son* represents a turning point both in Dickens's life and in his literary art. He had recovered the control of half his copyrights, and the continuing sale of earlier books combined with the splendid profits of *Dombey* made him prosperous beyond all further worry.[1] Despite his large family and lavish scale of living, his cheerfully improvident father and irresponsible brothers, and his own generous charities, from this time on Dickens always had several thousand pounds invested or in the bank.[2] And yet he was not at peace within himself. A deep inward dissatisfaction made his work laborious to him and drove him for relief to those stage excitements that enabled him to forget himself in the representation of some character quite different from his own.

His discontent had roots in personal emotion, but it was reflected too in his changing outlook on society. He expressed no consciousness of the reasons for his own restlessness, but he became steadily more analytical of the causes underlying the world's evils. His earliest books had assailed the debtors' prisons, the new Poor Law, the Yorkshire schools, and the slum breeding-grounds of disease and crime as if they were isolated abuses, dreadful but disconnected. Responsibility for them lay at the hands of individual knaves and dullards—ignorant parish officials, bullying magistrates, greedy usurers, brutal schoolmasters, lordly wastrels, dishonest lawyers, a misgoverning aristocracy. Even in *The Old Curiosity Shop* and *Barnaby Rudge* Dickens's warnings of labor violence and mob revolt endangering the social order

From *Charles Dickens: His Tragedy and Triumph* (New York: Simon and Schuster, Inc., 1952), II, 626–43. Copyright, 1952, by Edgar Johnson. Reprinted by permission of Simon and Schuster, Inc., Laurence Pollinger Limited, and the author.

implied no great complicity in society itself—hardly more, in fact, than a blind unawareness of the cruelties on which he strove to open men's eyes.

Somewhat later, *A Christmas Carol* had made Scrooge symbolize a whole social class and an entire economic philosophy. But Scrooge remained in his own person a mean and grasping old skinflint. The grotesque crew of commentators in *The Chimes*—the statistical Filer, Sir Joseph Bowley, "the Poor Man's Friend," and Alderman Cute— represented a savage showing-up of the hard-hearted economic rationalizations that supported business rapacity. The respectable businessman himself, however, Dickens had portrayed only in such figures as old Fezziwig, the Cheeryble Brothers, and Mr. Pickwick, benevolent old boys beaming through their spectacles in a warm mist of generous feeling. And from the beginning Dickens had had readers who wondered how Mr. Pickwick ever made enough money to retire on and who found the Cheerybles as fantastic as Scrooge.

What was the businessman really like, the City merchant, the rich banker, the prosperous middle-class citizen, subscribing his guineas to the proper charities, and behaving with complete rectitude according to conventional lights? By the time of *Dombey and Son* Dickens had heard him and scores of his fellows at hospital banquets expressing sentiments at which "any moderately intelligent dustman would have blushed through his cindery bloom." [3] Had they in their counting-houses no responsibility for the slums and the cholera and the starved laborer and the maimed factory child? What of the share the solid member of society had in allowing and fostering evils of which he was often smugly unaware? What, in short, of Mr. Dombey?

The troubled concern Dickens felt over these problems of modern society is reflected in the very period setting of *Dombey and Son.* The scene of *Pickwick* was almost contemporary with the time in which it was written,[4] and *Oliver Twist* if anything anticipated criticisms of the workhouse that were barely beginning to be made. But the books between *Pickwick* and *Dombey* remained in the *Pickwick* period or reverted to still earlier times, precisely during the years when the rapid changes of industrialism were making the world Dickens portrayed one of the past. *Nicholas Nickleby, The Old Curiosity Shop,* and *Martin Chuzzlewit* (except for its American episodes) are full of the old stagecoach days that were fast dying out, and drenched in the atmosphere of an old England and an old London. With *Dombey and Son,* however, Dickens leaps forward into the age of railway travel and jerry-built suburbs and company shares: little Paul is weaned while Euston Station is being constructed, old Sol Gills makes a comfortable fortune out of his investments, and most of the action takes place in the bustling forties.

The book vividly describes the building of the London and Birmingham Railway: "Houses were knocked down; streets broken through and stopped; deep pits and trenches dug in the ground; enormous heaps of earth and clay thrown up; buildings that were undermined and shaken, propped by great beams. Here, a chaos of carts, overthrown and jumbled together, lay topsy-turvy at the bottom of a steep unnatural hill; there, confused treasures of iron soaked and rusted in something that had accidentally become a pond. Everywhere were bridges that led nowhere . . . and piles of scaffolding, and wildernesses of brick, and giant forms of cranes, and tripods straddling above nothing. . . . Boiling water hissed and heaved within dilapidated walls; whence, also, the glare and roar of flames came issuing forth; and mounds of ashes blocked up rights of way, and wholly changed the law and custom of the neighbourhood." [5]

No less sharply noted are the effects on the outskirts of the city surrounding the construction, the new taverns called the "Railway Arms" and the "Excavators' House of Call" among the mud and ashes, the "frowsy fields, and cowhouses, and dunghills, and dustheaps, and ditches, and gardens, and summer-houses, and carpet-beating grounds," with "little tumuli of oyster shells in the oyster season, and of lobster shells in the lobster season, and of broken crockery and faded cabbage leaves in all seasons." [6] And farther out still, on the deserted great North Road, are places that were once rural but are now "only blighted country, and not town," with "a few tall chimneys belching smoke all day and night," and brickfields, tumble-down fences, and dusty nettles among a scrap or two of hedge.[7]

It is through this new world of change and speed and desolation and machinery that Mr. Dombey after the death of Paul takes his railway journey to Leamington. "Through the hollow, on the height, by the heath, by the orchard, by the park, by the garden, over the canal, across the river, where the sheep are feeding, where the mill is going, where the barge is floating, where the dead are lying, where the factory is smoking . . . away, with a shriek, and a roar, and a rattle, and no trace to leave behind but dust and vapour . . . Louder and louder yet, it shrieks and cries as it comes tearing on resistless to the goal: and now its way, still like the way of Death, is strewn with ashes thickly. Everything around is blackened. There are dark pools of water, muddy lanes, and miserable habitations far below. There are jagged walls and falling houses close at hand, and through the battered roofs and broken windows, wretched rooms are seen, where want and fever hide themselves in many wretched shapes, while smoke and crowded gables, and distorted chimneys, and deformity of brick and mortar penning up deformity of mind and body, choke the murky distance. As Mr. Dombey looks out of his carriage window, it is never in his thought that the monster who has brought him there has let the light of day in on these things: not made or caused them." [8]

Mr. Dombey himself is even more significant than the railroad showing up the horrors he and his kind have long suffered to exist hidden in obscurity. With him, Dickens has left behind those merchants like the Cheerybles, crude but kindly, eating with their knives, living in quarters above their place of business, and, like old Fezziwig, having their employees dwell with them in a relation of genial master and apprentice. Although Dombey's House is engaged in maritime commerce with England's colonial empire rather than with manufacturing industry, he represents the merchant-prince involved in close relations with bankers and industrialists and laying claims to an impressive magnificence. He displays a stiff propriety of manners, resides with bleak pomposity "in a tall, dark, dreadfully genteel street" [9] between Portland Place and Bryanston Square, rides to his offices on a smart pacer, and maintains a frigid detachment from all his employees. His associates—not friends, he has none—are wealthy East India directors and bank directors who boast with proud humility of their poor little hot-houses for pineapples and delightedly profess themselves unable to afford the opera. [10]

These slashing details brilliantly surpass anything of the kind that H. G. Wells was later to do in *Tono-Bungay* or Sinclair Lewis in *Babbitt,* and they are a portent of Dickens's altered judgment of the mercantile middle class. He no longer erects their virtues in opposition to a dissolute aristocracy represented by Sir Mulberry Hawk and Lord Frederick Verisopht or the dishonest trickery of upper-class governors like Mr. Gregsbury, M.P., and the icily egoistic Sir John Chester. Now he sees the broad group of businessmen as selfish, smug, and cold-hearted in their professional dealings, and realizes that they are as venally indifferent to the consequences of their behavior on social welfare and as harshly unsympathetic toward the poor as the most idly irresponsible of the aristocracy with whom they are beginning to intermingle and marry.

*　　*　　*　　*　　*

Dickens described the theme of *Dombey and Son* as pride, but Mr. Dombey's pride, though a dark and omnipresent strand in the story, is not its dominant principle. That principle is the callous inhumanity of an economic doctrine that strips Mr. Dombey's relations with everyone to an assertion of monetary power. He wants no ties of affection between his infant son and Polly Toodle, the wet nurse whom he engages for the child. "When you go away from here, you will have concluded what is a mere matter of bargain and sale, hiring and letting: and will stay away." [11] He is affronted to learn that Miss Tox, the poor toady on his grandeur, has dared to lift eyes of personal admiration to him and to dream that he might raise her to his side as his wife. It never enters his mind that he cannot hire the obedience of his subordinates to any of his commands, or that Mr. Carker, his Manager, even while he does his great chief's bidding, can resent being employed in degrading and humiliating ways. He believes that he can buy the respect and obedience of an aristocratic wife whose pride and beauty are to reflect luster on his greatness. Even his love for his son, though sincere and strong, is engendered in the doctrine that the wealth and pre-eminence of the House of Dombey and Son must go on forever.

The attitudes that Mr. Dombey displays toward those with whom he comes into immediate contact are also his attitudes toward society as a whole, and toward the welfare of society. "I am far from being friendly," he explains coldly, "to what is called by persons of levelling sentiments, general education. But it is necessary that the inferior classes should continue to be taught to know their position, and to conduct themselves properly. So far I approve of schools." [12] Fundamentally, however, Mr. Dombey agrees with his companion Major Bagstock, who distrusts all education for the poor: "Take advice from plain old Joe, and never educate that sort of people, Sir," says the Major. "Damme, Sir, it never does! It always fails!" [13]

Mr. Dombey is the living symbol of the nineteenth-century theory of business enterprise and its social philosophy. Not even the Lancashire industrialists who bitterly resisted the regulation of child labor and defied the law demanding the fencing-in of dangerous machinery exemplified a more relentless devotion to their own profits and power. Many factory owners, indeed, were decent enough men, devoted to their families, kind to those with whom they came in direct contact, and desirous of doing right by their workers. But they were helpless against ruthless competition and blinded by the belief that any protective interference with the operations of laissez-faire economics would be disastrous. Richard Oastler, the humane reformer who spent years trying to get the working man's day cut down to ten hours, explained the principles of competitive business to Dr. Thomas Chalmers: "Take advantage of another's poverty or ignorance, forcing or coaxing him to sell cheap; and when he is a buyer, using the same means to make him buy dear . . . get money any how, even at the cost of life and limb to those employed in his aggrandisement . . ." [14]

The entire complex development of *Dombey and Son* orchestrates these themes of callous indifference and social evil into a vast symphonic structure in which all the groups and individuals brought into contact with Mr. Dombey and his affairs are organically related. The group at the Wooden Midshipman, old Sol Gills, his bright, high-spirited nephew Walter Gay, simple-minded Captain Cuttle, the wooden-headed Bunsby; Polly Toodle and her apple-cheeked family; sharp-tongued Susan Nipper; poor, foolish, kind-hearted Mr. Toots; Cousin Feenix, with his willful legs and wandering speech—all display the warm humanity banished from the cold heart of Mr. Dombey. Even Miss Tox, toady though she is, reveals a disinterested loyalty and devotion ignored and despised by the object of her adulation. These characters surround with a glowing counterpoint the icy dissonances of Mr. Dombey's world.

The contrasts are developed with consummate artistry. Little Paul Dombey's christening is rendered entirely in glacial imagery: the freezing library with all the books in "cold, hard, slippery uniforms," Mr. Dombey taking Mr. Chick's hand "as if it were a fish, or seaweed, or some such clammy substance," [15] the chill and earthy church, the cold collation afterwards, "set forth in a cold pomp of glass and silver," the champagne "so bitter cold" as to force "a little scream from Miss Tox," the veal that strikes "a sensation of cold lead to Mr. Chick's extremities," Mr. Dombey as unmoved as if he were "hung up for sale at a Russian fair as a specimen of a frozen gentleman." [16]

From this silent, icy celebration the very next chapter plunges into the warm clamor of Polly Toodle's visit to her family in Stagg's Gardens with her "honest apple face . . . the centre of a bunch of smaller pippins, all laying their rosy cheeks close to it," [17] and all growing noisy, vehement, disheveled, and flushed with delight. Even the calmer scenes of everyday domesticity in the Toodle household are as different from those in the Dombey mansion as these two festive occasions. Mr. Toodle home from firing his locomotive engine recharges himself with innumerable pint mugs of tea solidified with great masses of bread and butter, with both of which he regales his expectant circle of children in small spoonfuls and large bites; snacks that "had such a relish in the mouths of these young Toodles, that, after partaking of the same, they performed private dances of ecstasy among themselves, and stood on one leg a-piece, and hopped, and indulged in other saltatory tokens of gladness." [18]

In the fierce sequence of climactic events centering around the flight of Edith, Mr. Dombey's second wife, with his treacherous Manager, Mr. Carker, Dickens designedly emphasizes the same contrasts. Again they occupy successive chapters, the heavy blow with which the marble-hearted father almost fells his daughter to the marble floor, her cry of desolation as she runs from that loveless and pitiless house, understanding at last that she has "no father upon earth"; [19] and then Captain Cuttle, trembling and "pale in the very knobs of his face," soothing the weeping girl with murmured endearments of "Heart's Delight," and "my pretty," as he tenderly raises her from the ground; [20] the freezing rancor of Mr. Dombey's gloomy board, and the little dinner the Captain prepares at the parlor fire.

There is a wonderful radiance in the Captain bustling about this meal, his coat off and his glazed hat on his head, making the egg sauce, basting the fowl, heating the gravy, boiling some potatoes, keeping his eye on the sausages "hissing and bubbling in a most musical manner," and at last removing his hat, putting on his coat, and wheeling up the table before Florence's sofa. "My lady lass," he begs her, "cheer up, and try to eat a deal. Stand by, my deary! Liver wing it is. Sarse it is. Sassage it is. And potato!" [21]

No less heart-warming is the Captain's endeavor to bestow on Florence the tin canister containing his savings of £14 2s. for any purchases she needs to make, his request to the shop girl to "sing out" if any more is required, his casually "consulting his big watch as a deep means of dazzling the establishment, and impressing it with a sense of property," and his disappointment when Florence does not use his money. "It ain't o' no use to *me*," he says. "I wonder I haven't chucked it away afore now." [22] What an illustration of the ludicrous forms goodness of heart can take without ceasing to be real goodness! No speech was ever more absurd, and yet no gentleman ever said anything more truly imbued with delicacy and generosity.

Captain Cuttle, together with Mr. Toots, is among the great portraits of the book, both irresistibly ridiculous and both at the same time possessed of a true dignity shining through all their absurdity. Poor Toots, with his "It's of no consequence whatsoever," his vapid chuckle, and trousers and waistcoats that are masterpieces of Burgess and Company, and his hopeless devotion to Florence, rises to heights of noble selflessness. And even when Captain Cuttle is scrambling quotations like a parody on T. S. Eliot and rambling through chains of dim association suggestive of Joyce's Molly Bloom, there is a heart of tender sanity in his nonsense. "If you're in arnest, you see, my lad," he comforts Toots, "you're a object of clemency, and clemency is the brightest jewel in the crown of a Briton's head, for which you'll overhaul the constitution as laid down in Rule Britannia, and, when found, *that* is the charter as them garden angels was a singing of, so many times over. Stand by!" [23]

Seen with no such gentle satire as the Captain and Toots, certain other characters represent disguised forms of Mr. Dombey's own cold egoism. Mrs. Skewton, Edith Dombey's mother, with her specious cult of the "heart," is a hypocritical parody of the sympathies that flow so sincerely in chuckle-headed Mr. Toots and the acidulous Susan Nipper; underneath the languishing phrases she is completely selfish and venal. Major Bagstock, "leering and choking, like an over-fed Mephistopheles," [24] covers a toadying malignance in a blustering pretense of blunt-spoken friendship.

The name of Dombey, the Major tells its owner, is one "that a man is proud to recognise. There is nothing adulatory in Joseph Bagstock, Sir. His Royal Highness the Duke of York observed on more than one occasion, 'there is no adulation in Joey. He is a plain old soldier is Joe. He is tough to a fault is Joseph'; but it's a great name, Sir. By the Lord, it's a great name!" [25] And Mrs. Skewton, reclining in her wheeled chair like Cleopatra in her gilded barge, wants to know what "we live for *but* sympathy! What else is so extremely charming! Without that gleam of sunshine on our cold cold earth, how could we possibly bear it? . . . I would have my world all heart; and Faith is so excessively charming that I won't allow you to disturb it . . ." [26]

As a part of her patter Cleopatra dotes upon the Middle Ages. "Those darling bygone times, Mr. Carker," she gushes, "with their delicious fortresses, and their dear old dungeons, and their delightful places of torture . . . and everything that makes life truly charming! How dreadfully we have degenerated!" There is no such Faith today, she goes on, as there was in the days of Queen Bess, "which were so extremely golden. Dear creature! She was all Heart!" And then there was her father, so bluff, so English, "with his dear little peepy eyes, and his benevolent chin!" [27] How appropriate that this creature of masks and attitudes should have detachable hair and a painted rosy complexion, and that when these are removed the little that is real of her should be put to bed "like a horrible doll." [28]

Grim parallels to Cleopatra and Edith Dombey are two figures from that dark lower world on which Mr. Dombey looked down from his railway carriage on the way to Leamington. But "Good Mrs. Brown" and her daughter, Alice Marwood, are linked to Mrs. Skewton and Edith by more than Dickens's desire for an artificial symmetry of plot. They symbolize the fatal mingling in society of those evils that creep from high to low like the greed-engendered cholera coiling from the slums into lordly homes. There is a deeper significance than mere accident in Alice Marwood's being the illegitimate daughter to an elder brother of Edith's father, and in her being seduced and abandoned by Carker, Mr. Dombey's Manager, as Edith has been bought in matrimony by Mr. Dombey himself. When the two mothers and their daughters meet by chance on the downs, Edith is fearfully struck by their dark resemblance to each other, and Mrs. Skewton guiltily jabbers her belief that Mrs. Brown is a good mother, "full of what's her name—and all that," "all affection and et cetera." [29] "No great lady," Alice has previously said with bitter irony, ever thought of selling her daughter, "and that shows that the only instances of mothers bringing up their daughters wrong, and evil coming of it, are among such miserable folks as us." [30] And looking after Edith, she exclaims, "You're a handsome woman; but good looks won't save us. And you're a proud woman; but pride won't save us." [31]

❖   ❖   ❖   ❖   ❖

On every level in the world of *Dombey and Son*, although not in every breast, the same forces are at work. From the stately mansions of the aristocracy on Brook Street and the pineries of Mr. Dombey's banker-associates down to the rag-filled hovel of Good Mrs. Brown, competitive greed and indifference to the welfare of others create a cynical economic system that spawns all the vices and cruelties of society. And of that system—it might even be called Dombeyism—Mr. Dombey is the symbolic embodiment. He is not, of course, directly and personally responsible for all the wrongs Dickens paints; and, despite grave defects of character, he is not even inherently vicious. He too has been shaped by the forces he now embodies. "When I thought so much of all the causes that had made me what I was," Edith says of Mr. Dombey, "I needed to allow more for the causes that had made him what he was." [32] But Dickens has also come to understand that, whatever the individual blame for the evils he is fighting, a statistically large proportion of them must be laid at the door of Dombeyism.

That is why even society's charities and generosities so often fail of their stated objects. They are not really directed toward human welfare, but are instruments of ostentation and keeping the poor in their place. So of the Charitable Grinders' School, to which Mr. Dombey nominated Polly Toodle's son Rob. Beaten daily by his master, "a superannuated old Grinder of savage disposition, who had been appointed schoolmaster because he didn't know anything, and wasn't fit for anything," [33] what wonder that Rob turns out a liar and a sneak? "But they never taught honour at the Grinders' School, where the system that prevailed was particularly strong in the engendering of hypocrisy. Insomuch, that many of the friends and masters of past Grinders said, if this were what came of education for the common people, let us have none. Some more rational said, let us have a better one. But the governing powers of the Grinders' Company were always ready for *them*, by picking out a few boys who had turned out well, in spite of the system, and roundly asserting that they could only have turned out well because of it. Which settled the business . . ." [34]

It is this emphasis on abstract forces that explains the diminished role of the villains in *Dombey and Son*. Though contemptible enough personally, they are not demonic creators of evil like Ralph Nickleby, Fagin, Quilp, Sir John Chester, and Jonas Chuzzlewit. They batten, not on the weakness of innocent victims, but on the vices of the powerful. Major Bagstock, "rough and tough old Joey," that hypocrite of truculence, exploits Mr. Dombey's snobbery and pride; but Mr. Dombey already had them, ripe for sycophancy. Mr. Carker, with his feline smile and those glittering teeth whose symbolic falseness Dickens is constantly suggesting without ever stating directly, flatters the demand for absolute abasement that Mr. Dombey was already making of all those about him. In a sense, Mr. Dombey may be said to have tempted and corrupted Carker rather than the reverse. Both the Manager and the blue-faced Major merely smooth a way that everything in Mr. Dombey's background and character predetermines he shall travel.

This way is hinted as early as the second page of the book and implicit in its very title. The three words "Dombey and Son," we are told, "convey the one idea of Mr. Dombey's life. The earth was made for Dombey and Son to trade in, and the sun and moon were made to give them light. Rivers and seas were formed to float their ships; rainbows gave them promise of fair weather; winds blew for or against their enterprises; stars and planets circled in their orbits, to preserve inviolate a system of which they were the centre." [35] His feeling about his first wife's death is hardly more than a sense of "something gone from among his plate and furniture, and other household possessions, which was well worth the having, and could not be lost without sincere regret." [36] He thinks of himself and his wealth as all-powerful. "The kind of foreign help which people usually seek for their children, I can afford to despise; being above it, I hope." [37] When his second wife asks if he believes he "can degrade, or bend or break" *her* "to submission and obedience," Mr. Dombey smiles, as if he had been asked "whether he thought he could raise ten thousand pounds." [38] Such is the nature of the man whom Carker maliciously describes as "the slave of his own greatness . . . yoked to his own triumphal car like a beast of burden." [39]

Given these elements in Mr. Dombey, it is natural that he should regard his daughter with indifference and bring whatever affection is in his chill nature to the son who may carry on his name and business. "He had never conceived an aversion to her: it had not been worth his while or in his humour." [40] But when he sees her fear of him and feels his exclusion from the tenderness between her and her dying mother, he cannot avoid knowing that it is a reproach to him. Later still, as he realizes that all the tenderness of his cherished son and heir is bestowed on his despised daughter, and observes in a moment of farewell the contrast between the limp and careless hand his boy gives him and the sorrowful face he turns to Florence, it is a bitter pang to the father's proud heart.[41] With what fateful steps it follows that as she reaps the love his riches cannot command his indifference should turn to jealous dislike! And that when Paul dies, he should see in her "the successful rival of his son, in health and life" and find it "gall to him to look upon her in her beauty and her promise"? [42]

In the course of the fierce duel between Mr. Dombey and his obdurate second wife, his resentment of his daughter deepens. While his bourgeois pride dashes itself in vain against the barriers of her aristocratic pride, who is it that wins his wife as she had won his boy, "whose least word did what his utmost means could not! Who was it who, unaided by his love, regard or notice, thrived and grew beautiful when those so aided died! Who could it be, but the same child at whom he had often glanced uneasily in her motherless infancy, with a kind of dread, lest he might come to hate her;

and of whom his foreboding was fulfilled, for he DID hate her in his heart." [43]

All this is handled with enormous skill and power. That the cancerous growth of Mr. Dombey's bitterness is delineated with absolute fidelity has never been denied. But there are readers who have not been convinced of his later change of heart. Their skepticism, however, ignores both the repeated psychological preparations Dickens makes for it in the book and the complex involutions of emotion in human beings. Is there anyone who has not often known, even as he sullenly persisted in a course of injustice, that his behavior was indefensible, and half longed to make the very change that he stubbornly resisted making? Does no one ever turn with unavailing remorse and belated affection to the memory of those he has wronged, and wish that he could make amends and win the love he has thrown away?

These emotions have struggled in Mr. Dombey from the very beginning. He has never been utterly without tender emotion, even for his daughter. Seeing her clasped in her mother's arms, he has felt an uneasiness that troubled his peace. On a later night he looks from his door upon his two children going to bed, and in the time thereafter his memory is haunted by the image of her small figure toiling up the stairs, singing to the baby brother in her arms.[44] Leaving his boy at Brighton with Florence, and bending down to kiss him good-by, his sight dimmed "by something that for a moment blurred the little face," he has a twinge of feeling about his injustice that makes his mental vision, "for that short time," Dickens tells us, "the clearer perhaps." [45]

Numerous impulses of contrition like these reach a culmination on the evening Mr. Dombey returns from Paris with his bride and, pretending to sleep, secretly watches Florence bent over her work from which she occasionally raises to him pathetic speaking eyes. "Some passing thought that he had had a happy home within his reach— had had a household spirit bending at his feet—had overlooked it in his stiff-necked arrogance, and wandered away and lost himself," [46] engenders a gentler feeling toward her. "As he looked, she became blended with the child he had loved" and "he saw her for an instant by a clearer and a brighter light, not bending over that child's pillow as his rival . . . but as the spirit of his home . . ." [47] Almost about to call her to him, he hears Edith's footstep on the stairs, and the moment is lost. Florence becomes a weapon in his struggle with his wife, and his softening hardens once again to resentment.

But after the flight of Edith and Florence, the bankruptcy of his business, and the loss of his fortune, as he sits alone in his desolate house, there is not one of these things that does not return to his memory. Again he sees the small childish figure singing on the stair, again he hears her heartbroken cry at the blow he struck her, and knows that if he had not thrown it away he would always have had her love, even now, in his fall, and "that of all around him, she alone had never changed. His boy had faded into dust, his proud wife had sunk into a polluted creature, his flatterer and friend been transformed into the worst of villains; his riches had melted away," but "she alone had turned the same gentle look upon him always. . . . She had never changed to him—nor had he ever changed to her— and she was lost." In his anguish, "Oh, how much better than this," he cries in his heart, "that he had loved her as he had his boy, and lost her as he had his boy, and laid them in their early grave together!" [48]

Even in Mr. Dombey's remorse, though, with a marvelous touch of psychological insight, Dickens shows him still his old self. If he had "heard her voice in the adjoining room," Dickens writes, "he would not have gone to her. If he could have seen her in the street, and she had done no more than look at him as she had been used to look, he would have passed on with his old cold unforgiving face, and not addressed her, or relaxed it, though his heart should have broken soon afterwards." [49] In their superb penetration these few vivid words, for all their brevity, are equivalent to paragraphs of intricate psychological analysis.

His misery is resolved only by the unhoped-for return of Florence, imploring his forgiveness instead of proffering the forgiveness he could never have forced himself to beg. "I was frightened when I went away, and could not think." [50] Although the mercy is undeserved, no reader who has understood the entire delineation of Florence's character could doubt it any more than he could disbelieve the behavior of Mr. Dombey. What wonder that the broken man exclaims, in a passion of grief, "Oh my God, forgive me, for I need it very much!" [51]

     ✿   ✿   ✿   ✿   ✿

Throughout all this personal drama of pride, heartache, and bankruptcy, Dickens has never lost sight nor allowed the reader to lose sight of the social bearings of his theme. On the crash of Dombey and Son, "The world was very busy now, in sooth," he writes, "and had a deal to say. It was an innocently credulous and a much ill-used world. It was a world in which there was no other sort of bankruptcy whatever. There were no conspicuous people in it, trading far and wide on rotten banks of religion, patriotism, virtue, honour. There was no amount worth mentioning of mere paper in circulation, on which anybody lived pretty handsomely, promising to pay great sums of goodness with no effects. There were no shortcomings anywhere, in anything but money. The world was very angry indeed; and the people especially, who in a worse world, might have been supposed to be bankrupt traders themselves in shows and pretences, were observed to be mightily indignant." [52]

Two-thirds of the way through the book, Dickens had sounded his own deeper indignation in a powerful outburst. "Hear the magistrate or judge admonish the unnatural outcasts of society; unnatural in brutish habits, unnatural in want of decency, unnatural in losing and confounding all distinctions between good and evil," Dickens exclaims; and then go "down into their dens, lying within the echoes of our carriage wheels," and look "upon the world of odious sights," at which "dainty delicacy, living in the next street . . . lisps 'I don't believe it!' Breathe the polluted air," he bids us: "And then, calling up some ghastly child, with stunted form and wicked face, hold forth on its unnatural sinfulness, and lament its being, so early, far away from Heaven—but think a little of its having been conceived, and born and bred, in Hell!

"Those who study the physical sciences," he goes on, ". . . tell us that if the noxious particles that rise from vitiated air were palpable to the sight, we should see them lowering in a dense black cloud above such haunts, and rolling slowly on to corrupt the better portions of a town. But if the moral pestilence that rises with them, and in the eternal laws of outraged Nature, is inseparable from them, could be made discernible too, how terrible the revelation! . . . Then should we stand appalled to know, that where we generate disease to strike our children down and entail itself on unborn generations, there also we breed, by the same certain process, infancy that knows no innocence, youth without modesty or shame, maturity that is mature in nothing but in suffering and guilt, blasted old age that is a scandal on the form we bear. Unnatural humanity! When we shall gather grapes from thorns, and figs from thistles; when fields of grain shall spring up from the offal in the by-ways of our wicked cities, and roses bloom in the fat churchyards that they cherish, then we may look for natural humanity and find it growing from such seed."[53]

In its faithfulness to the literal truths of human character and in its portrayal of their social consequences, *Dombey and Son* is a realistic development and elaboration of the themes fabulously set forth in *A Christmas Carol*. Like Scrooge, Mr. Dombey is symbolic, but he is also the mercantile reality of which Scrooge is a pantomime caricature. The picturesque glimpses in the *Carol* of humble courage and generosity, of evil and suffering, like brightly lighted scenes in a fairy tale, give way to fully detailed pictures of life on a dozen levels, from Mrs. Brown's slum to Portland Place, all suggested in their relation to each other. All the flashing intuitions of the *Carol* and *The Chimes* are richly worked out in the intellectual and emotional comprehension of *Dombey and Son*.

Though not, like them, an economic fantasy but a realistic study of contemporary society, it shares with them a curious strain of symbolism and symbolic imagery. To please his son and heir Mr. Dombey relieves the distress of Walter Gay's uncle, but then gratifies his own dislike of the courageous, high-spirited Walter by sending him forth on the voyage of the ominously named *Son and Heir*. Walter Gay survives, but the ship is lost—almost at the same time as the child who was always wondering what the waves were saying and who was in a way its namesake. The cold depths of the mahogany board at which Mr. Dombey sits just before his ill-fated marriage reflect vessels of dead-sea fruit riding there at anchor.[54] Beneath the picture that resembles Edith in Mr. Carker's dining parlor, there swings a chafing and imprisoned bird in "a pendant gilded hoop within the cage, like a great wedding-ring."[55] At Mr. Dombey's table a "long plateau of precious metal frosted . . . whereon frosted Cupids offered scentless flowers"[56] separates him from his second wife. Constantly Mr. Dombey's house and the meals there are described in terms of cold "and that unnecessary article in Mr. Dombey's banquets—ice."[57] And when his daughter takes her wounded heart to the Wooden Midshipman and its guardian, "A wandering princess and a good monster in a story-book," Dickens writes, "might have sat by the fireside and talked as Captain Cuttle and Florence thought—and not have looked very much unlike them."[58]

Such images—and there are many more of them—show that Dickens's creative powers were not working in naturalistic terms alone. With a surface observation almost as detailed as Balzac's and often far more brilliant, underneath there are always depths in which his vision pierces to something closely resembling myth and its mysterious power. These bold liberties with the canons of realism are no less exemplified by Dickens's melodrama at its best. It is as irrelevant to criticize some of the scenes between Edith Dombey and Carker by saying that people do not talk like that as to complain that Mirabell and Millamant converse in a shower of epigrams or that Iago distills his hate into a concentration of poisoned words. Drenched in theatricality, the interview in which Carker gives Edith Mr. Dombey's ultimatum is also tightly knit, loaded in every word with bitter suggestion and emotional intensity, and dramatically effective throughout every coil of its intricate subtlety.

The total achievement of *Dombey and Son* makes it one of Dickens's great books. With a creative vitality hardly surpassed by any of the books between it and *Pickwick,* it leaves all its predecessors far behind in structural logic, intellectual power, and social insight. His writing until now is the work of a brilliantly inspired youthful writer; *Dombey* is the first masterpiece of Dickens's maturity. Readers may prefer individual scenes in *Nickleby, Oliver,* or *Martin Chuzzlewit* to individual scenes in *Dombey*—although it is debatable that they contain anything really better than Captain Cuttle and Mr. Toots—but no one could say critically that they are better books. The problem of building a unified plot around a central theme so imperfectly tackled in *Chuzzlewit* is triumphantly solved in *Dombey.* None of Dickens's later books exhibit the loose improvisation with which he had begun; their elaboration is not that of planlessness but of a vast cathedral. And with *Dombey,* above all, Dickens has achieved a form by means of which he can convey the more detailed and philosophic social criticism that was to animate his work in the future.

NOTES

1. *Letters,* II, 102, Moir, 6/17/48. [Quotations from the published writings of Dickens and references to them are identified by their locations in *The Nonesuch Dickens,* edited by Arthur Waugh, Hugh Walpole, Walter Dexter, and Thomas Hatton, and published by the Nonesuch Press in 1938.]
2. Ibid.
3. Ibid., I, 518, Jerrold, 5/3/43.
4. *Pickwick Papers* was written in 1836-7, but, as has often been pointed out, its internal chronology is confused and ambiguous. The first chapter states that it is supposed to begin in 1827, but in the second Mr. Jingle refers to the Revolution of July, 1830. This was later covered up by

a joking footnote about "the prophetic force of Mr. Jingle's imagination." The imagined time of *Pickwick Papers,* on the whole, however, is hardly distinguishable from the period in which it appeared. And the main body of events in *Oliver Twist,* 1837–9, is almost completely current.

5. *Dombey and Son,* VI, 63–4.
6. Ibid.
7. Ibid., XXXIII, 474.
8. Ibid., XX, 283–4.
9. Ibid., III, 22.
10. Ibid., XXXVI, 514.
11. Ibid., II, 17.
12. Ibid., V, 60.
13. Ibid., XX, 281.
14. Driver, Cecil: *Tory Radical: The Life of Richard Oastler* (Oxford, 1946), p. 469, quoting Oastler, *The Champion,* I, 151.
15. *Dombey and Son,* V, 53.
16. Ibid., V, 58.
17. Ibid., VI, 66.
18. Ibid., XXXVIII, 538.
19. Ibid., XLVII, 668.
20. Ibid., XLVIII, 670.
21. Ibid., XLIX, 683–4.
22. Ibid., 687–8.
23. Ibid., XXXIX, 548.
24. Ibid., XX, 279.
25. Ibid., X, 128.
26. Ibid., XXI, 296.
27. Ibid., XXVII, 389.
28. Ibid., XXXVII, 531.
29. Ibid., XL, 577.
30. Ibid., LIII, 754.
31. Ibid., XL, 578.
32. Ibid., LXI, 873.
33. Ibid., VI, 69.
34. Ibid., XXXVIII, 543–4.
35. Ibid., I, 2.
36. Ibid., 5.
37. Ibid., V, 47.
38. Ibid., XL, 569.
39. Ibid., XLV, 630.

40. Ibid., III, 30.
41. Ibid., XI, 151.
42. Ibid., XVIII, 258.
43. Ibid., XL, 563.
44. Ibid., VIII, 97.
45. Ibid., XI, 151.
46. Ibid., XXXV, 505.
47. Ibid., 506.
48. Ibid., LIX, 841.
49. Ibid., 842.
50. Ibid., 845.
51. Ibid., 846.
52. Ibid., LVIII, 814.
53. Ibid., XLVII, 650.
54. Ibid., XXX, 431.
55. Ibid., XXXIII, 474.
56. Ibid., XXXVI, 515.
57. Ibid., 517.
58. Ibid., XLIX, 687.

CLAUDE T. BISSELL

Social Analysis in the Novels of
George Eliot

IF we were to limit our examination of George Eliot's powers of social analysis to those novels where she is concerned with expounding a political thesis, we would be forced to conclusions no less dispiriting to the historian of political and social ideas than to the literary critic. Fortunately, however, we should have scant material to work upon. *Felix Holt,* a conscientious attempt to write a didactic political novel, would be the major document. According to one of the conventions of the genre, this novel has as its hero a young, incorruptible man of the people who has pledged himself to a career of selfless devotion to a programme of reform. The action springs out of a political situation and follows the vagaries of party allegiance. George Eliot is striving to depict the turmoil and dislocation that arise even in the backwater of a small rural settlement in the days following the passing of the first Reform Bill, and, at the same time, she is pointing out and heavily underlining the moral inadequacies of philosophical radicalism. But even in *Felix Holt* this elaborate attempt to write a political novel cannot overcome the pull of other interests. Felix Holt's admirable sentiments, an amalgam of Carlyle, Comte and the Victorian conscience, are swamped by the intricacy of the plot and, more acceptably, by the firm and compassionate handling of the relationship between a mother and her estranged son.

Only once again was George Eliot led astray by her enthusiasm for a political programme. The results this time are even more disastrous to her art, although fortunately they are apparent in only one

From *ELH, A Journal of English Literary History,* XVIII (1951), 221–39. Reprinted by permission of the publisher and the author.

section of the novel. The hero of *Daniel Deronda* is, like Felix Holt, a young and incorruptible reformer. This time, however, he emerges from a vague and mysterious background and he moves darkly toward a vague and mysterious goal. The goal becomes palpable when Daniel learns that he is a Jew and that circumstances have made him a messianic leader who will summon his race to a political destiny of "separateness with communication." The political situation from which Felix Holt emerged was, at least, specific and real, but the hapless Daniel moves in a mist of sentimental idealism in which at times one can vaguely recognize sympathy for nationalistic aspirations, belief in the power of heredity and in racial solidarity and tempered interest in the programme of Zionism. The political section of the novel provides a catalogue of almost all the vices to which the novelist can succumb: the prose is wooden, with much reliance on abstractions and heavy, over-stuffed phrases; the characters are puppets in a dull charade, unfortunately endowed by their manipulator with the gift of endless speech. But, as I have suggested, George Eliot did not in this novel follow false lights unswervingly. Set aside the "Daniel Deronda" section, and the novel is George Eliot at her strongest and best, working in a social setting that she thoroughly understands and exploring a complicated network of motives with assurance and precision.

This inability to turn a political gospel into acceptable fiction does not mean that George Eliot was ill equipped to deal with social problems. Rather it serves to mark off sharply and to illuminate by contrast the area of social analysis in which she was most at home. It is the area that, it seems to me, properly belongs to the novelist whose imagination is kindled by the spectacle of man in society, who is concerned about the inter-relationship between the individual and the social groups and institutions of which he is a part. For such a novelist any exclusive concern with a particular programme is bound to be narrowing and may well be stultifying. George Eliot's role was to be that of recorder and reflective observer of man in society, and few English novelists have been better qualified to play it.[1]

On the basis of scope of knowledge and depth of intellectual curiosity George Eliot's qualifications for this role are unquestioned. I suppose that one must leap ahead to Mr. Aldous Huxley before one meets a novelist of such commanding erudition, though Mr. Huxley wears his learning a good deal less gracefully than the Victorian Sibyl. Regarded as a speculative thinker, she has, it is true, marked limitations. Her mind is not bold and adventurous; she is not impelled, as Meredith and Hardy were, towards the creation of metaphysics. She is at home only in those areas of thought where there is a solid basis in human experience—in the biological sciences, in religious and cultural history, in what today might be called sociology. But if this is a weakness for a philosopher, it may well be a strength for a novelist. She is inclined to be modest and tentative in her handling of knowledge, more prepared to examine the past carefully than to speculate about the future. Although she is skilled in analysis, in the uncovering of hidden causes and obscure motivations, she is free of the intellectual arrogance that often afflicts the Victorian agnostic. She fully realizes that this is an untidy and irrational world, that morals, manners and social institutions bear with them the superstitions and the prejudices as well as the enlightenments of the past. All these qualities then,—breadth of knowledge, intellectual curiosity, patience and skill in analysis, wisdom and compassion in judgment— at first precociously displayed in her early essays are transferred in subtler form to her work as a novelist.

Intellectual qualities such as these, admirable in themselves, do not, of course, ensure success in the writing of fiction. Indeed they may betray their possessor into writing novels that are merely historical documentaries or journalistic reports diluted with human interest. If George Eliot never sinks to this level, she does occasionally respond to a downward pull. The research worker and the novelist battle throughout *Romola* and there are not wanting uncharitable critics who award the victory to the former. But outside of this novel such a critical question does not seriously arise. What, I think, enables George Eliot to avoid the quality of the documentary in most of her novels is the fact that her material is bound to her by actual experience or by personal association and is transformed by memory and reflection. She is not simply stating facts that might be culled from a government report or recording the accurate impressions of the person who was there. She is giving her vision of a way of life that, although it is rooted in the past, continues to exist powerfully in her imagination.[2] This quality is most apparent in those passages where the autobiographical element is strong, in the opening chapters of *The Mill on the Floss,* for instance, where a brooding memory of her own childhood only gradually dissolves into the figure of an imaginary heroine.[3] This quest for a lost happiness is, however, a minor note. The appeal to the past is usually more impersonal and generalized, linking small recollections with broad historical events and forces. Here is such a passage, in which George Eliot summons up the memory of provincial society as it existed in the little town of St. Oggs in the late twenties of the nineteenth century:

> Everywhere the brick houses have a mellow look, and in Mrs. Glegg's day there was no incongruous new-fashioned smartness, no plate-glass in shop windows, no fresh stucco-facing or other fallacious attempt to make fine old red St. Ogg's wear the air of a town that sprang up yesterday. The shop windows were small and unpretending; for the farmers' wives and daughters who came to do their shopping were not to be withdrawn from their regular, well-known shops; and the trades-men had no wares intended for customers who would go on their way and be seen no more. Ah! even Mrs. Glegg's day seems far back in the past now, separated from us by changes that widen the years. War and the rumour of war had then died out from the minds of men, and if they were ever thought of by the farmers in drab great-coats, who shook the grain out of their sample bags and buzzed over it in the full market-place, it was as a state of things that belonged to a past golden age, when prices were high. Surely the time was gone for ever when the broad river could bring up unwelcome ships: Russia was only the place where the linseed came from—the more the better—making grist for the great vertical millstones with their scythe-like arms, roaring and grinding and carefully sweeping as if an in-forming soul were in them. The Catholics, bad harvests, and the mysterious fluctuations of trade, were the three evils mankind had to fear: even the floods had not been great of late years.[4]

Here past experience is not seen so much with the inward eye. The mood is one of clear-sighted objectivity in which past and present cast on each other an ironical glow.

The quality of objectivity that we have noted in this passage from *The Mill on the Floss* characterizes George Eliot's treatment of all her social material. It is present not only in her depiction of a his-torical era where, as we have seen, she is betrayed neither into a sentimental idealization of the past nor into a brash glorification of the present. It is at the heart of her analysis of various social classes. Here, an examination of her own happy relationship to the class structure of Victorian England will help us to understand why she can maintain this objective point of view. Recall the principal facts of her career. She grew up in the Warwickshire countryside. Her father was a workman of superior abilities who, like Caleb Garth in *Middlemarch*, was entrusted with a position of responsibility as the agent for a large country estate. Her family was on easy terms with the tenant farmers and agricultural labourers, and at the same time, enjoyed access to the homes of the gentry. Then, in the early forties, she and her father moved to Coventry, and she finds herself a member of a little middleclass group presided over by a successful industrialist with advanced views on a wide range of topics. Some ten years later, there is an even more dramatic shift. She is ushered abruptly into the London world of literature and journalism. After a painful false start, she quickly adjusts herself to new challenges and responsibilities. Within a short time, the provincial girl with an impressive but unbalanced intellectual background is the assistant editor of the most influential radical journal of the time and confidante of philosophers, scientists, and men of letters. Her union with George Henry Lewes in 1854 cuts her off for a short time from English society, both from the provincial society of her early years and the urban literary society she had known in London. But with her growing fame as a novelist in the sixties and seventies, suspicion and disapproval turn to acceptance and adulation. To respectability and fame has been added the grace of wealth. The most vivid picture we have of her in the final years is that given by young aspirants to a literary career like Henry James who gain admission to her celebrated London receptions where a spirit of gentility and reverence presides against a background of bric-a-brac.[5]

Even such a bald narration of facts provides material for a number of diverting biographical interpretations. For my present purpose, it will be sufficient to mention only one. Notice how George Eliot, by the strength of her personality and the happy alliance of circumstances, was never closely identified for any length of time with any one social group or any one class. She is, as it were, removed from the world of petty aspirations and petty conflicts that dog the author whose social status is a cause for personal concern. Not that she is unaware of these aspirations and conflicts. They are often the very stuff of her novels, but they are viewed with irony and detachment, never with the bitterness that springs from personal spleen. She is never tormented, as one suspects Thackeray and Meredith were, by the feeling that she doesn't quite belong to the élite.

This release from a class point of view makes, then, for objectivity. This objectivity is not to be confused, however, with aloofness and arid detachment. No other Victorian novelist moves more firmly and confidently through almost the entire range of nineteenth-century society. There are gaps, of course, but the total picture is a tribute to her catholicity of vision. Her success with rural types and with the world of middle-class commercialism is well known. Not so well known, perhaps, is her success with a more sophisticated and aristocratic society, the kind of society that Dickens entered at his peril. I do not refer here to those sketches of the amiable rural aristocracy that occur in *Felix Holt* and *Middlemarch*. These people do not constitute a world of their own; they are on the fringe of the provincial society with which in these novels George Eliot was primarily concerned. But in her last novel, *Daniel Deronda,* she made an upper-class world the center of her vision. It is in many respects the same world as the one that Henry James chose for his spiritual home, seen less plastically and less lovingly, but with a surer grasp, one suspects, of actualities and a sharper perception of social distinctions. Here is the kind of society in which the career of the heroine, Gwendolen Harleth, evolves toward its pathetic conclusion.

> A various party had been invited to meet the new couple: the old aristocracy was represented by Lord and Lady Pentreath; the old gentry by young Mr. and Mrs. Fitzadam of the Worcestershire branch of the Fitzadams; politics and the public good, as specialised in the cider interest, by Mr. Fenn, member for West Orchards, accompanied by his two daughters; Lady Mallinger's family, by her brother, Mr. Raymond, and his wife; the useful bachelor element by Mr. Sinker, the eminent counsel, and by Mr. Vandernoddt, whose acquaintance Sir Hugo had found pleasant enough at Leubronn to be adopted in England.[6]

George Eliot's insight into this cosmopolitan upper-class society is sharpened by her selection of a heroine who, lacking the pedigree of wealth and family name, can offer only beauty and a haughty temperament. But beauty and a haughty temperament can, if properly used, lead to the miracle of an aristocratic marriage. And to Gwendolen's relatives and friends such a marriage is an act of deep social piety. Her uncle, the local rector, reflects as follows on the opportunity this presented to his niece:

> This match with Grandcourt presented itself to him as a sort of public affair; perhaps there were ways in which it might even strengthen the Establishment. To the Rector, whose father (nobody would have suspected it, and nobody was told) had risen to be a provincial corn-dealer, aristocratic heirship resembled regal heirship in excepting its possessor from the ordinary standard of moral judgments. Grandcourt, the almost certain baronet, the probable peer, was to be ranged with public personages, and was a match to be accepted on broad general grounds national and ecclesiastical.[7]

Of course Gwendolen marries the young aristocrat. Her marriage swiftly and cruelly teaches her much about the moral reality that may underlie the charm and easy manners and the prestige of wide estates. Grandcourt, her husband, is a masterful analysis of what we might call the "infernal aristocrat" beside whom Lord Steyne is a genial and attractive Don Juan. I do not think that George Eliot wants us to look upon Grandcourt as a symbol of aristocratic decay; she was not given to symbolism and besides she was not naïve enough to suggest that moral qualities are simply the product of social background. Still, as the following passage shows, there is no doubt that she saw a relationship between Grandcourt's supercilious amorality and his general view of society.

> Grandcourt's importance as a subject of the realm was of the grandly passive kind which consists in the inheritance of land. Political and social movements touched him only through the wire of his rental, and his most careful biographer need not have read up on Schleswig-Holstein, the policy of Bismarck, trade-unions, household suffrage, or even the last commercial panic. He glanced over the best newspaper columns of these topics, and his views on them can hardly be said to have wanted breadth, since he embraced all Germans, all commercial men, and all voters liable to use the wrong kind of soap, under the general epithet of "brutes"; but he took no action on these much agitated questions beyond looking from under his eyelids at any man who mentioned them, and retaining a silence which served to shake the opinions of timid thinkers.[8]

Although the aristocratic world of *Daniel Deronda* is sharply observed and vividly recreated, it is true, none the less, that it lies outside the range of George Eliot's normal vision. In the novels on which her reputation chiefly depends she concentrates on rural and provincial England. And whereas *Daniel Deronda* is the novel in which she came closest to writing about her immediately contemporary world—it is set in the England of the sixties—she works most easily in an era that belongs to her own youth or to the youth of the preceding generation. She has, as it were, two historical centres towards which her imagination is strongly attracted. The first, and the less important, is the England of the turn of the century, an England that she thinks of as innocent of industrialism, as yet undisturbed by religious schism and social cleavage. This is the world of *Adam Bede* and *Silas Marner*. The second is the world that she recalls with all the warmth and immediacy with which she thinks of her own youth. It is the England of the late twenties and early thirties, of Catholic Emancipation and the first Reform Bill, an England moving quickly toward a new dispensation, an England where religion has hardened into habit or has split into sect, where the old social structure is feeling the pull of industrialism and new political faiths. This is the England of *The Mill on the Floss, Felix* and *Middlemarch.*

What I propose to do now is to examine in some detail the kind of social analysis and the function it plays in three of these novels—in *Adam Bede,* in *The Mill on the Floss* and in *Middlemarch.*

Adam Bede, as we have seen, takes us back to the opening years of the century, to an era that George Eliot did not, of course, know at first hand, but whose flavour was communicated to her by stories and reminiscences heard during her youth. As George Eliot's first extended work in fiction, it is relatively simple and uncomplicated in action, and the characters follow bold and obvious lines. Although George Eliot transposes it in a philosophical key, we immediately recognize the familiar story of the handsome, carefree squire who seduces the pretty, unsophisticated peasant girl and shatters what might have been an idyllic pastoral romance. As befits such a story and such a cast of characters, the society of *Adam Bede* harks back to a preceding age. It is paternalistic and feudalistic, with the squire at the top of the hierarchy, and with tenant farmers, independent artisans, and agricultural labourers arranged carefully in descending order. There is nothing harsh and oppressive about this society. Indeed, on a casual social level, a spirit of camaraderie prevails. But what enables this camaraderie between classes to flourish is not, of course, any spirit of egalitarian democracy, but simply an unquestioning acceptance of the need and of the justice of rigid class distinctions. In this best of all possible worlds there is no place for protest and no need of escape. For such old-world Toryism George Eliot has a slightly wistful admiration. It finds its most shining embodiment in her hero, the strong and incorruptible workman, Adam Bede:

> Adam was very susceptible to the influence of rank, and quite ready to give an extra amount of respect to every one who had more advantages than himself, not being a philosopher, or a proletaire with democratic ideas, but simply a stout-limbed clever carpenter with a large fund of reverence in his nature, which inclined him to admit all established claims unless he saw very clear grounds for questioning them. He had no theories about setting the world to rights, but he saw there was a great deal of damage done by building with ill-seasoned timber—by ignorant men in fine clothes making plans for outhouses and workshops and the like, without knowing the bearings of things—by slovenly

joiners' work, and by hasty contracts that could never be fulfilled without ruining somebody; and he resolved, for his part, to set his face against such doings. On these points he would have maintained his opinion against the largest landed proprietor in Loamshire or Stonyshire either; but he felt that beyond these it would be better for him to defer to people who were more knowing than himself.[9]

The society of *Adam Bede* is thus simple in structure and apparently self-contained and impervious to change.

A completely static world, however, is not any more possible in fiction than it is in life. The rural centre of Hayslope is disturbed not merely by the fatal conjunction of a handsome and genially indiscreet young squire and a pretty, light-headed milk-maid, but by the belated arrival from the world outside of a mildly revolutionary force known as Methodism. But Methodism is more an alien curiosity in this setting than a conquering gospel. Into the mouth of Dinah, the Methodist preacher, George Eliot puts an analysis of the social background of Methodism, all the more effective because the speaker is not conscious of the full implications of her comments.

> But I've noticed, that in these villages where the people lead a quiet life among the green pastures and the still waters, tilling the ground and tending the cattle, there's a strange deadness to the Word, as different as can be from the great towns, like Leeds, where I once went to visit a holy woman who preaches there. It's wonderful how rich is the harvest of souls up those high-walled streets, where you seemed to walk as in a prison-yard, and the ear is deafened with the sounds of worldly toil. I think maybe it is because the promise is sweeter when this life is so dark and weary, and the soul gets more hungry when the body is ill at ease.[10]

Dinah, it is to be noted, transcends the religious movement of which she is the spokesman. As the novel progresses, we think of her less as a Methodist and more as a practical saint divorced from sectarianism, as a warmly human embodiment of the essence of Christianity.

Although the social structure of *Adam Bede* is firmly and clearly indicated, it operates more as background than as an integral part of the problem posed by the action. Hetty's plight and Arthur's predicament are not given a social setting, outside of the fact, of course, that the wide separation in social status makes marriage impossible. If Hetty had been given more durable charms, if her aspirations to be a member of the great world had had a more realistic foundation, then we might have had a theme for social tragedy, not a study in the pathos of moral consequences. But that would be to ask for a level of sophistication that George Eliot at this time was not interested in achieving. *Adam Bede* is a folk story, given a realistic social setting and told in the light of advanced theories about the nature of human conduct.

Completely absent from *Adam Bede* are the sense of struggle, the grasping for security and social status, the frank acceptance of material values, the occasional note of protest that characterize the increasingly middle-class society of Victorian England. *The Mill on the Floss* ushers us immediately into such a world. It is, in some respects, George Eliot's most sustained analysis of English philistinism. The benevolent paternalism of *Adam Bede* is succeeded by a society where a certain measure of equality is within the grasp of all, provided one has a comfortable balance in the bank and the assurance of a good return on investments. With a few exceptions, the good citizens of St. Oggs—independent farmers, merchants, professional men—subscribe to the gospel of success whose characteristic virtues are diligence, frugality, and, if circumstances permit, honesty.

Since the characters in *The Mill on the Floss* have been partially released from a system of rigid class segregation, they are more sensitive to social status, more exposed to impersonal economic forces than were those in *Adam Bede*. We are now in a world that is dominated by the pursuit of financial security, a world that is to become increasingly familiar to us in English fiction. The passion for money runs through the story like a repulsive disease; the history of the Tulliver family, for instance, is charted in a series of financial crises. Beneath the casual pleasantries of social life lies a bedrock of economic necessity. It is a cause for wonder that no diligent Marxian critic, as far as I know, has extracted the following passage from *The Mill on the Floss* for appropriate comment:

> In writing the history of unfashionable families, one is apt to fall into a tone of emphasis which is very far from being the tone of good society, where principles and beliefs are not of an extremely moderate kind, but are always presupposed, no subjects being eligible but such as can be touched with a light and graceful irony. But then, good society has its claret and its velvet carpets, its dinner engagements six weeks deep, its opera and its faery ballrooms; rides off its ennui on thoroughbred horses, lounges at the club, has to keep clear of crinoline vortices, gets its science done by Faraday, and its religion by the superior clergy who are to be met in the best houses: how should it have time or need for belief and emphasis? But good society, floated on gossamer wings of light irony, is of very expensive production; requir-

ing nothing less than a wide and arduous national life condensed in unfragrant, deafening factories, cramping itself in mines, sweating at furnaces, grinding, hammering, weaving under more or less oppression of carbonic acid—or else, spread over sheepwalks, and scattered in lonely houses and huts on the clayey or chalky cornlands, where the rainy days look dreary. This wide national life is based entirely on emphasis—the emphasis of want, which urges it into all the activities necessary for the maintenance of good society and light irony: it spends its heavy years often in a chill, uncarpeted fashion, amidst family discord unsoftened by long corridors.[11]

A society such as this demands an approach radically different from that employed by George Eliot in *Adam Bede*. George Eliot is no longer the kindly romanticist describing a way of life whose disappearance she half regrets. She is now unsparingly analytical; she describes the solemn rites and customs of the Dodson family in the spirit almost of the anthropologist recording the peculiarities of a native tribe. And her tone is appropriately objective, enlivened by an irony that ranges from the playful to the mordantly serious. It is significant that Henry James—one of George Eliot's most discerning critics and a disciple, with qualifications—observed about *The Mill on the Floss* that "The portions of the story which bear upon the Dodson family are in their way not unworthy of Balzac. . . . We are reminded of him by the attempt to classify the Dodsons socially in a scientific manner, and to accumulate small examples of their idiosyncrasies." [12]

The picture of this sordid, materialistic world is not, of course, the whole story of *The Mill on the Floss*. I have referred already to the passages of poetic recollection where George Eliot sees her own childhood and youth in the childhood and youth of Maggie Tulliver. And Maggie's whole life is, you might say, a persistent attempt to escape from the cramping environment of St. Oggs. She is an early Dorothea, emotional, idealistic, striving to encompass certain vaguely benevolent ends. True, Maggie falls short of the heroic; her infatuation for one of George Eliot's school-girlish sketches of masculine charm might seem to be a pathetic climax to a life that, so we are told, "was full of eager, passionate longings for all that was beautiful and glad." Possibly the love affair between Maggie and Stephen is meant to be a crowning irony, George Eliot's final comment in the novel on the fragility of ideals in a materialistic society. But the problem is more complex than that. At the moment of her greatest weakness and, even more, at the moment of her greatest humiliation,

George Eliot wants us to look upon Maggie as inherently noble. We may be sure that she is not arguing romantically that Maggie merits our sympathy and praise because she has placed passion above social obligations. Rather the argument is that Maggie merits our sympathy and praise because she turns back to face the uncomprehending wrath of society at the call of a moral principle—a society, moreover, that is blind to spiritual subtleties and would have acquiesced in the easier solution of her problem. Maggie's action thus becomes a symbolic denial of the validity of utilitarian ethics. If she had obeyed her natural desires and had married Stephen, she would not, it is true, have brought the greatest happiness to the greatest number of people, but at least she would have brought the least pain to the least number of people. But Maggie scorns this compromise. She resolves on a course that can bring no approval from the community and only a troubled peace to her own conscience. The dilemma is too great for Maggie Tulliver and, one suspects, for George Eliot. The flood waters of the Floss provide a convenient solution.

What I want to emphasize, then, about social analysis in *The Mill on the Floss* is, first, that it is more complex and more pervasive than social analysis in *Adam Bede* and, consequently, bulks more significantly in the novel. In the second place, the analysis of social forces is here bound up closely with the working out of the theme. Whereas in *Adam Bede* society is simply framework or background, in *The Mill on the Floss* it is an active agent. Not merely must the heroine subdue the tumult in her own soul; she must fight against the collective prejudices of a society for which the greatest good can be reckoned only in terms of material success. Yet, in charting George Eliot's use of social analysis, *The Mill on the Floss* is only, as it were, a half-way house. She is still dealing with a relatively simple and undifferentiated society, one, moreover, that is innocent of ideas and is quarantined from the larger world outside. To demonstrate fully her power of social analysis, she needed a society more complex in its structure and more deeply implicated in the world of thought and controversy. In *Middlemarch,* the greatest of her novels, she created just such a society.

On the surface, *Middlemarch* seems to be merely a bulkier and more detailed examination of the same material that George Eliot had used in *The Mill on the Floss*—the provincial English town and the surrounding countryside of which it is the economic and cultural capital. But in reality the range of observation has become greater and the point of view has shifted notably. St. Oggs is one particular provincial town, clearly seen and vividly recreated; *Middlemarch* is English provincial society in the days just before the first Reform Bill. At the heart of this society, increasingly assertive and self-confident, is the prosperous middle-class, deriving wealth and prestige from commerce and banking and occasionally from a profession—the Vincys, the Bulstrodes and the Lydgates. From this centre we move upward into the squirarchy and the local families of established position—the Brookes and the Casaubons, and touch finally upon the life of the lesser, rural aristocracy. As we move downward from this same centre, we remain longest with a family like the Garths, honest and industrious folk who have not yet learned the catechism of success; we pause briefly to observe the repulsive entourage that gather around the expiring Featherstone—small, independent farmers of some means; and we listen from time to time to the voice of the tenant farmer and the agricultural labourer, raised bitterly and sometimes drunkenly against the ills of his lot. In this rural, midland society George Eliot had, of course, no place for the industrialized working class or for the artisans and colliers who appear in *Felix Holt*. Perhaps this is just as well. Like most of the Victorian novelists, she did not know the working man; she saw him at a distance, and at this remove he appeared less as an individual and more as a vague and disturbing element in society.

To this diversity of social class George Eliot in *Middlemarch* has added diversity of occupation and profession, so that social analysis is conducted from a multiple point of view. Thus, Casaubon is a study in the pathos of an arid and unimaginative scholarship. Lydgate, in his way, is a village Huxley who has dedicated his life to the ideals of disinterestedness and uncompromising veracity. Mr. Brooke is a politician, although inept in method and muddled in theory. Will Ladislaw is a free-lance intellectual, with an extensive if unorganized repertory of ideas. Even Dorothea, denied a profession and a rational education by the dictates of the age, tries to carve out a career as a humanitarian and philanthropist.

It is, of course, typical of George Eliot's art that, given characters such as these, she should try to relate them to their appropriate background. Casaubon and Lydgate emerge to the accompaniment of random observations on and brief sketches of the state of contemporary scholarship and medical science. The political material is even more prominent and often operates as a sort of central reference point for George Eliot's multiple approach. The livelier minds of the community look beyond the immediate and the personal and reflect on the

political problems of the day. Whereas St. Oggs had groped its way
into political consciousness only on the issue of Catholic emancipation
—not so much a realistic problem as a momentary return to the passions and prejudices of the past—*Middlemarch* is awake in a wide-
eyed and eagerly naïve fashion to the great issues of reform.

The increased scope and allusiveness of George Eliot's social analysis enables her to examine more fully than before the counterpoint of
class and social distinction. In *Adam Bede* wholly, and in *The Mill
on the Floss* mainly, the characters were placed against an unchanging social and political background; here, however, we are in the
midst of flux, in a world of rapid change that has swallowed many
of the old taboos and standards and is busily creating new ones. If
rural gentry and aristocracy mix more easily with solid middle-class
families, the solid middle-class families are more sensitive to distinctions within their own group. The vice of snobbery, unknown in
Adam Bede and incipient in *The Mill on the Floss,* has now emerged
and taken on cruel refinements. The Vincys, for instance, look down
upon the Garths because Mrs. Garth has taken in pupils and Mr.
Garth is financially unsound.

This is a world, moreover, where ideas, no less than economic
status and social position, can divide or unite. The reform movement
cuts boldly across class divisions and gathers in a diverse brood of
adherents. Enlisted under its banner are Bulstrode, wealthy banker
and pious dissenter, Farebrother, tolerant, this-worldly Church of
England clergyman, Vincy, prosperous merchant and genial man of
the world, and Will Ladislaw, bohemian and intellectual. The number
of malcontents, of those who try to burst out of their social mould,
has, in this novel, greatly increased. St. Oggs could throw up only a
Maggie and a Philip, but most of the leading characters in *Middlemarch* are jarred into dissatisfaction and sometimes even into active
rebellion. Usually, of course, the rebellion is abortive; circumstances
twine about the idealist and bind him securely to the commonplace
and the respectable. But still rebellion exists, and escape is not impossible.

Middlemarch might be described as a picture of a society where
two opposed principles struggle for dominance. The one we might call
the rigid or the static. It is embodied in the class structure, in the
prejudices and customs that make for division and segregation, in
the materialism that discourages thought and strangles aspiration.
The other we might call the flexible or the dynamic. It is embodied
in the social and intellectual movements that disdain the niceties of

class division and in the personal vision that sets at nought the things of this world. In George Eliot's reading of life, it was the former principle that more often than not triumphed, but not without a struggle.

I have tried to show the different roles that social analysis plays in three novels: how in *Adam Bede* it has a minor, background role; how in *The Mill on the Floss* it bulks much more significantly and strengthens and clarifies the theme; how finally in *Middlemarch* it helps to determine the choice of material, gives added depth to characterization, and provides one of the ideas by which a diverse and complex world takes on form and meaning. Yet I do not want to suggest that in *Middlemarch* the reader is being constantly reminded of the existence of a social context. If George Eliot has more powerfully than any other English novelist the social vision—the ability to embrace a diversity of social material: economic status, class division, professional characteristics, political divergences, she has at the same time, the power to fuse this material unobtrusively with her analysis of private motives. In *Middlemarch*, for instance, notice the way the political issue remains in the background, coming forward only to add colour and excitement to a scene or to sharpen conflicts that have already been established. I select as an example of this a scene in the novel that would appear to have a heavy political emphasis.[13] Lydgate and Ladislaw argue about electoral reform. A familiar antithesis is sharply and economically set forth in the exchange between the two men: Lydgate protests against "crying up a measure as if it were a universal cure, and crying up men who are part of the very disease that wants curing"; Ladislaw cheerfully admits that electoral reform is no cure-all and that reform candidates are often corrupt and ignorant, but argues that, after all, "your cure must begin somewhere." Now this dialogue is no doubt politically illuminating, but its real function in the novel lies elsewhere. The conversation takes place in the Lydgate drawing-room in the presence of Lydgate's wife, Rosamond, who looks upon it as a boring and vexatious interruption of the pleasant inanities of social life. As he talks, Lydgate is aware not only that his wife is bored but that she derives a pleasure from Ladislaw's innocent attentions that his own presence and conversation can no longer give. These disturbing thoughts force a more acrimonious note into his speech, which becomes stronger as he realizes the ironic cross-reference between his own relations with the hypocritical Bulstrode and his spirited protest against the linking of high, political goals with narrow measures and inferior men. This scene, then, emerges naturally from a private situation and illuminates character and conduct. Social analysis is the handmaiden, not the mistress, of George Eliot's art.

There are, it seems to me, two principal dangers to which the novelist deeply interested in the ways of society is exposed. One of these dangers is described by Mr. Edwin Muir in a comment he makes about the novels of H. G. Wells and John Galsworthy. "To Mr. Wells and Mr. Galsworthy," he writes, "society is essentially an abstract conception, not an imaginative reality; they do not recreate society, therefore, in their novels, they merely illustrate it, or rather their ideas about it. . . . To them society is there full grown as an idea at the beginning; it is not created by the characters, rather it creates them; but at the same time it is always beyond them, exists as a thing in itself, and cannot be adumbrated completely except by employing the arts of exposition." [14] The other danger is illustrated in the novels of Thackeray. Here there is no question of an abstract conception of society and of characters who are merely deduced from that conception. As Mr. Muir further observes, "Thackeray sets his characters going, he exhibits them continuously in a present not verbal but psychological, and at the end a picture of society has sprung up before our eyes." [15] But one should add that at the end of the Thackeray novel the characters he has so magnificently created tend to lose their identity and to disappear into the limbo of Vanity Fair. George Eliot, not the least accomplished of the Victorians in the art of compromise, avoids these two extremes. In *Middlemarch*, for instance, her vision of society and her vision of the individual never split asunder. They are bound together by an interlocking of the particular and the general, of the concrete and the theoretical, by a method of social analysis that has been refined into a subtle and complex art.

NOTES

1. This, I take it, is largely what Mr. F. R. Leavis has in mind when he refers to George Eliot's "Tolstoyan depth and reality." The whole passage from Mr. Leavis is worth quoting if only as an indication of the extent to which he will go in his effort at the critical rehabilitation of George Eliot. One regrets that his brilliant and perceptive critical analysis should be marred by a kind of literary Darwinism that marks out one novel-

ist for survival in a ruthless struggle for existence: "I . . . affirm my conviction that, by the side of George Eliot—and the comparison shouldn't be necessary—Meredith appears as a shallow exhibitionist (his famous 'intelligence' a laboured and vulgar brilliance) and Hardy, decent as he is, as a provincial manufacturer of gauche and heavy fictions that sometimes have corresponding value. For a positive indication of her place and quality I think of a Russian, not Turgenev, but a far greater, Tolstoy—who, we all know, is pre-eminent in getting 'the spirit of life itself.' George Eliot, of course, is not as transcendentally great as Tolstoy, but she *is* great, and great in the same way. . . . Of George Eliot it can be said that her best work has a Tolstoyan depth and reality." (F. R. Leavis. *The Great Tradition* (London, 1948), pp. 124–5.)

2. In the light of these comments, we can overcome the slight sense of shock occasioned by the critical juxtaposition of George Eliot and Proust. It is not merely a question of a somewhat similar use of memory. Proust knew the novels of George Eliot well and deeply admired them. For a discussion of the relationship between George Eliot and Proust see Franklin Gary, "In Search of George Eliot. An approach through Marcel Proust," *Symposium,* IV (1933), pp. 182–206; L. A. Bisson, "Proust, Bergson and George Eliot," *Modern Language Review,* XL (1945), pp. 104–14.

3. Gary (*op. cit.,* p. 184) quotes from a Proust letter: "Mais deux pages du *Moulin sur la Floss* me fait pleurer."

4. *The Mill on the Floss* (Everyman edition) Book I, Ch. 12, p. 108.

5. Henry James writes in a letter to William James, May 1, 1878: "The Leweses were very urbane and friendly, and I think that I shall have the right *dorénavant* to consider myself a Sunday *habitué.* The great George Eliot is both sweet and superior, and has a delightful expression in her large, long, pale, equine face. I had my turn at sitting beside her and being conversed with in a low, but most harmonious tone; and bating a tendency to *aborder* only the highest themes I have no fault to find with her." *The Letters of Henry James,* ed. Percy Lubbock (New York, 1920), i, 61.

6. *Daniel Deronda* (Library Edition) Book V, Ch. 35, pp. 291–2.

7. *Ibid.,* Book II, Ch. 13, pp. 99–100.

8. *Ibid.,* Book VI, Ch. 84, p. 423.

9. *Adam Bede* (Everyman edition) Ch. 16, p. 160.

10. *Adam Bede,* Ch. 8, p. 91.

11. *The Mill on the Floss* (Everyman edition) Book IV, Ch. 3, pp. 272–3.

12. Henry James, "The Novels of George Eliot" in *Views and Reviews* (Boston, 1908), pp. 31–32. The question of specific influences is a difficult one in considering a writer like George Eliot whose reading in the novel, as in most other fields of literature, was so extensive. Still it is significant that she had been reading and reflecting on the novels of Balzac just when she was beginning her career as fiction writer. On July 21, 1855, there appeared an article by her in *The Leader,* "The Morality of Wilhelm Meister," in which she referred to Balzac as "perhaps the most wonderful

writer of fiction the world has ever seen." She goes on, however, to say that Balzac has overstepped the limit of permissible realism and that "he drags us by his magic force through scene after scene of unmitigated vice, till the effect of walking among this human carrion is a moral nausea." The essay is reprinted in *Essays and Collected Papers* (Boston, 1909), pp. 305–09.

13. *Middlemarch* (Everyman edition) Book V, Ch. 46.
14. Edwin Muir, *The Structure of the Novel* (London, 1928), 122.
15. *Ibid.*

The Novels of Thomas Hardy

WHEN we say that the death of Thomas Hardy leaves English fiction without a leader, we mean that there is no other writer whose supremacy would be generally accepted, none to whom it seems so fitting and natural to pay homage. Nobody of course claimed it less. The unworldly and simple old man would have been painfully embarrassed by the rhetoric that flourishes on such occasions as this. Yet it is no less than the truth to say that while he lived there was one novelist at all events who made the art of fiction seem an honourable calling; while Hardy lived there was no excuse for thinking meanly of the art he practised. Nor was this solely the result of his peculiar genius. Something of it sprang from his character in its modesty and integrity, from his life, lived simply down in Dorsetshire without self-seeking or self-advertisement. For both reasons, because of his genius and because of the dignity with which his gift was used, it was impossible not to honour him as an artist and to feel respect and affection for the man. But it is of the work that we must speak, of the novels that were written so long ago that they seem as detached from the fiction of the moment as Hardy himself was remote from the stir of the present and its littleness.

We have to go back more than a generation if we are to trace the career of Hardy as a novelist. In the year 1871 he was a man of thirty-one; he had written a novel, *Desperate Remedies*, but he was by no means an assured craftsman. He "was feeling his way to a method," he said himself; as if he were conscious that he possessed all sorts of gifts, yet did not know their nature, or how to use them to advantage. To read that first novel is to share in the perplexity of its author. The imagination of the writer is powerful and sardonic; he is book-learned in a home-made way; he can create characters but he cannot control them; he is obviously hampered by the difficulties of his technique and, what is more singular, he is driven by some sense that human beings are the sport of forces outside themselves, to make use of an extreme and even melodramatic use of coincidence. He is already possessed of the conviction that a novel is not a toy, nor an argument; it is a means of giving truthful if harsh and violent impressions of the lives of men and women. But perhaps the most remarkable quality in the book is the sound that echoes and booms through its pages of a waterfall. It is the first manifestation of the power that was to assume such vast proportions in the later books. He already proves himself a minute and skilled observer of nature; the rain, he knows, falls differently as it falls upon roots or arable; he knows that the wind sounds differently as it passes through the branches of different trees. But he is aware in a larger sense of Nature as a force; he feels in it a spirit that can sympathize or mock or remain the indifferent spectator of human fortunes. Already that sense was his; and the crude story of Miss Aldclyffe and Cytherea is memorable because it is watched by the eyes of the gods, and worked out in the presence of Nature.

That he was a poet should have been obvious; that he was a novelist might still have been held uncertain. But the year after, when *Under the Greenwood Tree* appeared, it was clear that much of the effort of "feeling for a method" had been overcome. Something of the stubborn originality of the earlier book was lost. The second is accomplished, charming, idyllic compared with the first. The writer, it seems, may well develop into one of our English landscape painters, whose pictures are all of cottage gardens and old peasant women, who lingers to collect and preserve from oblivion the old-fashioned ways and words which are rapidly falling into disuse. And yet what kindly lover of antiquity, what naturalist with a microscope in his hand, what scholar solicitous for the changing shapes of language, ever heard the cry of a small bird killed in the next wood by an owl with such intensity? The cry "passed into the silence without mingling with it." Again we hear, very far away, like the sound of a gun out at sea on a calm summer's morning, a strange and ominous echo. But as we read these early books there is a sense of waste. There is a feeling that Hardy's genius was obstinate and perverse; first one gift would have its way with him and then another. They would not consent to

run together easily in harness. Such indeed was likely to be the fate
of a writer who was at once poet and realist, a faithful son of field
and down, yet tormented by the doubts and despondencies bred of
book-learning; a lover of old ways and plain countrymen, yet doomed
to see the flesh and faith of his forefathers turn to thin and spectral
transparencies before his eyes.

To this contradiction Nature had added another element likely to
disorder a symmetrical development. Some writers are born conscious
of everything; others are unconscious of many things. Some, like
Henry James and Flaubert, are able not merely to make the best use
of the spoil their gifts bring in, but control their genius in the act of
creation; they are aware of all the possibilities of every situation, and
are never taken by surprise. The unconscious writers, on the other
hand, like Dickens and Scott, seem suddenly and without their own
consent to be lifted up and swept onwards. The wave sinks and they
cannot say what has happened or why. Among them—it is the source
of his strength and of his weakness—we must place Hardy. His own
word, "moments of vision," exactly describes those passages of astonishing beauty and force which are to be found in every book that he
wrote. With a sudden quickening of power which we cannot foretell,
nor he, it seems, control, a single scene breaks off from the rest. We
see, as if it existed alone and for all time, the wagon with Fanny's
dead body inside travelling along the road under the dripping trees;
we see Troy flashing his sword round Bathsheba where she stands
motionless, cutting the lock off her head and spitting the caterpillar on
her breast. Vivid to the eye, but not to the eye alone, for every sense
participates, such scenes dawn upon us and their splendour remains.
But the power goes as it comes. The moment of vision is succeeded by
long stretches of plain daylight, nor can we believe that any craft or
skill could have caught the wild power and turned it to a better use.
The novels therefore are full of inequalities; they are lumpish and
dull and inexpressive; but they are never arid; there is always about
them a little blur of unconsciousness, that halo of freshness and margin of the unexpressed which often produce the most profound sense
of satisfaction. It is as if Hardy himself were not quite aware of what
he did, as if his consciousness held more than he could produce, and
he left it for his readers to make out his full meaning and to supplement it from their own experience.

For these reasons Hardy's genius was uncertain in development,
uneven in accomplishment, but, when the moment came, magnificent
in achievement. The moment came, completely and fully, in *Far from*

the Madding Crowd. The subject was right; the method was right; the poet and the countryman, the sensual man, the sombre reflective man, the man of learning, all enlisted to produce a book which, however fashions may chop and change, must hold its place among the great English novels. There is, in the first place, that sense of the physical world which Hardy more than any novelist can bring before us; the sense that the little prospect of man's existence is ringed by a landscape which, while it exists apart, yet confers a deep and solemn beauty upon his drama. The dark downland, marked by the barrows of the dead and the huts of shepherds, rises against the sky, smooth as a wave of the sea, but solid and eternal; rolling away to the infinite distance, but sheltering in its folds quiet villages whose smoke rises in frail columns by day, whose lamps burn in the immense darkness by night. Gabriel Oak tending his sheep up there on the back of the world is the eternal shepherd; the stars are ancient beacons; and for ages he has watched beside his sheep.

But down in the valley the earth is full of warmth and life; the farms are busy, the barns stored, the fields loud with the lowing of cattle and the bleating of sheep. Nature is prolific, splendid, and lustful; not yet malignant and still the Great Mother of labouring men. And now for the first time Hardy gives full play to his humour, where it is freest and most rich, upon the lips of country men. Jan Coggan and Henry Fray and Joseph Poorgrass gather in the malthouse when the day's work is over and give vent to that half-shrewd, half-poetic humour which has been brewing in their brains and finding expression over their beer since the pilgrims tramped the Pilgrims' Way; which Shakespeare and Scott and George Eliot all loved to overhear, but none loved better or heard with greater understanding than Hardy. But it is not the part of the peasants in the Wessex novels to stand out as individuals. They compose a pool of common wisdom, of common humour, a fund of perpetual life. They comment upon the actions of the hero and heroine, but while Troy or Oak or Fanny or Bathsheba come in and out and pass away, Jan Coggan and Henry Fray and Joseph Poorgrass remain. They drink by night and they plough the fields by day. They are eternal. We meet them over and over again in the novels, and they always have something typical about them, more of the character that marks a race than of the features which belong to an individual. The peasants are the great sanctuary of sanity, the country the last stronghold of happiness. When they disappear, there is no hope for the race.

With Oak and Troy and Bathsheba and Fanny Robin we come to

the men and women of the novels at their full stature. In every book three or four figures predominate, and stand up like lightning conductors to attract the force of the elements. Oak and Troy and Bathsheba; Eustacia, Wildeve, and Venn; Henchard, Lucetta, and Farfrae; Jude, Sue Bridehead, and Phillotson. There is even a certain likeness between the different groups. They live as individuals and they differ as individuals; but they also live as types and have a likeness as types. Bathsheba is Bathsheba, but she is woman and sister to Eustacia and Lucetta and Sue; Gabriel Oak is Gabriel Oak, but he is man and brother to Henchard, Venn, and Jude. However lovable and charming Bathsheba may be, still she is weak; however stubborn and ill-guided Henchard may be, still he is strong. This is a fundamental part of Hardy's vision; the staple of many of his books. The woman is the weaker and the fleshlier, and she clings to the stronger and obscures his vision. How freely, nevertheless, in his greater books life is poured over the unalterable frame-work! When Bathsheba sits in the wagon among her plants, smiling at her own loveliness in the little looking-glass, we may know, and it is proof of Hardy's power that we do know, how severely she will suffer and cause others to suffer before the end. But the moment has all the bloom and beauty of life. And so it is, time and time again. His characters, both men and women, were creatures to him of an infinite attraction. For the women he shows a more tender solicitude than for the men, and in them, perhaps, he takes a keener interest. Vain might their beauty be and terrible their fate, but while the glow of life is in them their step is free, their laughter sweet, and theirs is the power to sink into the breast of Nature and become part of her silence and solemnity, or to rise and put on them the movement of the clouds and the wildness of the flowering woodlands. The men who suffer, not like the women through dependence upon other human beings, but through conflict with fate, enlist our sterner sympathies. For such a man as Gabriel Oak we need have no passing fears. Honour him we must, though it is not granted us to love him quite so freely. He is firmly set upon his feet and can give as shrewd a blow, to men at least, as any he is likely to receive. He has a prevision of what is to be expected that springs from character rather than from education. He is stable in his temperament, steadfast in his affections, and capable of open-eyed endurance without flinching. But he, too, is no puppet. He is a homely, humdrum fellow on ordinary occasions. He can walk the street without making people turn to stare at him. In short, nobody can deny Hardy's power—the true novelist's power—to make us believe that his characters are fellow-beings driven by their own passions and idiosyncrasies, while they have—and this is the poet's gift—something symbolical about them which is common to us all.

And it is when we are considering Hardy's power of creating men and women that we become most conscious of the profound differences that distinguish him from his peers. We look back at a number of these characters and ask ourselves what it is that we remember them for. We recall their passions. We remember how deeply they have loved each other and often with what tragic results. We remember the faithful love of Oak for Bathsheba; the tumultuous but fleeting passions of men like Wildeve, Troy, and Fitzpiers; we remember the filial love of Clym for his mother, the jealous paternal passion of Henchard for Elizabeth Jane. But we do not remember how they have loved. We do not remember how they talked and changed and got to know each other, finely, gradually, from step to step and from stage to stage. Their relationship is not composed of those intellectual apprehensions and subtleties of perception which seem so slight yet are so profound. In all the books love is one of the great facts that mould human life. But it is a catastrophe; it happens suddenly and overwhelmingly, and there is little to be said about it. The talk between the lovers when it is not passionate is practical or philosophic, as though the discharge of their daily duties left them with more desire to question life and its purpose than to investigate each other's sensibilities. Even if it were in their power to analyse their emotions, life is too stirring to give them time. They need all their strength to deal with the downright blows, the freakish ingenuity, the gradually increasing malignity of fate. They have none to spend upon the subtleties and delicacies of the human comedy.

Thus there comes a time when we can say with certainty that we shall not find in Hardy some of the qualities that have given us most delight in the works of other novelists. He has not the perfection of Jane Austen, or the wit of Meredith, or the range of Thackeray, or Tolstoy's amazing intellectual power. There is in the work of the great classical writers a finality of effect which places certain of their scenes, apart from the story, beyond the reach of change. We do not ask what bearing they have upon the narrative, nor do we make use of them to interpret problems which lie on the outskirts of the scene. A laugh, a blush, half a dozen words of dialogue, and it is enough; the source of our delight is perennial. But Hardy has none of this concentration and completeness. His light does not fall directly upon the human heart. It passes over it and out on to the darkness of the heath and upon the trees swaying in the storm. When we look back into the room the group by the fireside is dispersed. Each man or woman is battling with the storm, alone, revealing himself most when he is least under the observation of other human beings. We do not know them as we know Pierre or Natasha or Becky Sharp. We do not know them in and out and all round as they are revealed to the casual caller, to the Government official, to the great lady, to the general on the battlefield. We do not know the complication and involvement and turmoil of their thoughts. Geographically, too, they remain fixed to the same stretch of the English country-side. It is seldom, and always with unhappy results, that Hardy leaves the yeoman or farmer to describe the class above theirs in the social scale. In the drawing-room and clubroom and ballroom, where people of leisure and education come together, where comedy is bred and shades of character revealed, he is awkward and ill at ease. But the opposite is equally true. If we do not know his men and women in their relations to each other, we know them in their relations to time, death, and fate. If we do not see them in quick agitation against the lights and crowds of cities, we see them against the earth, the storm, and the seasons. We know their attitude towards some of the most tremendous problems that can confront mankind. They take on a more than mortal size in memory. We see them, not in detail but enlarged and dignified. We see Tess reading the baptismal service in her nightgown "with an impress of dignity that was almost regal." We see Marty South, "like a being who had rejected with indifference the attribute of sex for the loftier quality of abstract humanism," laying the flowers on Winterbourne's grave. Their speech has a Biblical dignity and poetry. They have a force in them which cannot be defined, a force of love or of hate, a force which in the men is the cause of rebellion against life, and in the women implies an illimitable capacity for suffering, and it is this which dominates the character and makes it unnecessary that we should see the finer features that lie hid. This is the tragic power; and, if we are to place Hardy among his fellows, we must call him the greatest tragic writer among English novelists.

But let us, as we approach the danger-zone of Hardy's philosophy, be on our guard. Nothing is more necessary, in reading an imaginative writer, than to keep at the right distance above his page. Nothing is easier, especially with a writer of marked idiosyncrasy, than to fasten on opinions, convict him of a creed, tether him to a consistent point of view. Nor was Hardy any exception to the rule that the mind which is most capable of receiving impressions is very often the least capable of drawing conclusions. It is for the reader, steeped in the impression, to supply the comment. It is his part to know when to put aside the writer's conscious intention in favour of some deeper intention of which perhaps he may be unconscious. Hardy himself was aware of this. A novel "is an impression, not an argument," he has warned us, and, again

> Unadjusted impressions have their value, and the road to a true philosophy of life seems to lie in humbly recording diverse readings of its phenomena as they are forced upon us by chance and change.

Certainly it is true to say of him that, at his greatest, he gives us impressions; at his weakest, arguments. In *The Woodlanders, The Return of the Native, Far from the Madding Crowd,* and, above all, in *The Mayor of Casterbridge,* we have Hardy's impression of life as it came to him without conscious ordering. Let him once begin to tamper with his direct intuition and his power is gone. "Did you say the stars were worlds, Tess?" asks little Abraham as they drive to market with their beehives. Tess replies that they are like "apples on our stubbard-tree, most of them splendid and sound—a few blighted." "Which do we live on—a splendid or a blighted one?" "A blighted one," she replies, or rather the mournful thinker who has assumed her mask speaks for her. The words protrude, cold and raw, like the springs of a machine where we had seen only flesh and blood. We are crudely jolted out of that mood of sympathy which is renewed a moment later when the little cart is run down and we have a concrete instance of the ironical methods which rule our planet.

That is the reason why *Jude the Obscure* is the most painful of all Hardy's books, and the only one against which we can fairly bring the charge of pessimism. In *Jude the Obscure* argument is allowed to dominate impression, with the result that though the misery of the book is overwhelming it is not tragic. As calamity succeeds calamity we feel that the case against society is not being argued fairly or with profound understanding of the facts. Here is nothing of that width and force and knowledge of mankind which, when Tolstoy criticizes society, makes his indictment formidable. Here we have revealed to us the petty cruelty of men, not the large injustice of the gods. It is only necessary to compare *Jude the Obscure* with *The Mayor of Casterbridge* to see where Hardy's true power lay. Jude carries on his miserable contest against the deans of colleges and the conventions of sophisticated society. Henchard is pitted, not against another man, but against something outside himself which is opposed to men of his ambition and power. No human being wishes him ill. Even Farfrae and Newson and Elizabeth Jane whom he has wronged all come to pity him, and even to admire his strength of character. He is standing up to fate, and in backing the old Mayor whose ruin has been largely his own fault, Hardy makes us feel that we are backing human nature in an unequal contest. There is no pessimism here. Throughout the book we are aware of the sublimity of the issue, and yet it is presented to us in the most concrete form. From the opening scene in which Henchard sells his wife to the sailor at the fair to his death on Egdon Heath the vigour of the story is superb, its humour rich and racy, its movement large-limbed and free. The skimmity ride, the fight between Farfrae and Henchard in the loft, Mrs. Cuxsom's speech upon the death of Mrs. Henchard, the talk of the ruffians at Peter's Finger with Nature present in the background or mysteriously dominating the foreground, are among the glories of English fiction. Brief and scanty, it may be, is the measure of happiness allowed to each, but so long as the struggle is, as Henchard's was, with the decrees of fate and not with the laws of man, so long as it is in the open air and calls for activity of the body rather than of the brain, there is greatness in the contest, there is pride and pleasure in it, and the death of the broken corn merchant in his cottage on Edgon Heath is comparable to the death of Ajax lord of Salamis. The true tragic emotion is ours.

Before such power as this we are made to feel that the ordinary tests which we apply to fiction are futile enough. Do we insist that a great novelist shall be a master of melodious prose? Hardy was no such thing. He feels his way by dint of sagacity and uncompromising sincerity to the phrase he wants, and it is often of unforgettable pungency. Failing it, he will make do with any homely or clumsy or old-fashioned turn of speech, now of the utmost angularity, now of a bookish elaboration. No style in literature, save Scott's, is so difficult to analyse; it is on the face of it so bad, yet it achieves its aim so unmistakably. As well might one attempt to rationalize the charm of a muddy country road, or of a plain field of roots in winter. And then, like Dorsetshire itself, out of these very elements of stiffness and angularity his prose will put on greatness; will roll with a Latin sonority; will shape itself in a massive and monumental symmetry like that of his own bare downs. Then again, do we require that a novelist shall observe the probabilities, and keep close to reality? To find anything aproaching the violence and convolution of Hardy's plots one must go back to the Elizabethan drama. Yet we accept his story completely as we read it; more than that, it becomes obvious that his violence and his melodrama, when they are not due to a curious peasant-like love of the monstrous for its own sake, are part of that wild spirit of poetry which saw with intense irony and grimness that no reading of life can possibly outdo the strangeness of life itself, no symbol of caprice and unreason be too extreme to represent the astonishing circumstances of our existence.

But as we consider the great structure of the Wessex novels it seems irrelevant to fasten on little points—this character, that scene, this phrase of deep and poetic beauty. It is something larger that Hardy has bequeathed to us. The Wessex novels are not one book, but many. They cover an immense stretch; inevitably they are full of imperfections—some are failures, and others exhibit only the wrong side of their maker's genius. But undoubtedly, when we have submitted ourselves fully to them, when we come to take stock of our impression of the whole, the effect is commanding and satisfactory. We have been freed from the cramp and pettiness imposed by life. Our imaginations have been stretched and heightened; our humour has been made to laugh out; we have drunk deep of the beauty of the earth. Also we have been made to enter the shade of a sorrowful and brooding spirit which, even in its saddest mood, bore itself with a grave uprightness and never, even when most moved to anger, lost its deep compassion for the sufferings of men and women. Thus it is no mere transcript of life at a certain time and place that Hardy has given us. It is a vision of the world and of man's lot as they revealed themselves to a powerful imagination, a profound and poetic genius, a gentle and humane soul.

AUSTIN WARREN

Instress of Inscape

THE early Hopkins follows Keats and the "medieval school" (as he
called the Pre-Raphaelites). The latest Hopkins, who wrote the sonnets of desolation, was a poet of tense, economic austerity. Their
nearest parallel I can summon would be Donne's "holy sonnets":
"Batter my heart" and "If poisonous minerals." For mode in "Androm-
eda" and the later sonnets (1885–9), Hopkins himself projected "a
more Miltonic plainness and severity": he is thinking of Milton's
sonnets and the choruses of *Samson*. In 1887 he invoked another
name: "my style tends always more towards Dryden."

The middle period, which opens with the "Wreck of the Deutschland" (1875) and closes with "Tom's Garland" and "Harry Ploughman," both written in 1885, is the period of experiment. But it is
also the most Hopkinsian,—the most markedly and specially his.

Middle Hopkins startles us by its dense rich world, its crowded
Ark, its plentitude and its tangibility, its particularity of thing and
word. There is detailed precision of image ("rose moles all in stipple
upon trout that swim"). The poet is enamored of the unique, the
"abrupt self."

The exploration of Middle Hopkins,—its style, the view of life and
art implicit in its style,—may well start from the institutions and movements from which the poet learned, in which he participated. The
motifs are the Ritualist Movement, Pre-Raphaelitism, Aestheticism,
linguistic renovation, England, the Catholic Church. In Hopkins'

From *The Kenyon Review*, VI (1944), 369–82; reprinted in *Gerard Manley
Hopkins: By the Kenyon Critics* (Norfolk, Connecticut: New Directions,
1945), 72–88. Copyright 1944 by *The Kenyon Review*. Copyright 1945 by
New Directions. Reprinted by permission of New Directions and the author.

celebration of the sensuous, the concrete, the particular—his "instress of the inscapes"—all of these converge.

As a Catholic, Hopkins was an incarnationist and a sacramentalist: the sacraments are the extensions of the Incarnation. As a Catholic, he believed that man is a compound of matter and form, and that his body, resurrected, will express and implement his soul through all eternity. "Man's spirit will be flesh-bound when found at best. But unencumbered. . . ." Like all Catholic philosophers, he believed in an outer world independent of man's knowing mind—he was, in the present sense of the word, a "realist."

Hopkins was an Englishman, of a proud and patriotic sort. This is not always remembered, partly because he became the priest of a Church viewed by his compatriots as Continental, or Italian, or international. But there is an English way of being Catholic.[1] Hopkins was not an "old Catholic" of the sturdy, unemotional variety nourished on Challoner's *Garden of the Soul;* no convert could be that. But, like his admired Newman, and unlike Manning and Faber (also converts), he was "Gallican" not Ultramontane, British not Italian in his devotional life and rhetoric. He remembers when England was Catholic, when the pilgrims frequented the shrine of our Lady of Walsingham.

> Deeply surely, I need to deplore it,
> Wondering why my master bore it,
> The riving off that race
> So at home, time was, to his truth and grace
>
> That a starlight-wender of ours would say
> The marvelous Milk was Walsingham Way
> And one—but let be, let be;
> More, more than was will yet be.

The four real shapers of Hopkins' mind were all Britons; we might go further and say, all were British empiricists—all concerned with defending the ordinary man's belief in the reality and knowability of things and persons.

Two of them were encountered at Oxford. Pater, who remained his friend, was one of his tutors. In the abstractionist academic world, Pater boldly defended the concrete—of the vital arts and music of perception, of the unique experience. "Every moment some form grows perfect in hand or face, some tone on the hills or the sea is choicer than the rest. . . ." Though Hopkins could not conceivably have written so representatively, abstractly ". . . hills . . . sea . . .

choicer," the text pleads for a stressing of the inscapes. Hopkins followed some lectures by Pater on Greek philosophy: perhaps he heard, in an earlier version, Pater's lectures on Plato and Platonism, in which, with monstrous effrontery, the Doctrine of Ideas was praised as giving contextual interest to the concrete.

With Ruskin, whose *Modern Painters* he read early and admiringly, Hopkins shared the revolt against that neoclassical grandeur of generality praised by Johnson and expounded by Reynolds. The influence of Ruskin—art medievalist, devout student of clouds, mountains, trees —is pervasive in Hopkins' sketches (five of which are reproduced in the *Note-Books*) and in his journalizing—his meticulously technical descriptions of church architecture (often neo-Gothic) and scenery.

Hopkins follows the general line of Ruskin in more than art. Remote from him is the old "natural theology" which finds the humanly satisfactory and well furnished world such an effect of its Creator as the watch of the watchmaker. Nor does he, after the fashion of some mystics and Alexandrians, dissolve Nature into a system of symbols translating the real world of the spirit. Like Ruskin, he was able to recover the medieval and Franciscan joy in God's creation. And like Ruskin he protested against an England which is "seared with trade . . . and wears man's smudge." His political economy, as well as it can be construed, was Ruskinian; what may be called Tory Socialist or Distributist.

It was to Newman, his great predecessor, that Hopkins wrote when he decided to become a Roman Catholic. And Newman's closest approach to a philosophical work, his *Grammar of Assent* (1870), interested Hopkins so far that in 1883 he planned to publish (should Newman agree) a commentary on it. There were marked temperamental and intellectual differences between the men. Newman, much the more complex and psychologically subtle, could feel his way into other men's minds as Hopkins could not. Hopkins was the closer dialectician and scholar. He did not share Newman's distrust of metaphysics, including the scholastic, his tendency to fideism; but he was, like Newman (in words the latter used of Hurrell Froude), "an Englishman to the backbone in his severe adherence to the real and the concrete."

The great medieval thinker who most swayed Hopkins' spirit to peace, Duns Scotus, was also a Briton, had been an Oxford professor. He was "Of reality the rarest-veinéd unraveler": he was able to analyze, disengage from the complex in which they appear, the thinnest, most delicate strands ("vein" may be either anatomical or geological). Perhaps "rarest-veinéd unraveler" is a kind of *kenning* for the philosopher's epithet, the Subtle Doctor. Scotus, the Franciscan critic of the Dominican Thomas Aquinas, was centrally dear to Hopkins by virtue of his philosophical validation of the individual. St. Thomas held that, in the relation of the individual to his species, the "matter" individuates, while the "form" is generic: that is, that the individuals of a species reproductively multiply their common originative pattern. Scotus insisted that each individual has a distinctive "form" as well: a *haecceitas,* or thisness, as well as a generic *quidditas,* or whatness.

After meeting with this medieval Franciscan, Hopkins, taking in "any inscape of sky or sea," thought of Scotus. The word, of Hopkins' coinage, occurs already in his Oxford note-books. Suggested presumably by "landscape": an "inscape" is any kind of formed or focussed view, any pattern discerned in the natural world. Being so central a word in his vocabulary and motif in his mental life, it moves through some range of meaning: from sense-perceived pattern to inner form. The prefix seems to imply a contrary, an outer-scape—as if to say that an "inscape" is not mechanically or inertly present, but requires personal action, attention, a seeing and *seeing into.*

The earliest "Notes for Poetry" cite "Feathery rows of young corn. Ruddy, furred and branchy tops of the elms backed by rolling clouds." "A beautiful instance of inscape *sided* on the *slide,* that is successive sidings on one inscape, is seen in the behavior of the flag flower. . . ." In 1873, two years before the "Deutschland," he "Saw a shoal of salmon in the river and many hares on the open hills. Under a stone hedge was a dying ram: there ran slowly from his nostrils a thick flesh-coloured ooze, scarlet in places, coiling and roping its way down so thick that it looked like fat."

He made notes on ancient musical instruments and on gems and their colors: "beryl—watery green; carnelian—strong flesh red, Indian red. . . ." His love of precise visual observation never lapsed. Nor did his taste for research. Like Gray, he had a scholarly, fussy antiquarianism, adaptable to botany or archaeology. He liked "Notes and Queries," details, studies in place-names, amateur etymologies.

What is perhaps his most brilliant prose celebrates the self and its wonders: "That taste of myself, of I and me above and in all things, which is more distinctive than the taste of ale or alum. . . ." Other selves were mysterious. As a shy man, he found it easier to reach natural "inscapes" than to know other selves. He hadn't Newman's psychological finesse; wrote no psychic portraits matching by their sharpness and delicacy his notations of ashtrees. The men in his poems are seen as from a distance—sympathetically but generically.

But he gloried in the range and repertory of mankind. Like Chesterton, who was concerned that, in lying down with the lamb, the lion should "still retain his royal ferocity," Hopkins wanted monks to be mild and soldiers to be pugnacious. He imagined Christ incarnate again as a soldier. He didn't want other men to be like himself—scholarly, aesthetic, neurotic: he was drawn to soldiers, miners, Felix Randall the blacksmith and Harry the Ploughman, to the rough and manly manual laborers. And each of these selves he wished to be functioning not only characteristically but intensely, violently, dangerously—on their mettle, like the Windhover, like Harry Ploughman, like the "Eurydice's" sailor who, "strung by duty, is strained to beauty. . . ."

In poetry, he desired both to record inscapes and to use words so that they would exist as objects. His was a double particularity.

Poetry, he wrote, shortly before the "Deutschland," is "speech framed to be heard for its own sake and interest even over and above its interest of meaning. Some [subject] matter and meaning is essential to it but only as an element necessary to support and employ the shape which is contemplated for its own sake. Poetry is in fact speech for the inscape's sake—and therefore the inscape must be dwelt on."

In 1862, he was already collecting words—particularistic, concrete words. The earliest entries in the *Note-Books* are gritty, harshly tangy words, "running the letter," "grind, gride, grid, grit, groat, grate . . ." and "crock, crank, kranke, crick, cranky. . . ." He is also aroused by dialectal equivalents which he encounters: *whisket* for *basket*, *grindlestone* for *grindstone*. He notes linguistic habits: an observed laborer, when he began to speak "quickly and descriptively, . . . dropped or slurred the article." He attends to, and tries to define, the sundry schools of Latin pronunciation—this while the priests say mass. He inquires concerning the character of the Maltese language; wants to learn Welsh—not primarily in order to convert the local Wesleyans back to their ancestral faith.

As a beginning poet, Hopkins followed Keats and the "medieval school." Even in his middle style, there remain vestiges of the earlier decorative diction, frequent use of "beauty," "lovely," "dear," "sweet" ("that sweet's sweeter ending"). But already in 1866, "The Habit of Perfection," though dominantly "medieval," anticipates the later mode:

> This ruck and reel which you remark
> Coils, keeps, and teases simple sight.

"The Wreck of the Deutschland" (1875) inaugurates Hopkins' middle period (his first proper mastery). The diction is as remarkable as the rhythm. Characteristic are homely dialectal words, words which sound like survivors from Anglo-Saxon, and compound epithets. From the concluding stanzas of the "Deutschland" come these lines:

> Mid-numbered He in three of the thunder-throne!
> Not a dooms-day dazzle in his coming nor dark as he came;

and

> Dame, at our door
> Drowned, and among our shoals,
> Remember us in the roads, the heaven-haven of the
> Reward: . . .

From "The Bugler's First Communion":

> Forth Christ from cupboard fetched, how fain I of feet
> To his youngster take his treat!
> Low-latched in leaf-light housel his too huge godhead.

Modern readers take it for granted that Hopkins was influenced by Old English poetry. In his excellent *New Poets from Old: A Study in Literary Genetics*, Henry Wells notes that all the technical features representative of that poetry appear conspicuously in Hopkins; judges him far nearer to Cynewulf than to Chaucer; finds a plausible parallel to a passage in *Beowulf*. But by his own statement, Hopkins did not learn Anglo-Saxon till 1882, and seems never to have read either *Beowulf* or Cynewulf. There need of course be no pedantic mystery here. Hopkins knew something of *Piers Plowman* and is likely to have known some specimens of Old English versification.

In any case, Hopkins was already a student of Welsh poetry and an attentive reader of linguistic monographs; and he belongs among the poets who can be incited to poetry by scholars' prose.

In 1873–4, he taught "rhetoric" at Manresa House, wrote the observations on that subject collected in the *Note-Books*. His notes lead us to the *Lectures on the English Language*, published in 1859 by the versatile American scholar, George P. Marsh. This book is full of matter calculated to excite a poet, for Marsh has a real interest in the future (as well as the past) of the language and a real interest in the literary (as well as the pragmatic) use of words. The whole direction of his book suggests that literary experiment can find much in its purpose in literary history, that new poetry can come from old. Ending his lecture on "Accentuation and Double Rhymes," he urges:

"We must enlarge our stock [of rhyming words] by the revival of obsolete words and inflections from native sources," or introduce substitutes for rhyme; in the following, the 25th Chapter, he incitingly discusses alliteration (with illustrations from *Piers Plowman*), consonance—e.g., "bad, led"; "find, band" (with illustrations from Icelandic poetry and invented English examples), and assonance (with illustrations from the Spanish). Hopkins' quotations from *Piers* are Marsh's; only in 1882 did he study *Piers*, and then without admiration, regarding its verse as a "degraded and doggrel form of Anglo-Saxon sprung rhythm.

To both Bridges and Dixon, curious concerning the new poetic method of the "Deutschland," Hopkins says nothing of Old English nor of *Piers Plowman* but speaks of nursery rhymes, the choruses of *Samson*, and of his reading in Welsh poetry (which he began studying in 1875). "The chiming of the consonants I got in part from the Welsh, which is very rich in sound and imagery." H. I. Bell, a recent student of Welsh poetry, distinguishes four types of *cynghanedd*—two offering consonantal sequences (like "*N*igh*t* may *d*are / *not* my dearest"), another with a pattern of internal rhyme ("If to the *grove* she *rove*th"), and a fourth combining internal rhyme and alliteration ("*Dais*ies *bl*oom, and *ros*es *bl*ow"). Traits common to Old English and Middle Hopkins (scant use of articles, prepositions, and pronouns; constant use of compound words) are shared by both with Welsh poetry.

Then there is a third line for Hopkins' diction. He derives, through Barnes and Furnivall at least, from an imprecisely defined group of historians and philologists who may be called Teutonizers and who challenged the dominance of the Latin and Romance—the "civilized," learned, and abstract elements in our language. These linguistic protestants were motivated by nationalist or regionalist feeling or by anti-intellectualism or both.

One of these protestants was the Oxford historian, E. A. Freeman, who chronicled the Norman Conquest and himself resisted it. As early as 1846, he was praising the Teutonic part of our language as affording "expression mostly of greater strength than their romance synonyms for all purposes of general literature"; and he used the phrase "pure English" for a diction purged of these synonyms. Later, he purged and prodded. In 1872 he writes to a disciple on style: "Don't be afraid . . . I find that fifteen or sixteen years back, I talked of 'commencement,' 'conclusion,' and 'termination.' I really believe that, in these times, simplicity of style comes only by long practice." Another

Anglicizer was F. J. Furnivall, a founder, in 1864, of the Early English Text Society, and a constant editor of texts, for which he wrote Forewords (not prefaces) and Afterwords. He began his intellectual career under the influence of Ruskin and Maurice, was active in the Working Men's College, and protested that his interest in early literature was not linguistic but social.

Another founder of the EETS, R. C. Trench, published in 1855 his engaging *English, Past and Present*. The second lecture considers "English as it might have been" had the Normans not invaded. Admitting that there have been gains in the mixture of linguistic stocks, Trench is concerned with defining the losses. He argues that, while our present cerebral and technical words derive from the classical languages, the Anglo-Saxon might have developed—chiefly by compounding, as German has done—such a vocabulary. Even *impenetrability* could have been matched, by *unthoroughfaresomeness*, an ungraceful word but an accurate equivalent. Theological language would be intelligible to farmhand as well as scholar if we said *again-buying* for *redemption, middler* for *mediator,* "Christ fellow-feels for His people" instead of "He sympathizes."

In the tradition of Trench, but much more violent, William Barnes lamented the linguistic Conquest of English and declared the old stock still capable of extension by compounding. Instead of *photograph,* we should say *sunprint* or *flameprint*. Indeed, all our current Latinisms we should replace out of the "wordstores of the landfolk." Barnes's nominations are all flavorsome; samples are *wordrich* (copious of speech), *overyearn* (commiserate), *gleecraft* (music), *outclear* (elucidate), *faithheat* (enthusiasm), *footkeys* (pedals), *withwrinkling* (spiral), *sleepstow* (dormitory), and *craftly* (technical). He regretted the loss of *inwit* in place of *conscience;* and to serve instead of *subjective* and *objective* (those psychological-philosophical terms which Coleridge introduced from Germany) he suggested *inwoning* and *outwoning*.

Barnes had something of a following among literary people; was publicly praised by Patmore, Gosse, Bridges, Hardy. His poetry, early read, Hopkins preferred to Burns's—liked its "West country instress"; but he learned most from the prose. Barnes's *Speechcraft* [i.e., Grammar] says Hopkins in 1882, is "written in an unknown tongue, a soul of modern Anglosaxon, beyond all that Furnival in his wildest Forewords ever dreamed. . . . [Evidently Hopkins was familiar with the publications of the Early English Text Society.] It makes one weep to think what English might have been, for in spite of all that Shake-

speare and Milton have done with the compound ["impure" English]
I cannot doubt that no beauty in a language can make up for want
of purity. In fact, I am learning Anglosaxon and it is a vastly superior
thing to what we have." He cites Barnes's wondrous "pitches of such-
ness" (for "degrees of comparison"): "We *ought* to. call them so,
but alas!" [2]

Hopkins' characteristic critical and philosophical terminology follows closely the counsel of Trench and Barnes: that is, it is a compounding of Old English roots and suffixes to suit new needs and to
replace Latinic terms. *Inwit* (for *conscience*) and Barnes's *inwoning*
(subjective) suggest *instress* and *inscape*. Hopkins explains his special
use of *sake* (the being a thing has outside itself) by analytic parallel
of the compounds *forsake, namesake, keepsake*. The terminology of
the *Comments on the Spiritual Exercises* (1880) is particularly Hopkinsian (e.g., *pitch, stress, burl*). Says Pick, "He uses almost a new
language and doesn't provide a dictionary." To Bridges, Hopkins wrote
of his manuscript book on rhythm, "It is full of new words, without
which there can be no new science."

His doctrine of the language for poetry, nowhere exposited, was
assuredly different. Archaism—the use of obsolete words for literary
effect—he repudiated. His oddities (like "pashed," "fashed," "tucked,"
"degged") are generally dialectal; and it is safe to assume that his
words of Old English lineage were collected and used by him as
dialectal, still spoken, English: not "inkhorn" terms but folkspeech.
Even when he thought he was improvising he was—at least in one
instance—remembering: his alleged coinage, "louched" (slouched,
slouching), was, as Bridges observed, to be found in Wright's Dialect
Dictionary.

Whenever Hopkins explains his words (as he stands always ready
to do to his friends), the particularity of the words, their compactness
and detail, is made manifest. "Stickles—Devonshire for the foamy
tongues of water below falls."

He defends "bole" thus: "It is not only used by poets but seems
technical and *proper* [i.e., exactly belonging to] and in the mouth of
timber merchants and so forth." Of "flit," called into question by a
correspondent, he writes: "I myself always use it and commonly hear
it used among our people. I think it is at least a North Country word,
used in Lancashire, for instance. . . ."

His compoundings are another matter. Though analogues can be
offered from Browning, Hopkins came to them (I suppose) by way of
medieval poetry, English and Welsh, and by way of Marsh, Trench,

and Barnes. Here the vindication would be that to compound freely was to restore to the English language that power it once had possessed: the words compounded, or the root and suffix or prefix, were separately familiar and oral. He writes "spendsavour salt" (the salt which is spending its savour and on its way to being the Biblical salt which has lost its savour), *bloomfall, trambeam, backwheels,* "Though worlds of *wanwood* [dark or pale trees] *leafmeal* [cf. "piecemeal": the suffix means "by bits," "by portions"] lie."

Judged by its effect and its internal intent, Hopkins' poetry finds partial parallels in Holst, Delius, and Vaughan Williams. As (without the precise imitation of Warlock or the archaism of Dolmetsch) they sought to resume "English" music where its genuine succession was interrupted, at the Restoration, and to go creatively back to the English glory of folksong, madrigal, the modes, to Dowland, Bull, and Byrd—so Hopkins seems to be reaching back, while he reaches forward, to an "English" poetry. Probably we may add, to an English Catholic poetry; and suppose that his pushing back of the Elizabethans had some incentive in his desire to get back of the Reformation to the day when all England was at once Catholic and English.

Like the poetry of the bards and the scops, Hopkins' poetry was to be oral but not conversational, formal and rhetorical without being bookish. It used dialectal words without attempting, like Barnes's *Poems of Rural Life,* to be local and homely; it uses folk-words in "serious" poetry. Hopkins' poems intend, ideally, an audience never actually extant, composed of literarily alert countrymen and linguistically adept, folk-concerned scholars; he had to create by artifice what his poetry assumed as convention. "The Wreck" and "Tom's Garland" suggest, adumbrate, a greater poetry than they achieve.

To create an English and Catholic convention of poetry and poetic language: this was too grand an order for one Victorian poet. The experiments are yet more important than the achievement; the comparative failures more interesting than the good whole poems.

The ideal of poetry must be to instress the inscapes without splintering the fabric of the universe, and, expressionally, to make every word rich in a way compatible with the more than additively rich inclusive structure of the whole poem.

In Hopkins' poems, the word, the phrase, the local excitement, often pulls us away from the poem. And in the more ambitious pieces, the odes as we may call them ("The Wreck," "Spelt from Sibyl's Leaves," "Nature is a Heraclitean Fire"), there is felt a discrepancy between texture and structure: the copious, violent detail is matched by no corresponding mythic or intellectual vigor. Indeed, both the Wrecks are "occasional," commissioned pieces which Hopkins works at devotedly and craftfully, as Dryden did at his *Annus Mirabilis,* but which, like Dryden's poem, fail to be organisms. Hopkins wasn't a storyteller, and he was unable to turn his wrecks into myths of Wreck: they remain historical events enveloped in meditations. "The Bugler-Boy" and other poems suffer from the gap between the psychological naïveté and the purely literary richness. To try prose paraphrases of the middle poems is invariably to show how thin the thinking is. Hopkins' mind was first aesthetic, then technical: he thought closely on metaphysical and prosodic matters: his thinking about beauty, man, and Nature is unimpressive.

The meaning of the poems hovers closely over the text, the linguistic surface of the poems. The rewarding experience of concern with them is to be let more and more into words and their linkages, to become absorbed with the proto-poetry of derivation and metaphorical expansion, to stress the inscapes of our own language.

NOTES

1. Cf. The English Way: *Studies in English Sanctity from St. Bede to Newman* (ed. M. Ward, 1933) and the studies of Dom Augustine Baker, Lingard, and Hopkins—by Fr. D'Arcy—in *Great Catholics* (ed. C. Williamson, 1939).

2. *Arabia Deserta* (1888) was written partly, says Doughty, to show "my dislike of the Victorian English." In order to show there was an alternative, he devised an idiom making large use of pre-Miltonic words (after the model of Old English, Trench, and Barnes). "Doughty's English" is the subject of a Society for Pure English Tract (no. 51, 1939). Bridges admired Doughty's work; Hopkins, who did not, but who knew it only in excerpts, took the view that all archaism is an affectation and hence bad.

WILLIAM IRVINE

Carlyle and T. H. Huxley

Kicked into the world a boy without guide or training, or with worse than none, I confess to my shame that few men have drunk deeper of all kinds of sin than I. Happily, my course was arrested in time . . . and for long years I have been slowly and painfully climbing . . . towards better things. And when I look back, what do I find to have been the agents of my redemption? The hope of immortality or of future reward? I can honestly say that for these fourteen years such a consideration has not entered my head. No, I can tell you exactly what has been at work. *Sartor Resartus* led me to know that a deep sense of religion was compatible with the entire absence of theology. Secondly, science and her methods gave me a resting-place independent of authority and tradition. Thirdly, love opened up to me a view of the sanctity of human nature, and impressed me with a deep sense of responsibility.[1]

HUXLEY wrote these words on September 23, 1860. His four-year-old son, then an only child, had died but a few days before. The tragedy had occasioned an epistolary exchange of peculiar significance, for the bereaved father was already a notorious "agnostic" and his correspondent was the churchman Charles Kingsley, who, though a complete stranger, had with characteristic courage written a letter of sympathy. Huxley's reply is at once a personal confession and a statement of faith. As he was a man of much less than average turpitude, the confession is not to be taken very seriously. It is probably the attempt of a deeply moral nature, frantic with grief, to explain his loss according to some sort of moral justice. The statement of faith which closes

From *Booker Memorial Studies: Eight Essays on Victorian Literature in Memory of John Manning Booker, 1881-1948*, edited by Hill Shine (Chapel Hill: The University of North Carolina Press, 1950), pp. 104-121. Reprinted by permission of the publisher and the author.

the paragraph is interesting chiefly because of the basic importance assigned to the influence of Carlyle.

Perhaps too little has been made of Huxley's loss of faith. Certainly, the warfare between Huxley and religion was essentially fratricidal. By temperament and destiny he was a cleric who began as a partial non-conformist and ended as very nearly a complete one. By nature he was a superb teacher who deeply reverenced his profession in youth and in maturity exercised it from nearly every platform but the pulpit. As a child he admired Sir Herbert Oakley, the local rector. Once—if the event is of any significance—he turned his pinafore around backwards to represent a surplice, and delivered a sermon in the manner of his hero to the maids in the kitchen.[2] A few years later, listening to another clergyman, he heard "dark allusions to 'sceptics' and 'infidels,'" and "from the horror of the tone in which they were mentioned," wondered whether they "belonged to the criminal classes."[3] Soon afterwards he began that course of amazingly rapid desultory reading, which, growing always more intensive and systematic and continuing throughout life, made him one of the most learned, and the least Anglican, of Victorians. He had a boy's eye for big titles, from Hutton's *Theory of the Earth* to Sir William Hamilton's "Philosophy of the Unconditioned"; nor was his eye bigger than his stomach. And as knowledge increased, reverence dwindled. He noticed that village parsons frequently used bad grammar, and used it to little purpose, except to reveal ignorance and prejudice. It was Hamilton's article, which he found in an old volume of *The Edinburgh*,[4] that finally explained everything, and released him from any further need to take parsons seriously. Sir William ponderously undermines all conditioned and finite knowledge in order to establish the Scottish Kirk in the transcendental sublimity of the unconditioned. Huxley abandoned the Kirk, but embraced the scepticism. At the age of fifteen he found, probably with some complacency, that he had developed the opinions of the criminal classes.

But if he felt very clever, he must also have felt rather lonely in those opinions. It is not easy to be sceptical when most people believe. Moreover, he was not, like so many nowadays, comfortably accustomed to a universe locked up in transience and death. As a child he had known a Creation with a window looking up to a Creator and a door opening out on immortality. He could not have seen the door and the window closed without some bitterness and fear. He never suggests that agnosticism is a cheerful creed, and he refers with some contempt to clergymen who help themselves over the problem of life with the sleeping pill, or "anesthetic," of a conventional faith.[5] As late as 1847, in the first year of his long cruise in the *Rattlesnake*, he wrote:

"Ich kann nichts anders! Gott hilfe mir!" Morals and religion are one wild whirl to me—of them the less said the better. In the region of the intellect alone can I find free and innocent play for such faculties as I possess. And it is well for me that my way of life allows me to get rid of the "malady of thought" in a course of action so suitable to my tastes, as that laid open to me by this voyage.

And in 1849 he adds, beside the same entry: "Is it better with me now? A little." [6]

This passage suggests that he took comfort in Carlyle's doctrine of work. In any case, what prevented his religious problem from ever coming to an acute crisis was probably devotion to Carlyle, who was the chief hero of his youthful reading. Unfortunately, his statements of indebtedness are nearly as vague as they are emphatic. He gives evidence of having read *Sartor Resartus, Past and Present,* the *Latter-Day Pamphlets,* and "Characteristics," as well as others of the *Critical and Miscellaneous Essays.* One gathers that he gained from Carlyle sympathy for the poor, a hatred of shams, devotion to work, the impetus to study German language and literature, and—as the letter to Kingsley acknowledges—a deep sense of religion divorced from theology.[7] In spite of the evidence, one may well ask, what could a cool, clear-headed rationalist like Huxley see in a hot, steamy-headed moralist like Carlyle? The answer is that Huxley was not always so cool and clear-headed as he seemed; that when he read Carlyle he was very young, with some of a young man's romanticism; and that he was also Victorian, with all a Victorian's earnestness.

Carlyle's vast contemporary fame depended on the moral and literary grandeur with which he invested ambiguous answers to contemporary dilemmas. Of the religious dilemma Huxley had been painfully aware, and probably very much in Carlyle's terms. For if he found virtue in Carlyle's cure, he must have suffered from Carlyle's disease. If he embraced Carlyle's stentorian moralism, half naturalistic, half Calvinistic, so fervently that its effects are traceable in his whole later career, he must at one time or another have received dark intimations of the "Everlasting No." Again, he had marked literary sensitivity. If his hero could not provide logical answers, at least he provided poetical ones. Finally, Huxley was the kind of man who, if he did not need theological certainty, undoubtedly craved ethical direction and significance in his life. He had a moralist's conscientiousness without a moralist's gift for introspection. He either dreaded or did not care or was unable to look inward. For such a man, Carlyle's crude apotheosis of action, with its convenient sacrifice of ultimate and interior knowledge to efficiency and service, must have seemed at once a justification and the answer to a spiritual need.

What the two men had in common was, fundamentally, the search for truth; and since the older man's achievement was in large degree the younger man's inspiration, it might be well to recall Carlyle's own early development. Like Huxley, he passed from orthodoxy to scepticism. Logic, matter, and David Hume made him an infidel. To a mind like Carlyle's doubt was loathsome, not simply because he infinitely preferred a live universe to a dead one and an heroic one to a mechanical, but because he preferred strength to weakness.[8] He felt that he was a prophet able to instruct mankind. Doubt meant division, humiliation, paralysis. Or, more accurately, the tragedy was intensely personal. Having dramatically proclaimed in the person of Teufelsdröckh that he would die for cosmic truth, Carlyle shifts almost at once to "Alas! the fearful Unbelief is unbelief in yourself."[9] Not to know God was not to have an intelligible theater in which to develop one's potentialities. It is not surprising that he invented a universe to set off his own talents, fashioning it in the image of his ambitions, tastes, tradition, and—one is tempted to say—his indigestion. The subjectivity of the German idealists provided him with an instrument and a framework. He decided that matter was "but an air-image," "the reflex of our own inward Force";[10] and logic, which he now hated as a disease, but the instrument of the understanding, of a lower, earthly kind of reason. The higher reason was intuition, direct insight into the mind of God through the transparent "air-images" which were the world of man and nature. His treatment of this faculty is confused. Sometimes his intuition is ethical and Calvinistic, exalting moral law in God and man, and enjoining reverence and obedience. Sometimes it is romantic and expansive, exalting force and dynamic spontaneity, and enjoining the virtues of wonder and intensity. Yet whatever it is, Carlyle's intuition is always aesthetic and in a curious pragmatic way realistic. Since every fact is fundamentally symbolic, its meaning depends on an effort of the individual imagination and its validity on passionate expression or effectual action. Since the whole world is fundamentally symbolic, its precise, literal meaning becomes less important; so that, as potential knowledge, it is only secondarily a museum for investigation and primarily a battle ground of imaginative subjectivities, where poetry proposes and will disposes. History is the unfolding of divine ideas in the lives of great men, of which there are two kinds—poets who persuade and strong men who act. They are the intermediaries between dream and reality, thought and deed. Truth is not so much discovered, as conceived and made. It is poetry that prevails in practical life. In the long run, it is what vividly survives, as action or idea, in the vast competition which is history.

These ideas seem very far from the smooth agnosticism of Huxley, in whom matter, logic, and David Hume eventually did their worst.[11] And yet the difference between Hume and Huxley might, in large degree, be summed up as the influence of Carlyle.

As a boy in his 'teens, Huxley seems to have accepted such works as "Characteristics" and *Sartor Resartus* with little reservation. Negatively, they confirmed him in his agnosticism, leading him to reject revelation and all divine metaphysics in the old dogmatic sense.[12] Positively, they provided him with a belief which probably softened the impact of scepticism and taught him that "a deep sense of religion was compatible with the entire absence of theology." What this sense of religion involves one may guess from his enthusiasm for the German essays, among which the "Novalis" contains a lengthy discussion of Kantian and post-Kantian idealism. A quotation from "Characteristics," copied down in his journal at the age of seventeen, betrays him even into a minor heresy against science: "The healthy understanding, we should say, is neither the argumentative nor the Logical, but the Intuitive, for the end of the understanding is not to prove and find reasons but to know and believe." [13]

Probably Carlyle also awakened the young man's literary sense. One is tempted to ask why he did no more, why he did not turn so fine a literary talent permanently to literature. As a matter of fact, he did not even stimulate it to temporary action. For Huxley, writing was always an instrument. It meant the art of clarity, the art of controversy, which, particularly in later years, he cultivated as a virtuoso, but always for the purposes of the scientist and the social critic. Literature in the narrow sense could hardly have claimed him, partly because he was too practical and utilitarian to care for mere art and partly because he was not sufficiently interested in its characteristic subject matter, which is man as such. He could become absorbed in man as a physical mechanism, as an anthropoid ape, as a citizen and social animal, as a delicate machine for the discovery of scientific truth; but not in man as a personality and a human being. With all his splendid talents for friendship and affection, he remained, from the deeper psychological point of view, indifferent to people. In fact, as I have indicated, he was not even interested in himself. Seldom has so vivid and articulate a writer had so little of importance to say, even in his most intimate letters, about himself.

A few months after foreswearing logic and evidence in the idiom of "Characteristics," Huxley embraced them with a fanaticism that increased with increasing years. He was converted to science by the eminent anatomist and physiologist Wharton Jones, under whose influence he came in his first term as a medical student at Charing Cross Hospital. From Jones he learned exact, painstaking scientific method in the search for truth. His sense of discipline had found its most typical expression.

Huxley, like Carlyle, had an imperative personal need for certainty, for in him the will to achieve and dominate was perhaps equally strong, though less self-conscious and dramatic. He was also magnificently endowed for the life of action. Swiftness and clarity of thought, as he himself observes,[14] were the essential qualities of his mind; and he had all the coolness, the sureness, and the self-confidence which accompany them. He was always mobilized for action. He never hesitated, was never less than himself. He was a rapid and voluminous reader, a ready and eloquent speaker, a facile and brilliant writer. In short, he possessed the obvious virtues in nearly as much splendor as Macaulay. Sir Mountstuart Grant Duff correctly remarked that he might have been one of the most successful politicians of his age [15]— and perhaps he was. But like all strong men conscious of their strength and eager to exert it, he needed a rock, "a resting place," [16] from which to spring. This he found in science.

Both Carlyle and Huxley had begun by recognizing the difference between final and contingent knowledge. Both had set up truth as the key to life, but whereas Carlyle's truth was poetic and pragmatic, Huxley's was scientific and verifiable. They emphasized alternate instruments of the Kantian system. Carlyle chose *Vernunft*, and regarded the world as a luminous symbol of Eternity. Huxley chose *Verstand*, and regarded the world as likely to be very solid and opaque. Carlyle attempted to discredit the understanding by emphasizing its limitations.[17] Huxley rested in those limitations with a truly heroic firmness. He attained his heaven by denying it.

And in this denial there is a Puritan rigor which must have been encouraged by the reading of Carlyle. He turned science and the agnosticism which is its philosophical equivalent into a principle of self-abnegation, extracting from the very sternness of scientific method and the very nullity of scientific pretensions to spiritual knowledge, a measure of spiritual consolation. As an agnostic he professed no opinions on ultimate questions. Nevertheless, he was inclined to disbelieve in immortality because it was an idea flattering to human wishes.[18] Particularly when pressed in controversy, he willingly enlarged on the uncertainty of knowledge. The laws of nature might suddenly be abrogated, or nature itself, as we know it through the senses, might be a phantasm, having no relation to any genuine reality. In his scientific work, whether of teaching or research, he was a fanatic of method, submitting not only his own results but even the hallowed platitudes of textbooks to careful testing.[19] For him, science embodied a Calvinistic imperative. Had Carlyle been a scientist, he would probably have been such a scientist as Huxley.

Apparently Huxley felt that science exerts spiritual force in three ways, all more or less related: it imposes a discipline of accuracy and fairmindedness; it provides a knowledge of nature; and it frees the mind from prejudice and superstition. He nowhere asserts that intellectual discipline naturally becomes moral discipline, but he does say that science is truth-telling and that truth-telling is the basis of all the virtues.[20] Science is not only organized common sense but organized honesty. Does not its immense success offer the spectacle of a poetic justice which may eventually regenerate mankind? But with all his confidence in science as discipline, Huxley seems to have expected more from an increased knowledge of nature. "Learn what is true," he wrote of such knowledge, "in order to do what is right."[21] To know nature is probably an aid to virtue, but to know man and society is certainly a much greater aid. This introduces the question of what Huxley meant by *nature*.

Late in life a careful reading of Rousseau showed him the dangers of deducing an ethical system from the natural order. In such essays as "Natural and Political Rights" (1890) and "Evolution and Ethics" (1893) he makes a clear distinction between nature and human society, the law for brute and the law for man. Up until 1890, however, he regarded man simply as a part of nature, into which, under the influence of Carlyle and probably of Wordsworth, he read important moral and aesthetic values. If nature is beautiful, obviously it is an ennoblement of the mind, and therefore a moral help, to study her. If she is moral, she becomes, quite simply, a peculiarly long and complicated treatise on morals. To study her is to become learned in virtue.

So far as Huxley's own career is concerned, the beauty of nature must have been an inspiration not only to good conduct but to scientific study. Books like *Sartor Resartus*, merely as nature poetry, must have given an aesthetic impetus to the biological investigations pursued on the *Rattlesnake* and to the geological observations carried on with Tyndall in the Alps. But books like *Sartor* and *Past and Present* were probably even more influential in determining his ideas about nature as a moral and spiritual entity. In many respects, his attitude closely parallels that of Carlyle. There is the same tendency to see God in nature, the same tendency to merge ethical and natural law. In the famous letter to Kingsley, for example, he refers in so many words to the "Divine Government" as embodied in nature and the system of things, and declares that it is "wholly just." "As we live we are paid for living." [22] But perhaps what is written in the extremity of grief should not be taken too exactly. The great bulk of Huxley's writings indicates that he was not a theist. It also indicates, however, that, with all his scrupulous detachment, he was not sufficiently self-critical to be altogether consistent. He steadily maintained that, whereas religion was anthropomorphic, science was entirely impersonal; yet high and solid as he built the walls of his impersonality, he was constantly smuggling God into his citadel in a metaphor. For example, the famous metaphor of the hidden chess player concludes:

> The chess-board is the world, the pieces are the phenomena of the universe, the rules of the game are what we call the laws of Nature. The player on the other side is hidden from us. We know that his play is always fair, just and patient. But also we know, to our cost, that he never overlooks a mistake, or makes the smallest allowance for ignorance. To the man who plays well, the highest stakes are paid, with that sort of overflowing generosity with which the strong shows delight in strength. And one who plays ill is checkmated—without haste, but without remorse. [23]

Here science is very close to anthropomorphism. The passage is not easy to interpret, but the general sense seems to be that if you know the laws of nature and play the game well and strongly, you will obtain justice. To the soured modern reader this may seem nothing but a very sweet, Victorian way of saying that in nature the law of strength and cunning prevails. I am inclined to think, however, that Huxley did not know quite what he meant. In the poetic overtones of the passage there is a distinct suggestion that justice inheres in the physical order. Huxley's words are strikingly similar to those describing nature as a sphinx in *Past and Present*. [24]

Almost as much quoted, and perhaps even more interesting, is another pronouncement on nature from the Kingsley letter:

Sit down before fact as a little child, be prepared to give up every preconceived notion, follow humbly wherever and to whatever abysses nature may lead, or you shall learn nothing. I have only begun to find content and peace of mind since I have resolved at all risks to do this.[25]

But to sit down before fact as a little child, with humility, trust, and reverence, is perhaps to read something into fact. It is to sense the infinite in the finite, the boundless mystery in the little flower in the crannied wall. Apparently, matter does not need to be dialectically exorcised to become transparent. Here Huxley's facts threaten to become as insubstantial and infinitely suggestive as Carlyle's symbols. The passage expresses spiritual detachment, but not quite scientific impersonality. Its implications are not necessarily anthropomorphic, but they tend to be spiritual and other-worldly. Here Huxley apprehends fact with *Vernunft* as well as *Verstand*.

And yet he steadily refused to see the consequences of his attitude. Why? The question takes us back to the Victorian dilemma, which was critical for both Huxley and Carlyle. A brave new world of thought and action was rapidly unfolding which, as it revealed more and more glittering possibilities, came into even more drastic contradiction with traditional ethics and religion. The new world had no ultimate spiritual rationale. The old ethics and religion had no practical content. Most Victorians solved the problem by keeping very busy and allowing contradictions to creep back into the dictionary. Carlyle elaborated this procedure into a moral doctrine: "Work, and a real intelligible universe will grow up around you." While Carlyle's doctrine of work was undoubtedly an inspiration to Huxley, inevitably it meant somewhat different things to men so different.

It might (rather extravagantly) be argued that the greatest influences on Carlyle were Hume and Gibbon: they contributed so much to make him what they were not. Certainly their neat logical scepticism was the focus which projected the contradictions of the age into his mind with a persistent, gnawing sharpness, producing at length a general inward conflict in which intellectual vanity was at war with worldly ambition, personal integrity with duty to parents, logic with common sense, and reason with spiritual inclination.[26] It is no wonder that thereafter logic gave him indigestion and self-inquiry seemed to him a disease. His doctrine of work suffers the consequences. It is at once the most imposing and heroic formulation of the Victorian faith in process, and a curious conglomerate of Scottish peasant industriousness, utilitarian optimism, artistic self-consciousness, romantic rainbow-questing, and Christian meditation without inwardness. It declares all labor sacred with little regard to kind or to the end envisaged. On the analogy of the potter's wheel, it asserts that movement creates its own adequate stability and control, that environment and especially the laws of nature provide a sufficient moral discipline. It proclaims a faith in man's future without offering any coherent theory either of man or the future. Here it is closely related to the ambiguities in Carlyle's picture of history, which suggests a cyclical morality drama in which God, while inculcating the broad, rough principles of justice, strains rather self-consciously for artistic effect. All that partakes of the infinite is divine. As historical symbols are divine in their infinite, indefinite suggestiveness, so all human effort is divine in its infinite possibility. The splendid picture of Columbus sailing into the vastness of the western ocean appropriately culminates Carlyle's most elaborate treatment of the subject of labor.[27] At its best, his doctrine represents great moral courage with great moral blindness. At its worst, it suggests a reluctance to define for fear the definition may not be titanic enough.

Other than to acknowledge indebtedness to Carlyle, Huxley nowhere attempts any formulation of his ideas on this subject, yet his faith in process, in activity as such, is striking. As a personal resource, work was for him, as for Carlyle, a means of gratifying ambition, satisfying a sense of duty, and escaping from inward contradictions. As a doctrine, it represents one thing—faith in the future of science. To work at science was to work for the certainty of almost unlimited human knowledge and power.[28] By discovering the laws of social organization, science will answer the questions of Carlyle's sphinx and eventually solve the problem of poverty itself.[29] By revealing the laws of nature and by thus enabling man to place himself, in Carlyle's sense, more closely under natural discipline, it will improve human virtue and make moral progress a reality. By pursuing matter to its ultimate intricacies in the nerve cells of the human brain, it will probably unlock the mysteries of spirit and throw light on the great problems of epistemology.[30] Though admitting there is no proof that matter is the key to reality, Huxley is a devoted materialist. His materialism is part of his optimism, even of his idealism. If matter is real, then indeed miracles become not impossible, but probable and almost certain.

Science will also continue to destroy sham, prejudice, superstition, and hypocrisy, achieving truth by the elimination of error. Acting on this conviction, Huxley entered on the Scriptural controversies which earned him his own epithet of *episcopophagus* and brought him his most characteristic fame. In the one explicit reference to Carlyle's emphasis on work, he says:

> There is nothing of permanent value . . . , nothing that satisfies quiet reflection—except the sense of having worked according to one's capacity and light, to make things clear and get rid of cant and shams of all sorts. That was the lesson I learned from Carlyle's books when I was a boy, and it has stuck by me all my life.[31]

Carlyle's hatred of shams was not only puritan but romantic and primitivistic. They represented artificiality as opposed to nature, mechanism as opposed to spontaneity, shallow self-consciousness as opposed to the creative profundities of the unconscious. Moreover, mechanical pretense inhibits the natural flow of creative reality. According to Carlyle's cyclical conception of history, the shams of a decadent age must be cleared away before the vitalism of a constructive one can assert itself.[32] Hence the usefulness of Humes and Voltaires, otherwise so contemptible:

> Of our Modern Metaphysics, accordingly, may not this already be said, that if they have produced no Affirmation, they have destroyed much Negation? It is a disease expelling a disease: the fire of Doubt, as above hinted, consuming away the Doubtful; that so the Certain come to light, and again lie visible on the surface.[33]

The moral inspiration of Carlyle encouraged Huxley to continue the destructive work of Voltaire. He was not actuated by a cyclical or romantic theory of history. Rather, his negative attitude toward religion proceeded in large degree from the nature of his position. As the champion of science he was necessarily the hostile critic of revelation. He had to attack the Pentateuch because it contradicted the discoveries of Lyell and Darwin. He had to wage war on demons and miracles because they contradicted the principle of the uniformity of nature, on which all science is founded. He discomfited bishops and archdeacons because their mode of argument was often hypocritical and unscientific. Yet his interests went beyond the mere exploding of superstition and prejudice. Thanking Edward Clodd for his *Jesus of Nazareth*, he wrote in 1879:

> In spirit, matter, and form it appears to me to be exactly what people like myself have been wanting. For though for the last quarter of a century I have done all that lay in my power to oppose and destroy the idolatrous accretions of Judaism and Christianity, I have never had the

slightest sympathy for those who, as the Germans say, would "throw the child away with the bath"—and when I was a member of the London School Board I fought for the retention of the Bible, to the great scandal of some of my Liberal friends.[34]

What Huxley wanted to preserve was the best moral teaching of the Bible. In his "Evolution of Theology," [35] he explores the field of comparative religion at some length to show that the higher the religion, the more ethics and the less dogma and ceremony.

But when every allowance has been made for the nature of his position and the breadth of his sympathies, it must be confessed that much of his writing, particularly on religion, is negative and critical in emphasis. Through many years of brilliant warfare against Noah's Ark and the Gadarene swine, he never once attempts to define either Jesus's teaching or its relation to modern life. Behind his scriptural controversies, as behind John Stuart Mill's defense of free speech in *Liberty*, lies the conception, which utilitarian argument so often implies yet so seldom expresses, that in the competition among opinions truth survives as an accumulating residue. "The struggle for existence," wrote Huxley of *The Origin of Species* after defending it triumphantly for twenty-one years, "holds as much in the intellectual as in the physical world. A theory is a species of thinking, and its right to exist is coextensive with its power of resisting extinction by its rivals." [36] Carlyle's "fire of Doubt . . . consuming away the Doubtful; that so the Certain come to light" is very close to this idea, for it is obviously part of the broader idea, applied in so many fields of nineteenth-century thought, that competition produces excellence.

And so Huxley labored mightily at pumping off the gases of religious error in order that religious truth might eventually become visible as a tiny speck of near-certainty in a great vacuum of opinion. His justification was Carlyle's, minus the cyclical theory of history: He was preparing the ground for sounder beliefs—presumably for a religion with scientific ethics and no theology. Such a prospect is perfectly legitimate, except that Huxley pays too little attention to it. Sometimes he seems simply too much exhilarated by the pleasant excitement of window-smashing to think much about what to do with the empty spaces. Sometimes he seems positively unwilling to think about them. The Comtists, for example, who attempted to construct a scientific religion, draw some of his most deadly fire; and while no doubt they deserved it, still his sharpness is significant. Here again, Huxley is open to the accusation of believing rather blindly in process, of postponing his problems to the future. Basically, his fault—and that of many other Victorians, including Carlyle—is a reluctance to define. Carlyle was sufficiently constructive, but he avoided the final responsibilities of construction by an ambiguous use of words, particularly such words as *nature* and *intuition*. Huxley took refuge not only in ambiguities, but in the bright, reassuring clarity of negative criticism. As an agnostic he was prepared to define the magnitude of his ultimate ignorance, but not, as a moralist, to define any minimum of ultimate knowledge.

> Few men [wrote Huxley shortly after Carlyle's death in 1881] can have dissented more strongly from his way of looking at things than I; but I should not yield to the most devoted of his followers in gratitude for the bracing wholesome influence of his writings when, as a very young man, I was essaying without rudder or compass to strike out a course for myself.[37]

In other words, Carlyle, though a moulding force upon Huxley's youth, was a diminishing one upon his maturer career. We must therefore not expect any close relationship between the ideas of these two men on educational, political, and social theory, with which Huxley was largely occupied in later years. Carlyle regarded society as an organism ruled by imagination, which expresses itself in various kinds of hero worship. Huxley regarded society as a body of individuals historically united by an implicit social contract and ruled ultimately by reason and expediency, which are ideally embodied in science. Nevertheless, early influences are persistent, and though he differed radically on fundamentals, Huxley may have owed certain broad convictions and tendencies, at least in part, to his early reading of Carlyle. These are, on the one hand, distrust of laissez-faire and of extreme democracy;[38] and, on the other, belief in the importance of genius[39] and of moral education.

Had he never read Carlyle, Huxley would probably have been less confused, less poetic, and considerably more utilitarian. What Carlyle chiefly contributed was not ideas but temperament. He developed the Victorian in Huxley. And in the Victorian age what could have been more important? He strengthened the moral fervor and the sense of discipline which gave to Huxley's strenuous advocacy of science an invaluable respectability at a time when science was confronted with the serried ranks of righteousness. Carlyle did not greatly change Huxley's mind, but he probably made it more influential.

NOTES

1. Leonard Huxley, *Life and Letters of Thomas Henry Huxley* (New York, 1900), I, 237.

2. Thomas Henry Huxley, "Autobiography," *Methods and Results* (New York, 1896), p. 5.

3. Thomas Henry Huxley, "Prologue," *Science and Christian Tradition* (New York, 1896), p. 21.

4. A review of M. V. Cousin's *Cours de Philosophie*, L (1829), 194–221.

5. "The Evolution of Theology: An Anthropological Study," *Science and Hebrew Tradition* (New York, 1897), p. 287.

6. Julian Huxley, ed., *T. H. Huxley's Diary of the Voyage of H.M.S. Rattlesnake* (London, 1935), p. 38.

7. L. Huxley, *Life and Letters*, I, 9, 10, 16, 237; II, 285; Leonard Huxley, "Carlyle and Huxley: Early Influences," *The Cornhill Magazine*, LXXI (1932), 290–302.

8. *Sartor Resartus, Carlyle's Works*, Edition de Luxe (Boston, 1884), I, 125. When a volume number is given after a Carlyle title, it will be understood that this edition is referred to.

9. *Ibid.*, I, 126.

10. *Ibid.*, I, 42.

11. See Huxley's *Hume, With Helps to the Study of Berkeley* (New York, 1897).

12. "Characteristics," XIV, 365–69; *Sartor Resartus*, I, 146–47.

13. L. Huxley, *Life and Letters*, I, 14.

14. "Autobiography," *Methods and Results*, p. 4.

15. L. Huxley, *Life and Letters*, I, 381.

16. See the quotation that opens this article.

17. *Sartor Resartus*, I, 28, 40–42, 193–95.

18. John Fiske, "Reminiscences of Huxley," *Annual Report of the Board of Regents of the Smithsonian Institution*, 1900, p. 720.

19. L. Huxley, *Life and Letters*, I, 254–55.

20. Leonard Huxley, "Home Memories," *Nature*, CXV (1925), 699.

21. William K. Brooks, *Annual Report of the Board of Regents of the Smithsonian Institution*, 1900, p. 705.

22. L. Huxley, *Life and Letters*, I, 236. See also T. H. Huxley, *Scientific Memoirs*, Michael Foster and E. Ray Lankester, eds. (London, 1891), I, 307, 311.

23. "A Liberal Education; and Where to Find It," *Science and Education* (New York, 1897), p. 82.

24. *Past and Present*, XII, 8–9.

25. L. Huxley, *Life and Letters*, I, 235.

26. David A. Wilson, *Carlyle Till Marriage* (London, 1923), pp. 78–79, 109–11, 145–49, 248–52.

27. "Labour" in *Past and Present*.

28. "Six Lectures to Working Men 'On Our Knowledge of the Causes of the Phenomena of Organic Nature,'" *Darwiniana*, pp. 359–60.

29. "Evolution and Ethics," *Evolution and Ethics* (New York, 1896), p. 218.

30. "Prologue," *Science and Christian Tradition*, pp. 46-47.

31. Letter to W. Platt Ball, Oct. 27, 1890, in L. Huxley, *Life and Letters*, II, 285.

32. Hill Shine, *Carlyle and the Saint-Simonians: The Concept of Historical Periodicity* (Baltimore, 1941), pp. 2, 19, 24, 25, 30-33 ff.

33. "Characteristics," XIV, 381.

34. L. Huxley, *Life and Letters*, II, 9.

35. *Science and Hebrew Tradition*, pp. 287-372.

36. "The Coming of Age of 'The Origin of Species,'" *Darwiniana* (N.Y.: D. Appleton, 1897), p. 229.

37. Letter to Lord Stanley of Alderly, in L. Huxley, *Life and Letters*, II, 36-37.

38. See "Administrative Nihilism," *Methods and Results*, pp. 251-89.

39. *Ibid.*, p. 256.

A. L. ROWSE

———◆———

Macaulay's *Essays*

Not the least among the number of remarkable books whose publication distinguished the year 1843 was Macaulay's *Essays*. We owe their appearance at that time to the Americans. Macaulay had previously considered publishing his reviews in book form and turned the idea down. For all his cocksure certainty he was a modest man. He did not think so highly of his essays as the public did. "The public judges, and ought to judge, indulgently of periodical works," he wrote to the editor of the *Edinburgh Review*. "They are not expected to be highly finished. Their natural life is only six weeks." But his hand was forced in the matter. When, not content with collecting and publishing his reviews (without permission or remuneration) in the United States, American publishers sent over copies in their hundreds to this country, Macaulay was forced to act. We have reason to be grateful. So far from being confined to a natural life of only six weeks, the *Essays* have survived a hundred years. Few works have been so severely criticised, or shown to have more serious errors; and yet there is no doubt that they will go gaily on to their second century. To what do they owe their survival?

First and last, they owe it to their immense readability. The inscription upon Macaulay's statue in the ante-chapel of Trinity at Cambridge, which says that he was the first to write annals in such a way that the truth was more readable than fiction, has an element of exaggeration in it, when you think of Gibbon and Hume before him, not to mention Tacitus. But all the same it lays hold of the essential fact about Macaulay: he is the most readable of historians.

From *The English Spirit: Essays in History and Literature* (New York: The Macmillan Company, 1946), pp. 228–32. Reprinted by permission of Macmillan & Co. Ltd. (London) and the author.

The difficulty with him is not, as with some others (the uncongenial Freeman, for example), to take him up, but to put him down: the eye races through those exciting, easy pages, fearful lest the chapter or the essay come to an end too soon. And the *Essays,* though not up to the standard Macaulay reached in the *History,* reveal this particular quality at its highest.

Whatever we may think of his point of view, and however much we must take exception to what he says, there is no doubt about the pleasure he has given now to generations and will continue to give. Sir G. O. Trevelyan says that the demand for Macaulay varies with the demand for coal. It is a pleasant nineteenth-century thought. But I can imagine no more cheerful and stimulating companion for winter evenings in war-time, in conditions of the black-out. As Macaulay himself says of the pleasures of reading: "Plato is never sullen. Dante does not stay too long."

And the *Essays* are incomparable for young people who are just beginning to take an interest in things of the mind. How many people owe their first intellectual stimulus to the *Essays!* (The appreciation of the *History,* a maturer work, comes later.) Arthur Balfour, in his *Autobiography,* has expressed the obligation of those hundreds of people, with minds worth speaking of, for whom the *Essays* opened a door to higher things. One can see why this should be: for all that Macaulay was a man of affairs, and even a man of the world, there was something curiously unadult, ungrown-up about him. After Dickens the most famous writer of his day, he remained something of a boy to the end of his life. (Some people—it is obvious that Strachey was one of them—have the impression that we do not know all there is to be known about Macaulay.)

What, then, are the qualities which make the *Essays* such a prodigious success?

They have a power of holding the attention in a most extraordinary way. And this arises from the fact that their style is essentially conversational—but the conversation is dramatic, declamatory, exciting. In fact the *Essays* are debates. Macaulay in his usual generous way gave Southey the credit for first hitting upon this form of historical essay; he merely said that he had improved upon it. But what life and vivacity Macaulay gave to it! You can hear the voice, the torrent of that astonishing conversation, which made some people protest (cf. Greville's *Memoirs*), though, like Greville, they usually ended by submitting, fascinated, conquered by him. Again and again one has the sensation of listening to a wonderful discussion among that brilliant circle of young men at Cambridge, or to the famous talk at Holland House. There is all the dramatic excitement of opposing ideas being argued out. There are the intellectual high spirits on every page—always an irresistible quality. There is plenty of good knock-about fun. One cannot but enjoy his attack on Montgomery's *Poems*—would there were someone with a pen like his to deal with the Montgomerys of our day!—or his onslaught upon the intolerable pro-lixity of Professor Nares:

> The work of Dr. Nares has filled us with astonishment similar to that which Captain Lemuel Gulliver felt when first he landed in Brob-dingnag, and saw corn as high as the oaks in the New Forest, thimbles as large as buckets, and wrens of the bulk of turkeys. The whole book, and every component part of it, is on a gigantic scale. The title is as long as an ordinary preface: the prefatory matter would furnish out an ordinary book; and the book contains as much reading as an ordinary library. We cannot sum up the merits of the stupendous mass of paper which lies before us better than by saying it consists of about two thousand closely printed quarto pages, that it occupies fifteen hundred inches cubic measure, and that it weighs sixty pounds avoirdupois. Such a book might, before the Deluge, have been considered as light reading by Hilpa and Shallum. But unhappily the life of man is now three-score years and ten; and we cannot but think it somewhat unfair of Dr. Nares to demand from us so large a portion of so short an existence.

And so on.

I used to think that this might be somewhat unfair on poor Dr. Nares; but having tried to read his book, I now sympathise with Macaulay.

Besides high spirits, ceaseless vivacity, great sense of phrase, a vivid historical imagination, clear-cut and accurate, something more is needed to explain his success as a writer. On the technical side the clue is to be found in his admirable, his infallible power of construc-tion. Whatever it may be, whether argument, or scene, or narrative, he carries the reader irresistibly along with him. Other factors help to explain his almost unexampled success with the public in his own time. He was a deeply conventional man, a Philistine of genius; his work appealed to, was the very expression of, the conventionalism, the Philistinism of the Victorian age. He was a moralist of a rather crude kind; he spoke straight to the heart of a society which, almost inex-plicably to us, saw everything in crudely moral terms. To him, as to them, everything was either black or it was white. And so we get the fatiguing antitheses in which he saw, altogether too simply, the characters of Warren Hastings, Clive, Marlborough, Bacon, Dr. Johnson, Horace Walpole. Whatever we may think of it as history, there is no doubt that it makes for good reading.

Macaulay's defects were the defects of his qualities. He was very square-cut, definite, downright. Altogether too much so. He had much of the positiveness of the eighteenth century about him. His taste was formed on Addison, that proto-Victorian, and the writers of the age of Queen Anne. This meant a great limitation of sympathies —though, even then, those were broader than many of his latter-day critics realise. It was Macaulay, somewhat surprisingly, who said: "We know no spectacle so ridiculous as the British public in one of its periodical fits of morality." (If it had not been for that magisterial "we," it might have been Matthew Arnold speaking.) His essay on the Restoration dramatists shows him a good deal less sympathetic to Puritanism than might have been feared from the son of Zachary Macaulay, brought up in the strictest circle of the Clapham sect, the darling child of Hannah More.

The pity is that Macaulay had such power, such unique vividness, that when he was wrong, as he often was, he has impressed his own version upon the English mind more firmly than the truth. His treatment of Warren Hastings and Marlborough are outstanding cases in point. One might almost say that his misrepresentation of Hastings was responsible for the Indian attitude towards the history of our rule in India. What people other than the English would have been so careless of their own case, so unjust to themselves, as to prescribe the reading of Macaulay's essay on Warren Hastings in their schools and universities? The English have a singular faculty for depreciating their great men. (Is it perhaps a form of superiority-complex?) Most people must still be under the impression that Marlborough, though a great soldier, was a bad hat. That is the view that Macaulay has fixed upon us. It is quite untrue that he was a bad man: he was a cold, wonderfully controlled man; but in addition to his genius, he was not without a heart. The Prime Minister's life of his ancestor has disproved Macaulay once and for all.

Nevertheless, the exaggeratedly high standards which Macaulay stood for were an important element in forming the Victorian outlook. Though the Victorians kidded themselves a lot, they were genuinely high-minded; which we are not—and we lose something by it.

It is interesting to note Macaulay's own modest estimate of his *Essays*:

In spite of the applause and the profit, neither of which I despise, I am sorry that it had become necessary to republish these papers. There are few of them which I read with satisfaction. Those few, however, are generally the latest, and this is a consolatory circumstance. The most hostile critic must admit, I think, that I have improved greatly as a writer. The third volume seems to me worth two of the second, and the second worth ten of the first.

That gives a very useful little clue to the correct estimation of the *Essays*. What is needed is a dependable guide to them for the use of the unwary.

WALTER F. WRIGHT

Richard Feverel's Tragic Ordeal

> You burly lovers on the village green,
> Yours is a lower, and a happier star!
> (*Modern Love*)

WHEN Meredith began *The Ordeal of Richard Feverel*, he had behind him *The Shaving of Shagpat* and *Farina* and the 1851 edition of *Love in the Valley*, all three rarefied distillations of life in the manner of allegory and pastoral. The characters and the incidents were derived from reality and were translatable again into actual life, but they were clothed in the metaphor of poetic romance. He was now concerned to give his fiction a local habitation, to show human passion at play in nineteenth-century English settings. In *The Ordeal* he achieved some of his finest scenes of pathos and tragedy.

The novelist was still, however, very much interested in tracing the design, as one might in a tapestry, and in making it conspicuous amid the multiplicity of detail. His propensity for outlining the pattern and giving comic designations to its features was to remain with him throughout his writing career. It was especially apparent, however, in the first, 1859, version of *The Ordeal;* and though in revising he excised many of the more farcical elements, his final, 1875, version begins with a comic framework, retains comic terminology while moving through pastoral romance, and is loath, indeed too loath, to relinquish its witty commentary as the narrative plunges toward its tragic end.

To stress the fact that, despite its peculiar variations, what happened to an English family in the nineteenth century was as generic

From *Art and Substance in George Meredith: A Study in Narrative* (Lincoln, Nebraska: University of Nebraska Press, 1953), 147–61. Reprinted by permission of the publisher and the author.

as anything in the history of Shibli or Bhanavar or of Farina and the Cologne monk, the author repeatedly inserted allegorical labels. Most prominent, as the title itself indicates, is the concept of Feverel life as an ordeal. Though the novel is to conclude as the tragedy of Richard, the first version begins in a tone even lighter than that used later to introduce Sir Willoughby's comedy. Each of various Feverels is facetiously caricatured as the victim of Mrs. Malediction, and Sir Caradoc has emphasized a "special Ordeal" as the distinguishing characteristic of Feverel fate. Sir Austin sentimentally regards his wife's desertion as his ordeal and enjoys having been considered worthy of persecution by the "Fates and Furies." Losing of a leg in a cricket match and suffering from dyspepsia are variant manifestations of the ordeal.

Still in a light vein comes the introduction of Richard and, by way of "The Pilgrim's Scrip," the label which superficially indicates his ordeal. The Pilgrim's Scrip is a complex improvement upon the choral rhymes in *The Shaving of Shagpat*. Written by the pseudo-wise Sir Austin, it contains many aphorisms which imply shrewd sense, for the sentimentalist, Meredith liked to point out, can speak aptly against the very sin which he commits. But it also has cynical worldly wisdom expressive of Sir Austin's pique against the woman who left him for a worthless rhymester. It is the Wise Youth who, seeing clearly another's sins though never his own, christens the Scrip "The Great Shaddock Dogma"—shaddock, or grapefruit, being understood by those who are clever to be the forbidden fruit to which Eve introduced Adam in Eden. Before Richard has dreamed of love Sir Austin has written with bitterness of what Meredith here and again later calls the "Apple-Disease." With further involvement of the metaphor, the novelist says (in a passage deleted in the revised version) that Sir Austin plans to guard Richard "like a Tree of Eden; by advancing him to a certain moral fortitude ere the Apple-Disease was spontaneously developed, there would be seen something approaching to a perfect Man." Thus before the lad starts on his career the novelist has designated the paternal interference which will create his *ordeal*. Near the end the term is again to become prominent when Adrian in specific allusion to the malediction of Sir Austin's Shaddock Dogma once quips, "O Richard of the Ordeal!"

In a manner strongly reminiscent of *The Shaving of Shagpat*, others besides Richard and the Wise Youth are characterized under the terms of comedy or allegorical romance. Benson, the butler, who protects Sir Austin during the siege by female admirers, is both "the Great

Shaddock Dogma condensed in a look" and the "Saurian": "As Dragons of old guarded the dwellings of beautiful princesses, Heavy Benson stood sentinel over the Baronet." (This passage too was deleted.) The dissipated old sinner Hippias, who glamorizes his illness as his ordeal, is simply "the Dyspepsy." Sir Miles Papworth, candidate for Parliament, is two circles set upon stumps. There are scores of caricatured women who, with a motherly tenderness that does not preclude marriage, idolize Sir Austin for what they believe is sweetness concealed within the acerbity of his Scrip. Particularly there is Mrs. Grandison, a caricature of misguided mothers and of all the female descendants of Sir Charles.

The labels and motifs extend to the personification of attitudes. In a dialogue of Sir Austin and Richard, for example, the two are "Cold Blood" and "Hot Blood." Once when Sir Austin is debating with himself the negative arguments are spoken by the devil. Simplicity in feeling as contrasted with sophistication is a manifestation of nature personified; the change that takes place in Richard when he walks in the German forest comes under the chapter title "Nature Speaks." A rather arbitrary symbol is the cypress, which for the young lovers is always, as might be expected, a foreboding of ill.

Significant too are the allusions to literature, especially to Shakespeare and to classical comedy. In "Ferdinand and Miranda" the novelist indicates the standard his readers are to accept in reading his great love scene. For a commentary on the wooing of Richard by Bella, after a scene reminiscent of *Faust*, he rephrases the famous lines in *Richard III*, giving to his Richard the lady's role: "Was ever hero in this fashion won?" The first reference to "the new Comedy" (later deleted) is without a capital *n*, and the term describes what the unlettered Tom Bakewell feels engaged in. The second, with a capital, refers to Ripton's anticipation of an adventure involving lover, beloved, and disapproving father, an adventure, in short, suggestive of Terence and of what Meredith knew of Menander. Again, a chapter title includes "the Last Act of the Comedy." A reference also to Sir Austin as having been "the God of the machine" admits a parallel that Meredith certainly recognized between the denouement of his tragedy and Greek drama.

Most of these allegorical designations and commentaries were retained in the final draft of the novel, but their total was substantially —though still not sufficiently—reduced in frequency and form. The caricatures, including those of the besieging ladies, were either stricken out entirely or compressed to passing allusions. An entire chapter on

Sir Austin's visit to Mrs. Grandison was omitted, and with it scattered paragraphs elsewhere referring to the Grandisons and the paragon Sir Charles. The excised passages, which are mainly in the opening scenes, indicate the transitional nature of *The Ordeal*. The novelist could not determine what attitude to take toward his characters and theme, and the story altered as he wrote. When he began to enter deeply into the conflict in Sir Austin's mind and into the passions of Richard he must have perceived that his apparatus tended to reduce his characters to superficial comic types. The most striking evidence of Meredith's increasing depth within the first version itself is the fact that Richard's tragedy develops into something much more serious than Adrian's quip implies; so that the very word *ordeal* as employed by the Wise Youth is an ironic understatement of an experience which, far from being peculiar to a fated few, symbolizes the eternally repeated process of man's coming spiritually of age. Entertaining though the light comedy is, it represents no advance over Meredith's earlier work. It is only when the tragedy becomes ominous that the wittiness develops depth and the elements fuse into a unified story.

For Richard the tragic denouement is the more intense because it springs from and contrasts with romance. In a pastoral world—and Meredith liked to contemplate such an ideal realm—the young heroes lead wholesome lives. They may suffer love sickness, even jealousy, and, as in *Sandra Belloni,* they may break heads in open but transitory wrath. They may have to war against evil, and they will endure the natural, inevitable sorrow of a Moschus for Bion. But there is no place for an ordeal. The pastoral is an unreal world, of course, to the extent that the heroes are free of life's petty frustrations and their spiritual problems are reducible to order. But though in this sense unreal, the pastoral is the norm by which to judge actual human error. No more than Milton could Meredith dispense with a garden of Eden.

Richard Feverel begins his career therefore, not as a burly lover on the village green, to be sure, but as a romantic boy for whom a pastoral sequence would seem appropriate. The poaching, the rick burning, and, as a climax to all, the discovery of Lucy by the stream are adventures which belong in a serpentless meadow. But though Richard has not yet tasted of the knowledge of good and evil, there is guarding him a saurian, Sir Austin, who having found the shaddock bitter, believes Eden itself to be inherently satanic. Nature to Sir Austin is indiscriminately rank, breeding riotously and recklessly wasting; man must protect himself against its licentious extravagance, and his duty extends to the careful watching of others, who must not be allowed to eat of the shaddock until they are mature, yet must miraculously accept the wisdom of one who has eaten.

Sir Austin is so replete with contradictions that it is impossible to decide at times whether to blame more his theory of education or his frequent violations of it. Like the later Sir Willoughby he has contempt for poetry and glorifies what he believes is science. In the name of science he exposes Richard to the vice of London, convinced that he is thus gradually bringing the boy to readiness for the apple. He stresses the scientific impersonality with which he withholds forgiveness from Richard when he is actually avenging his own wounded pride.[1] In the belief that nature must be followed he expects Lucy to nurse her baby when she is ill, and in disregard for nature, he reproaches her though she is mentally distraught. His essential sin, however, from which the lesser evils spring, is sentimental egoism. Having tasted of the gall of the Roc, he has lost all appetite for adventure and become defensive. He will risk nothing lest he lose again, and instead jealously guards his one possession, the son whom his deserting wife has left him. Richard must belong to him completely; there is no place for Clare and none for Lucy unless she will belong to him too and serve his purpose with Richard. He will shut out the world from the castle where he has imprisoned Richard and will take the youth on what he believes are guarded tours outside the walls to prove why he should return within.

At one level Sir Austin's folly exemplifies the erring of civilization when it denies the natural coursing of the blood and becomes a negation of adventure; this, as we have seen, Meredith was consistently to deplore in nineteenth-century England. More profoundly, it is a study of the ubiquitous tendency toward the supreme evil, the desire to possess another's soul and to act for it the part of a god.

Another form of evil is meant to be typified by the cynic Adrian. In the 1859 edition Adrian's sensual indulgence with a servant girl is explicit, and his hypocritical pretense is ridiculed by the girl. When revising, Meredith struck out the reference to licentiousness in the comic bucolic dialogue, and he otherwise trimmed the sketch of Adrian, still depicting him as a callous sensualist, but stressing rather his disbelief in human goodness and his assumption that living is primarily a game of intrigue. Body and intellect are divorced in him except as intellect provides plans for bodily indulgence. Wit is for Adrian a refuge against the intrusion of any moral or emotional consideration. Like other minor characters in Meredith's works, the Wise Youth is worthy of a larger portrait, for he is essentially a miniature of Mephistopheles as wit. His vanity is ludicrous, especially when he believes that his sophisticated manner will win Lucy's admiration. Yet laughable though he is, Adrian is a satanic imp. His example in cynicism is harmful to the impressionable Richard, and his advice, which ignores human longings, helps prevent reconciliation of father and son.

Not all the minor exemplifications of folly have an important effect on Richard's life, but they do fill in a background of egoism and error. Such are the ordeal-suffering Algernon and Hippias, the unfaithful Berry, Mrs. Grandison, and the feckless Sandoe. Pure sensuality, on the other hand, in the form of Lord Mountfalcon, is of major importance both as a touchstone by which to judge Richard and as the immediate cause of the catastrophe. . . . Mountfalcon is utterly comic. He is as obedient as any Ovidian seducer to Lucy's will, but instead of being rewarded with physical tokens of compassion, he is subjected to tedious instruction in virtue. To keep the sensuality of Mountfalcon dominant Meredith avoided giving him all the other wickedness which a villain might show; when, for example, he is challenged by Richard, he is indeed coerced into taking part in the nonsensical duel. As a sensualist Mountfalcon is not only a cause of evil to others; he is himself as unfortunate as the later Algernon Blancove. Desiring only pleasure, he is actually wretched; and indolent by nature, he is feverishly occupied.

It is in the world represented by these secondary characters that Richard's personality and his ordeal take on meaning. Because it is meant to be inclusive the life of Richard shows resemblances to the lives of various minor characters who are merely personifications of one or another attitude. Its most tragic errors parallel those of Sir Austin, Adrian, and Mountfalcon. Like his father, Richard is at times possessed by egoism, especially in his thoughtless cruelty to Clare and to Lucy. He is the victim of Mephistophelean doubt, which he cannot dismiss with the Wise Youth's urbane dispassion. And he plunges into sensuality, from which, unlike Mountfalcon, he recoils with tragicomic revulsion.

It is because he lives in a world where he is surrounded by unpropitious examples—for he has learned even of sensuality long before meeting Mountfalcon or Bella—that the youth finds encouragement to err. The direction of his folly is very much determined by the meddling of his father. When in the rick-burning affair Sir Austin undermines his heroism by secret intrigue, a breach begins; with the destruction of his poetry it becomes too wide for bridging. Richard is left with suspicion of his father, whom he would love if he could, and so he learns none of the wisdom which was intended to see him safely through the apple-disease. In a limited sense his ordeal is that he must spend most of his life from early adolescence onward as a victim of the disease, for disease it is for Richard. He is dominated by preoccupation with women; indeed he has no other career. And yet he comes to each new situation in helpless ignorance. Shut out as he is from knowledge of the actual natures of women, he creates idealized abstractions; and his tragedy stems from his not seeing the inferiority of the idealizations to the realities themselves.

When Richard is seven years old he wakes to find a lady bending over his bed. As she is his mother, the action becomes symbolic of her shadow upon his soul. There is an unspoken feeling in Richard that sinister things have occurred, and in the light of what happens later it is clear that he suspects his father of being to blame. When he does finally rescue his mother the young man is so involved in new perplexities with Lucy and Bella that Meredith scants the incident, leaving obscure the effect upon Richard himself. The quest for a mother is shown to have been as deeply inspired, however, as the longing for a father's understanding, and yet Lady Feverel has been for Richard an idealized lonely sufferer untouched by commonplace actuality.

It is sight of Lady Blandish's bonnet that causes the boy to lose his swimming match, and it is overhearing what Richard—and she too for a while—thinks is Sir Austin's wooing of her that gives him notions on courtship. She is just enough removed from him to allow chivalric transformation; she might as easily be a lady in a book of fashions, for the lad never thinks of her as a pathetic and subtly perceptive woman.

There is, of course, the natural adolescent dreaming of ideal loves, and it is from this that Richard is suddenly transported to a yet more intense dream of Lucy. The Ferdinand-Miranda relationship is for Meredith as for Shakespeare of enchanting beauty. He would not have Richard at once bound to earth by practical considerations. But whereas Lucy can be idealistic and practical too, Richard has no understanding of her as a person. Clare has been taken from him, he has known no girls well, and he has only an imagined concept into which he tries to make Lucy fit.

In the first edition Carola Grandison, a young girl who wishes she were a boy, gains Richard's affection when he is confused by Lucy's being taken from him. The incident is plausible and it prepares for later defection after his marriage. The author may have cut it because he was eliminating the chapter on the Grandison family, or simply because, though believable, it came too early in his presentation of Richard's infidelity and could not be allowed interesting development. Significantly, when with Carola, Richard is utterly imperceptive; he likes her for her seeming boyishness and never appreciates the drama of rebellion within her mind.

It is after he has undiscerningly separated from Lucy and after a Thames holiday with women of uncertain character that Richard starts out to rescue lost women, who, he imagines, are waiting to be redeemed to virtue and security. But he once more sets up an idealization that keeps him from seeing the actual. Bella is a fallen soul, then she is a fascinating witch, and soon Richard thrills to the voluptuous thought that she and he are fated to be supremely wicked together and to join the damned in Hell. The real Bella is no saint, but unlike Richard she can fall in love, and it is too late before Richard awakens to the cruelty he has committed in ignorance of her true nature.

The death of Clare might well be the climax to a tragic hero's education, for Richard undergoes deep contrition of spirit when he reads Clare's diary. But he soon descends again into insane folly, from which he must be rescued anew. It was a conviction of Meredith that man and woman are not only not limited to one love, but in the struggle to find their own identities in the social universe are often unconsciously wasteful of the souls which love them. In this respect Clare is the victim of Richard's extravagance. As a girl she has been banished from his company by the barbarous egoism of Sir Austin, and as a young woman she has been wedded to a dolt because her mother knew no alternative to marriage. In Clare as in Lucy, Meredith provides an ironic contrast to Richard. His career is meteoric, hers outwardly colorless and submissive to fate. And yet it is Clare whose passions have been unceasingly of heroic magnitude. The discovery of the truth can bring nothing but shame to Richard, because in his self-indulgent acceptance of Clare's devotion he has actually been toying with her very life.

Though the recognition that the real Clare was not a passionless, bloodless abstraction is like seeing a miracle for Richard, Meredith had not said all he wished of man's ordeal. Richard's thoughtless cruelty to Clare is the outgrowth of Sir Austin's egoistic attempt to keep him from loving her. But although as in Donne's poem we can add to the father's sins those which he has led Richard to sin, by the time of Clare's suicide Richard himself is blindly egoistic. Sobering as the shock is to him, he is still unable to see a living woman as he sees the dead one. There follows a friendly association with Judith Feltre, unhappily wedded to a "decrepit lord" and seeking distraction on the continent. But even when he wins sympathy from Judith, Richard never has more than a superficial awareness of her suffering. His thoughts are still fixed painfully upon himself.

The youth does come to pity Lucy and to yearn for forgiveness; but far from telling her the whole truth, he flees from her to commit yet another infidelity. For the duel itself is a disloyalty to Lucy and reveals how little Richard comprehends her love. The Richard who insists that Mountfalcon give him satisfaction is tragicomic. He has committed acts of which he is intensely ashamed, and he wants to regain integrity. Yet, like any sentimentalist, he does not want to pay an honest price. He dramatizes his guilt to Lucy, but he is still his own hero, determined to make circumstance, in the form of Mountfalcon, the villain. Lucy's virtue and reputation are unsullied; she has not been emotionally harmed by the attempt at seduction. Richard's seduction of Bella, on the other hand—for he actually wins her love rather than she his—is a very real tampering with another's soul; and the fact that Bella is ennobled by her love in no way mitigates Richard's guilt. Yet he will fight a duel as if destruction of a villain would remove all sin from himself and leave him freed from his past. He has suffered for his treatment of Clare, and during his walk in the German forest, including the finding and nursing of the leveret, he has sensed his cruelty to Lucy. Nevertheless it is only a finer abstraction than before from whom he asks forgiveness, while withholding the secret of his last, worst sin of all.

At the end, as in all tragedy, we see how far we have come. The eating of the shaddock is a symbol no longer limited to the apple sickness. Through his futile quest to find in Sir Austin a true father and through perceiving the anguish that he has caused—for Clare's and Lucy's deaths will forever weigh his spirit—he has come to the irrevocable knowledge of good and evil. Lucy's death is indeed the incident which signifies his irreparable loss of Eden. His few years have brought him not increased relish of good things, but the terrifying vision of his father's error and of his own. He does have one precious awareness which the Sir Austins of this world can never know. When dying, Lucy has cried out against the egoist's cold harshness, and Lady Blandish pictures him as a creature in Hell. Sir

Austin's sensation is at best negative. He cannot feel the kind of shame that brings purification; he knows only bafflement and bitter loss. In contrast, though he has not found a father and though he will forever suffer remorse for his own guilt, Richard has as never before in his mind the image of Lucy, and in its essence it is now a true image. Like Othello, he sees finally how much better she was than any of his idealizations of woman.

From the vantage point of the tragic ending we can judge both the framework of the novel and the qualities which make the story significant. In the abstract concept of its design the comedy and tragicomedy are conspicuous, even in the final draft. In so far as the story is of Sir Austin it follows a pattern ranging from farce in the early pages to the later tragicomedy, in which an inflexible egoist comes at last to see that he has made mistakes in judgment but remains the victim of his own unimaginative attitude. It is bitter irony that the baronet's attempt to be a god to his son loses his affection entirely, that his unappreciative acceptance of women's adoration is succeeded by their denunciation of his cruelty.

There are major aspects of Richard's career which, as we have seen, are comic. His patronizing of Lucy as if she were an innocent child at the very time that he is scolding her for lack of courage, his tasting forbidden fruit as a self-appointed moralist, his self-castigation with which he gets pity from Lucy instead of the full penance he deserves, and his egoistic risking of Lucy's happiness in a duel to defend his *amour-propre*—all these are the stuff of bitter comedy. Indeed it is essentially comic that the boy who was to be guided by his father with scientific wisdom does not shape his life according to any intellectually conceived order, but instead rushes headlong, finding bliss only to desert it and career into folly, and, like all the other Feverels, blaming fate for his ordeal, until the final overthrow, when the tragicomic muse at last waves him "for the loftier lyre."

The excellence of the novel is, however, in the psychological insight and in the subtle poetic tone, by means of which, even when the comedy is most rampant, the author never allows us to forget the spirit of romance or to doubt that Richard does have within him the capacity for tragic purification. As a lad he represents eternal boyhood, with its love of adventure, its humiliations, and its heroic loyalties. As a youth he is a knight-errant, with his passion and folly and his inherent decency. Finally, his is the tragic sorrow of a sensitive and noble mind.

Because of Meredith's indifference to tight dramatic structure

222

Richard is sometimes a shadowy figure, whose actions are reported as having happened, with only general hints as to their motivation. But he becomes vividly real whenever we see him immediately before us and feel that we know the impressions in his mind. It is the novel's penetration of a mind rather than its surface pattern which makes it distinctive. We know what dreams Richard brings to the weir and the lyric exaltation which sustains him in a world of romance. We sense the images in his mind which inspire the pummeling of Benson, who would destroy that world. As he reads Clare's diary we know what the life is that he recalls; the diary itself is replete with images each of which can evoke companion images in Richard's mind. With his memory of his infidelity to Lucy, Richard is so vividly before us in the German forest that we experience with him both the memory and the urge to flee it. We see into the mind of the youth who has tried to make of wandering and distraction a refuge from his guilty thoughts, and we feel suddenly a hope when the discovery of the little hare brings a new group of images into his mind, images fraught with positive tenderness instead of negative remorse.

Richard has been wandering as if he were a lost soul, but the chance incident makes him a man of action, impelled by his love of his wife. When we are almost ready to believe that the reawakened love will triumph over the bitterness, Meredith tears Richard's mind apart by news of Mountfalcon's perfidy, which introduces yet a different pattern, involving both remorse and desire for action madder and more tragic than before. Finally, when fever has blotted out many images and has killed all passion to act, Richard lies before us stripped of illusion. Here Meredith, through Lady Blandish's letter, gives only the briefest statement of his hero's sense of shame and of his deepened love; for Richard is now completely tragic, and, so far as sensitive, experienced minds are concerned, his thoughts and feelings are universal.

The ornamental framework of the novel possesses a certain charm, though one would prefer a more Doric simplicity, and it does remind one that the novelist is not naïve—that he is wiser than the Wise Youth, that he sees with scientific analysis the fallacy of Sir Austin, the pretender to scientific wisdom, that he can discourse philosophically of life's passions, in short, that he draws on the disciplines of reason and common sense. But the psychological beauty is what transcends these. As we live in Richard's thoughts we feel anew that youth, adventure, love are magical qualities. We are forced relentlessly to admit that life may be a ruthless destroyer of the magic; and yet, in the paradox of tragedy, we perceive that through the chill, melancholy disillusionment about his own volatile nature and the mutability of a star-crossed fate man may still apprehend, however poignantly, a beauty which is not mutable.

NOTES

1. In "The Artistic Unity of 'Richard Feverel': Chapter XXXIII," *Nineteenth Century Fiction*, VII (1952), 119–23, W. E. Buckler demonstrates that Sir Austin's motives prevent the working of any system. Cf. also W. R. Mueller "Theological Dualism and the 'System' in *Richard Feverel*," *Engl. Lit. Hist.*, XVIII (1951), 138–54.

MARTIN J. SVAGLIC

———◆———

The Structure of Newman's *Apologia*

THE *Apologia pro Vita Sua* is not the autobiography of Newman from
1801 to 1845. It tells us nothing of the family life, the student activities, the intellectual and artistic interests of its complex subject. Nor
is it even a spiritual autobiography of those years except in a limited
sense. We must turn to the *Letters and Correspondence*, with their
"Autobiographical Memoir," to supplement the bare account given
in the *Apologia* of Newman's conversion to Evangelical Christianity.
The *Apologia* is primarily a work of rhetoric designed to persuade a
body of readers or "judges," English, Protestant, and suspicious of a
convert to an unpopular religion, that Newman, whom Kingsley had
made a symbol of the Catholic priesthood, was a man not of dishon-
esty but of integrity. Newman chose autobiography as his method
because of his lifelong English preference of the concrete to the
abstract, his vivid realization of the role in persuasion of personal
influence: "I am touched by my five senses, by what my eyes behold
and my ears hear. . . . I gain more from the life of our Lord in the
Gospels than from a treatise *de Deo*." [1] "The heart is commonly
reached, not through the reason, but through the imagination, by
means of direct impressions, by the testimony of facts and events, by
history, by description. Persons influence us, voices melt us, looks
subdue us, deeds inflame us." [2] It was his conversion to Catholicism
after a long puzzling delay, many predictions of the event, and even
charges of treachery to the Church of England that had created the
atmosphere of suspicion in which his character had been impugned.
Therefore he would confine the autobiography principally to a brief
explanation of how he arrived, to begin with, at what so many re-

From *Publications of the Modern Language Association of America*, LXVI
(1951), 138–48. Reprinted by permission of the publisher and the author.

garded with suspicion and fear: Anglo-Catholic principles; and to a detailed one of how, having accepted them and devoted himself to propagating them, he became convinced that the principles which had led him thus far must lead him farther still, into the Catholic Church. "I am but giving a history of my opinions, and that, with the view of showing that I have come by them through intelligible processes of thought and honest external means" (p. 27). If that history of opinions, in spite of its limited scope, has so much of the richness and variety of great autobiography, it is because Newman held that the means by which we arrive at belief, all of which he would try to chronicle for his own life so far as that was possible, were multiform and complex.

Newman, with his extraordinary memory for personal affairs, his strong affections, and his fondness for musing on the past—that great revealer of God's providence—was peculiarly equipped to tell his story; and, as we have indicated, the scope of that story was carefully limited by his rhetorical purpose. But what kind of material was to be used, and how was it to be expressed and arranged? Newman's theories of belief and of biography, closely related, provided the answer to the first question, and his conception of life and of conversion to the second.

"It is the concrete being that reasons," Newman tells us in the *Apologia* (p. 153), and the remark sums up his approach to the problem of belief, which dominates so much of his thinking from his early days as an Oxford preacher to the last years of his life, from the *University Sermons* to the *Grammar of Assent*. Since the man who assents to any given proposition is far more than a mere dialectician, an intellect in a void, the account of his reasoning (which cannot be the same as the reasoning itself) must include all the forces at work in creating his state of mind so far as they can be specified. Many of these must remain implicit; the explicit account may be syllogistic in form or may "designate particular methods of thought, according to which the mind reasons (that is, proceeds from truth to truth)" and "particular states of mind which influence its reasonings. Such methods are antecedent probability, analogy, parallel cases, testimony, and circumstantial evidences; and such states of mind are prejudice, deference to authority, party spirit, attachment to such and such principles, and the like." As Walter E. Houghton remarks, this passage, written in 1840, reads like "Directions for Writing the *Apologia*." [3] The syllogistic method was designed for a simpler psychology than Newman's. The effect of St. Augustine's verdict, "securus iudicat orbis terrarum," for example, would be far greater on one who was deferential to authority than on one who was not. In 1841, writes a well-known historian, "one of those events occurred whose full horror it requires a clerical mind to appreciate. The State Churches of England and Prussia combined to set up a bishopric of Jerusalem. The idea of such communion between Christ's followers, on the scene of Christ's passion, was too much for Newman. 'It was one of the blows that broke me,' he confessed in his *Apologia*." [4] For the ironic "clerical mind" substitute "attachment to such and such principles" (belief in dogmatic religion, a visible church with rites and sacraments as the channels of grace, and the episcopal system, as Newman is careful to explain at the beginning of Chapter Two) and the comment, apart from its tone, is quite in harmony with Newman's thought. How did he come to hold such principles in the first place? The various "methods of thought" and "states of mind" of the first chapter supply the answer.

As we come to realize the magnitude and complexity of the task Newman set out to perform in a short space and a shorter time, we can begin to understand the expressions of difficulty which recur in the *Apologia*. As for his great "revolution of mind," he confesses (pp. 84–85):

> I feel overcome with the difficulty of satisfying myself in my account of it, and have recoiled from the attempt, till the near approach of the day, on which these lines must be given to the world, forces me to set about the task. For who can know himself, and the multitude of subtle influences which act upon him? And who can recollect, at the distance of twenty-five years, all that he once knew about his thoughts and his deeds, and that, during a portion of his life, when, even at the time, his observation, whether of himself or of the external world, was less than before or after, by very reason of the perplexity and dismay which weighed upon him. . . . It is both to head and heart an extreme trial, thus to analyze what has so long gone by, and to bring out the results of that examination.

Newman's own reticence, unusual even for an Englishman, increased the difficulty. Yet he is confident of success, for he goes on to say: "I have done various bold things in my life: this is the boldest; and, were I not sure I should after all succeed in my object, it would be madness to set about it." We can see now that far more is involved here than a rather melodramatic introduction to a chapter of crisis.

Memory alone, however, even Newman's, would be inadequate to such a task; hence the great importance of contemporary letters and documents for reliably and vividly portraying the mind in action at any given time in the past. In reading a biography, Newman said, he looked for "the secret heart"—"the *interior*." [5] And it was in the lives and letters of the ancient saints like John Chrysostom that he especially found it, for they "left behind them just that kind of literature which more than any other represents the abundance of the heart, which more than any other approaches to conversation; I mean correspondence." Thus it is that the Duke of Wellington's "despatches on campaign . . . tell us so much more about him than any panegyrical sketch." These lines were written in 1859. Five years later Newman followed his own precepts by giving us a life replete with letters and "despatches on campaign." A "silent Saint," he had written, "is the object of faith rather than of affection. If he speaks, then we have the original before us. . . ." The *Apologia* is both colloquial and dramatic in tone. The original is decidedly before us. And he impresses the reader, as Newman holds it the proper object of a "Life" to do, "with the idea of moral unity, identity, growth, continuity, personality." As he converses with us, we are "conscious of the presence of one active principle of thought, one individual character, flowing on and into the various matters which he discusses, and the different transactions in which he mixes." [6]

That the *Apologia* is vividly dramatic in style was perhaps first pointed out, and with some regret, by the *Times* in its original review, which felt that the book lacked

> some of the graces and proper characteristics of a retrospect. It has not the calmness and serenity of a distant survey of life. . . . The writer is mentally too near the times and the controversies which he describes, and the rush of thought which carries him along is often more like a conversational explosion on the subject of an event or scene of yesterday than a recall of distant memories, and a train of feelings and relations of the past. From the freshness and vividness with which he reawakens the struggle of that occasion, it is difficult to believe that No. 90 was not condemned last week. Everybody has, however, his own way of doing things, and if Dr. Newman's autobiography wants the calm grace of a retrospect, it has all the fire of a description of the present moment [June 16, 1864, p. 12]

Precisely! For the dramatic way is indeed Newman's way and one main source of his great hold on hearer or reader. He never wrote anything truer than the remark in 1833, in the midst of a merciless self-analysis which events were to prove unduly severe, that "I have a vivid perception of the consequences of certain admitted principles, have a considerable intellectual capacity of drawing them out, have the refinement to admire them, *and a rhetorical or histrionic power to represent them*. . . ."[7] The piercing subtlety of his perceptions, his command of metaphor as well as of simple, direct speech, his sense of ironical contrasts and vivid climax—all are employed in the realization of a conception of life which rests on the "main Catholic doctrine of the warfare between the city of God and the powers of darkness" (pp. 5–6).

From boyhood to old age Newman loved drama. He acted as a youth at Ealing in the plays of Terence, and in his declining years he adapted those plays for the students at his beloved Oratory school near Birmingham. He constantly saw life in dramatic terms. God's relations with the Jewish people were to him a "grand drama." [8] The fourth century, that critical and formative period of Christianity to which above all others his mind and heart returned for inspiration, was

> [a]n eventful century, a drama in three acts, each marvellous in itself, each different from the other two! The first is the history of the Roman Empire becoming Christian; the second, that of the indefectible Church of God seeming to succumb to Arianism; the third, that of countless barbarians pouring in upon both Empire and Christendom together. And, as the great convulsions of the earth involve innumerable commotions in detail and local revolutions, and each district and neighbourhood has its own story of distress and confusion, so, in the events of the social world, what is done in the camp or synod vibrates in every town and in every bishopric. From one end of the century to the other, the most momentous changes and the most startling vicissitudes took place; and the threshold of the Apostles was now darkened by messengers of ill, and now lit up with hope and thanksgiving.
>
> So it was in the fourth century; so will it be to the end. . . . [*Historical Sketches*, II, 1–2]

And so it was in the story of his own life. Various writers like the *Times* reviewer, Bishop Samuel Wilberforce, and Lewis E. Gates have spoken of the dramatic quality of the *Apologia*.[9] Walter E. Houghton has given us the first pointed analysis of the dramatic devices of the style.[10] However, little or nothing appears to have been said about the basic structure of the work as a whole, which so heavily affects the style of the narrative and is determined by Newman's conception of life and of the nature of conversion. The editors of Newman's *Correspondence with John Keble* have likened the four chapters of the narrative proper in the *Apologia* to "four seasons of the year," not as "a piece of cheap rhetoric, but as a serviceable peg for the memory." [11] But there is no need of apology. They are more than four stages of the year: they are four acts in the drama of Newman's conversion, carefully and skillfully planned as such.

As the protagonist of the drama, what kind of role does Newman play? The role he always admired so greatly in this world of symbols as perhaps the supreme type of the life of a Christian in the Church Militant: the soldier. It is no mere eccentricity or paradox that Newman eagerly followed the careers of his early hero Wellington, of Napoleon, and of General Gordon; or that Walter Scott was his favorite novelist; or Southey's *Thalaba* one of his best-loved poems. The despatches of the Iron Duke, J. A. Froude tells us, drew Newman's confession that they made one "burn to have been a soldier." [12] Froude likened Newman's face to Julius Caesar's and said Newman gave one the impression that he might have been a great general. Newman himself always preferred the society of men who exemplified the view he derived ultimately from the *Ethics* of Aristotle and the Epistles of St. Paul: that life is for action. Our Lord founded, he says, "not merely a religion, but (what was then quite a new idea in the world) a system of religious warfare, an aggressive and militant body, a dominant Catholic Church, which aimed at the benefit of all nations by the spiritual conquest of all; and . . . this warfare, then begun by it, has gone on without cessation down to this day, and now is as living and real as ever it was. . . ." [13]

It was not only at the start of the Oxford Movement, when he led the fight for the Catholic Church as he then conceived it, that Newman, in choosing with Hurrell Froude the motto of Achilles, sounded "the true note of the chieftain settling his own high purposes before he gathers up his closest retainers to do battle with detested and overmastering powers." [14] It is almost the dominant note of his life and work. He is always the man with a mission: to spread the truth; and to spread the truth is "warfare." [15] Long before the Oxford Movement, he had sounded the note in an awkward little poem for his brother's twenty-first birthday:

> Dear Frank, we both are summon'd now
> As champions of the Lord;—
> Enroll'd am I, and shortly thou
> Must buckle on thy sword;
> A high employ, nor lightly given,
> To serve as messengers of heaven! . . .

Till in the end of days we stand
As victors in a deathless land.[16]

Ultimately, of course, he drew this conception of life as a drama in which Christians were the warriors of the God of Revelation, from the Bible, which from childhood he knew almost entirely by heart, and especially from St. Paul, to him the "special herald and chief pattern" of grace.[17] It was St. Paul who had warned that we (like Thalaba) "wrestle not against flesh and blood, but against principalities and powers, against the world-rulers of this darkness, against the spirits of wickedness in the high places." It was St. Paul who had flung out the ringing challenge: "Therefore take unto you the armour of God, that you may be able to resist in the evil day, and to stand in all things perfect. Stand therefore, having your loins girt about with truth, and having on the breast-plate of justice, and your feet shod with the preparation of the gospel of peace; in all things taking the shield of faith, whereby you may be able to quench all the fiery darts of the wicked. And take unto you the helmet of salvation and the sword of the Spirit, which is the Word of God." [18]

If the Church spreads the truth by warfare and conquest, then the man who receives or is converted to it must be a man who is conquered by truth. And this is precisely what he is for Newman: a convert to him is a man *subdued by* the word or "the force of truth." (Hence the special irony of Kingsley's charge that truth for its own sake was not a virtue with Newman.) Thus, Gregory of Neocaesarea, under the influence of Origen, was in A.D. 231 "overcome by the force of truth." [19] How was England converted? The "word of truth came to our ancestors in this island and subdued them to its gentle rule." As for the converts of the Oxford Movement, each of them "was lovingly subdued by the sweet mysterious influence which called him on." To prospective converts Newman says: "We do but wish to subdue you by appeals to your reason and to your heart; give us but a fair field. . . ." [20] And so we are prepared to read in the Preface that the *Apologia* is the story of the process whereby the Catholic religion was able to "subdue the reason and overcome the heart, without the aid of fraud and the sophistries of the schools." [21] In short, the *Apologia* is the drama of a soldier who, through defeat and submission, at last finds peace: a loving defeat ostensibly by his enemies but in reality by the "sweet mysterious influence which called him on."

The first chapter or first act of the drama, "History of My Religious Opinions to the Year 1833," sets the scene for the battle and supplies the inciting force. Here we find Newman gradually learning the Catholic conception of the Church from Anglican sources and then resolving to restore that conception to an establishment now weak, divided, and state-ruled, as the only possible means of preserving her from the ultimate infidelity of liberal rationalism. The Bill for the Suppression of the Irish Sees is a portent of what the Church can expect from those coming into power in the aftermath of the reforms of 1829 and 1832. "*Exoriare aliquis!*" Hamlet and Thalaba and Dido calling for vengeance all spring to his mind. "I began to think that I had a mission." Hurrell Froude and he choose for a motto the words of Achilles on returning to the battle: "You shall know the difference, now that I am back again." The chapter ends with a swiftly-paced description of his return to England ("Lead, Kindly Light") just in time for Keble's sermon on "National Apostasy." He has "ever considered it the start of the religious movement of 1833"—perhaps because it was preached on July 14.

In fitting contrast, the second act begins on a quiet note: "In spite of the foregoing pages, I have no romantic story to tell." Superficially that is true—but he will make it as romantic as possible, both to keep his readers interested in the subtleties of his theological position and because his conception of life is, as we have seen, in some ways definitely romantic. "You read, my brethren," he tells us, "in the lives of Saints, the wonderful account of their conflicts, and their triumphs over the enemy. They are . . . like heroes of romance, so gracefully, so nobly, so royally do they bear themselves." [22] Military imagery becomes more and more predominant. The chapter as a whole, covering the years 1833 to 1839, is the rising action: the period of confidence and strength, "in a human point of view, the happiest time of my life. I was truly at home. . . . We prospered and spread" (p. 69). Newman outlines his first principles, trusting like Orestes in the race to the *event,* and gives an account of how, wanting "to bring out in a substantive form a living Church of England," he published such works as the *Prophetical Office* and the *Lectures on Justification,* outlining the theory of the *Via Media.* How were the Thirty-nine Articles to be reconciled with such a view? Tract 90 would give the answer. It is discussed in this chapter, although not published until 1841, because the speculations on which it is based arose well before that date and thus belong to the period of confidence. [23] In the concluding pages, however, Newman does anticipate material of the next chapter by recalling the reception of Tract 90. Rumors of its contents had got into "the hostile camp; and not a moment was lost in proceeding to action, when I was actually fallen into the hands of the Philistines."

He was "denounced as a traitor who had laid his train and was detected in the very act of firing it against the time-honoured Establishment." Echoing Othello, he tells us that "my occupation was gone."

The third act, from 1839 to 1841, is the crisis. It begins with superbly dramatic foreshadowing of "that great revolution of mind," then detains the reader for many pages of setting the mental scene. His own confident estimate of the Movement is illustrated at length by an article from the *British Critic* of April 1839. Then the issue and status of the unavoidable controversy with Rome are analyzed, with the admission that this "will involve some dry discussion; but it is as necessary for my narrative, as plans of buildings and homesteads are at times needed in the proceedings of our law courts" (p. 95). The strong point of Rome is universality; but she has added to the primitive faith. England, though regrettably separated from the great body of Christians, has kept that faith. Union with Rome was a matter of expedience rather than of necessity. "As time went on, without doubting the strength of the Anglican argument from Antiquity, I felt also that it was not merely our special plea, but our only one" (p. 103). The *Via Media* embodied it. Yet this, he makes it clear, is still a theory, not yet a certitude.

The heart of the chapter opens with the quietly portentous remark, "The Long Vacation of 1839 began early." Then all at once, in his study, appears the first "ghost"—the analogy revealed to him by the history of the Council of Chalcedon between the position of modern Anglicans and fifth-century Monophysites. "I saw my face in that mirror, and I was a Monophysite" (p. 104). Then come the words of St. Augustine—"securus iudicat orbis terrarum!"—in which perhaps the greatest oracle of antiquity testifies in favor of the judgment of the universal Church. By these words, he laments, "the theory of the *Via Media* was absolutely pulverized." Nevertheless, the errors and abuses of Rome remain, and on these he now concentrates his force. Perhaps much can yet be said for the Anglican Church as a repository of Catholic truth. The whole thing needed more study, and he was becoming calm again. Meanwhile the Articles were the apparent stumbling-block: Did they exclude Catholic truth, as so many took for granted? In Tract 90, an "experimentum crucis," he would show that they did not; it would be like "proving cannon." In fact, though for a time the Church appeared to have stood the test, with the Tracts stopped but not condemned, it turned out to be a case of "hoisting the engineer with his own petard." Between July and November, 1841, he received the "three blows which broke" him (p. 126): The ghost came a second time with the analogy of the semi-Arians; the Bishops issued formal condemnations of Tract 90; and at the same time, they endorsed Protestant heresy by the scheme of the Jerusalem Bishopric.

The last act, 1841 to 1845, is the resolution and denouement: the period of the dying soldier, "on my death-bed, as regards my member-ship with the Anglican Church," though becoming aware of the fact only by degrees. Highly complex and heavily documented, this chapter may be summarized only very crudely. There was as yet no thought of leaving Anglicanism. He retired to Littlemore, this priestly Wellington: "I called Littlemore my Torres Vedras, and thought that some day we might advance again within the Anglican Church, as we had been forced to retire" (p. 134). But for him the hope was to be in vain. In a theory to fit the need, since he cannot go to Rome with the view he holds of its abuses, he takes refuge in the note of sanctity and likens the Church of England to Samaria cut off from the temple, yet touched by God's grace. Meanwhile the young pro-Roman wing of the Move-ment drives him on remorselessly with its logic; and the Protestant foe—editors, heads of houses, even bishops—spies on him and spreads false reports of his movements. In anger and sorrow he flings back a challenge:

> [T]hey persisted: "What was I doing at Littlemore?" Doing there! have I not retreated from you? have I not given up my position and my place? am I alone, of Englishmen, not to have the privilege to go where I will, no questions asked? am I alone to be followed about by jealous prying eyes, which take note, whether I go in at a back door or at the front, and who the men are who call on me in the afternoon? Cowards! if I advanced one step, you would run away; it is not you that I fear: "Di me terrent et Jupiter hostis." [24] It is because the Bishops still go on charging against me, though I have quite given up; it is that secret misgiving of heart which tells me that they do well, for I have neither lot nor part with them: this it is which weighs me down. I cannot walk into or out of my house, but curious eyes are upon me. Why will you not let me die in peace?

"This was the keen feeling which pierced me," he tells us, "and, I think, these are the very words in which I expressed it to myself" (pp. 155–156). Newman was a born dramatist.

Meanwhile he tries to keep young men in his charge faithful to Anglicanism and holds Catholics at a distance. Gradually, however, through books provided by one of these (Dr. Russell of Maynooth) and through reflection of his own, he comes to see that devotion to the saints in the Roman Church does not interfere with the worship due solely to God; and that the principle of doctrinal development might account for what seemed on the surface unwarranted Roman additions to primitive Christianity. The way to Rome is now open to him, though he is not yet certain of his conclusions. He retracts his harsh sayings against her and resigns his living in September 1843. The liberals had beaten him in a fair field, he says; the Bishops had "seethed the kid in his mother's milk." And he concludes the account with the words Lucan applied to Pompey, beaten by the tyrant Caesar but dear to that embodiment of honor and truth, Cato: "Victrix causa diis placuit, sed victa Catoni" (p. 194). The remainder of the chapter, covering the two years in which opinion became conviction, treats largely of how he tried to prepare his friends for the pain he knew he would cause them. It ends in the haunting sadness of his farewell to Littlemore ("Obliviscere populum tuum et domum patris tui"), to his friends, and to his beloved Trinity College.[25]

The minor motif of the imagery now reappears, like that of the battle ultimately Pauline in origin: faith as a journey in response to a vision, a voyage on the sea. "I realize more that we are leaving Littlemore," he writes to a friend, "and it is like going on the open sea" (p. 214). We hear the note in "Lead, Kindly Light" and other verses of the *Lyra Apostolica*. Newman elaborates it in Chapter III of the *Apologia* (p. 108):

> And first, I will say, whatever comes of saying it, for I leave inferences to others, that for years I must have had something of an habitual notion, though it was latent, and had never led me to distrust my own convictions, that my mind had not found its ultimate rest, and that in some sense or other I was on journey. During the same passage across the Mediterranean in which I wrote *Lead, kindly light,* I also wrote the verses, which are found in the *Lyra* under the head of *Providences,* beginning, "When I look back." This was in 1833; and, since I have begun this narrative, I have found a memorandum under the date of September 7, 1829, in which I speak of myself, as "now in my rooms in Oriel College, slowly advancing . . . and led on by God's hand blindly, not knowing whither he is taking me."

From St. Paul's warning against "those, who, having 'rejected a good conscience,' had 'made shipwreck of their faith' " [26] the imagery of the sea appears to take its origin. Newman elsewhere describes the converts of the Oxford Movement in the same figure:

> He came as a spirit upon the waters; He walked to and fro Himself over that dark and troubled deep . . . hearts were stirred, and eyes

were raised in hope, and feet began to move towards the Great Mother. . . . First one, and then another, sought the rest which She alone could give . . . each drawn by divine power, and against his will, for he was happy where he was. . . . One by one . . . silently, swiftly, and abundantly, they drifted in. . . .[27]

And thus it is that he brings his own story to a close: "it was like coming into port after a rough sea; and my happiness on that score remains to this day without interruption" (p. 216).

Now at last, in his fifth and final chapter, Newman is ready for a direct answer to some of the principal charges of Kingsley and his friends. And now, of course, it will not be easy to resist him.

NOTES

1. Introduction to "St. Chrysostom," *Historical Sketches*, II, 217. All references except those to the *Apologia* are to the standard edition of Newman's *Works* (London, 1891–1903). References to the *Apologia* are to the edition of Charles Frederick Harrold (New York, 1947).

2. *Discussions and Arguments*, p. 293.

3. "Implicit and Explicit Reason," *University Sermons*, p. 258; cited by Houghton, *The Art of Newman's "Apologia"* (New Haven, 1945), p. 28 (an admirable study, to which I am much indebted).

4. Esmé Wingfield-Stratford, *The Victorian Tragedy* (London, 1931), p. 174.

5. Introduction to "St. Chrysostom," *Historical Sketches*, II, 218, 219. This essay has received considerable attention in recent years. See Fernande Tardivel, *La Personnalité littéraire de Newman* (Paris, 1937), pp. 231–38; and Houghton, pp. 14–20.

6. *Historical Sketches*, II, 221–22, 224, 227.

7. *Letters and Correspondence*, I, 366. Italics mine.

8. *A Grammar of Assent*, p. 436.

9. Wilberforce's review, which originally appeared in the *Quarterly* (CXVI [1864], 528–73) is reprinted in his *Essays Contributed to the "Quarterly Review"* (London, 1874), I, 334–93. For the comments of Gates, see his *Selections from the Prose Writings of John Henry Cardinal Newman* (New York, 1895), pp. xvii–xviii.

10. Op. cit., pp. 46–47.

11. *Correspondence of John Henry Newman with John Keble and Others: 1839–1845*, edited at the Birmingham Oratory (London, 1917), p. 165.

12. See Wilfrid Ward, *The Life of John Henry Cardinal Newman* (London, 1912), I, 61–62.

13. *A Grammar of Assent*, p. 444.

14. Wilberforce in the *Quart. Rev.*, CXVI (1864), 549.

15. *Sermons Preached on Various Occasions*, p. 178 (hereafter referred to as *Occasional Sermons*).

16. *Verses on Various Occasions,* p. 15.

17. *Parochial and Plain Sermons,* V, 76.

18. Quoted from Eph. vi. 12–17, *Occasional Sermons,* p. 306.

19. *The Arians of the Fourth Century,* p. 67.

20. *Occasional Sermons,* pp. 127, 136, 160.

21. *Apologia,* p. 391. Originally the end of Part II of the 1864 edition but part of the preface to the revised edition of 1865. It is this latter edition, revised slightly in subsequent impressions, which most readers know.

22. *Discourses to Mixed Congregations,* pp. 98–99.

23. See *Apologia,* p. 71. It appears that Newman originally intended the story proper to consist of three parts but changed his mind in the process of composition. This may account for his ending the second chapter with the reception in 1841 of Tract 90. See Henry Tristram, "Note au bas d'un grand texte," *La France franciscaine,* IIIe Série, XXII (1939), 43–44.

24. The words of Turnus, about to be slain. *Aeneid* XII. 895.

25. The elegiac note which pervades the *Apologia* and culminates in the unforgettable ending of Ch. V is perhaps the great secret of its irresistible appeal even to those who regret Newman's departure from the Church of England. Like the conception of life and conversion we have been discussing, it is all the more effective as a rhetorical device in being first a deeply genuine sentiment. Compare the effect of the *Apologia* with that of *Phases of Faith,* the spiritual autobiography of Newman's brother Francis, who refused to be *subdued by* anything outside of himself and in whom there is nothing which might be called elegiac.

26. See *Occasional Sermons,* p. 73.

27. Ibid., pp. 136–37.

T. S. ELIOT

Arnold and Pater

ALTHOUGH Pater is as appropriate to the 'seventies as to the 'eighties, because of the appearance of *Studies in the History of the Renaissance* in 1873, I have chosen to discuss him in this volume [1] because of the date 1885, the middle of the decade, which marks the publication of *Marius the Epicurean*. The first may certainly be counted the more "influential" book; but *Marius* illustrates another but related aspect of Pater's work. His writing of course extended well into the 'nineties; but I doubt whether any one would consider the later books and essays of anything like the importance, in social history or in literary history, of the two I have mentioned.

The purpose of the present paper is to indicate a direction from Arnold, through Pater, to the 'nineties, with, of course, the solitary figure of Newman in the background.

It is necessary first of all to estimate the aesthetic and religious views of Arnold: in each of which, to borrow his own phrase against him, there is an element of *literature* and an element of *dogma*. As Mr. J. M. Robertson has well pointed out in his *Modern Humanists Reconsidered*, Arnold had little gift for consistency or for definition. Nor had he the power of connected reasoning at any length: his flights are either short flights or circular flights. Nothing in his prose work, therefore, will stand very close analysis, and we may well feel that the positive content of many words is very small. Culture and Conduct are the first things, we are told; but what Culture and Conduct are, I feel that I know less well on every reading. Yet Arnold does still hold us, at least with *Culture and Anarchy* and *Friendship's*

Garland. To my generation, I am sure, he was a more sympathetic prose writer than Carlyle or Ruskin; yet he holds his position and achieves his effects exactly on the same plane, by the power of his rhetoric and by representing a point of view which is particular though it cannot be wholly defined.

But the revival of interest in Arnold in our time—and I believe he is admired and read not only more than Carlyle and Ruskin, but than Pater—is a very different thing from the influence he exerted in his own time. We go to him for refreshment and for the companionship of a kindred point of view to our own, but not as disciples. And therefore it is the two books I have mentioned that are most readable. Even the *Essays in Criticism* cannot be read very often; *Literature and Dogma, God and the Bible,* and *Last Essays on Church and Religion,* have served their turn and can hardly be read through. In these books he attempts something which must be austerely impersonal; in them reasoning power matters, and it fails him; furthermore, we have now our modern solvers of the same problem Arnold there set himself, and they, or some of them, are more accomplished and ingenious in this sort of rationalizing than Arnold was. Accordingly, and this is my first point, his Culture survives better than his Conduct, because it can better survive vagueness of definition. But both Culture and Conduct were important for his own time.

Culture has three aspects, according as we look at it in *Culture and Anarchy,* in *Essays in Criticism,* or in the abstract. It is in the first of these two books that Culture shows to best advantage. And the reason is clear: Culture there stands out against a background to which it is contrasted, a background of definite items of ignorance, vulgarity and prejudice. As an invective against the crudities of the industrialism of his time, the book is perfect of its kind. Compared with Carlyle, it looks like clear thinking, and is certainly clearer expression; and compared with Arnold, Ruskin often appears long-winded and peevish. Arnold taught English expository and critical prose a restraint and urbanity it needed. And hardly, in this book, do we question the meaning of Culture; for the good reason that we do not need to. Even when we read that Culture "is a study of perfection," we do not at that point raise an eyebrow to admire how much Culture appears to have arrogated from Religion. For we have shortly before been hearing something about "the will of God," or of a joint firm called "reason and the will of God"; and soon after we are presented with Mr. Bright and Mr. Frederic Harrison as foils to Culture; and appearing in this way between the will of God and

Mr. Bright, Culture is here sufficiently outlined to be recognizable. *Culture and Anarchy* is on the same side as *Past and Present* or *Unto this Last*. Its ideas are really no clearer;—one reason why Arnold, Carlyle and Ruskin were so influential, for precision and completeness of thought do not always make for influence. (Arnold, it is true, gave something else: he produced a kind of illusion of precision and clarity; that is, maintained these qualities as ideals of style.)

Certainly, the prophets of the period just before that of which I am supposed to be writing excelled in denunciation (each in his own way) rather than in construction; and each in his own fashion lays himself open to the charge of tedious querulousness. And an idea, such as that of Culture, is apt to lead to consequences which its author cannot foresee and probably will not like. Already, in the *Essays*, Culture begins to seem a little more priggish—I do not say "begins" in a chronological sense—and a little more anaemic. Where Sir Charles Adderley and Mr. Roebuck appear, there is more life than in the more literary criticism. Arnold is in the end, I believe, at his best in satire and in apologetics for literature, in his defence and enunciation of a needed attitude.

To us, as I have said, Arnold is rather a friend than a leader. He was a champion of "ideas" most of whose ideas we no longer take seriously. His Culture is powerless to aid or to harm. But he is at least a forerunner of what is now called Humanism, of which I must here say something, if only to contrast it and compare it with the Aestheticism of Pater. How far Arnold is responsible for the birth of Humanism would be difficult to say; we can at least say that it issues very naturally from his doctrine, that Charles Eliot Norton is largely responsible for its American form, and that therefore Arnold is another likely ancestor. But the resemblances are too patent to be ignored. The difference is that Arnold could father something apparently quite different—the view of life of Walter Pater. The resemblance is that literature, or Culture, tended with Arnold to usurp the place of Religion. From one point of view, Arnold's theory of Art and his theory of Religion are quite harmonious, and Humanism is merely the more coherent structure. Arnold's prose writings fall into two parts; those on Culture and those on Religion; and the books about Christianity seem only to say again and again—merely that the Christian faith is of course impossible to the man of culture. They are tediously negative. But they are negative in a peculiar fashion: their aim is to affirm that the emotions of Christianity can and must be preserved without the belief. From this proposition two different types of man can extract two different types of conclusion: (1) that Religion is Morals, (2) that Religion is Art. The effect of Arnold's religious campaign is to divorce Religion from thought.

In Arnold himself there was a powerful element of Puritan morality, as in most of his contemporaries, however diverse. And the strength of his moral feeling—we might add its blindness also—prevented him from seeing how very odd might look the fragments of the fabric which he knocked about so recklessly. "The power of Christianity has been in the immense emotion which it has excited," he says; not realizing at all that this is a counsel to get all the emotional kick out of Christianity one can, without the bother of believing it; without reading the future to foresee *Marius the Epicurean,* and finally *De Profundis.* Furthermore, in his books dealing with Christianity he seems bent upon illustrating in himself the provincialisms which he rebuked in others. "M. de Laveleye," he says in the preface to *God and the Bible,* with as deferential a manner as if he were citing M. Renan himself, "is struck, as any judicious Catholic may well be struck, with the superior freedom, order, stability, and religious earnestness of the Protestant Nations as compared with the Catholic." He goes on complacently, "Their religion has made them what they are." I am not here concerned with the genuine differences between Catholic and Protestant; only with the tone which Arnold adopts in this preface and throughout this book; and which is in no wise more liberal than that of Sir Charles Adderley or Mr. Roebuck or "Mr. Tennyson's great broad-shouldered Englishman." He girds at (apparently) Herbert Spencer for substituting *Unknowable* for *God;* quite unaware that his own Eternal not ourselves comes to exactly the same thing as the Unknowable. And when we read Arnold's discourses on Religion, we return to scrutinize his Culture with some suspicion.

For Arnold's Culture, at first sight so enlightened, moderate and reasonable, walks so decorously in the company of the will of God, that we may overlook the fact that it tends to develop its own stringent rules and restrictions.

> Certainly, culture will never make us think it an essential of religion whether we have in our Church discipline "a popular authority of elders," as Hooker calls it, or whether we have Episcopal jurisdiction.

Certainly, "culture" in itself can never make us think so, any more than it can make us think that the quantum theory is an essential of physical science: but such people as are interested in this question at all, however cultured they be, hold one or the other opinion pretty strongly; and Arnold is really affirming that to Culture all theological and ecclesiastical differences are indifferent. But this is a rather positive dogma for Culture to hold. When we take *Culture and Anarchy* in one hand, and *Literature and Dogma* in the other, our minds are gradually darkened by the suspicion that Arnold's objection to Dissenters is partly that they do hold strongly to that which they believe, and partly that they are not Masters of Arts of Oxford. Arnold, as Master of Arts, should have had some scruple about the use of words. But in the very preface to the second edition of *Literature and Dogma* he says:

> The *Guardian* proclaims "the miracle of the incarnation" to be the "fundamental truth" for Christians. How strange that on me should devolve the office of instructing the *Guardian* that the fundamental thing for Christians is not the Incarnation but the imitation of Christ!

While wondering whether Arnold's own "imitation" is even a good piece of mimicry, we notice that he employs *truth* and *thing* as interchangeable: and a very slight knowledge of the field in which he was skirmishing should have told him that a "fundamental truth" in theology and a "fundamental thing" in his own loose jargon have nothing comparable about them. The total effect of Arnold's philosophy is to set up Culture in the place of Religion, and to leave Religion to be laid waste by the anarchy of feeling. And Culture is a term which each man not only may interpret as he pleases, but must indeed interpret as he can. So the gospel of Pater follows naturally upon the prophecy of Arnold.

Even before the 'seventies began Pater seems to have written, though not published, the words:

> The theory, or idea, or system, which requires of us the sacrifice of any part of this experience, in consideration of some interest into which we cannot enter, or some abstract morality we have not identified with ourselves, or what is only conventional, has no real claim upon us.[2]

Although more outspoken in repudiating any measure than man for all things, Pater is not really uttering anything more subversive than the following words of Arnold:

> Culture, disinterestedly seeking in its aim at perfection to see things as they really are, shows us how worthy and divine a thing is the religious side in man, though it is not the whole of man. But while recognizing the grandeur of the religious side in man, culture yet makes us eschew an inadequate conception of man's totality.

Religion, accordingly, is merely a "'side' in (*sic*) man"; a side which so to speak must be kept in its place. But when we go to Arnold to enquire what is "man's totality," that we may ourselves aim at so attractive a consummation, we learn nothing; any more than we learn about the "secret" of Jesus of which he has so much to say.

The degradation of philosophy and religion, skilfully initiated by Arnold, is competently continued by Pater. "The service of philosophy, and of religion and culture as well, to the human spirit," he says in the 1873 conclusion to *The Renaissance,* "is to startle it into a sharp and eager observation." "We shall hardly have time," he says, "to make theories about the things we see and touch." Yet we have to be "curiously testing new opinions"; so it must be—if opinions have anything to do with theories, and unless wholly capricious and un-reasoning they must have—that the opinions we test can only be those provided for our enjoyment by an inferior sort of drudges who are incapable of enjoying our own free life, because all their time is spent (and "*we* hardly have time") in making theories. And this again is only a development of the intellectual Epicureanism of Arnold.

Had Pater not had one gift denied to Arnold, his permutation of Arnold's view of life would have little interest. He had a taste for painting and the plastic arts, and particularly for Italian painting, a subject to which Ruskin had introduced the nation. He had a visual imagination; he had also come into contact with another generation of French writers than that which Arnold knew; the zealous Puritan-ism of Arnold was in him considerably mitigated, but the zeal for culture was equally virulent. So his peculiar appropriation of religion into culture was from another side: that of emotion, and indeed of sensation; but in making this appropriation, he was only doing what Arnold had given license to do.

Marius the Epicurean marks indeed one of the phases of the fluctuating relations between religion and culture in England since the Reformation; and for this reason the year 1885 is an important one. Newman, in leaving the Anglican Church, had turned his back upon Oxford. Ruskin, with a genuine sensibility for certain types of art and architecture, succeeded in satisfying his nature by translating everything immediately into terms of morals. The vague religious vapourings of Carlyle, and the sharper, more literate social fury of Ruskin yield before the persuasive sweetness of Arnold. Pater is a new variation.

We are liable to confusion if we call this new variation the "aesthete." Pater was, like the other writers I have just mentioned (except Newman), a moralist. If, as the *Oxford Dictionary* tells us, an aesthete is a "professed appreciator of the beautiful," then there are at least two varieties: those whose profession is most vocal, and those whose appreciation is most professional. If we wish to understand painting, we do not go to Oscar Wilde for help. We have specialists, such as Mr. Berenson, or Mr. Roger Fry. Even in that part of his work which can only be called literary criticism, Pater is always primarily the moralist. In his essay on Wordsworth he says:

> To treat life in the spirit of art, is to make life a thing in which means and ends are identified: to encourage such treatment, the true moral significance of art and poetry.

That was his notion: to find the "true moral significance of art and poetry." Certainly, a writer may be none the less classified as a moralist, if his moralising is suspect or perverse. We have today a witness in the person of M. André Gide. As always in his imaginary portraits, so frequently in his choice of other writers as the subjects of critical studies, Pater is inclined to emphasize whatever is morbid or associated with physical malady. His admirable study of Coleridge is charged with this attraction.

> More than Childe Harold (he says of Coleridge), more than Werther, more than René himself, Coleridge, by what he did, what he was, and what he failed to do, represents that inexhaustible discontent, languor, and homesickness, that endless regret, the chords of which ring all through our modern literature.

Thus again in Pascal he emphasizes the malady, with its consequences upon the thought; but we feel that somehow what is important about Pascal has been missed. But it is not that he treats philosophers "in the spirit of art," exactly; for when we read him on Leonardo or Giorgione, we feel that there is the same preoccupation, coming between him and the object as it really is. He is, in his own fashion, moralizing upon Leonardo or Giorgione, on Greek art or on modern poetry. His famous dictum: "Of this wisdom, the poetic passion, the desire of beauty, the love of art for art's sake has most; for art comes to you professing frankly to give nothing but the highest quality to your moments as they pass, and simply for those moments' sake," is itself a theory of ethics; it is concerned not with art but with life. The second half of the sentence is of course demonstrably untrue, or else being true of everything else besides art is meaningless; but it is a serious statement of morals. And the disapproval which greeted this first version of the Conclusion to *The Renaissance* is implicitly a just recognition of that fact. "Art for art's sake" is the offspring of Arnold's Culture; and we can hardly venture to say that it is even a perversion of Arnold's doctrine, considering how very vague and ambiguous that doctrine is.

When religion is in a flourishing state, when the whole mind of society is moderately healthy and in order, there is an easy and natural association between religion and art. Only when religion has been partly retired and confined, when an Arnold can sternly remind us that Culture is wider than Religion, do we get "religious art" and in due course "aesthetic religion." Pater undoubtedly had from childhood a religious bent, naturally to all that was liturgical and ceremonious. Certainly this is a real and important part of religion; and Pater cannot thereby be accused of insincerity and "aestheticism." His attitude must be considered both in relation to his own mental powers and to his moment of time. There were other men like him, but without his gift of style, and such men were among his friends. In the pages of Thomas Wright, Pater, more than most of his devout friends, appears a little absurd. His High Churchmanship is undoubtedly very different from that of Newman, Pusey and the Tractarians, who, passionate about dogmatic essentials, were singularly indifferent to the sensuous expressions of orthodoxy. It was also dissimilar to that of the priest working in a slum parish. He was "naturally Christian"—but within very narrow limitations: the rest of him was just the cultivated Oxford don and disciple of Arnold, for whom religion was a matter of feeling, and metaphysics not much more. Being incapable of sustained reasoning, he could not take philosophy or theology seriously; just as being primarily a moralist, he was incapable of seeing any work of art simply as it is.

Marius the Epicurean represents the point of English history at which the repudiation of revealed religion by men of culture and intellectual leadership coincides with a renewed interest in the visual arts. It is Pater's most arduous attempt at a work of literature; for *Plato and Platonism* can be almost dissolved into a series of essays. *Marius* itself is incoherent; its method is a number of fresh starts; its content is a hodge-podge of the learning of the classical don, the impressions of the sensitive holiday visitor to Italy, and a prolonged flirtation with the liturgy. Even A. C. Benson, who makes as much of the book as any one can, observes in a passage of excellent criticism:

But the weakness of the case is, that instead of emphasizing the power of sympathy, the Christian conception of Love, which differentiates Christianity from all other religious systems, Marius is after all converted, or brought near to the threshold of the faith, more by its sensuous appeal, its liturgical solemnities; the element, that is to say, which Christianity has in common with all religions, and which is essentially human in character. And more than that, even the very peace which Marius discerns in Christianity is the old philosophical peace over again.

This is sound criticism. But—a point with which Dr. Benson was not there concerned—it is surely a merit, on the part of Pater, and one which deserves recognition, to have clarified the issues. Matthew Arnold's religion is the more confused, because he conceals, under the smoke of strong and irrational moral prejudice, just the same, or no better, Stoicism and Cyrenaicism of the amateur classical scholar. Arnold Hellenizes and Hebraicizes in turns; it is something to Pater's credit to have Hellenized purely.

Of the essence of the Christian faith, as Dr. Benson frankly admits, Pater knew almost nothing. One might say also that his intellect was not powerful enough to grasp—I mean, to grasp as firmly as many classical scholars whose names will never be so renowned as that of Pater—the essence of Platonism or Aristotelianism or Neo-Platonism. He therefore, or his Marius, moves quite unconcerned with the intellectual activity which was then amalgamating Greek metaphysics with the tradition of Christ; just as he is equally unconcerned with the realities of Roman life as we catch a glimpse of them in Petronius, or even in such a book as Dill's on the reign of Marcus Aurelius. Marius merely *drifts* towards the Christian Church, if he can be said to have any motion at all; nor does he or his author seem to have any realization of the chasm to be leapt between the meditations of Aurelius and the Gospel. To the end, Marius remains only a half-awakened soul. Even at his death, in the midst of the ceremonies of which he is given the benefit, his author reflects "often had he fancied of old that not to die on a dark or rainy day might itself have a little alleviating grace or favour about it," recalling to our minds the "springing of violets from the grave" in the Conclusion to *The Renaissance,* and the death of Flavian.

I have spoken of the book as of some importance. I do not mean that its importance is due to any influence it may have exerted. I do not believe that Pater, in this book, has influenced a single first-rate mind of a later generation. His view of art, as expressed in *The Renaissance,* impressed itself upon a number of writers in the 'nineties, and propagated some confusion between life and art which is not wholly irresponsible for some untidy lives. The theory (if it can be called a theory) of "art for art's sake" is still valid in so far as it can be taken as an exhortation to the artist to stick to his job; it never was and never can be valid for the spectator, reader or auditor. How far *Marius the Epicurean* may have assisted a few "conversions" in the following decade I do not know: I only feel sure that with the direct current of religious development it has had nothing to do at all. So far as that current—or one important current—is concerned, *Marius* is much nearer to being merely due to Pater's contact—a contact no more intimate than that of Marius himself—with something which was happening and would have happened without him.

The true importance of the book, I think, is as a document of one moment in the history of thought and sensibility in the nineteenth century. The dissolution of thought in that age, the isolation of art, philosophy, religion, ethics and literature, is interrupted by various chimerical attempts to effect imperfect syntheses. Religion became morals, religion became art, religion became science or philosophy; various blundering attempts were made at alliances between various branches of thought. Each half-prophet believed that he had the whole truth. The alliances were as detrimental all round as the separations. The right practice of "art for art's sake" was the devotion of Flaubert or Henry James; Pater is not with these men, but rather with Carlyle and Ruskin and Arnold, if some distance below them. *Marius* is significant chiefly as a reminder that the religion of Carlyle or that of Ruskin or that of Arnold or that of Tennyson or that of Browning, is not enough. It represents, and Pater represents more positively than Coleridge of whom he wrote the words, "that inexhaustible discontent, languor, and homesickness . . . the chords of which ring all through our modern literature."

NOTES

1. A volume entitled *The Eighteen-Eighties*. Edited by Walter de la Mare for the Royal Society of Literature. Cambridge.
2. In quoting from *The Renaissance* I use the first edition throughout.

C. M. BOWRA

The House of Life

WITH the death of Keats in 1821 and of Shelley in 1822 the main
movement of English Romanticism came to an end. It is true that
Coleridge had another twelve years to live and Wordsworth another
twenty-eight, but, so far as Romantic poetry was concerned, their
work was done. Both were still to write good poems, but neither was
any longer inspired by the visions which had once made him great.
The Romantic genius seemed to have been buried beside the Pyramid
of Caius Cestius in the Protestant Cemetery in Rome. The new poetry
turned from vast mysteries and intoxicating ideas to delicate sentiment and careful description. A greater sense of security grew as the
shocks of the French Revolution and the Napoleonic Wars receded
into the past, and the emergence of a new moneyed class, conscious
of its worth and its destiny, hushed the eager, searching questions
which had troubled rebellious aristocrats like Shelley and Byron.
Poetry contracted its ambitions and was content to combine mild
instruction with grace and charm. As its worst it produced the pompous platitudes of Martin Tupper, at its best the noble and serious art
of Tennyson. Though Tennyson learned much from the Romantics, he
was not of their number. The familiar world was good enough for
him, and, even when he sought to pierce behind the veil, he did
so in a practical way as a man who is puzzled by something which
he does not understand, not as an explorer who advances into the
unknown because of the mysterious lure which it has for him. If sentiment was the dominant note of early Victorian poetry, it was soon

Reprinted by permission of the publishers from C. M. Bowra, *The Romantic
Imagination*, Cambridge, Mass.: Harvard University Press, Copyright, 1947,
by The President and Fellows of Harvard College. Permission granted also
by the Oxford University Press, London, and the author.

countered to some degree by a realism which made a disturbing appearance in 1840, when Browning published *Sordello* and said farewell to his youthful admiration for Shelley. Tennyson and Browning became the protagonists of English poetry, and the Romantic generation passed into history.

Such indeed was the general picture, but the Romantic spirit was not dead and was before long to make a new appearance in the Pre-Raphaelites. In different ways the two Rossettis, Swinburne, and Morris had drunk deep from the Romantic well and felt more sympathy for Keats and Coleridge than for the generation which immediately preceded their own. They were not hostile to Tennyson and Browning, but their spiritual needs were satisfied neither by the grave sentiment of the one nor by the realism and the didacticism of the other. Unlike these two poets, they were in revolt against their age and needed a special gospel. They sought a life richer than contemporary conditions seemed able to give, and they found it in the construction of imaginary worlds. If they owed much to a vision of an ideal past, whether in Italy or Greece or the Middle Ages, their special debt was to great literature and great painting. They found a selection from human experience at an exalted level and tried to live up to it. They believed that by absorbing the spirit of great art they would find an intenser vision and a less confused approach to the present. Like Keats, they rebelled against the scientific spirit, and, like Coleridge, they savoured the lure of the remote and the unfamiliar. In their search for an ideal which should be an extension of experience and at the same time throw light on many neglected aspects of actual life, they continued in reduced circumstances the work of the great Romantics.

The Pre-Raphaelites were the conscious inheritors of the Romantic outlook, but they adapted it to new needs and, in so doing, narrowed it. When we turn to them, we feel that we are in a more circumscribed world and that poetry, to save itself, has had to make considerable sacrifices. Nor is this due merely to an inferiority of talent. It may well be true that none of the Pre-Raphaelites has the sweep of the great Romantics, but their work was limited by other factors. First, though they were poets of revolt, they revolted not against a scheme of society in the hope of replacing it by something better, but against the whole spirit of an urban and industrial world. They were poets of escape not into a bright future but into happy day-dream and exalted fancy. At the very start they admitted defeat, and even Morris, most delightful and most courageous of reformers, was in his poetry an advocate of flight into a world which never existed on earth and was the more attractive for that reason. The Pre-Raphaelites lacked the adventurous curiosity of the Romantics, and the result is a contraction of confidence and energy. Secondly, the different imaginary worlds which they fashioned for their consolation were on the whole built less from an immediate experience of life than from art and literature. They thus lacked the vigour which comes from direct contact with the living scene. They gave their attention to the masterpieces of the past, and this made their work in some degree derivative. They transcended this by the intensity of their devotion and the strength of their personal vision, but their work is none the less narrower than the best work of the Romantics. Thirdly, whereas the Romantics, in their belief in a world beyond the senses, made little attempt to define it exactly or to know precisely its nature, the Pre-Raphaelites tried to find out what it was, to see within what limits its manifestations appeared, and to relate it to some coherent plan. The result was a lack of that cloudy magnificence which permeates the work of the Romantics, and its replacement by something which is perhaps easier and more intelligible but is also less magical and less alluring. Though the Pre-Raphaelites revolted against realism, they were touched by it to the extent that they wished even their wildest longings to be directed to some definable goal.

The most imposing figure of the Pre-Raphaelites was Dante Gabriel Rossetti. In his own circle his position was paramount. He was the master, whose work was an inspiration to others and whose criticisms were gratefully and dutifully accepted. Alike to his sister, Christina, and to his friend, Swinburne, he was the most eminent poet of the time, and he left indelible marks on their work. He meant little to Tennyson or Browning or Arnold, and, though his poetry found admirers from the start, he did not enter into his full renown until after his death. The reasons for this are not far to seek. Rossetti differed from the other great Victorians not merely in his foreign origin but in his uncompromising doctrine of what poetry ought to be. For them the poet had duties to society and must not only delight but instruct and improve; but as William Michael Rossetti said, "in all poetic literature anything of a didactic, hortatory, or expressly ethical quality was alien from my brother's liking." [1] Rossetti was as unusual a figure in England as Baudelaire was in France. Just as Baudelaire set his cult of Ideal Beauty against such eminent figures as Victor Hugo, who too often treated poetry as an instrument of propaganda, so Rossetti concentrated on the beautiful and gave himself to its service. In this he was undoubtedly strengthened by the example of Keats, for whom he had an almost unqualified admiration. He accepted Keats not with reservations as Tennyson and Swinburne did, but with his whole heart as a man who sought beauty and nothing else. This was an imperfect view of Keats, but it was what Rossetti believed, and he justified his own practice by it. Such an ideal was not to the usual Victorian taste, and Rossetti went his own way in pursuit of it. In an age of uncertain technique, he was a rigorous technician and an exacting critic both of his own and of others' work: religious passions left him cold, and such religion as he had was instinctive and intermittent; though he was brought up in an electrically political atmosphere, he never took any interest in politics; and, though he lived through years in which science assumed an ever increasing importance, he followed Blake and Keats in wishing "Confusion to the memory of Newton." [2]

Though Rossetti was inspired by Keats in his devotion to poetry, his actual field of creation lay elsewhere. His ballads owe something to Coleridge, and his more realistic poems to Browning, but the essential quality of his work must be understood in relation to his Italian origins and especially to his love for that poetry which preceded Dante and found its culmination in him. Though modern European poetry came into existence when the love-songs of Provence moved to Sicily in the time of Frederick II, and though what poets then wrote set the lines on which poetry was to move until almost our own time, at its beginning this poetry had a special and indeed startling character. It was inspired and shaped by the ideal of courtly love. In the language of feudal homage, poets sang of their mistresses in an allusive manner which suggested the union of physical love to some divine devotion. This was preëminently a poetry of love, and of a special kind of love, in which a human passion both keeps its earthly strength and is transcended by its attachment to a celestial order. The service of a living lady passes into the service of God and of an ideal world. Rossetti learned of this poetry from his father. He studied it with a scholar's care and translated it with an extraordinary accomplishment. His literary art might owe something to Keats, but its roots were in mediaeval Italy. He was in some sense a troubadour born out of due time, a child of that early Italian world which found in the cult of ideal love a satisfying field for its energies and was not afraid to speak freely about the flesh because somehow it was the visible image of the soul.

Rossetti's cult of beauty may be traced to this Italian poetry. He assumed the existence of an ideal world and sought to find it through beautiful things. He was a kind of Platonist both by nature and by education. In the Italian Middle Ages he found a way of life which he recognized as his own because it answered his innermost needs. And in this sense he was a Romantic, different indeed from his English predecessors in the special concentration of his genius on a limited goal, but like them in his assumption that the ideal world makes sense of the actual and is to be sought through it. Rossetti's pursuit of the ideal was his metaphysics, his gospel, his scheme of life, and his hope of salvation. To it he gave his powerful intellect and his no less powerful senses. He never wavered in his devotion to it, and it was the purity of this devotion, no less than his own commanding gifts, which gave him a predominant place in his own circle. In his life he paid a heavy price for it. His tragic marriage, his troubling and troubled passions, his last years of broken health and haunting hallucinations, all arose directly from his inflexible outlook. For him anything that contributed to the creation of beauty was right, and to this he sacrificed his health, his happiness, and something of what lesser men might call his honour.

In such a career any document which throws light on its determining principles has a special interest, and such Rossetti has left in the hundred and three sonnets of *The House of Life*. The title, drawn from astrology, suggests that these were intended to reveal Rossetti's complete view of life, and, though this is to claim too much, they occupy a special place in his work and provide a centre to which his other poems can be related. *The House of Life* occupied Rossetti at intervals through almost his whole career. The earliest sonnet in it, "Retro me, Sathana," was written in 1847, when he was nineteen years old, and the latest, "True Woman," in 1881, a year before his death. In *The House of Life* Rossetti presented his innermost convictions on almost all matters which really concerned him. The range of themes is not large, but in his devoted cult of beauty Rossetti restricted himself to a comparatively narrow field, and his strength lay less in range than in intensity. What matters is that these sonnets reveal a highly unusual personality in those moments when he abandoned narrative-poetry for communion with himself and spoke of what lay nearest his heart. More even than in his lyrical poems, Rossetti gives in the sonnets his most considered and most intimate conclusions about his life and his life-work.

The House of Life is not, strictly speaking, what Rossetti calls it, a sonnet sequence. It differs not merely from those Elizabethan series of sonnets, by Shakespeare or Drayton or Daniel, in which a kind of story, whether real or fictitious, is presented, but also from the sonnet sequences in which some Victorian poets recorded a crisis in their lives, as did Elizabeth Barrett in *Sonnets from the Portuguese*, Christina Rossetti in *Later Life,* and Wilfrid Blunt in *Esther.* Rossetti's sonnets reflect not a crisis but a lifetime, and through them he tells what his most enthralling discoveries have been. Although they are based on actual experience, and it may in some cases be possible to trace them to their source, there is no need to do this, and it is almost an irrelevant task, since Rossetti transmutes particular occasions into moments of universal interest and is concerned only with their lasting and essential appeal. The sonnets are arranged not according to some chronology, whether real or imaginary, but according to subject; and the subjects are divided into two main parts, which Rossetti calls "Youth and Change" and "Change and Fate." The first is almost entirely concerned with love, the second with a variety of matters which rise from Rossetti's outlook and the issues which it forces upon him. *The House of Life* is a unity because it reflects a consistent and closely knit personality and shows its progress along a clearly marked path. It needs no story to hold it together, and, because it has no story, it is all the more impressive as a personal record.

Rossetti had clear views on the nature and the function of a sonnet. For him it is an independent unit which presents as fully as possible a single exalting experience:

> A Sonnet is a moment's monument,—
> Memorial from the Soul's eternity
> To one dead deathless hour.

So, when he arranges his sonnets in a series, it is not with the intention of making them mere parts of a whole. Each sonnet is complete and fulfils its own task. Nor is it concerned with common or trivial subjects. It is reserved for moments of crisis, whether to celebrate some rapturous moment or to lament some dark catastrophe. And more than this, inside its unity it has a twofold function. It concerns the soul, but it must also place the soul in relation to whatever powers govern it:

> A Sonnet is a coin: its face reveals
>   The soul,—its converse, to what Power 'tis due:—
> Whether for tribute to the august appeals
>   Of Life, or dower in Love's high retinue,
> It serve; or, 'mid the dark wharf's cavernous breath,
> In Charon's palm it pay the toll to Death.

Rossetti believed that a sonnet must do more than unlock the heart: it must treat of those moments when through some intense experience he sees himself in relation to supernal powers and realizes that, before the mysteries of love or life or death, he can best express himself in this special kind of poetry which concentrates on some distilled thought or passion and pours all its strength into a narrow vessel.

Having decided to put his most intimate thoughts into sonnets, Rossetti proceeded to apply with rigour some of his most considered convictions about the composition of poetry. He gave much thought to technique and formulated clear views of it. In the first place, he said that poetry must be "intense." The word, which he may have got from Keats, passed into common currency and provided excellent jokes against the votaries of the Aesthetic Movement in the eighties and nineties, but for Rossetti it had a real meaning. It meant a full concentration on every theme, and implied that a rigorous discrimination must govern the composition of a poem. He developed his thesis when he said:

> It seems to me that all poetry, to be really enduring, is bound to be amusing . . . as any other class of literature; and I do not think that enough amusement to keep it alive can ever be got out of incidents not amounting to events.[3]

By "amusing" Rossetti means "lively"—the positive quality which redeems from dullness and triviality. In his view a poet should choose not minor, unimportant incidents, but events which are in themselves attractive or exciting. Rossetti applied this doctrine in *The House of Life*. Its subjects are the perennial subjects of poetry, the high moments when a man feels that his whole being is engaged by some enthralling occurrence. Such matters must be treated "intensely," that is, with a full awareness of their worth and a desire to make every word contribute fully to the total result. Such an ambition rules out on the one side the spacious ease of Tennyson, with its tendency to make much of incidents which are in themselves trivial, and on the other side the crowded, tumultuous sweep of Browning, with his lack of care for individual words and his many lapses from a truly poetical mood. But Rossetti gained other advantages than these. In his concern with ideal beauty, he acted in almost a religious spirit, to which his special kind of intensity was well suited. It reflected the special quality and strength of his feelings as he looked at visible things and saw in them a manifestation of the ideal.

This conception of poetry explains some marked characteristics of

Rossetti's style in *The House of Life*. He was a slow worker, who envied Swinburne's gift of rapid composition and said of himself:

> I lie on the couch, the racked and tortured medium, never permitted an instant's surcease of agony until the thing on hand is finished.[4]

Even when "the thing on hand" was finished, Rossetti did not leave it alone, but was continually turning back to it and changing it. This method of writing emphasized what Rossetti believed: that a poem must be charged with as much meaning as possible. He would use dictionaries of rhymes and of synonyms to get the words which he wanted, and of course the result is elaborate and self-conscious. At first sight his sonnets may seem rather too burdened with meaning, too stiff, and too slow in their movement. Part of this effect comes from their vocabulary, to which Rossetti's taste for resounding words of Latin origin gives a more than Miltonic weight. Yet these words are necessary for the majesty at which he aims and are part of his protest against the artificial simplicity of some Victorian poetry. Nor are his Latin words usually pompous or alien. He combines them with short words of Anglo-Saxon breed in such lines as

> Blazed the momentous memorable fire

or

> As the cloud-foaming firmamental blue,

and the result is both English and his own. Rossetti needed an unusual vocabulary because his subject itself was highly unusual. In approaching matters remote from the common world, he had to stress their almost hieratic character. No doubt this manner was largely natural to him, but he enhanced it through his deliberate, slow art and emphasized its strangeness. He had something uncommon to say, and for him this was the right way to say it.

The same elaboration can be seen in the way in which Rossetti fashions a sentence. His space is limited to the fourteen lines of a sonnet, and into this he puts as much as he can. To keep his architectural structure, he will combine several themes into a single sentence. The result is that he is often difficult to understand at a first reading, and that, even when we understand him, he seems to be trying to do too much. This manner has a marmoreal, Latin quality, reminiscent in some ways of Horace's Odes. It might well be argued that a language which has so few inflexions as English should not be modelled on an inflected language like Latin, and perhaps in the last resort Rossetti tried to do too much with his sentences. Yet we can see why he composed as he did. Since a sonnet is "a moment's monument," it must present as much as possible of such a moment, and present it in a monumental form. The various elements of an experience must be fused into a single whole, and, if this demands some excess of syntax, it cannot be helped. The result at its best is certainly grave and serious and rich in sound and meaning, and this is what Rossetti thought poetry ought to be.

In the second place, Rossetti thought that poetry must be pictorial and explained what he meant:

> Picture and poem must bear the same relation to each other as beauty in man and woman; the point of meeting where the two are most identical is the supreme perfection.[5]

If for painting this means that the subject of a picture must have a literary or poetical appeal, for poetry it means that a poem must have an appeal to the eye as well as to the ear and the understanding. For Rossetti poetical experience is complete only when it is presented through images which convey pictorially what is beyond the power of abstract words to convey in its full nature. No doubt he thought this because he was a painter and because his imaginative vision passed readily into concrete, pictorial shapes. He wished to do in poetry what he did in painting, to achieve through the medium of words an effect comparable to what he achieved through line and colour. This is of course quite different from making poetry imitate painting by an objective description of visible objects. Rossetti was no Parnassian. He sought in poetry the same end as in painting, but he knew that the two arts have different methods and materials. In both he hinted at concealed beauties, and in poetry he used visual effects to make them more vivid. Through images he transforms thoughts and feelings into solid shapes. For instance, in "The Hill Summit" he tells how towards evening he climbs a hill, and this careful account of what looks like an actual occasion has a symbolical purpose. The arrival at the hill-top is his own arrival at middle age. He keeps his symbols clear and consistent and creates by visual means the atmosphere of such a situation with its imaginative appeal to him:

> And now that I have climbed and won this height,
>   I must tread downward through the sloping shade
> And travel the bewildered tracks till night.
>   Yet for this hour I still may here be stayed
>   And see the gold air and the silver fade
> And the last bird fly into the last light.

This is how Rossetti, at a turning-point of his life, pauses while he looks back to the past and forward to the future. The situation needs no comment from him, since it is complete in itself and belongs to common experience.

Unlike much of Rossetti's work, the sonnets of *The House of Life* deal with events which take place largely in the mind. He might of course have conveyed their character by describing their external symptoms, and at times he does so. But to limit himself to such a method would be to leave unsaid much that means a good deal to him. Indeed, though Rossetti introduces natural scenes, it is usually as a prelude to something else. He sets his figures in their visible surroundings, and then advances from the sight of them to their significance. Thus he begins "Youth's Spring-Tribute":

> On this sweet bank your head thrice sweet and dear
> I lay, and spread your hair on either side,
> And see the newborn woodflowers bashful-eyed
> Look through the golden tresses here and there.

This is more than a background; it prepares the way for a situation in which the poet feels the spring both in nature and in himself and hears a summons to love. The physical setting is transcended as it becomes the symbol for a spiritual condition. So too in "Silent Noon" Rossetti begins by describing himself and his beloved at noon in the silence of the king-cups and the cow-parsley. But this external situation is the visible image of the flawless peace which he and his beloved feel:

> Deep in the sun-searched growths the dragon-fly
> Hangs like a blue thread loosened from the sky:—
> So this winged hour is dropt to us from above.
> Oh! clasp we to our hearts, for deathless dower,
> This close-companioned inarticulate hour
> When twofold silence was the song of love.

In the visible scene Rossetti sees hints of the spiritual state which is born from it and is so much a part of it that, when he seems to do no more than describe, he is also speaking in symbols.

Rossetti used this technique for his cult of the beautiful. Like the great Romantics, he was glad to lose himself in some ulterior scheme of things, to penetrate beyond the familiar world to secrets and mysteries, to find that even the most casual phenomena hold the key to unknown places of the spirit. Some sight might so captivate his senses and his intelligence, so excite and exalt him, that he was forced out of his habitual ways of thought into flights of imagination and moments of clairvoyant vision. When he defined the twofold task of the poet, he knew that his creative duty was to present both the immediate experience which engaged him and the remoter mystery which lurked in it. In responding to such calls his whole being was transformed. This was the most enthralling thing that he knew, and in "Soul's Beauty" he spoke of it with religious reverence:

> Under the arch of Life, where love and death,
>> Terror and mystery, guard her shrine, I saw
>> Beauty enthroned; and though her gaze struck awe,
> I drew it in as simply as a breath.

He believed that he was chosen by nature to absorb the influences of beautiful things, but he found them in the actual world. He did not share Baudelaire's conception of a remote ideal with its hatred of movement and its detachment both from laughter and from tears. But like Baudelaire, he knew how wayward and unpredictable the appearances of beauty are. It may be a single law which binds sea and sky and woman, but it is unaccountable in its comings and goings, as it lures men after it and exacts a life-long service from them:

> This is that Lady Beauty, in whose praise
>> Thy voice and hand shake still,—long known to thee
>>> By flying hair and fluttering hem,—the beat
>>> Following her daily of thy heart and feet,
>> How passionately and irretrievably,
> In what fond flight, how many ways and days!

Though Rossetti moves from one beautiful sight to another and is enslaved by each in turn, he believes that behind them all is the same celestial power, which irresistibly draws him and gives a direction and a pattern to his existence.

The pursuit of beauty was Rossetti's predominant passion and provides the main theme of *The House of Life*. The subject develops and expands and opens new prospects, but it remains his constant concern. It is inevitably connected with love. Rossetti's Southern blood freed him from most Victorian and English restraints, and his inevitable response to beautiful sights made him a ready victim to the beauty of women. In his first poem, "Love Enthroned," he speaks of the appeal which hope, fame, youth, and life make to him, but he goes on to say that love is more important than any of them:

Love's throne was not with these; but far above
    All passionate wind of welcome and farewell
He sat in breathless bowers they dream not of;
    Though Truth foreknow Love's heart, and Hope foretell,
    And Fame be for Love's sake desirable,
And Youth be dear, and Life be sweet to Love.

For Rossetti love has a paramount position because it brings him into contact with beauty in the most direct and most absorbing way. In his outlook we naturally expect to find the influence of Dante, and there are certainly traces of it. Just as Dante in the *Vita Nuova* makes love a principle of life and goodness, so does Rossetti, though of course his conception of goodness is not at all like Dante's. But here the resemblance ends. While Dante sees in love a divine power which brings man nearer to God, Rossetti is content that it should bring him nearer to beauty. He may be religious in his devotion to an ideal and in his sense of another, superior order of being, but he is not Christian like Dante. Perhaps he has more in common with Dante's predecessors, who were franker about the bodily claims of love and denied that it could or should be merely ideal. Rossetti is a Platonist in so far as he believes that love wakes the soul to enchanting visions and stirring enterprises, but he has nothing of the true Platonist's contempt for the flesh. Behind him lay centuries of Mediterranean life in which love, exalted to a very special cult, had been victorious over attempts to reduce it to an ethical discipline or to confine it to sanctified wedlock. To Rossetti love was a necessity both of the body and of the soul, and it satisfied the soul largely because it satisfied the body. Through it all his faculties were set to work, and he lived in that exalted awareness of the beautiful which was the spring of his creative being.

Many English poets have sung of love and have had new things to say of it. At one extreme are those, like Donne, who are not shy of speaking of its physical aspects, and find in it something alluring and fierce and exciting. Such poets do not attempt to glorify it or to claim that it belongs to anything but the body. At the other extreme are those like Shelley for whom love is the quintessence of ethereal flame, a union of souls in some unearthly sphere of harmony. But few have resembled Rossetti in his fusion of both elements and in his ability to make the best of both worlds, of the flesh and the spirit. If he was denounced by Robert Buchanan for his fleshliness, others have found him deplorably idealistic and remote from actuality. Both counts are unfair. Though Rossetti often describes physical beauty and its effect on him, though he is sometimes startlingly candid, he is never coarse. He redeems and transforms bodily passions by his sense of a spiritual world to which he penetrates through them, and by the exalted mood which is always his even when he is enraptured by his mistress's hair or eyes or body. Conversely, he never loses himself, as Shelley does, in an atmosphere so rarefied that it seems to have no relation to any familiar world. Rossetti knew that there is one beauty of the flesh and another beauty of the spirit, but he believed that in the end both are united in a single harmony and that each fulfils and glorifies the other. If he sought for the unseen beauty which lies in visible things, he knew that such glimpses of it as are permitted to men are to be found in this earth through the flesh which is the garment of the soul.

Rossetti's outlook gives a special quality to his poetry of love. It is never wild or ecstatic, and though it beats with powerful emotions, it keeps them in control and does not allow them to upset the prevailing balance. In his approach to love Rossetti is as grave as any of his early Italians, and his gravity is uniformly sustained. In his poetry there are always evidences of that "fundamental brainwork" which he claimed to be necessary for poetry.[6] His is a highly premeditated art, because he was able to exploit creative impulses only after a considerable struggle with himself and his emotions. He had first to extract all that he could from them, put them in order and see them in their right perspective, then relate them to his ideal of beauty and interpret their particular manifestations through some wider idea or more comprehensive vision. With him even physical passion is disciplined to this end, and Rossetti's poetry of it, outspoken as it often is, is always redeemed by the conviction that passion in itself is not enough but must be treated as a means to discover something beyond it.

The result is that even in those poems which most shocked Rossetti's contemporaries, the poetry passes beyond physical appetite to something exalting. As Rossetti meditated on his experience and related it to his own kind of metaphysics, he gave to it a new character and new depths. Take, for instance, "Nuptial Sleep," which Rossetti omitted from certain editions of *The House of Life* because some readers found in it "an unpleasant excess of realism." [7] The octet presents the actual situation with Rossetti's usual truthfulness, but what counts is the prevailing mood, and this is certainly much more than physical satiety. Even so, it is only an introduction to what follows, and should not be treated as if it contained the whole substance of the poem. In the sestet Rossetti passes to something else, to the sense of wonder and restored life which the situation brings, and in the magnificent image in which he portrays this, he conveys its essential mystery, its hints of a half-revealed world beyond the present occasion:

> Sleep sank them lower than the tide of dreams,
>   And their dreams watched them sink, and slid away.
> Slowly their souls swam up again, through gleams
>   Of watered light and dull drowned waifs of day;
> Till from some wonder of new woods and streams
>   He woke, and wondered more: for there she lay.

The search for beauty, which began in physical sensations, has passed to something else which illuminates them and gives them a new character.

The truth is that, when Rossetti fell in love, he felt himself in the presence of something so wonderful that he could not understand it or feel anything but awe before it. For him the women whom he loved were not so much human beings as visible manifestations of eternal beauty, embodiments of spiritual perfection, starry creatures of grace and tenderness. He found it almost impossible to believe that he, who was none of these things, could be so inexplicably privileged. It was as if the secrets of the universe were suddenly revealed to him in a flashing splendour and he was allowed to consort with beings from a celestial world. Before such a revelation he felt his inability to grasp all that was shown to him, and he saw how much more it meant than he could say:

> Not I myself know all my love for thee:
>   How should I reach so far, who cannot weigh
>   To-morrow's dower by gage of yesterday?
> Shall birth and death, and all dark names that be
> As doors and windows bared to some loud sea,
>   Lash deaf mine ears and blind my face with spray;
>   And shall my sense pierce love,—the last relay
> And ultimate outpost of eternity?

With an idealism entirely natural and sincere, Rossetti saw in his beloved not merely her visible self but great impersonal powers which move the world. He believed that his particular love was an individual manifestation of something sublime and eternal and universal. This vision he saw not as a philosopher but as a poet, and he gave his powers to showing what enchantment it put on him:

> Sometimes thou seem'st not as thyself alone,
>   But as the meaning of all things that are;
>   A breathless wonder, shadowing forth afar
> Some heavenly solstice hushed and halcyon;
> Whose unstirred lips are music's visible tone;
>   Whose eyes the sun-gate of the soul unbar,
>   Being of its furthest fires oracular;—
> The evident heart of all life sown and mown.

In moments like this Rossetti felt that he had pierced beyond the visible to the invisible and had begun to fathom its secrets.

Through love Rossetti found the ideal beauty which gave direction to his life's work. The story of his actual career has its painful and humiliating chapters, but it has little relevance to the interpretation of his poetry. In this we see him at his best, and most truly himself; for it presents all that he took most seriously. His poetry moves in a world not of fact but of imagination. Through the chequered events of his life he found something permanent and satisfying. But absorbing and exalting as his scheme was, it could not always be maintained at its highest level, and even in his most glorious moments Rossetti felt its insecurity and feared for its collapse. He was fully aware of the gulf between the ideal and the actual, between the high rapture when he found beauty and the black, bleak moments when he was alone with himself and empty and afraid:

> What of the heart without her? Nay, poor heart,
>   Of thee what word remains ere speech be still?
>   A wayfarer by barren ways and chill,
> Steep ways and weary, without her thou art,
> Where the long cloud, the long wood's counterpart,
>   Sheds double darkness up the labouring hill.

Even when he was most in love, Rossetti might fear that it could not last and that he would before long be robbed of everything that mattered most to him. For him the loss of love was much more than a personal sorrow; it meant that he was cut off from the main aim of his existence and from the vision which sustained him. It is not surprising that, when he thought of this, he was assailed by something close to despair and turned his thoughts to death:

> O love, my love! if I no more should see
> Thyself, nor on the earth the shadow of thee,
>   Nor image of thine eyes in any spring,—
> How then should sound upon Life's darkening slope,

The ground-whirl of the perished leaves of Hope,
The wind of Death's imperishable wing?

Rossetti's ideal beauty was a fugitive and inconstant power, and he knew that at times it would abandon him and leave him alone with his fears.

This uncertainty was the flaw in Rossetti's scheme of things. Beauty was his goal, and love the means by which he found it, but he had no assurance that love would always be his and that he would not suffer from defeat or frustration or some failure in himself to give all that he could or should. He might of course still find solace and inspiration in beautiful things and be moved by them to write poetry. But this was a second-best course. Physical nature and dramatic events meant much to him and provided him with excellent material for his art, but they touched only the fringes of his creative self and not its centre. His most characteristic and most authentic art was inspired by love, and he could not be sure that it would always be his. Of course, all poets are in a high degree dependent on the whims of inspiration, but with Rossetti the problem was more serious. Love gave him not only inspiration but his whole philosophy, since through it he found beauty. It was only natural that at times he should question his system of life and doubt if he had chosen the right way. At the outset of his career he saw the problem and shaped it into the three sonnets of "The Choice." With impartial justice he speaks in turn with the voices of the voluptuary, the religious ascetic, and the enquiring thinker. He comes to no explicit conclusion and makes no declared choice between the three lives. Each case is treated with an imaginative insight into its claims. The first catches the glamour of love and wine, the second the appeal of a life dedicated to self-denial in the hope of celestial reward, the third the driving optimism of thought which is never satisfied but always looks for more horizons beyond the known. There was something of each element in Rossetti. He knew the absorbing lure of women and wine; he had his moments of dark humiliation, when the world and its glories seemed to be nothing; he knew the restless ambitions of the creative mind. Ideally, perhaps, all three might be included and transcended in the cult of the beautiful, but in practice this was not possible, and it is not surprising that Rossetti wondered which course he ought to pursue. In effect he rejects the first and the second and gives his approval to the third. He puts it last, and with it alone he ends on a note of confident effort:

Nay, come up hither. From this wave-washed mound
    Unto the furthest flood-brim look with me;
Then reach on with thy thought till it be drown'd.
    Miles and miles distant though the last line be,
And though thy soul sail leagues and leagues beyond,—
    Still, leagues beyond those leagues, there is more sea.

No doubt a courageous hope of this kind sustained Rossetti through many hours of defeat, but he did not always hold to it, and there were times when it was of little help to him.

In shaping his life so deliberately to an end which suited many elements in his nature, Rossetti did not take full account of other elements which were discordant and intractable. For all his neglect of conventions, he was not able to rid himself of a very human sense of guilt. Artist and aesthete as he was, he was not beyond considerations of good and evil. Of course, he never seriously doubted that the pursuit of beauty was good, but he did doubt whether he had always been as eager and as energetic in it as he might have been. He, who knew so well the glory and the glitter of life, knew also at times its other side and was deeply distressed by his own shortcomings. In "The Sun's Shame" he speaks of the discords and shams and failures of the world, of power and success given to the corrupt or the feeble, of love unrequited and lives ruined by poverty, but, though he is indignant against these flaws and faults, he knows that he himself is in no way superior to those whom he condemns, and ends with a confession of his own inadequacy:

Beholding these things, I behold no less
The blushing morn and blushing eve confess
The shame that loads the intolerable day.

Rossetti was perfectly honest with himself and saw that in an imperfect world he too had his share of imperfections.

The most persistent and most painful remorse which assailed Rossetti was that he had not given all that he might have to his chosen work. He was so purely an artist that in the last resort devotion to art was his standard of behaviour, and he judged himself by it. Lost opportunities and failures due to sloth or cowardice haunted him as they haunt other men and brought sharp pangs of regret and re- pentance:

Look in my face; my name is Might-have-been;
I am also called No-More, Too-Late, Farewell.

He knew that there is no final protection against such feelings and that, though he might for the moment find peace, it would be only for the moment, and the cruel presences would again harry him. He brooded over them and asked what they meant. The religious faith of his childhood came back to him and intensified his sense of guilt, as he wondered how his failures would be judged in the afterworld when they would be seen in their naked reality. He felt that he, who had possessed remarkable gifts, had so neglected and squandered them that he had ruined himself and would rightly be denounced by all his murdered selves:

> I do not see them here; but after death
>   God knows I know the faces I shall see,
> Each one a murdered self, with low last breath.
>   "I am thyself,—what hast thou done to me?"
>   "And I—and I—thyself," (lo! each one saith,)
>   "And thou thyself to all eternity!"

Just as Baudelaire found that, in his devotion to an ideal beauty, he himself fell woefully below his standards, so too did Rossetti. Though he indulged himself in many ways and had no great respect for established morality, he had his own moral system, which was part of his whole system of life, and it was no less exacting than other more traditional codes.

This was the price which Rossetti had to pay for his convictions. No doubt, as his powers began to fail, such moments became more frequent and more harassing. But he would not have been himself without them, and they give a special depth to his poetry. They provide a contrast to his ecstatic flights and enable us to see against what difficulties he contended in his struggle to find an ideal world. They make him appreciate the ideal all the more keenly when he has glimpses of it and knows that his efforts have not been in vain, that he has in part lived up to his standards. They introduce a note of anguish into what might otherwise be rather remote and impersonal. Nor in the end did Rossetti allow himself to be defeated by them. Like all men of strong emotions and exacting ambitions, he had his dark hours of depression and defeat, and they were all the darker because he felt that he himself was to blame for them. But his outlook was not pessimistic. After all, he had his sublime rewards and knew that they more than compensated for anything that he might suffer. He was fully justified when he closed *The House of Life* with a sonnet which is indeed far from jubilant, but which displays his courageous persistence in his task. To this he had given everything, and in the end he might well ask if it had been worth while:

> When vain desire at last and vain regret
> Go hand in hand to death, and all is vain,
> What shall assuage the unforgotten pain
> And teach the unforgetful to forget?

He looks forward to another world and asks if he will find peace in it or perhaps even joy. Beyond the present he hopes for a consolation, a chance that something will survive and reward him, and in this he puts his final trust:

> Ah! let none other alien spell soe'er
> But only the one Hope's one name be there,—
> Not less nor more, but even that word alone.

Though Rossetti does not explicitly say so, it is legitimate to infer that the hope which sustains him is that after death his longing for love, and for beauty through love, will be realized, and that at last he will know in perfection what he has hitherto known uncertainly and fragmentarily.

The House of Life presents what was most powerful in Rossetti's creative being. These sonnets stand apart in his work because they reflect something which is not common at any time and which Rossetti possessed in a high degree. He pursued the beautiful more vigorously and more consistently than Ruskin or Pater, and his aestheticism was a much sterner discipline than Wilde could have endured. There is something noble and impressive in this dedication of a life to an ideal end, and in this determination to follow an exacting gospel without fear of consequence. Though Rossetti lacks the sweep and the scope of the great Romantics, though at times he seems remote or exotic, too enclosed in his special outlook and too careless of the world about him, he stands in the true Romantic tradition because of his belief in the mystery of life. His place is secure because in his pursuit of the beautiful he gave all his powers to an ideal which he valued beyond everything else and felt in his inner being to be sacred. If at times he thought that he had failed, he mastered his doubts through his command of his art and his unfailing sincerity with himself, and his confessions of weaknesses give to his poetry another dimension which adds greatly to its strength and brings him closer to us.

NOTES

1. *The Collected Works of Dante Gabriel Rossetti,* ed. by William M. Rossetti (1 vol., rev. ed.; London, 1911), p. 671.

2. *Dante Gabriel Rossetti, His Family-Letters,* with a Memoir by William M. Rossetti (2 vols.; Boston, 1895), II, 328. Letter of D. G. Rossetti to his mother: "There is also a splendid anecdote of Keats' proposing as a toast at a gathering—'Confusion to the memory of Newton!' and, on Wordsworth's wishing to know *why* he drank it, the reply was 'Because he destroyed the poetry of the rainbow by reducing it to a prism.' That is magnificent." The story comes from Haydon's *Autobiography.*

3. *Ibid.,* I, 420.

4. A. C. Benson, *Rossetti* (London, 1904), p. 74.

5. *Collected Works of Dante Gabriel Rossetti,* p. 15.

6. Hall Caine, *Recollections of Dante Gabriel Rossetti* (London, 1882, 1928), p. 248.

7. William Sharp, *Dante Gabriel Rossetti* (London, 1882), p. 413.

◆

John Ruskin

RUSKIN's early career was that of a singularly brilliant if singularly erratic art critic, one of whose most distinctive convictions was that the arts should be regarded as an expression of the society that produces them. At about forty, Ruskin shifted his main interest and henceforth wrote books chiefly about the problems of his society, though he found room in them for comments on art and, as a matter of fact, on almost every topic one could name. Ruskin's social criticism dates from about 1860 to the end of his productive life in the eighteen-eighties. Twenty-four years younger than Carlyle, and coming later in life to social criticism than Carlyle did, he reflects little of the tension and alarm that marked the period of the Reform Bill and of Chartism. Though born the year before Arnold, Ruskin was immunized by a sheltered home life, by Evangelicalism, and by his preoccupation with art from the understanding of the eighteen-forties and fifties that appears in Arnold's work. The period to which he is to be related as a social critic is the boom period of industrialism, the mid-years of the golden age of British capitalism.

Ruskin said he gave up criticism of art for criticism of society because no man could go on painting pictures in a burning house—an observation that reminds us that the most prosperous Victorian years could impress a contemporary as anything but serene. "For my own part . . . I have seceded from the study not only of architecture, but nearly of all art; and have given myself, as I would in a besieged city, to seek the best modes of getting bread and water for its multitudes, there remaining no question, it seems to me, of other than such grave

From *Perplexed Prophets: Six Nineteenth-Century British Authors* (Philadelphia: University of Pennsylvania Press for Temple University Publications, 1953), pp. 86–103. Reprinted by permission of the publishers and the author.

business for the time." [1] The shift in interest came at a time of personal crisis for Ruskin. It was at this time, for one thing, that he abandoned the faith in which he had been brought up. The conflict between science and religion had troubled him as early as 1851: "If only the Geologists would let me alone, I could do very well, but those dreadful hammers! I hear the clink of them at the end of every cadence of the Bible phrases." [2] When he mét Holman Hunt in Venice in the sixties he declared himself an atheist, giving it as his belief that there is no eternal father and that man must be his own helper and only resource. [3] Not that Ruskin remained consistent in this view, any more than he did in any other view. Yet it is clear that Ruskin is one of the many Victorians who turned with a new seriousness to social questions when they found that traditional religious belief had failed them.

The crisis of 1860, however, was mainly an inner crisis occasioned by the belated, partial, and extremely costly revolt against the domination of that part of his own nature which had been patterned by parental influence. As with Carlyle, Ruskin's attitudes were shaped in the main by powerful internal conflicts; he did not, like Arnold, have sufficient relative integration so that the conflicts the age imposed were among the most serious that beset him. Ruskin's parents, discovering that they had a genius on their hands, had devoted themselves to his nurture with the self-dedication of people whose lives are incomplete. In their handling of the boy they combined affection and strict discipline in such a way as to attach the child to his parents with bonds that proved for many years stronger than he could sever. It was not till Ruskin was twenty-six and famous that he was allowed to go abroad for the first time without his parents—and even then it was arranged that he should be accompanied by a valet, a guide, and a traveling servant. [4] The letters that passed between Ruskin and his parents, as Amabel Williams-Ellis remarks, resemble lovers' letters in their minute analysis of misunderstandings and grievances and unintended offenses. "There is something terrible in such minuteness of memory on both sides. We seem to see two spirits handcuffed together." [5]

It is to this abnormal relationship with his parents that one must trace the unhappy story of Ruskin's unconsummated marriage, his frantic tirades against sex, which far surpass the norms even of a prudish age, and his emotional attachments, as a middle-aged man, to very young girls, the most notable example of which was his pitiable infatuation with Rose La Touche, to whom he proposed when he was forty-seven and she seventeen. Charles Eliot Norton understood well that Ruskin suffered from what today would be called neurosis, as he shows when he says that "the deepest currents of his life ran out of sight, but it was plain that they did not run calmly, and their troubled course became manifest now and then in extravagances of action and paradoxes of opinion." [6] Usually Ruskin fought against admitting any weakness in himself; often he compensated for the unconscious realization of weakness by delusions of omniscience and infallibility; yet sometimes he shows a grasp of the malady from which he suffered. When he remarks that "it seems to be the peculiar judgment-curse of modern days that all their greatest men shall be plague-struck," [7] one has no doubt that he has himself in mind. No one can read Ruskin's writing or his biography without feeling pity for this greatly talented but tortured spirit.

R. H. Wilenski [8] regards the malady which eventually culminated in recurrent periods of insanity as manic-depressive psychosis; Louis Bragman,[9] T. M. Mitchell,[10] and Louise Nelson [11] confirm this view. In reading Ruskin one must constantly make allowances for the psychic disturbances reflected in his work. In *Fors Clavigera*, written during the seventies and early eighties, the reader learns to pay little attention when Ruskin announces that he will take up a certain subject; he seldom does so. Even the work of the sixties is marked by endless caprice and irrelevancy. The fact is that in his social criticism Ruskin was often not dealing primarily with outer reality, but was resolving tensions and releasing aggressions of his own subconscious nature. He seldom achieved that disciplined fidelity to outer fact that is indispensable for satisfactory literary construction. One must make allowances also for an arrogance that would strike the reader as intolerable if he were not aware of its neurotic origins. When Ruskin in his moods of manic exaltation offered blueprints for the total reconstruction of society, he laid down the most minute regulations as to the conduct of life in the new era. Permission to marry, for example, was to be granted publicly at village festivals held twice a year, in spring and autumn.[12] He prescribes the dress to be worn by different groups in the community, the degree of purity to be used in metals for coinage, and the stampings and inscription for each coin.[13] He prescribes that a bishop or overseer shall be in charge of each one hundred families and render an account for each individual.[14] Farmers, he decides, will be permitted to use the power only of animal or man, or wind and water—direct natural forces —not of machines.[15] In the new society, he says, "I will allow no man to admonish anybody, until he has previously earned his own dinner by more productive work than admonition" [16]—a rule for which much might be said, to be sure, though one cannot help thinking how much admonishing Ruskin himself was in the habit of doing though he admitted on another occasion that he "never did a stroke of work in my life worth my salt, not to mention my dinner." [17] All this apocalyptical blueprinting, however, would prove an almost intolerable exasperation to a reader unaware of its pathological origin.

One must make allowances, again, for a great amount of hostility—directed as often as not toward the reader. Ruskin was capable of great "sweetness and delicacy," of great kindness, as we see, for example, in the letter in which he offered financial help to Rossetti: "It seems to me that, amongst all the painters I know, you on the whole have the greatest genius, and you appear to me also to be—as far as I can make out—a very good sort of person. I see that you are unhappy, and that you can't bring out your genius as you should. It seems to me, then, the proper and *necessary* thing, if I can, to make you more happy, and that I should be more really useful in enabling you to paint properly and keep your room in order than in any other way. If it were necessary for me to deny myself, or to make any mighty exertion to do this, of course it might to you be a subject of gratitude, or a question if you should accept it or not. But as I don't happen to have any other objects in life, and as I have a comfortable room and all I want in it (and more), it seems to me just as natural I should try to be of use to you as that I should offer you a cup of tea if I saw you were thirsty, and there was plenty in the tea-pot, and I had got all I wanted." [18] Yet, though he was able at times to show the finest and most delicate feeling for people, as this passage indicates, at other times Ruskin was impelled by his internal malady to lunge out savagely against those about him. He was fighting a desperate battle—a losing one, in the end—for mental security; he attacked his neighbors, his contemporaries, and his readers in an effort to save himself from inner collapse. He turns to address the workingmen of England in *Time and Tide*, only to be overcome by a storm of hatred and contempt: "Your voices are not worth a rat's squeak," he cries, "either in parliament or out of it." [19]

Ruskin used his pen "to explain away his self-indulgences and to relieve his obsessions" [20] to such an extent that he frequently lost sight of the effect he must be having on the reader. While explaining to the workingman audience the evils of an unplanned economy he says he has recently felt compelled to give a hundred pounds to this needy case and another hundred pounds to that, with the result that both he and England will suffer because he will have to give up a trip to Switzerland "to examine the junctions of the molasse sandstones and nagelfluh with the Alpine limestone." [21] Reading passages of this sort one can hardly help being more impressed with the petulant old maid in Ruskin than with the point he is supposedly making. Similarly, Ruskin illustrates the decline of European civilization by complaining of the service he has received in a Paris hotel. Breakfast comes later than in the old day, he says; when it arrives, "it looks all right at first,—the napkin, china, the solid silver sugar basin, all of the old regime. Bread, butter,—yes, of the best still. Coffee, milk,—all right too. But, at last, here is a bit of the new regime. There are no sugar-tongs; and the sugar is of beetroot, and in methodically similar cakes, which I must break with my finger and thumb if I want a small piece, and put back what I don't want for my neighbor, tomorrow." [22] Only a man pathologically absorbed in his own conflicts could cite the absence of sugar-tongs in a Paris hotel as a grievance calculated to impress the English factory worker.

But the experience that gave rise to Ruskin's pathology was at the same time a source of strength in his social criticism, a criticism in some ways the most powerful produced in England in the nineteenth century. The strength of Ruskin's social criticism lies in the clarity and force with which he assails the irrationalities of the industrial system and the debasement of human nature for which he holds it responsible. Here Ruskin's magnificent intelligence, though recurrently entrammeled by obsessional drives as always, was able to work with great freedom and his incomparable gift of language was used to the finest effect. But we are constantly aware of deeper and more intimate sources of power than the rational intelligence plus command of the instrument of expression. The patterns of human relationship Ruskin had made his own in childhood had exceptional importance for him, since he had adopted them at the cost of suppressing his spontaneous self. Like Carlyle, he used an image of human relationship generated within the family—the image of an organic, tightly related, responsible society—as a criterion by which to judge the social relationships of contemporary England. The divergence between the image and the actuality gave rise to the anxiety, dismay, and fury a man feels when a conception that has neurotic importance for him is threatened. At the same time the intensity of feeling that accompanied the revolt of long-suppressed instinctual drives was diverted toward the object of immediate attack in his criticism. The tone, the emotional power, and to a great extent the ideas of Ruskin's social criticism are to be explained, then, in terms of his neurotic nature.

Comparing the Victorian spectacle of poverty amid plenty with his private image of the rationally ordered human family, Ruskin sweeps to the attack on a society where every plus sign of wealth is balanced by a minus sign of poverty, but where the pluses "make a very positive and venerable appearance in the world," while "the minuses have, on the other hand, a tendency to retire into back streets, and other places of shade,—or even to get themselves out of sight into graves."[23] "Though England is deafened with spinning wheels," he exclaims, "her people have not clothes—though she is black with digging fuel, they die of cold—and though she has sold her soul for gain, they die of hunger."[24] Comparing the ethics of the new society, in which self-interest has become a virtue, with the humane ethics he had acquired as a child, he denounces the "thrice accursed, thrice impious doctrine of the modern economist, that 'to do the best for yourself, is finally to do the best for others.'"[25] "So far as I know," he says, "there is not in history record of anything so disgraceful to the human intellect as the modern idea that the commercial text, 'Buy in the cheapest market and sell in the dearest,' represents, or under any circumstances could represent, an available principle of political economy."[26] The assertion that the predatory instinct is "one of the conditions of man's nature and, consequently, of all arrangements of civilized society" he describes as the "most vile sentence which I have ever seen in the literature of any country or any time."[27] He reminds the reader constantly that the pursuit of material gain, which the economy views as the foundation of national welfare, is for Christianity the root of all evil.[28] Your religion, he says, tells you to love your neighbor, but "you have founded an entire science of political economy, on what you have stated to be the constant instinct of man—the desire to defraud his neighbor."[29] You "mock Heaven and its Powers, by pretending belief in a revelation which asserts the love of money to be the root of *all* evil, and declaring, at the same time, that [you are] actuated . . . in all chief national deeds and measures, by no other love."[30] "I know no previous instance in history of a nation's establishing a systematic disobedience to the first principles of its professed religion."[31]

With savage elation Ruskin strips away the humbug through which men disguise from themselves the injustices from which they profit. To those who say the poor should bear with patience the burdens placed upon them by Providence, he retorts: "You knock a man in the ditch, and then you tell him to remain content in the 'position in which Providence has placed him.'" [32] "It is the merest insolence of selfishness," he insists, "to preach contentment to a laborer who gets thirty shillings a week, while we suppose an active and plotting covetousness to be meritorious in a man who has three thousand a year." [33] When the economist justifies lavish expenditures by the rich on the ground that they give employment to the poor, Ruskin sets the record straight by asserting that the rich do not support the poor by their spending; the poor support the rich by their work: "There is something to be said in favor of the present arrangement," he adds, "but it cannot be defended in disguise; and it is impossible to do more harm to the cause of order, or the rights of property, than by endeavors . . . to revive the absurd and, among all vigorous thinkers, long since exploded notion of the dependence of the poor upon the rich." [34]

These subjects arouse in Ruskin at times an effective form of fury-tinged humor. Quoting the remark that some of the new wealth of the country is now "filtering downwards to the actual workers," for example, he asks: "But whence, then, did it filter down to us, the actual idlers?" [35] Referring to the economist's contention that payment of interest is to be regarded as a reward for abstinence, compensation for risk, and wages for the labor of superintendence, Ruskin remarks that his fifteen thousand pounds of bank stock have not brought "the slightest communication from the directors that they wished for my assistance in the superintendence of that establishment"; as for compensation for risk, "I put my money into the bank because I thought it exactly the safest place to put it in"; and as for the interest's being a reward for abstinence, "If I had not my fifteen thousand pounds of Bank Stock I should be a good deal more abstinent than I am" and "nobody would talk of rewarding me for it." [36] It is in this fashion that Ruskin disposes of the cant of the political economist. As for the economist's assertion that economic depressions are caused by overproduction, this, says Ruskin, is "accurately the most foolish thing, not only hitherto said by men, but which it is possible for men ever to say, respecting their own business. No foolish being on earth will ever be capable of saying such another foolish thing, through all the ages." [37]

Ruskin displays a great gift not only for stripping off the disguises which hide the true relationship between man and man in an industrial society but for presenting these relationships in the most graphic form. If interest, for example, is not reward for abstinence, compensation for risk, or wages for superintendence, what is it? It is a device, says Ruskin, by means of which one man gets another to do his work. Seven thousand pounds which he has in government bonds, he tells his workingman audience, entitle him to a white slip of paper with some marks on it "which gives me a right to tax you every year, and make you pay me two hundred pounds out of your wages; which is very pleasant for me; but how long will you be pleased to do so?" [38] The loans floated by the Thiers government in 1871, Ruskin says, mean "that all the poor laboring persons in France are to pay the rich idle ones five per cent annually, on the sum of eighty millions of sterling pounds, until further notice." Furthermore, the government will have to keep the army in good shape to ensure that the interest is paid, so that the poor man will be required not only to pay the interest but to support the army that compels him to pay this interest: "He must pay the cost of his own roller." [39]

If interest is a device for getting another to do one's work, wealth, according to Ruskin, equals power over men. "What is really desired, under the name of riches, is, essentially, power over men; in its simplest terms, the power of obtaining for our own advantage the labor of servant, tradesman, and artist; in wider sense, authority of directing large masses of the nation to various ends." [40] A man cannot acquire a large fortune through "fair pay for fair labor" but only "by obtaining command over the labor of multitudes of other men, and taxing it for [his] own profit." [41] It would be a good thing, Ruskin said, using the device of intentionally naïve illustration which he handled so well, if every rich man could be addressed in his youth in some such words as these: "You are likely to be maintained all your life by the labor of other men. You will have to make shoes for nobody, but some one will have to make a great many for you. You will build houses and make clothes for no one, but many a rough hand must knead clay, and many an elbow be crooked to the stitch, to keep that body of yours warm and fine. Now remember, whatever you and your work may be worth, the less your keep costs, the better. It does not cost money only. It costs degradation. You do not merely employ these people. You also tread upon them. It cannot be helped; —you have your place, and they have theirs; but see that you tread as lightly as possible, and on as few as possible." [42]

"Nearly every problem of State policy and economy, as at present understood and practised," Ruskin says in another effective instance of naïve illustration, "consists in some device of persuading you laborers to go and dig up dinner for us reflective and aesthetical persons, who like to sit still, and think, or admire." [43] For when we get to the bottom of the matter, we will find that the inhabitants of the earth fall into two great classes. The first is the peasantry—the working people—the "original and imperial producers of turnips." Then, "waiting on them all round," is the other group, "a crowd of polite persons, modestly expectant of turnips, for some—too often theoretical—service. There is, first, the clerical person, whom the peasant pays in turnips for giving him moral advice; then the legal person, whom the peasant pays in turnips for telling him, in black letters, that his house is his own; there is, thirdly, the courtly person, whom the peasant pays in turnips for presenting a celestial appearance to him; there is, fourthly, the literary person, whom the peasant pays in turnips for talking daintily to him; and there is, lastly, the military person, whom the peasant pays in turnips for standing, with a cocked hat on, in the middle of the field, and exercising a moral influence upon the neighbors." [44]

Penetrating and impassioned as was Ruskin's criticism of contemporary society, when it came to offering a remedy his thinking became less coherent and less forceful. Often such proposals as he makes come as a bewildering anticlimax after the storm of his denunciation. He follows a dramatic picture of the way England is squandering her wealth in manufacture, for example, by asking: What can we do about it? And his answer is: With what you can spare from charity "buy ever so small a bit of ground . . . but buy it *freehold*, and make a garden of it, by hand-labor. . . . If absolutely nothing will grow in it, then have herbs carried there in pots." [45]

The principal reason for Ruskin's ineffectiveness in constructive criticism was that, like Carlyle, he was imprisoned by the psychic authoritarianism of his upbringing. It is true that at the time when he turned to social criticism, his spontaneous self was forcing its way to the surface; sometimes it carried him surprisingly far toward affirmation of the drive of the masses toward independence and a fuller life. It is in a sense extraordinary that a patrician like Ruskin should have turned away entirely from his own class to address himself to the working class. He turns to the workingmen, he says, because he knows that they "must for some time be the only body to which we can look for resistance to the deadly influence of moneyed power." [46] "What would have been the use of writing letters only for the men who have been produced by the instructions of Mr. John Stuart Mill?" [47] Ruskin's appeal to the workers was motivated in part also by the fine feeling he was capable of displaying on occasion for ordinary humanity. One recalls the way he encouraged stonemasons to carve what they would on the walls of the Oxford Museum—an attractive contrast, as William Gaunt remarks, with Whistler's reluctance to let the ordinary workman do so much as mix paints for the decoration of a room.[48]

But Ruskin could never for long think of the free drives of man's nature as anything but dangerous. He returned always to the conviction that just as the individual must master his instinctive impulses, so people in general must be held in check by a strict, if kind, authority. Unable to construct an image of the good society except in the guise of the wise paternalism of his home, Ruskin could not, save for sporadic flashes of insight, consider a democratic solution to the problems of Victorian society; he reverted instead to the image of a hierarchy where each man gives orders to those below him and in turn carries out in obedience the wishes of captain, leader, bishop, or king. For those who did not fit into such a scheme, repression or punishment was the only treatment. Like Carlyle, Ruskin regards the criminal not with understanding but with the same vindictiveness as he directs toward his own unsanctioned impulses. Criminals, he says, "are partly men, partly vermin; what is human in them you must punish—what is vermicular, abolish." [49] The worst misleaders of the people, he says, are those who say: "Stand up for your rights—get your division of living—be sure that you are as well off as others, and have what they have!—don't let any man dictate to you—have not you all a right to your opinion?—are you not all as good as everybody else?—let us have no governors, or rather—let us all be free and alike." [50] "My own teaching has been, and is," he repeats, "that Liberty, whether in the body, soul, or political state of man, is only another word for Death, and the final issue of Death, putrefaction." [51]

Because Ruskin often wrote on impulse and said whatever happened to be uppermost in his mind at the moment, one can find almost any view in his work. "Ruskin calendars," says R. W. Wilenski, "can be compiled by Tories, Fascists, and Communists, by photographic painters and Cubist artists, by Chauvinists and Pacifists, by parsons and agnostics. All can claim him as their man." [52] But the dominant point of view is an authoritarian one—and in this fact lies the source of his failure as a constructive critic. The only workable solution for the problems Ruskin faced was increased democracy. In the context in which he wrote, an authoritarian gospel had either to be ineffectual or, as an anticipation of twentieth-century fascism, vicious. Perhaps there is reason to rejoice that in his attempt at constructive criticism Ruskin was as ineffectual as he was.

Aware as he necessarily became of the inadequacy of his constructive proposals, Ruskin resorted commonly to an appeal for individual reform. F. W. Bateson's comment that "the evils the Victorians denounced were always individual, and the 'heart,' the conscience, was always their cure"[53] applies to Ruskin even more than to Carlyle or Arnold. Ruskin, like Carlyle, writes constantly in such a way as to imply that social problems have their source in personal ethics and can be solved through an appeal to the individual conscience. He says, for example, that competition in commerce is caused by personal jealousy,[54] and appears not to have considered that personal jealousy might be caused by competition in commerce. He censures businessmen for acquisitiveness and workingmen for shiftlessness; "The masters cannot bear to let any opportunity of gain escape them, and frantically rush at every gap and breach in the walls of Fortune, raging to be rich, and affronting, with impatient covetousness, every risk of ruin; while the men prefer three days of violent labor, and three days of drunkenness, to six days of moderate work and wise rest."[55] That the structure of society, rather than personal weakness, may make the businessman acquisitive and the worker shiftless Ruskin appears not to consider. He reads the businessmen lectures on how they should interest themselves, not in profit, but in the purity of the product and the welfare of their employees.[56] "It is no more [the manufacturer's] function to get profit for himself . . . than it is a clergyman's function to get his stipend."[57] That a manufacturer may sacrifice both the purity of his product and his employees' welfare to profit not because he wants to but because he must, Ruskin again appears not to consider.

We can see today more clearly than anyone could see in Ruskin's time that the economic practices of the day were determined by the evolving structure of society rather than by any set of thinkers. The role of the economists, at best, was to give a theoretical justification to practices which men adopted because they had little choice. Those who cited the authority of the economists in support of their actions were finding an ideological justification for what they were impelled to do by circumstance. But Ruskin, permitting himself to believe that everything could be changed if one could only reach the individual conscience, tried to deliver his contemporaries from the false teaching of the economists. "When I accuse Mill of being the root of nearly all the immediate evil among us in England," he said, "I am in earnest." [58] The lack of cogency in much of Ruskin's writing has its source in this mistaken assumption that abstract principles, rather than the necessities of an evolving society, determine the form of economic conduct.

Even when writing about war, Ruskin assumes that the problem can be solved by an appeal to the individual understanding or conscience. He uses all the rhetorical devices at his command to exhibit the absurdity of modern warfare. The nations today are like neighbors, he says, who instead of enjoying one another's society, employ their ingenuity and money in trying to excel one another in the manufacture of steel traps with which each hopes to catch the other if he ventures to trespass. [59] For England to spend a hundred and fifty times as much money on arms as on art, again, is as if a private gentleman should spend 164 pounds on pictures and then think nothing of spending 24,000 pounds for private detectives to watch the shutters. [60] The "essential character" of every war can be understood, says Ruskin, if we think of it as a fight between men of neighboring counties. The Franco-Prussian War of 1871, for example, might be regarded as a struggle between Lancashire and Yorkshire for the line of the Ribble. In the course of the quarrel Lancashire demands from Yorkshire the townships of Giggleswick and Wigglesworth. Over this question the men of both counties pour out their wealth and their blood. [61] We see today that the wars of the nineteenth century, like its economic conduct, were brought about by forces originating in the structure of society rather than by any failure of the intellect to grasp their absurdity or by any atrophy of the private sense of justice; they were fought despite the fact that people saw them to be wasteful and wrong, not, as Ruskin's rhetoric implies, because they failed to see this.

It may seem unfair in a sense to take Ruskin to task for belonging to his century rather than to ours. It was much less easy for Ruskin's contemporaries than for ours to see that by the mid-nineteenth century British society had developed a dynamic partly independent of men's conscious desires, with the result that God-fearing men paid their employees starvation wages, men privately disposed to co-operative enterprise engaged in destructive forms of competition, selfless men devoted their lives to acquisitive accumulation, and peaceloving men supported policies designed to protect investments, commandeer sources of raw material, and safeguard lines of trade by force of arms. Yet it is not only from the vantage point of the mid-twentieth century that Ruskin's failure to take account of this independent social dynamic becomes apparent. "Though in relation to nature he is a true naturalist," *The Spectator* said of Ruskin in 1877, "in relation to human nature [he] has in him nothing at all of the human naturalist. It never occurs to him apparently that here, too, are innumerable principles of growth which are quite independent of the will of man, and that it becomes the highest moralist to study humbly where the influence of human will begins and where it ends, instead of rashly and sweepingly condemning, as due to a perverted morality, what is in innumerable cases a mere inevitable result of social structure." [62] Ruskin's failure to apprehend rightly the relationship between the individual and society could not be better formulated. How far Ruskin was from accepting this form of criticism as pertinent may be seen from his infuriated reply: "England at this time has no 'social structure,' whatsoever; but is a mere heap of agonizing human maggots, scrambling and sprawling over each other for any manner of rotten eatable thing they can get a bite of." [63] Whistler, with characteristic malice, once said that the artists thought Ruskin a great political economist and the economists thought him a great artist.[64] One would be inclined to agree with the economists that Ruskin lacked capacity for the subject he was dealing with—provided, of course, that such agreement did not imply that the orthodox economists had greater competence.

Ruskin's appeal to the individual conscience prompted him to write many purple passages of somewhat facile inspirationalism—passages in which he evidently supplied the age with something it needed. It was this aspect of Ruskin's work that Prince Leopold selected for praise in a speech delivered in 1879. Ruskin had shown the English artisans, the Prince said, how they could draw "the full measure of instruction and happiness from this wonderful world on which both rich and poor gaze alike." His great lesson is "that the highest wisdom and the highest pleasure need not be costly or exclusive, but may be almost as cheap and as free as air,—and that the greatness of a nation must be measured, not by her wealth or her apparent power, but by the degree in which all her people have learnt to gather from the world of books, of Art, and of Nature, a pure and ennobling joy." [65] The passages of vague uplift to which the Prince refers now embarrass more than they inspire. In making an anthology of Ruskin selections fit to endure, one would omit every one of them.

No one can fail to be impressed with Ruskin's account of the manner in which his own society had lost its bearings. Yet the deepest impression made by Ruskin's social criticism as a whole is one of the pathos of an immense and tragic failure. It was a failure of which he himself was keenly aware. Unable either to shelve or to solve the problems of his age, he fell victim, he told Charles Eliot Norton, to a "daily maddening rage." [66] He gives way to "the unmeasured anger against human stupidity" which can often be, as John Morley finely says, "one of the most provoking forms of that stupidity." [67] He rages at the "money theory" of modern times, which "corrupts the Church, corrupts the household, destroys honor, beauty and life throughout the universe. It is *the* death incarnate of Modernism, and the so-called science of its pursuit is the most cretinous, speechless, paralyzing plague that has yet touched the brains of mankind." [68] He takes the preachers to task for giving support to Mill and to Mammon. [69] He lashes at his countrymen for letting "the destinies of twenty myriads of human souls" be determined by "the chances of an enlarged or diminished interest in trade." [70] His invectives become increasingly violent until they reach the point of hysteria: "We English, as a nation, know not, and care not to know, a single broad or basic principle of human justice. We have only our instincts to guide us. We will hit anybody who hits us. We will take care of our own families and our own pockets; and we are characterized in our present phase of enlightenment mainly by rage in speculation, lavish expenditure on suspicion or panic, generosity whereon generosity is useless, anxiety for the souls of savages, regardlessness of those of civilized nations, enthusiasm for liberation of blacks, apathy to enslavement of whites, proper horror of regicide, polite respect for populicide, sympathy with those whom we can no longer serve, and reverence for the dead, whom we have ourselves delivered to death." [71] Sometimes the invective turns into a shriek of loathing for "this yelping, carnivorous crowd, mad for money and lust, tearing each other to pieces, and starving each other to death, and leaving heaps of their dung and ponds of their spittle on every palace floor and altar stone." [72] When we read Ruskin we are often made to feel, as Leslie Stephen said, that we are "listening to the cries of a man of genius, placed in a pillory to be pelted by a thick-skinned mob, and urged by a sense of his helplessness to utter the bitterest taunts he can invent." [73]

NOTES

1. *The Complete Works of John Ruskin* (Philadelphia: Reuwee, Wattlee and Walsh, 1891), V, 357 (*The Study of Architecture*).

VICTORIAN LITERATURE: MODERN ESSAYS IN CRITICISM

2. E. T. Cook, *The Life of John Ruskin* (London: Allen, 1911), II, 19–20.

3. William Gaunt, *The Pre-Raphaelite Tragedy* (New York: Harcourt, Brace, 1942), p. 175.

4. Amabel Williams-Ellis, *The Exquisite Tragedy: an Intimate Life of John Ruskin* (Garden City, N. Y.: Doubleday Doran, 1929), p. 76.

5. *Ibid.*, p. 86.

6. *Letters of John Ruskin to Charles Eliot Norton,* ed. Charles Eliot Norton (Boston: Houghton, Mifflin, 1904), I, 17.

7. Thomas Earle Welby, *A Study of Swinburne* (London: Faber and Gwyer, 1926), p. 19.

8. R. H. Wilenski, *John Ruskin: an Introduction to Further Study of His Life and Work* (New York: Frederick A. Stokes, 1933).

9. Louis J. Bragman, "The Case of John Ruskin: A Study of Cyclothymia," *American Journal of Psychiatry,* 91 (March, 1935), 1137–59.

10. T. M. Mitchell, review of R. H. Wilenski's *John Ruskin* in *British Journal of Medical Psychology,* XIII (December, 1933), 354–59.

11. Louise A. Nelson, "Why John Ruskin Never Learned How to Live," *Mental Hygiene,* XII (October, 1928), 673–705.

12. *Works,* XIV, 203 (*Time and Tide*).
13. *Works,* IX, Letter LVIII (*Fors Clavigera*).
14. *Works,* XIV, 170 (*Time and Tide*).
15. *Works,* XIV, 217 (*Time and Tide*).
16. *Works,* XIV, 189 (*Time and Tide*).
17. *Works,* XVIII, 270 (*Arrows of the Chase*).
18. Quoted by Evelyn Waugh, *Rossetti, His Life and Work* (London: Duckworth, 1928), p. 69.
19. *Works,* XIV, 133 (*Time and Tide*).
20. Bragman, *op. cit.,* p. 1158.
21. *Works,* XIV, 197 (*Time and Tide*).
22. *Works,* VIII, Letter XLVIII (*Fors Clavigera*).
23. *Works,* VI, 208 (*Unto This Last*).
24. *Works,* XII, 272 (*Lectures on Art*).
25. *Works,* XV, 63 (*The Crown of Wild Olive*).
26. *Works,* VI, 175–76 (*Unto This Last*).
27. *Works,* VIII, Letter XLII (*Fors Clavigera*).
28. *Works,* VI, 57 (*Sesame and Lilies*).
29. *Works,* VII, Letter V (*Fors Clavigera*).
30. *Works,* VI, 57 (*Sesame and Lilies*).
31. *Works,* VI, 177 (*Unto This Last*).
32. *Works,* XV, 34 (*The Crown of Wild Olive*).
33. *Works,* XIV, 130 (*Time and Tide*).
34. *Works,* XVIII, 268–69 (*Arrows of the Chase*).
35. *Works,* VII, Letter IV (*Fors Clavigera*).
36. *Works,* VII, Letter XVIII (*Fors Clavigera*).
37. *Works,* VII, Letter II (*Fors Clavigera*).
38. *Works,* VII, Letter IV (*Fors Clavigera*).
39. *Works,* VII, Letter VIII (*Fors Clavigera*).
40. *Works,* VI, 168–69 (*Unto This Last*).
41. *Works,* XIV, 177 (*Time and Tide*).

282

42. *Works*, XIV, 205 (*Time and Tide*).
43. *Works*, VII, Letter XI (*Fors Clavigera*).
44. *Works*, VII, Letter XI (*Fors Clavigera*).
45. *Works*, VIII, Letter XLIII (*Fors Clavigera*).
46. *Works*, XIV, 219 (*Time and Tide*).
47. *Works*, VIII, Letter XXXVI (*Fors Clavigera*).
48. William Gaunt, *The Aesthetic Adventure* (New York: Harcourt, Brace, 1945), p. 98.
49. *Works*, VIII, Letter XLVIII (*Fors Clavigera*).
50. *Works*, XIV, 234 (*Time and Tide*).
51. *Works*, IX, Letter LVII (*Fors Clavigera*).
52. Wilenski, *op. cit.*, p. 188.
53. Frederick Wilse Bateson, *English Poetry and the English Language: an Experiment in Literary History* (Oxford: Clarendon Press, 1934), p. 101.
54. *Works*, XV, 48 (*The Crown of Wild Olive*).
55. *Works*, VI, 159 (*Unto This Last*).
56. *Works*, VI, 163 (*Unto This Last*).
57. *Works*, VI, 163 (*Unto This Last*).
58. *Letters to Norton*, I, 245.
59. *Works*, XV, 49 (*The Crown of Wild Olive*).
60. *Works*, XIV, 136–37 (*Time and Tide*).
61. *Works*, VII, Letter I (*Fors Clavigera*).
62. *Works*, IX, Letter LXXXV (*Fors Clavigera*).
63. *Works*, IX, Letter LXXXV (*Fors Clavigera*).
64. E. R. and J. Pennell, *The Life of James McNeill Whistler* (Philadelphia: J. B. Lippincott Co., 1919), p. 167.
65. Cook, *op. cit.*, II, 184.
66. *Letters to Norton*, II, 78.
67. Morley, *Life of Cobden*, I, 213.
68. Cook, *op. cit.*, II, 129. Letter to Dr. John Brown, August, 1862.
69. *Works*, VIII, Letter XXXVI (*Fors Clavigera*).
70. *Works*, XVIII, 220 (Letter to *The Scotsman*, August 6, 1859, *Arrows of the Chase*).
71. *Works*, XVIII, 225 (*Arrows of the Chase*).
72. *Works*, VIII, Letter XLVIII (*Fors Clavigera*).
73. Leslie Stephen, "Mr. Ruskin's Recent Writings," *Fraser's Magazine*, June, 1874.

LESLIE A. FIEDLER

◆

The Master of Ballantrae

"That Angel was the Devil."

R. L. S. at the age of seven.

MODERN prose fiction has moved toward the myth in two quite different ways: one way, that of James Joyce, for instance, leads from the inward novel of character, through psychological naturalism, to symbolism, to the truly mythic (that is to say, from *Dubliners* to *Ulysses* to *Finnegans Wake*); the other begins with the outward romance of incident, the boys' story or the fairy tale, and moves through allegory, often elusive, to myth. To the latter group belong such different writers as Herman Melville, Charles Williams, Graham Greene—and Robert Louis Stevenson. It is typical of the latter group that they preserve the story and its appeal intact; in them the picturesque never yields completely to the metaphysical—and they can always be read on one level as boys' books or circulating-library thrillers. To understand and examine Stevenson as a writer of this kind is at once to take him seriously and to preserve the integrity of his romance as romance.

Moreover, when we have come to see Stevenson's artistic progress toward exploiting ever more deeply the universal meanings of his fables, with the least possible surrender of their logic and appeal as "howling good tales," we will be able to understand, perhaps better than the author ever did, certain contradictions of tone and intent in the later books. Indeed, Stevenson was a writer who understood him-

Introduction by Leslie A. Fiedler to Robert Louis Stevenson's *The Master of Ballantrae,* Rinehart Edition. Copyright 1954 by Leslie A. Fiedler. Reprinted by permission of Rinehart & Company, Inc., New York, Publishers, and the author.

self singularly little; he was saved by a stubborn faith in his stories "as they came" that preserved him from the shallow literary virtues he proposed: the avoidance of all "griminess," a contempt for the "artificial" world of city and drawing room in favor of the "real, male world" of outdoors, the pursuit at all costs of the picturesque and the cheerful. At only one point was R. L. S.'s inner necessity at one with his avowed aesthetic principles: in his distrust of the "particular," his rejection of the faith that in painstaking literal detail is truth, from which we are just now recovering.

> How to get over, how to escape from the besotting *particularity* of fiction. "Roland approached the house; it had green doors and window blinds; and there was a scraper on the upper step." To hell with Roland and the scraper!—*From a letter of R. L. S.*

In the mythic, Stevenson found a way successfully to get over the "besotting particularity" of the novel, a way to another order of truth; and in the mythic, too, he found unity. He is pre-eminently a latter-day maker of myths, and it is in the realm of myth that we must look for his unity and meaning.

Over and over again since his reputation was first questioned, critics have asked: Is there in Stevenson's work a single motivating force, beyond the obvious desire to be charming, to please, to exact admiration—qualities that seem to us now a little shallow and more than a little coy? It is a double question, really, though a single answer will perhaps suffice, a question of technique and a question of morality: What device makes a unified whole of the several scenes and observations in books like *Dr. Jekyll and Mr. Hyde, Treasure Island,* and *The Master of Ballantrae,* all patchworks of shifting points of view, intruded documents, and supplementary narratives? And what compelling vision, what felt unity of discrimination or illumination maintains their relevance for us? Frank Swinnerton found in only one book, *Jekyll and Hyde,* a "unifying idea." But "idea" is a misleading word; a single felt myth gives coherence, individually and as a group, to several of Stevenson's long fictions—and it is the very myth explicitly stated in *Jekyll.* The other books are *Treasure Island, Kidnapped, The Master of Ballantrae,* and *The Weir of Hermiston;* the organizing mythic concept might be called the Beloved Scoundrel, or the Devil as Angel, and the books make a series of variations on the theme of the beauty of evil—and conversely, the unloveliness of good.

To be sure, there is no single theme which sums up *all* the meanings of Stevenson's long fictions, but the Beloved Scoundrel is a continuing and crucial motif in every one of his more important novels (I exclude those inferior "machines" done in collaboration with Lloyd Osbourne), and it is certainly the theme most completely realized in *The Master of Ballantrae*. The appealing rogue makes his debut as Long John Silver in *Treasure Island*, a tale first printed, it is worth noticing, in a boys' magazine, and written to explain circumstantially a treasure map drawn for a child's game that Stevenson had been playing with his stepson.

There can be little doubt that, in part at least, Stevenson married to become a child; to find himself at the age of thirty at long last a child enabled him unexpectedly to become for the first time a real creative writer, that is, to sustain a successful long fiction. All of Stevenson's major loves had been older, once-married women, which is to say—mothers. There was his "Madonna," Mrs. Sitwell, who in the end married his friend Sidney Colvin and to whom he used to sign his letters of passionate loneliness "Your Son"; there was the agreeably alien and mature Mme. Garschine, whom he assured "what I want is a mother"; and there was, at last, the woman he actually wed, Fanny Osbourne, some eleven years older than he, the mother of three children.

His marriage to Mrs. Osbourne gave him a mother to replace his own from whom he felt estranged and to whom he could not utterly commit himself without feelings of guilt toward his father; at the same time it provided him for the first time with a brother in the form of his twelve-year-old stepson Lloyd. An only child and one isolated by illness, Stevenson had never been able to feel himself anything but a small adult (his parents observed him, noted down his most chance remarks with awful seriousness); against the boy Lloyd he was able to define himself as a boy. Together they *played* at many things: toy soldiers, printing (they founded the Davos Press to publish accounts of their mock warfare)—even writing. Before Lloyd had fully matured, he and Stevenson had begun their collaboration with *The Wrong Box*. To R. L. S. writing seemed always a kind of childish sport: "To play at home with paper like a child," he once described his life's work, with a glance over his shoulder at his disapproving forebears, good engineers and unequivocal adults. But there is in such a concept of art not only the troubled touch of guilt, but the naïve surge of joy; and Stevenson's abandonment to childhood meant his release as an artist—it produced *Treasure Island*, *Kidnapped*, and *A Child's Garden of Verses*.

Long John Silver is described through a boy's eye, the first of those fictional first-person singulars who are a detached aspect of the author. It is Jim Hawkins who is the chief narrator of the tale, as it is Jim who saves the Sea-Cook from the gallows. For the boy, the scoundrel par excellence is the Pirate: an elemental ferocity belonging to the unfamiliar sea and uncharted islands hiding blood-stained gold. Vain, cruel, but astonishingly courageous and without self-doubt, able to compel respect, obedience, and even love—that is John Silver; and set against him for a foil is Captain Smollett, in whom virtue is joined to a certain dourness, an immediate unattractiveness. Not only Jim, but Stevenson, too, finds the Pirate more lovable than the good Captain. In one of his *Fables* written afterward, he sets before us Alexander Smollett and John Silver, debating with each other while their author rests between Chapters XXXII and XXXIII: and Captain Smollett is embarrassed by the Sea-Cook's boast that their common creator loves him more, keeps him in the center of the scene, while he keeps the virtuous Captain "measling in the hold." Jim and Stevenson are one —good boys, both, they like for a little while to play at pirates.

Kidnapped, like *Treasure Island*, was written for a boys' magazine, and both are consequently innocent of sex. In *Kidnapped*, however, the relation of the Boy and the Scoundrel, treated as a flirtation in the earlier book, becomes almost a full-fledged love affair, a presexual romance; the antagonists fall into lovers' quarrels and make up, swear to part forever, and remain together. The Rogue this time is Alan Breck Stewart, a rebel, a deserter, perhaps a murderer, certainly vain beyond forgiveness and without a shred of Christian morality. The narrator and the foil in this book (technically the most economical; perhaps, in that respect, the best of Stevenson) are one: David Balfour is Jim Hawkins and Captain Smollett fused into a single person. David must measure the Scoundrel against himself, and the more unwillingly comes to love that of which he must disapprove. Here good and evil are more subtly defined, more ambiguous: pious Presbyterian and irreverent Catholic, solid defender of the *status quo* and fantastic dreamer of the Restoration; in short, Highlander and Lowlander, Scotland divided against itself. It is the Lowlander that Stevenson *was* who looks longingly and disapprovingly at the alien dash, the Highland fecklessness of Alan through the eyes of David (was not Stevenson's own mother a Balfour?); but it is the Highlander he *dreamed* himself (all his life he tried vainly to prove his father's family was descended from the banned Clan MacGregor) that looks back. The somber good man and the glittering rascal are both two and one; they war within Stevenson's single country and in his single soul.

In *Dr. Jekyll and Mr. Hyde,* which Stevenson himself called a "fable," that is, a dream allegorized into a morality, the point is made explicit: "I saw that of the two natures that contended in the field of my consciousness, even if I could rightly be said to be either, it was only because I was radically both." It is the respectable and lonely Dr. Jekyll who gives life to the monstrous Mr. Hyde; and once good has given form to the ecstasy of evil, the good can only destroy what it has shaped by destroying itself. The death of evil requires the death of good. *Jekyll and Hyde* is a tragedy, one of only two tragedies that Stevenson ever wrote; but its allegory is too schematic, too slightly realized in terms of fiction and character, and too obviously colored with easy terror to be completely convincing.

In *The Master of Ballantrae,* Stevenson achieves the full tragedy he merely indicated in *Jekyll.* In the greater book he dramatically splits in two what is morally one: unlovely good and lovely evil; and he further splits, as in *Treasure Island,* the good protagonist into an actor and a narrator, localizing in the latter all the ambivalence toward the Rogue. For this book the boys' Scoundrel, one-legged Pirate, or kilted Highland Rebel will not do; there must be an adult villain, though he must live and die in terms of a "howling good tale." Such is James Durrisdeer, the Master of Ballantrae.

He is, like John Silver or Alan Breck, absolutely brave and immediately lovable, though unscrupulous and without mercy, two-faced and treacherous, inordinately proud and selfish. But he is all these conventionally villainous things in an absolute sense; he is the very maturity, the quintessence of evil. He is for a time like Long John a Pirate, like Alan a Rebel (and like the later Frank Innes a Seducer), but these are for him mere shadowy forms of what he is ideally. Stevenson, as if to make sure we understand, brings the Master face to face first with the protagonist of *Kidnapped,* "Alan Black Stewart or some such name," and next with Teach himself, the infamous Blackbeard—surely a fit surrogate for Silver and all his crew—and shows each of these in turn shamefully outwitted by the Master. Alan's conduct in their encounter is described as "childish," and Teach, called first "a wicked child" meets his defeat at the Master's hand "like a wicked baby." Beside ultimate villainy, the Pirate and the Highland Rebel seem scarcely adult; theirs is the rascality of the nursery, laughable rather than terrible—and they serve at last only to define the Master's "deadly, causeless duplicity," that final malevolence which must be called "beautiful," the "nobility of hell."

In a letter in which he first discusses his plans for the book, Stevenson writes, "The Master is all I know of the devil," and later to Henry James, "The elder brother is an INCUBUS!" One of the happiest strokes of invention in *The Master* is the presentation of elemental good and evil as brothers: Esau and Jacob in their early contention, Cain and Abel in their bloody ending. It is an apt metaphor of their singleness and division.

Henry, the younger brother of the Master, James, is patient, loyal, kind though not generous, at first more than reasonably pious and humble. He has, however, the essential flaw of Stevenson's virtuous men: the flaw of Alexander Smollett, who was "not popular at home," perhaps even of R. L. S. himself appealing to his "Madonna" to assure him that he is not "such cold poison to everybody." Henry does not compel love, not his father's nor that of Alison, the woman who marries him believing that her real beloved, his malefic brother, is dead. He feels his lack of appeal as a kind of guilt, and when his wife is morally unfaithful to him (he is like the hero of *Prince Otto*, in everything but physical fact a cuckold), he can reproach only himself.

Ephraim Mackellar, called "Squaretoes," the Steward of Durrisdeer and the loyal supporter of Henry, is everything that his Lord is—exaggerated toward the comic—and a pedant and a coward to boot. It is through his dry, finicky prose (with the exception of two interpolated narratives by the Chevalier Burke, the comic alter ego of James) that the story unfolds, and it is in his mind that the conflict of feeling—repulsion and attraction—toward the Master is played out.

There is no question of James Durrisdeer having some good qualities and some bad; it is his essential quality, his absolute evil, that is *at once* repellent and attractive. The Master *is* evil, that imagined ultimate evil which the student Stevenson naïvely sought in the taverns and brothels of Edinburgh, another Mackellar, his notebook in hand! It is the quality that, Stevenson found, women and unlettered people instinctively love—the dandiacal splendor of damnation that even a Mackellar must call at one point "beautiful!" The study of such double feeling is not common in the nineteenth century, which preferred melodrama to ambivalence; and it is the special merit of Stevenson to have dealt with a mode of feeling so out of the main stream of his time.

From the beginning of the book, the diabolical nature of the Master is suggested, at first obliquely and almost as if by inadvertence. "I think you are a devil of a son to me," the old father cries to James; it is merely a commonplace figure of speech, but later it becomes more explicit. Henry, veiledly telling his young son of his duel with the Master, speaks of "a man whom the devil tried to kill, and how near he came to kill the devil instead." They are the words of one already half-mad with grief and torment, but the eminently sane Mackellar is driven to concur in part: "But so much is true, that I have met the devil in these woods and have seen him foiled here." All leads up to the moment of recognition and unwilling praise, when Mackellar says of James: "He had all the gravity and something of the splendor of Satan in the 'Paradise Lost.' I could not help but see the man with admiration. . . ."

But if James is in any real sense the Devil, he must be immortal; his defeats and deaths can be only shows—and this, indeed, the younger brother comes to believe: "Nothing can kill that man. He is not mortal. He is bound upon my back to all eternity—to all God's eternity!" Actually—which is to say according to the account of Mackellar—at the point where Henry breaks forth into near hysteria at the news of yet another presumed death, the Master has been falsely thought dead twice. "I have struck my sword throughout his vitals," he cried. "I have felt the hilt dirl on his breastbone, and the hot blood spirt in my very face, time and again, time and again! But he was never dead for that. . . . Why should I think he was dead now!" And truly, he is to rise once more. Which account is then *true?* Mackellar's dry literal report, or the younger brother's hallucinated sense of the moment of strife, the unreal death repeated again and again through all time—James and Henry, Esau and Jacob, Cain and Abel?

It is Stevenson's difficult task to juggle both truths: to contain in a single tale the eternally re-enacted myth and the human story, the historical event—and to do it in "Mackellarese"! Small wonder if he felt his problem almost impossible, and if, to some degree, he failed. I do not think he understood the precise nature of his difficulty ever (there is a price to pay for choosing to be a child), but he sensed its presence. "My novel is a tragedy. . . ." he wrote to Henry James. "Five parts of it are bound [sound?], human tragedy; the last one or two, I regret to say, not so soundly designed; I almost hesitate to write them; they are very picturesque, but they are fantastic; they shame, perhaps degrade, the beginning. I wish I knew; that was how the tale came to me however. . . . Then the devil and Saranac suggested this *dénouement,* and I joined the two ends in a day or two of feverish thought, and began to write. And now—I wonder if I have not gone too far with the fantastic? . . . the third supposed death and the manner of the third re-appearance is steep; steep, sir. It is even very steep, and I fear it shames the honest stuff so far. . . ."

The "honest stuff," the "sound, human tragedy" is the story of the hatred of two brothers and its genesis: the love of Alison for the Master; his supposed death at Culloden; her marriage to Henry, who has all the while loved her; and the Master's reappearance. It is an episode doubtless suggested in part by the actual experience of Stevenson's wife, whose first husband, presumed dead, had reappeared to his supposed widow. Indeed, Samual Osbourne seems to have been in his own right a scoundrel worthy of sitting for James Durrisdeer. This aspect of his novel Stevenson has handled with great psychological accuracy: the Master's reappearance causing the disconcerting transformation of what had been a touching loyalty to the dead into a living infidelity; the Master's two faces, graceful charm for Alison and his father, careless scorn for Henry and the Steward; the timid rage of Mackellar mounting toward the climactic moment at sea when he discovers he is not quite the coward—or the Christian—he has thought himself, and prays blasphemously in the midst of a storm for a shipwreck that will destroy him and the Master together.

But the "steep" denouement that joined itself to the soundly human story, one freezing night at Saranac, impelled the original material toward allegory, in the direction of the mythical. In that remote context, Stevenson had remembered a story told him by an uncle many years before: a tall tale of an Indian fakir who could, by swallowing his tongue, put himself into a state of suspended animation that would permit his being buried alive and later exhumed without any permanent ill effects. The last presumed death of the Master was to be such a deliberate East Indian sham, translated to the Province of Albany. To justify so "fantastic" a conclusion in terms other than the merely picturesque, Stevenson would have had frankly to abandon ordinary standards of credibility, to make the Master *really* a devil, and to risk the absurdity of a myth of the deathlessness of evil. But that would have impugned the *human* tragedy he had already blocked out, and he dared be in the end only fantastic enough for a yarn, that is to say—far from too fantastic—not fantastic enough. Even in *Jekyll* Stevenson had felt bound to explain the transformation to Hyde in the "scientific" terms of a graduated glass and a compound of salts— and that story he considered an outright "Fable"—immune to the human limitations of the novel.

Stevenson will have the fabulous, but he will have it rationally explicable too. The Master must be provided with an Indian servant, must indeed have been in India himself; and there must even be an interpolated narrative to give us a glimpse of him there. The voice which frankly terms him supernatural, which asserts, "He's not of this world. . . . He was never canny!" must be that of a man nearly mad. If *The Master* seems to pull apart a little at the seams, it is this timidity on the part of its author that is the cause, rather than the fact, customarily insisted upon, that the book was begun in upstate New York and only completed after a lapse of inspiration in Honolulu. After all, the beginning and the end, whenever actually written, were *conceived* together. Perhaps the real trouble was that Stevenson, unlike his characters, did not really believe in Hell.

And yet the ending is effective all the same. The Master, who had seemed to die at Culloden, and had turned up again only to be apparently killed in a duel with his younger brother, is carried off by smugglers, healed, and returns once more to pursue his brother on two continents; but Henry, finally tormented out of humility and reason, turns on James, who, at last trapped by the cutthroats his younger brother has hired to kill him, "dies" and is buried in the midwinter American wilderness. Dug up by his Hindu servant under the eyes of his brother, the Master revives for a moment, just long enough to cause the death by heart failure of the onlooking Henry, and to ensure their burial under a single marker in that remote waste.

The point is the point of *Jekyll:* evil will not die until it has corrupted the good to its own image and brought it down by its side to a common grave. "He is bound upon my back to all eternity—to all God's eternity!" Henry had prophetically cried; and Mackellar, noting the universal meaning of his degeneration, its relevance to that struggle of us all—in which combating evil we come to resemble it— said, "I was overborne with a pity almost approaching the passionate, not for my master alone but for all the sons of man."

Toward the end of his life, Stevenson seems to have lost faith in the worth of *The Master,* though the book had received great critical acclaim, and he had begun with a sense of its being "top chop," "a sure card!" One of his last recorded remarks about the book is that lacking "all pleasureableness," it was "imperfect in essence"—a strange judgment surely, for it is precisely a pleasureable story, a work of real wit: a tragedy seen through the eyes of a comic character. Much more just seems to us the comment of Henry James, written out of his first enthusiasm: "A pure hard crystal, my boy, a work of ineffable and exquisite art." The word "crystal" is peculiarly apt; it is a winter's tale throughout, crystalline as frost, both in scene, from the wintry Scottish uplands to the icy, Indian-haunted Albanian forest; and in style, the dry, cold elegance of "Old Squaretoes"—preserved in a subzero piety in which nothing melts.

The quality of the writing alone—the sustained tour de force of "Mackellarese," that merciless parody of the old maid at the heart of all goodness and of Stevenson himself, which makes style and theme astonishingly one in this book—is the greatest triumph of Stevenson's art.

In the unfinished *Weir of Hermiston*, alone among his important novels, R. L. S. attempts to write in the third person, in his own voice —and consequently, there is in that book, as there is never in *The Master*, downright bad writing. Stevenson's instinctive bent was for first-person narrative; and when in his last book he attempts to speak from outside *about* his fiction, his style betrays him to self-pity (we *know* Archie is really the author, and the third-person singular affects us like a transparent hoax), sentimentality, and the sort of "fine" writing he had avoided since *Prince Otto*.

The *Weir* presents several fascinating problems: it is the only one of Stevenson's books to deal at all adequately with a woman and with sexual love (Alison in *The Master* quickly becomes a background figure; and the earlier efforts along these lines in *Catriona* and *Prince Otto* were failures, sickly or wooden). Even here the most successfully realized female character is not the Ingenue, but Old Kirstie, the epitome of all Stevenson's foster mothers from his Nurse, Cummy, to his wife. It is, too, the only explicit formulation of the conflict between father and son so important in Stevenson's life and so ignored in his major fiction until the *Weir*.

For our present purposes, however, the *Weir* is chiefly interesting for the final appearance of the Lovable Rogue, this time as the Seducer, Frank Inncs, a school friend of, and foil to, the protagonist Archie Weir, the prototype of all those "good" Stevensonian characters who are somehow unworthy of love. The Master, who contains in himself all of Stevenson's lesser scoundrels, had already foreshadowed the Seducer, in intent upon his brother's wife, and in fact upon the village girl Jessie Broun, casually abandoned after a brief and brutal amour by the older brother, but provided for by the kindness of the younger. Young Kirstie in the *Weir* is something of Alison and something of Jessie, a Cressida at heart, neither untouchable nor yet a harlot.

In the book as originally planned, Young Kirstie, baffled by the principled coldness of Archie who loves her but whom she cannot understand, was to be got with child by Frank Innes, who would then be killed by Archie, and Archie in turn would be condemned to die on the gallows by his own father, a hanging judge of terrible integrity. It is the ending of *Jekyll* and *The Master* all over again—good destroying itself in the very act of destroying evil—but Stevenson relented. In the projected ending reported by his amanuensis and much deplored by most of his critics, Archie was to have broken prison just before the day of his execution, and to have escaped with Kirstie to America, making her his wife and taking as his own the child she was carrying, the by-blow of the Scoundrel he has killed.

It was to be a complete merging of good and evil, not as before in mutual destruction and the common grave, but in the possession of a single woman able to love—though in different senses—both; and in the seed which virile evil is able casually to sow, but which only impotent virtue can patiently foster. To cavil at this as an unmotivated "happy ending," and to wish that Stevenson had survived once more to change his mind, is to miss utterly the mythic meaning of the event: a final resolution of man's moral duality this side of the grave.

E. K. BROWN

◆

Swinburne: A Centenary Estimate

THE centenary of Swinburne's birth falls at a time when the excellences of Swinburne's poetry are unlikely to receive their due. In a recent study (1931), Mr. W. R. Rutland, writing as a professed admirer, suggests that Swinburne is as remote as the Elizabethans; he belongs to the past, as unquestionably as Hardy belongs to the present. He has not been dead thirty years; and yet it is not easily remembered that for the last ten years of his life he was currently accepted as the greatest living English poet. It is even more difficult to recall that from 1870 on to the end of the century his lyrical poetry was the purest written in England. Of all the great Victorian poets it was he who made the most direct attack upon the idols of his time, upon the sentimental conception of love, upon bourgeois democracy, upon the institutional expressions of the Christian religion. For his daring he has paid heavily: a sulphurous cloud still hangs over his name, his work has always had about it the aroma of heresy, revolt, and evil. He is the poet of passion, the poet of absolute liberty, the poet of evolution, the poet of tumultuous music. Passion is not now the staple of great literature that it was accounted ten years ago; absolute liberty is dismissed as a chimera, and those who believe in it may soon be obliged to follow Conrad's *Garibaldino* to the mythical republic of Costaguana; the emotional implications of evolution are no longer formative; tumultuous music seems vulgarly emphatic, like the nudes of Ingres and the landscapes of Turner. Swinburne is in danger of becoming a forgotten poet; and it is when a writer is in danger of

From *University of Toronto Quarterly*, VI (1937), 215–235. Reprinted by permission of the publisher and Margaret Brown.

being forgotten that his centenary should be seized upon as an occasion for evoking his achievement, turning it leisurely before our eyes and deciding whether or not literature will be served by quietly allowing him to recede into a mere name in the anthologies along with Campbell and Rogers. There is still time enough, however, if Swinburne's achievement seems to justify it, for his place to be in greater company—with Byron, Keats, and Shelley.

Since his death, it must be said, he has had interpreters and advocates of greater capacity and fervour than Tennyson has had, or Browning or Arnold. Sir Edmund Gosse wrote his biography, a masterpiece of discretion; Mr. T. J. Wise has collected and described a vast Swinburne library; there are the critical studies of T. Earle Welby, of Mr. S. C. Chew, of M. de Reul, of Mr. Harold Nicolson, and of Mr. Rutland, all of them sympathetic and penetrating, one, at least, a work of great brilliance and power; finally, in 1928, M. Georges Lafourcade, in his two-volume work, *La Jeunesse de Swinburne*, has made for him the mightiest monument that any of our Victorian poets has yet received, and it is fitting that the definitive work on Swinburne's youth should be written in France.[1] Other interpreters there have been, and most of them enthusiastic. The public and the world of critical readers, however, have not been enthusiastic; and Swinburne's champions must have felt themselves to be at work against heavy odds. They have not won their cause; they have barely told upon opinion.

I

One power Swinburne is generally allowed to have possessed: the power of passionate song. It is with this quality of his poetry that it is best to begin the progress towards a general estimate. By it the poet himself set great store. Writing to E. C. Stedman in 1875, he insists on the primary importance of the singing power, if one would write poetry. Stedman had sent him a copy of one of his works on American poetry; and Swinburne passes in review the poets represented there. Two extracts from his letter will tell the whole story. Speaking of Bryant and Lowell he insists:

> I cannot say that either ["Thanatopsis" or the "Commemoration Ode"] leaves in my ear the echo of a single note of song. It is excellent good speech, but if given us as song its first and last duty is to sing. The one is most august meditation, the other a noble expression of deep and grave patriotic feeling on a supreme national occasion; but the thing more necessary, though it may be less noble than these, is the pulse,

the fire, the passion of music—the quality of a singer, not of a solitary philosopher, or a patriotic orator.

It is not important that Swinburne may have been wrong in his estimate of Lowell's greatest poem, which so captious a judge as W. C. Brownell has placed with the patriotic passages of Shakespeare. What is important is to note the exactness with which he states the function and relative place in poetry, of substance, emotional and intellectual, and of form. That a poet should like Bryant be capable of august meditation, or like Lowell of an expression of deep feeling on a great subject, is nobler than that he should have the power to sing; but, if he cannot sing, neither meditation nor deep feeling will make of him a poet. And, Swinburne goes on to say, complaining of Emerson's lack of the singing power:

> It is a poor thing to have nothing but melody, and be unable to rise above it into harmony, but one or the other, the less if not the greater, you *must* have. Imagine a man full of great thoughts and emotions and resolved to express them in painting, who has absolutely no power upon either form or colour. Wainwright the murderer,[2] who never had any thought or emotion above those of a pig or a butcher, will be a better man for us than he.

Clearly, Swinburne does not believe that the power to sing is the whole of poetry, he values nobility of substance, intensity of emotion, as much as Ruskin himself; but he dissents from the Ruskinian view— a view seldom consciously held nowadays, but one which moulds to an amazing degree the current notions of poetry—that great substance suffices to create great poetry.

In lyric poetry always, and usually in epic and dramatic, the power to sing was what Swinburne sought for first. The poets he most admired were those who were great singers and also great prophets: Marlowe, Shelley, Hugo, and Shakespeare (who is the supreme expression of the English race and as such an unconscious prophet). The prophets whose song was wheezy and harsh could never satisfy him; indeed they were less precious to him than the singers who were incapable of thought. He valued highly his own power of song. There is an amusing record of a conversation at Jowett's tea-table, in which, on being asked who among the English poets had the best ear, Swinburne said: "Shakespeare, without doubt; then Milton; then Shelley; then, I do not know what other people would do, but I should put myself." Indeed, unless one wishes to give the fourth place to Spenser, it is difficult to defend another choice. From the first lines of the first chorus in his first great poem:

> When the hounds of spring are on winter's traces,
>   The mother of months in meadow or plain
> Fills the shadows and windy places
>   With lisp of leaves and ripple of rain . . .

to so late a poem as "England: An Ode," with such lines as these which a few years ago, when quoted in the House of Commons, set that body in an uproar:

> All our past acclaims our future: Shakespeare's voice and Nelson's hand,
> Milton's faith and Wordsworth's trust in this our chosen and chainless
>   land, . . .

always he is a master of song.

The charge laid against his singing is that of monotony. This charge rests upon a misapprehension of the nature of great lyric poetry. Most great lyrists have a personal style, a formed and permanent manner; Petrarch has such a style and manner, and Shelley and Leopardi. Whatever the metre and stanza may be, whatever the mood expressed, the poem is unmistakeably theirs—it has their accent, the imprint not merely of a personality but of a style. So it is with Swinburne. Whether his subject is passion, or political idealism, or the misdeeds of Mr. Henry Buxton Forman, he writes in a highly personal way, which nevertheless is always, or almost always, appropriate to his theme. When it is objected that his verse is monotonous, what is really under attack is not the continued presence of a style and manner (which are in Swinburne no more uniform than in most other great lyrical poets) but the fact of his diffuseness, or else, it may be, that the critic finds Swinburne's style and manner intrinsically disagreeable, and the more he reads the more, of course, he is exasperated. But diffuseness is not necessarily monotony; and only an indolent mind will confuse a fundamental dislike of a style and manner with an impression that a dislike develops only because a style and manner are exhibited at unusual length.

To many people his style and manner are disagreeable. Why they are found disagreeable, Mr. Eliot, following and clarifying Welby's view, has explained in his essay, "Swinburne the Poet." Besides being diffuse, Swinburne dwells, not in a world of objects, but in a world of words. If one looks in his poetry for the clear shapes of particular things, which stand forth in soft outline in the poems of Rossetti, one will be not only disappointed but exasperated. If one expects that each line, or even each stanza, will make its specific, isolable contribution to the statement of an idea or communication of an emotion or

sensation, one will be expecting what does not exist. The effect which
Swinburne seeks to produce is a total effect; and in producing this
effect he relies (apart from the intellectual content) chiefly upon
sound. Mr. Eliot has quoted a passage from "The Triumph of Time"
which, so far as a brief passage can, admirably illustrates Swinburne's
lack of particularization and his dependence on sound:

> There lived a singer in France of old
> By the tideless dolorous midland sea.
> In a land of sand and ruin and gold
> There shone one woman, and none but she.

And he comments: "It is the word that gives him the thrill, not the
object." "Gold" and "dolorous" and "ruin" and "shone"; the phrases
"midland sea" and "France of old"; the movement of the lines, too;
it is by such devices as these that Swinburne communicates the mysterious sadness which is the soul of the passage. This is not the way of
the English poets; and the reader, if unaccustomed to Swinburne—or
the French poets—is upset by a sense that all is vague to him, and
feels that he must grope towards a meaning that so far has eluded
him. In its greatest periods, English poetry has followed the doctrine
of Keats that "the poet should have distinctness for his luxury," that
is, for his supreme glory. A taste formed in reading the Elizabethans,
Milton, and the poetry of our nineteenth century, will demand such
distinctness. It is not to be had from Swinburne. "He dwells in a
world of words"; they gave him the thrill and it is only through them
that he can communicate it to us.

As Mr. Richards remarks, it is foolish to ask for distinctness. He
quotes a stanza from "Before the Mirror," a characteristic Swinburne
stanza:

> There glowing ghosts of flowers
>   Draw down, draw nigh;
> And wings of swift spent hours
>   Take flight and fly;
> She sees by formless gleams,
> She hears across cold streams,
>   Dead mouths of many dreams that sing and sigh.

Mr. Richards says appropriately: "Little beyond vague thoughts of
the things the words stand for is required." He insists that the
absence of vivid imagery is no better a ground for depreciating a
poem which depends on other effects, than the absence of profound
thought would be. But the English reader, unaware of the narrowness

of the range of his taste and fatigued by a long succession of stanzas resembling that quoted, will doubtless go on saying that Swinburne's verse is monotonous, when all he really means is that he finds Swinburne's style and manner unacceptable because they lack distinctness.[3]

Not only does Swinburne rely on words and the harmony of words beyond the custom of our poets; but he also delights—to return to Mr. Eliot's second point—in diffuseness. Relying on sound, he wishes, as Spenser did, to protract his poems so that they may become irresistible incantations, the movement finally lulling the reader into a condition in which he receives the emotional effect at which the poet aims. Swinburne's lyrics, unlike those of great pictorial poets such as Keats and Gautier, have little structural design. A single stanza could be abstracted at almost any point from "Hertha," or "Faustine," or "Dolores," and the poem would suffer very small damage. Of "Dolores," indeed, Swinburne wrote, significantly, to Howell: "I have added yet four more jets of boiling and gushing infamy to the perennial and poisonous fountain of 'Dolores.'" In a postscript he announces "ten more verses."[4] "Dolores" is indeed a perennial fountain; there seems no need for it ever to cease; its stanzas are separate "jets," each a unit, and scarcely any in intimate relation with its neighbours. Still almost every one of the fifty-five stanzas communicates intense emotion; the cumulative effect is almost intolerably strong; and yet it is impossible for a sympathetic reader to rise from reading the last stanza without wishing, and wishing ardently, that there were more, and yet more, to maintain one in elation.

The vagueness and the diffuseness, the riot of mellifluous words, all play their part in producing the emotional effect; but they are not the whole of Swinburne's manner and style. They are auxiliaries to his matchless rhythm, a rhythm which depends more than that of any other English poet on anapaests and choriambics and upon lavish use of alliteration and assonance. It is to Swinburne's rhythm that the analyst must finally appeal in the attempt to account fully for the shock of pleasure that his poetry can give, to the "new and resounding rhythms," in Professor Grierson's phrase, to the melodies in which, says M. Lalou, "the rhythm actually acquires the strength of a perfume."

Swinburne's most novel rhythms are those which are extremely speedy, and those which are extremely languorous. To perceive how vast his range of rhythm is, one need only set side by side a stanza from "Dolores":

> I have passed from the outermost portal
>   To the shrine where a sin is a prayer;
> What care though the service be mortal?
>   O our Lady of Torture, what care?
> All thine the last wine that I pour is,
>   The last in the chalice we drain,
> O fierce and luxurious Dolores,
>   Our Lady of Pain.

and one from "A Forsaken Garden":

> All are at one now, roses and lovers,
>   Not known of the cliffs and the fields and the sea.
> Not a breath of the time that has been hovers
>   In the air now soft with a summer to be.
> Not a breath shall there sweeten the seasons hereafter
>   Of the flowers or the lovers that laugh now or weep,
> When as they that are free now of weeping and laughter
>   We shall sleep.

Whether the anapaestic movement be swift as a Bacchanalian dance, or slow and grave as a dirge, it is always fervent and intense, it is always the measure of a "prosodist magician." In the dazzling light of beauty such as this, it seems time wasted to reason about the lyrical power of Swinburne; it is wiser perhaps to say with Saintsbury: "If anybody wants something finer . . . let him seek noon at fourteen o'clock, and when he has found it, sit down and eat better bread than is made of wheat." As a greater than Saintsbury has said, and one whose admiration for Swinburne was profound: when we are solicited by the impressions of such beauty, "we shall hardly have time to make theories."

II

But the power of passionate song is not enough to make the greatest poetry, as Swinburne wisely said. How insistent he was in requiring more, appears in his attitude towards Keats, of which M. Lafourcade has given a full account in the introduction to his edition of Swinburne's *Hyperion*. To Keats, as painter of nature and master of imagery, Swinburne gave warm praise, saying that he was unrivalled "in that especial field of work where all the giants and all the gods of art would fail to stand against him for an hour." But more than imagery, and pictorial art generally, is needed; and more Keats does not, in Swinburne's view, have. What is needed is a passionate belief in ideas and a wish to express them with all the magical splendour of great song. Speaking of Arnold's view that all great poetry is a criticism of life, he asserts: "All sane men must be willing to concede the truth of an assertion which [Arnold] seems to fling down as a challenge . . . that a school of poetry divorced from any moral idea is a school of poetry divorced from life."

What, then, are the ideas which Swinburne himself sings?

The *Poems and Ballads* of 1866 are dedicated not simply to the description of passion but to the praise of the idea of passion. "Rightly considered," remarks Professor Beach, "the sensualism of his first volume of *Poems and Ballads*, the worship of Venus, is but one article in the creed of naturalism." It is commonly said that Swinburne is not a great poet of love: "Of love," says Professor Grierson, "he knows only one mood." This is very chastely said; but it is well, I think, to speak more plainly. Swinburne's letters abound in allusions to the Marquis de Sade, and in quotations from his novel *Justine;* and the records of his life, many of which are still withheld, establish that during the years when he was writing his greatest love-poems he associated in practice as well as in theory the emotion of love with the infliction of pain.[5] In "Anactoria" and "Félise" and "Faustine" and "Dolores," the picture of love is in the main a sadist's picture. In such poems he may indeed be said to know only one mood of love. But there are others. "The Triumph of Time," for example, is usually associated with his rejection by Jane Faulkner. In that poem there are scattered images of cruelty and pain; but the poem records, chiefly, in phrases and rhythms of mastered agitation, the sense that without Jane the world is an empty and withered place. It is a supremely effective expression of a mood of love which is utterly remote from the ecstasies over Dolores and her strange sisterhood: the mood is one that Yeats and Housman have both expressed. "The Year of the Rose," in which the mood is different again, is no less genuine, scarcely less beautiful. Summarily stated, the truth is that Swinburne was the first poet to sing one perverted form of love, but was not by this peculiarity incapacitated from singing other forms with a power not inferior to that of the great love-poets of the age. Even of the Dolores group M. Lafourcade has rightly said (the remarks of Swinburne's contemporary critics confirm the view): "Whatever the secret springs of his inspiration, we must recognise that Swinburne managed (and this was an artistic *tour de force*) to give us the crystal flow of the rushing stream and conceal its painful origins . . . ; we shall find little which will strike the uninitiated as strange or suspicious." The judgment on a poem is to be rendered on what it contains and can communicate, not on what we read into it after a study of the poet's life.

The idea of passion which dominates the first collection was not long to reign over the poet. "The impulse," as he says, "ceased." One of the most amazing transformations in the history of our poetry was to come over him in the months which followed the publication of *Poems and Ballads*. This transformation Sir Edmund Gosse has described with gentle humour. Jowett, who had not ceased to exercise a protective friendship over his former pupil, is assumed to have called a council of the poet's more respectable friends; Giuseppe Mazzini was consulted; an effort was made to discover "what could be done *with* and *for* Algernon." The upshot was that Mazzini wrote to Swinburne, expressing his admiration for the "Ode on the Insurrection in Candia"; that Swinburne called on Mazzini; and that Jowett's manœuvres led to Swinburne's becoming the greatest political poet of his time and place. So runs the story, entertaining, rich in the irony that Gosse loved; unfortunately for ironists, M. Lafourcade makes short work of demolishing it. Swinburne was already acquainted with Mazzini; and immediately after the publication of *Poems and Ballads* he had written to W. M. Rossetti, saying that he was tired of the poetry of passion and that it was now his chief consolation that he believed firmly in the ideal of liberty, as he had always done, and cared fervently for the future of Italy. *Songs before Sunrise* are accordingly the expression of one of the strongest and, as it was to prove, one of the most permanent elements in his mind.

It is upon them that his reputation as a prophet, an intellectual poet comparable with Shelley and Hugo, chiefly rests. In the organ-notes of "The Prelude," Swinburne describes the change that has occurred within him, his repudiation of the rose-gathering attitude—the search for intense sensation—which had ruled his youth; and in the grave rhythms of the long but simple stanza which he has here selected, he affirms his belief in the supreme greatness of man, the greatest form of universal life, his dedication to political idealism, his conversion to the solemn frame of mind of those

> . . . who rest not; who think long
> Till they discern as from a hill
> At the sun's hour of morning song,
> Known of souls only, and those souls free,
> The sacred spaces of the sea.

He flicks with scorn those degenerate Italians who, acquiescing in their political servitude, live a life of sensual luxuriance, a life which recalls the paganism of *Poems and Ballads:*

> And they slept and they rioted on their rose-hung beds
> With mouths on flame,
> And with love-locks vine-chapleted, and with rose-crowned heads
> And robes of shame.

He upbraids the French for their desertion of the ideals of the Revolution and their abject submission to Napoleon the Little; he upbraids the English for their recreancy to the principles of the Commonwealth, and their deafness to the prophetic voices of Milton, Shelley, and Landor. Nowhere else in English verse does the hatred of the autocrat blaze with so scornful a rage as in such stanzas as these from "A Marching Song":

> And thou, whom sea-walls sever
> From lands unwalled with seas,
> Wilt thou endure for ever,
> O Milton's England, these?
> Thou that wast his Republic, wilt thou clasp their knees? . . .
>
> These princelings with gauze winglets
> That buzz in the air unfurled,
> These summer-swarming kinglets,
> These thin worms crowned and curled,
> That bask and blink and warm themselves about the world; . . .
>
> These limbs, supine, unbuckled,
> In rottenness of rest,
> These sleepy lips blood-suckled
> And satiate of thy breast,
> These dull wide mouths that drain thee dry and call thee blest; . . .
>
> Lest thine own sea disclaim thee,
> Lest thine own sons despise,
> Lest lips shoot out that name thee
> And seeing thee men shut eyes,
> Take thought with all thy people, turn thine head and rise.

The absence of oppression is, for Swinburne as for Mill, prerequisite to all virtue. It is instructive to consider *Songs before Sunrise* as the rendering in poetry of the substance of the essay *On Liberty,* of which Swinburne wrote some few years later: "Ever since his *Liberty* came out it has been the text-book of my creed as to public morals and political faith." All the main aspects of Mill's essay are developed in the *Songs:* admiration of the Greek world; doubt as to the total effect of Christianity on the moral nature of men; hatred of the tyranny of the majority; insistence on the supreme value to the community and to the universe of freely developing individuals; almost mystical faith in the ideal of liberty, liberty of thought, liberty of discussion, liberty of action, liberty for everyone, always, everywhere:

> For where Freedom lives not, there live no good things.

To the spirit of the *Songs* the later political poetry of Swinburne appears to be in irreconcilable contrast. From a revolutionary idealist he appears to have become an aggressive nationalist, almost a jingo. The customary explanation of the shift is the influence of Theodore Watts-Dunton, a convenient scapegoat for all in the later Swinburne which deserves censure. But there are other elements in the poet's position after 1879 which must be given their weight. He had in his songs deplored the autocracy of Louis Napoleon and the disunion of Italy. Now Louis Napoleon had been driven from the throne and a republican regime instituted in France, among whose first actions had been the revocation of Hugo's banishment. Italy, if it had not killed or exiled its sovereigns, had at least clipped their wings; and the *risorgimento* had furnished it with at least the appearance of unity. Iniquity was no longer in the saddle. If Swinburne could no longer burn with rage at the sight of a recreant France and a prostrate Italy, he continued to attack the autocrats of other European countries, notably the Czars.

Towards England, indeed, his attitude had changed, although the state of England had scarcely altered. He was an enemy of the Irish and the Boers; he was the advocate of oppressive policy abroad. The explanation of the new tone in his political utterances about England, lies, I suggest, in his immersion in the literature of the Elizabethan age. He came to feel that Elizabethan drama was the greatest form of the greatest period of the greatest literature that the world had ever seen. Between his mind and the English oppression of the Irish and the Boers came the loved and shadowy figures of Chapman and Marlowe, of Shakespeare and Milton. He was thinking about the England of these, especially of Shakespeare, when he appeared to be talking of the England of Disraeli and Chamberlain:

> More than that sovereign lordship of the sea
> Bequeathed to Cromwell from Elizabeth . . .
> More than all deeds wrought of thy strong right hand,
> This praise keeps most thy fame's memorial strong,
> That thou wast head of all these streams of song,
> And time bows down to thee as Shakespeare's land.

And who were the Boers, who were the Irish (among whom he saw, moreover, too many priests for his peace of mind) that they should contest the will of the sons of Shakespeare?[6] When Swinburne spoke of the domestic situation, of the claims of the House of Lords to impede the popular will, he kept the tone of his early revolutionary poetry: the Lords he taunts, in celebrated lines, as men

> Who are Graces by grace of such mothers
> As brightened the bed of King Charles.

Songs before Sunrise is his central book. "Other books are books," he has said, "*Songs before Sunrise* is myself." It is his central book because, beside the lyrics of liberty, he there gives us his conception of the universe in the poems which may be associated with "Hertha." He believes that all is one, abjuring with Emerson and Meredith the dualism of the elder Victorian poets and freeing himself from the coil of problems with which they were wrestling. It is in this belief in the unity of all, rather than in his attitude towards passion, that he is perhaps most modern. His view of the universe is one easily reconcilable with the fullest implications of the evolutionary hypothesis; and yet, in the crash of ideals that this involved, Swinburne's is a valiant note. For him, man is a being of unfathomed greatness; with the reform of society, the rooting out of false ideas about the nature of the universe and the function of humanity, man will achieve ends of perfect beauty and perfect goodness. Again, Swinburne is speaking with the essay *On Liberty* in his mind. His political faith, like his faith in passion, is but one tenet in his doctrine of naturalism. If man will but believe in the greatness of his nature he will speedily set to the bloody work of destroying shams and tyrannies, with a sense that the cause is holy and the enemy doomed from the outset. In the poem significantly named "Messidor" he bids man begin:

> The dumb dread people that sat
>   All night without screen for the night,
>   All day without food for the day,
>   They shall give not their harvest away,
> They shall eat of its fruit and wax fat:
>   They shall see the desire of their sight,
>   Though the ways of the seasons be steep,
>   They shall climb with face to the light;
> Put in the sickles and reap.

Urging that the sickles be raised, Swinburne in a dozen poems seeks to cheer man with the sense that he is the greatest element in the universe, ringing the changes on the theme,

Glory to Man in the highest, for Man is the Master of things.

III

When Swinburne published *Songs before Sunrise*, he was four years beyond the age of Shelley's death and within two years of the age of Byron's. He had before him thirty-eight years, more than the whole life-span of either, and his mind was to be unclouded to the end. What in these years was he to do?

He was to become a scholar in Elizabethan drama, and to do for Chapman, Jonson, and others what only a mind which was both erudite and creative could do. He was to write seven tragedies in the Elizabethan manner—he had already written two—and some narrative poems. He was also to continue the composition of lyrical poetry. And yet he was not to justify his early promise.

The critical works of Swinburne, whether on Elizabethan or modern themes, are often penetrating and usually scholarly; but they lack the precision of impression and design of Pater and the balance and wisdom of Arnold; they are more properly to be compared with the critical papers of Symonds, whose zeal and verbosity they rival. Swinburne's criticism is, in the main, of the kind Shelley might have written in middle age. It consists of pleas and harangues rather than judgments.

For all his saturation in the literature of the Elizabethan age, his tragedies lack the primitive force of the great Elizabethans. They have but few lifelike characters, and too many "megaphones" for the author, as Mr. Granville-Barker says; few scenes which capture the emotions. They are, moreover, quite unadapted for performance in the theatre; in one of them John Knox is permitted to rant for four hundred lines and in general there is too little action, too much speech. His diffuseness serves Swinburne ill in the drama. He recognized the chasm between such plays and the modern stage: "When I write plays," he remarks, "it is with a view to their being acted at the Globe, the Red Bull, or the Blackfriars," which is to say, with a view to their being acted only on the stage of sympathetic imaginations. His distaste for the modern stage went so far as to make him averse to witnessing performances of the plays of Shakespeare or Hugo.

But in the last half of his life, as in the first, he wrote a very large amount of lyrical poetry; and this has been under-estimated by the world, as has the later poetry of Tennyson, and, in our own time, of Yeats. One of the great themes of his younger days is completely absent from the later collections—the theme of passion. But much of the political and philosophical poetry of the later years is in no degree inferior, either in intellect or in music, to what he had written in his first volumes. "The Armada" and the Hugo birthday ode, to name but two of his later lyrics, show his singing and his prophetic power at the height, or very close to it. In place of the passion, which had given wings to so much of his best poetry, there is now, in "A Nympholept" for example, intense poetry of nature for which there is no parallel in his earlier work. In "The Armada," the theme of political freedom, the theme of philosophical naturalism, and the theme of natural beauty are combined in a perfect whole. The Spaniards represent the forces of evil, the tyrants, the supernaturalists; the English represent the new order, lovers of liberty and nature (in its philosophical as well as its aesthetic sense). The English are victors because Nature, expressed in the sea (now the chief of Swinburne's symbols), has determined to annihilate its enemies:

> Earth's hosts are with them, and with them is heaven: but with us is
> the sea.

It is Hertha herself who fights against the Spaniards; and against the Nature-goddess the forces of Spain—the might of the Spanish God and the might of erring and misapplied human intelligence—are powerless. The triumphant ring of the verse celebrates no mere English victory; it celebrates the victory of that mysterious deity which appears more distinctly in the Hugo birthday ode. And "The Armada" is rich with natural splendour.

Still, taking the later lyrics as a whole, the early promise is not fulfilled. Swinburne does not renew himself as Hugo does; he is singing the old themes with an accent which has less intensity, with a rhythm which has less sweep, less of the dizzy speed of his early days. Old age is no boon to a lyrical poet.

IV

The greatest lyrical force to appear in English poetry since the death of Shelley—that is the estimate of the most eminent of living Swinburnians, M. Lafourcade. There will not, I think, be any dissent from the suggestion, which in this essay I have assumed to be true, that Swinburne's claims to greatness rest upon his lyrics and the lyrical passages in his narratives and tragedies. His lyricism expresses itself without much assistance from two qualities which, in English poetry at least, usually characterize the masters of the lyric—firm composition, and distinct, vivid imagery. Shelley, too, lacks these qualities, if not altogether, certainly in very large part. In compensation Swinburne and Shelley offer luxuriant song and vehement thought. Swinburne's thought, like Shelley's, is that of a revolutionary idealist; it is without hesitations or nuances; it is simple, bold, and passionate; and to those who are out of tune with revolutionary idealism it seems superficial, ignorant, and appropriate only to lands beyond the moon. "The ideas of Shelley," says Mr. Eliot, "seem to me to be always the ideas of adolescence." He goes on to call them "feeble," "shabby," "repellent"; and to assert that, not because he does not share them, but because he cannot even respect them, he is obliged to leave Shelley unread. Some such view is, I suspect, taken of Swinburne's thought in our time; and this is one of the reasons why his poetry is little read. But his ideas are intellectually respectable: such doctrines as the unity of man with nature, the dignity of humanity, the supreme value of liberty, are not easily dismissed as feeble or shabby. They are typical doctrines of John Stuart Mill; and if some one chooses to say that Mill is no longer intellectually respectable, I throw up my hands, and am content to leave Swinburne, as thinker, in his company. Appropriately, Swinburne's revolutionary idealism is clothed in verse which moves as swiftly as the wings of thought, which stirs a tumult of feelings so great that the reader is eager to relieve an overburdened spirit by violent action. At his best, between Swinburne's thought and his art there is perfect harmony: a multiplicity of straining, intense particles are caught and held in a strange unity. The effect produced is not complex or fine but it is strong; and even those who resent its furious strength cannot, if they expose themselves to it, resist its impact.

NOTES

1. His subsequent *Swinburne, A Literary Biography*, is relatively disappointing.

2. Wainwright was Swinburne's favourite example of the immoral artist. An admirer of Blake, himself a painter and critic, he murdered his sister-in-law to collect £18,000 of life insurance.

3. It is significant that the critic who has most earnestly sought to vindicate Swinburne's imagination is a Frenchman, M. Lafourcade. See *La Jeunesse de Swinburne*, II, pp. 542 ff.

4. The manuscript discloses that the first draft of the poem was entirely chaotic. The variants of this and other poems frequently suggest that for Swinburne the tonality of the word was the chief consideration. In the twenty-second stanza of "Ilicet" he rejected the succession "unprofitable," "unperishable," "unfathomable," "inexorable," "unconquerable," "inevitable," in favour of his final choice, "unalterable," in the line "Of the old unalterable gods."

5. M. Lafourcade has furnished unassailable evidence (*La Jeunesse de Swinburne*, I, p. 265, n. 109, and *Swinburne, A Literary Biography*, p. 196). English critics have been extremely reluctant to consider the question.

6. Even republican France was odious to him in later years; he mistrusted French policy towards England.

ARTHUR J. CARR

Tennyson as a Modern Poet

"MODERN fame is nothing," said Tennyson to William Allingham. "I'd rather have an acre of land. I shall go down, down! I'm up now. Action and reaction."

"Action and reaction" only partly account for Tennyson's fall. We cannot help feeling in the bard of Farringford and Aldworth, in the author of "The May Queen," "Enoch Arden," and "The Promise of May," that depressing sense of an imagination "more saved than spent," which made Henry James breathe, "Oh, dear, oh, dear," upon discovering that Tennyson himself "was not Tennysonian."

Not until after the great dividing years of 1914–18 was it possible to view the dead laureate with some composure and to wish to retrieve at least the part of his work that was not official and "Victorian." For an age that demanded of poetry "reality of emotional impulse," Harold Nicolson boiled the essential Tennyson down to "a morbid and unhappy mystic," "afraid of death, and sex, and God." A little later, T. S. Eliot boldly called him "a great poet," because of his "abundance, variety, and complete competence." When W. H. Auden made up a selection of Tennyson's poetry very much as Nicolson had specified, he conceded that Tennyson "had the finest ear, perhaps, of any English Poet"; then he added, "he was undoubtedly the stupidest; there was little about melancholia that he didn't know; there was little else that he did."

In the presence of such a figure it is no wonder that critics who are also poets grow nervous and exasperated. They see in Tennyson not an open but a covert capitulation, perhaps involuntary though not

From *University of Toronto Quarterly*, XIX (1950), 361–82. Reprinted by permission of the publisher and the author.

altogether unconscious. Yet he is our true precursor. He shows and hides, as if in embryo, a master theme of Joyce's *Ulysses*—the accentuated and moody self-consciousness and the sense of loss that mark Stephen Dedalus. He forecasts Yeats's interest in the private myth. He apprehended in advance of Aldous Huxley the uses of mysticism to castigate materialistic culture. And in *Maud*, at least, he prepared the way for the verse of Eliot's "Preludes" and "Prufrock." At some crucial points Tennyson is a modern poet, and there are compelling reasons why we should try to comprehend him. Our uneasiness, our reluctance to acknowledge the relationship is understandable, and it explains how little we advance toward seeing what Tennyson's poetry is like.

Seeing what it is like, discerning the essentials without "essentializing," as Kenneth Burke would ask, demands that criticism breathe a mixed atmosphere, neither wholly aesthetic nor wholly biographical. It is not a question of choosing to consult biography in order to chart the poem or of preferring to ignore the private reference. In Tennyson's poetry the private and public worlds are fused. In the presence of such poetry, criticism must act upon life as well as upon art. Tennyson's double nature does not divide itself between the poet and the man; his poetry has a double nature and reveals not only itself but the poet. This is the truth that Hallam Tennyson confessed in his preface to the *Memoir* of his father's life: ". . . but besides the letters of my father and of his friends there are his poems, and in them we must look for the innermost sanctuary of his being. For my own part, I feel strongly that no biographer could so truly give him as he gives himself in his own works." Although we must look to the man to find the poet, we shall find the man in his poems.

The artistic and cultural crisis which underlies the swervings and sudden drops in his long career was clearly sketched for Tennyson while he was at Cambridge, from 1828 to 1831. It was the protean question that the members of the Apostles Club debated, and that some of them attempted to resolve in action. The ill-fated Torrijos expedition, vigorously recounted by Carlyle in his *Life of John Sterling*, was a point of focus. With a handful of exiled Spaniards around General Torrijos, a few of "the young Cambridge democrats" joined in a pitifully brave and futile attempt to restore constitutional monarchy to Spain by simultaneous uprisings in the north and south. In the summer of 1830 Alfred Tennyson and Arthur Hallam carried messages through southern France to leaders of the northern conspiracy. At the same moment Torrijos and his compatriots were land-ing at Gibraltar with Tennyson's friends John Mitchell Kemble (later the editor of *Beowulf*) and Richard Chenevix Trench (later the Archbishop of Dublin).

Perhaps more lucidly than the other English youths, Trench saw it as a desperate venture of sensibility that charged the external political motives and the physical danger with symbolic drama concerning the role of the individual in society and the role of the artist in a disordered culture. To another of the Apostles, W. B. Donne, Trench wrote on the eve of his departure from England:

> But the future, the future—who shall question that? What will one be? What will this age be? Must one end in a worldling; and our age, will it prove the decrepitude of the world? Are we not gathering up the knowledge of past generations because we are adding nothing ourselves? Do we not place the glory of our century in the understanding of past ages, because our individual energy is extinct, and we are ourselves nothing? After one or two revolutions in thought and opinion, all our boasted poetry, all, or nearly all, of Keats and Shelley and Wordsworth and Byron, will become unintelligible. When except in our times, did men seek to build up their poetry on their own individual experiences, instead of some objective foundations common to all men? [1]

The question of "objective foundations" permeates Tennyson's career and binds his poetry to the crisis of the arts in our century. Tennyson took in the sickening fact that the continental areas of common values were breaking up. Myths, rituals, slogans, accustomed loyalties and animosities, the classic procedures of politics and warfare, the classic mysteries of philosophies, the groundwork of rational history and rational science, the themes and modes of art—all cemented by hallowed ethical and economic traditions—were coming loose fast. The sense of this fact is the atmosphere of his poetry and is present everywhere. It is evident in his exploitation of a multitude of traditional poetic forms, in the question of electing a tradition and in the desperate virtuosity of his style; in his private use of the public domain of myth and legend as he turns from the formal and familiar elements to the inward and particular. We may trace it in his anxiety to keep up with the thought of his day and to draw it—drag it, if necessary—into his poetry; in his quest for symbols; in his perplexity over the artist's involvement in affairs ("The Palace of Art" sprang from Trench's ultimatum, "Tennyson, we cannot live in art"); and in his sad conviction that his work would fail.

Only a little altered in the fashion of their dress, these questions still pace our critical reviews and galleries of art. Tennyson's awareness of these issues, which the century since the publication of *In Memoriam* has tiresomely expounded, was never lucidly conceived. His ideas flow in the current of his melancholic sensibility. When that sensibility was fed, enormously, by such a loss as the death of Arthur Hallam, Tennyson's poetry swept the entire range of crisis.

The theme of loss appeared very early in Tennyson's poetry as the talisman of imaginative energy. Whenever this theme reappears, even after *In Memoriam*, it works its magic. This fact may explain why Tennyson often seems to force himself to remember the loss of Hallam, enclosing him in the figure of King Arthur in *Idylls of the King*, performing again the ritual of loss and recovery in "Vastness," "In the Valley of Cauteretz," "Merlin and the Gleam," and "Crossing the Bar," and implicitly in many other poems. When the private sensibility was not stirred, the awareness was wanting, and "stupid" "Alfred Lawn Tennyson," the Victorian, wrote masterly bathos.

Tennyson is the most "occasional" of poets, but the occasions were not public, even when he made them so. His imagination rose only to its own promptings or to the lure of an event that suggested or reproduced the subjective drama of loss, defeat, and disappointment. Then manner and matter would unite, and even in the placid years he could write the "Ode on the Death of the Duke of Wellington," of a man who reminded Tennyson of the statesman latent in Arthur Hallam, and *Idylls of the King*, which broods over the disintegration of an ideal society and the fall of a heroic lay-figure. Such a survival of imagination in spite of all that was wasted taught Henry James to observe: "As a didactic creation I do not greatly care for King Arthur; but as a fantastic one he is infinitely remunerative." As Trench saw, there is a romantic entanglement of poet and poem. The concinnity of Tennyson's art rests on his "individual experiences," rather than upon "some objective foundations common to all men."

II

The genetic view of Tennyson's poetry naturally swings toward his early work in search of the components of his sensibility. James Spedding had remarked in 1835 that his friend Tennyson was "a man always discontented with the Present till it has become the Past, and then he yearns toward it and worships it, and not only worships it, but is discontented because it is past." Many years later, Tennyson himself, speaking to Sir James Knowles about "Tears, Idle Tears," said, "It is what I have always felt even from a boy, and what as a boy I called the 'passion of the past.' And so it is with me now; it is the distance that charms me in the landscape, the picture and the past, and not the immediate to-day in which I move."

Yet such moods of melancholy, sometimes mellow, sometimes acute, generate Tennyson's poetry. T. S. Eliot saw in Tennyson "emotion so deeply suppressed, even from himself, as to tend rather towards the blackest melancholia than towards dramatic action." It is a response to frustration not only felt but expressed, embodied in art and in the problems of art, in the search for theme and for symbols.

In the early poems the underlying theme of the "divided will" is charged with the highest imaginative excitement, and most of the issues that were to be explored later are set forth. In what is possibly Tennyson's earliest poem, "Armageddon," [2] the theme is a transcendent mystical revelation, like that which Tennyson said that he experienced repeatedly later in life. The poem approaches the instant of transcendental disclosure only through passages of ominous imagery and a sense of deep anxiety and awe. The hour is the typical Tennysonian twilight when sun and moon stand in opposition. Then the poet enters the realm of the deeper consciousness and finds delight in himself:

> Yea! in that hour I could have fallen down
> Before my own strong soul and worshipp'd it.

Later, in "The Mystic," in the crucial lyric 95 of *In Memoriam*, in "The Holy Grail," and "The Ancient Sage," Tennyson would have recourse to this theme. The ominous images and the sense of awe denote a dialectic clash between the attraction of the deepest subjective levels and the resistance and restraint of other sectors of reality.

Dream, memory, and desire come to represent in these early poems the modes of imaginative freedom that is restrained by forces not explicitly represented except as a category called "conscience" or "fear." The dialectic is perfectly realized in the lyric "In Deep and Solemn Dreams" (in *Unpublished Early Poems*), that forecasts the tonality and the problem of *In Memoriam*. The dreamer meets "sunny faces of lost days . . . Forms which live but in the mind":

> And we speak as we have spoken
> Ere our love by death was broken.

But the wind of dawn shakes "The large leaves of the sycamore" and breaks the "sacred charm of tearless sleep":

> Dear lips, loved eyes, ye fade, ye fly,
> Even in my fear yet die,

> And the hollow dark I dread
> Closes round my friendless head.

Even in that strained and rhetorical poem "Remorse" (in *Poems by Two Brothers*) there are sudden disclosures, though the cause of remorse is kept in mystery. The poet cursed "With too much conscience to have rest, Too little to be ever blest," recoils from himself:

> I would I'd been all-heartless! then
> I might have sinn'd like other men

and turns avidly toward the image of a final sleep in death, safe from "the thrill of conscious fear."

In "Sense and Conscience" and "Memory" (in *Unpublished Early Poems*), Tennyson deals more objectively with the dialectic issues. The first of these is a fragment of an allegory suggesting the theme of *Idylls of the King*. "Conscience" is laid asleep by "Sense" in the midst of "pleasurable flowers," often associated by Tennyson with erotic themes. He is visited by "Delicious dreams" and "witching fantasies," "Lovely with bright black eyes," "And lips which moved in silence." But "Memory" and "Pain" arouse him:

> Rage seized upon him then
> And grasping with both palms his wondrous blade,
> Sheer through the summit of the tallest flowers
> He drave it. . . .
>   The ivy from the stem
> Was torn, the vine made desolate; his feet
> Were crimson'd with its blood, from which flows joy
> And bitterness, first joy from bitterness,
> And then again great bitterness from joy.

No relief is obtained by laying waste the pleasurable flowers, whose blood is like his own; and he lives with Memory and Pain. To deny and stamp out Sense only leads to a repression of desire, and Conscience suffers all the more. Nor would Tennyson ever attempt again to reach an answer by annihilating one of the sources of his inspiration as well as of his pain.

The poem "Memory" [3] almost succeeds in formulating the imaginative strife:

> Wherefore do I so remember
> That Hope is born of Memory
> Nightly in the house of dreams? . . .

Why at break of cheerful day
Doth my spirit faint away
Like a wanderer in the night?
Why in visions of the night
Am I shaken with delight
Like a lark at dawn of day?

If memory becomes an avenue of desire, like dreams themselves, it must still turn and agonize around conscience and the wakeful forces of restraint. Hence the painful irony and paradox that Tennyson phrased distinctly.

As a recurrent poetic strategy, with its own dialectic equation, the interchanging play of memory and desire seems a mask of the personality. In an excellent detailed study of erotic and symbolic elements in Tennyson's early verse,[4] Professor W. D. Paden has called this strategy "the mask of age." In it the face of desire and anxiety appears as memory and regret. No doubt Tennyson was simply borrowing at first a Byronic attitude. The desirable future and the frustrations of the present come forth as the vanished past—recapturable in memory. The thirst of youth is presented as the dryness of age. The feelings of guilt inseparable from dream are costumed as remorse and self-reproach for what is gone and cannot be helped. The advantage of the strategy is that it marches toward some degree of objectivity: the imaginative forces are brought under partial control. Yet Tennyson's discovery of "the magic cirque of memory" would be of only passing interest in his development did not the mask of age show forth again in poems of his best hours: in "Ulysses," the hero about to embark on a voyage of desire toward reunion with "the great Achilles, whom we knew"; in "Tithonus," the immortal, aging lover trapped by senility in a heaven of erotic ease that he can taste only in memory; in "Tears, Idle Tears"; in the "mad scenes" of *Maud;* above all in the nature of *In Memoriam.*

If the strategy of the mask of age both conceals and connotes anxiety, it is also sufficient to bind together the elements of a divided sensibility. The war of sense and conscience is no simple opposition between frustration and desire. The dialectic plays in both the inner and the outer worlds at once. There are the arrows of conscience and the chains of obligation. There are the demands of duty and the commands of love. Consequently, the objects of sense pass swiftly into symbols of desire, and the laws of dreams are cast outward over the objects of sense. In these terms Tennyson continues to explore the premises of romantic art, following Byron, then Keats and Coleridge, and even Shelley, in employing egocentric melancholy and the sensuous and supersensuous imagery of dream, and in debating the role of the artist in society. But he is not simply imitative. He accepts a tradition and goes beyond it to take what he can from whatever touches him in Western art.

Poems, Chiefly Lyrical (1830) and *Poems* (1833) display Tennyson's rapid and thorough engagement of his characteristic themes and, in particular, his concern with erotic motives to unfold the dialectic of sense and conscience. Fantasy beckons and repels. The gates of desire are defended by danger and wakeful fears. In "Recollections of the Arabian Nights," the poet voyages through a sub-tropical paradise that opens only as he enters "another night in night" and, in a dream within a dream, hears the Keatsian nightingale,

> Not he, but something which possess'd
> The darkness of the world, delight,
> Life, anguish, death, immortal love,
> Ceasing not, mingled, unrepressed. . . .

"Entranced," he gazes on the "amorous" Persian girl alone. The poem closes deep within the dream; there is no painful waking.

"A Dream of Fair Women" is a finer and more anxious poem. It begins with visions of

> Beauty and anguish walking hand in hand
> The downward slope to death.

Chaotic images of warfare, resembling the opening lines of "Armageddon," culminate as the poet lifts his arm "to hew down" a cavalier who is abducting a lady; then sleep and dream come upon him, and he is in the midst of an ominous and familiar forest, deadly still. It is just before dawn. The regressive stride into a deeper dream is made at once:

> The smell of violets, hidden in the green,
>   Pour'd back into my empty soul and frame
> The times when I remember to have been
>   Joyful and free from blame.
>
> And from within me a clear undertone
>   Thrill'd thro' mine ears in that unblissful clime,
> "Pass freely thro'; the wood is all thine own
>   Until the end of time."

Yet the dangers and distress are not so easily exorcized. The interviews with Helen of Troy, Iphigenia, Cleopatra, and other famous ladies are not lacking in overtones of awe, and the dream ends abruptly with the coming of dawn (as with "In Deep and Solemn Dreams") and assumes the mask of age:

> As when a soul laments, which hath been blest,
> Desiring what is mingled with past years,
> In yearnings that can never be exprest
> By sighs or groans or tears. . . .

Significantly, the ladies of the dream are dead ladies. With remarkable persistence death becomes in all these poems the ambivalent counterpoise to love and desire. It embodies the hostility between sense and conscience and guards the thresholds of fantasy. Regression to a deeper level of consciousness must pass the danger of death; yet to reach the level of fantasy is to triumph over death. The symbol death has a double nature: frustration of desire is a kind of death; yet persistence of desire rouses the conscientious phantom of death. Nor are the deeper levels of dream free from phantoms. They haunt the idyllic museum of Western culture in "The Palace of Art," and drive the Soul, for a while at least, into the world until she shall purge her "guilt." Only in those rare and brief disclosures of transcendental reality are the penalties of desire delayed, and even there the dark freedom of the mind is soon "stricken through with doubt."

Regression and withdrawal continue to mark Tennyson's later poetry. He sometimes falls back to a mental posture from which the return to erotic enjoyment and moral victory is facilitated. In *The Princess*, the Prince, "Of temper amorous" and subject to sudden trances when aggression threatens, at first disguises his sex to enter the cloister of art and learning where Princess Ida keeps her college for young ladies. When the Prince, like the dreamer in "A Dream of Fair Women," is striking a blow in battle to win the Princess, he is wounded, falls, and lies, embryo-like, "silent in the muffled cage of life." The Princess nurses him, assuming a role more maternal than erotic; then "Leapt fiery Passion from the brinks of death," and without courtship the Prince wins his bride. King Arthur, too, after renouncing Guinevere and being mortally wounded, recedes into the valley of Avilion, from which he will emerge in fresh power.

In such poems as "Fatima" and "Mariana" Tennyson attempted the delineation of erotic moods without recourse to dreams. But neither Fatima nor Mariana is a personality. They encase fevers of frustration and desire prolonged to the point of statuesque agony. There is no shadow of alleviation. Fatima is frozen at the point of hot desire, and in "Mariana" the lines between inner and outer reality are obliterated and her house becomes a house of dreams, disappointment, and death.

One could make it a simple equation that the more complete is the damming up of desire, in the moods and situations of these poems, the more certain to rise is a Keatsian lushness of imagery and diction. This is the root of Tennyson's "ornate" style in which, as Walter Bagehot noted, "everything has about it an atmosphere of something else," suitable to subjects of "half-belief" and to "dubious themes." Tennyson had learned to embody a problem in a mood and the mood in evocative, concrete, and disturbed imagery. To this ability he would soon add the use of myth and legend that made a hard and brilliant surface of traditional substance under which the private sensibility moved as if through water.

Tennyson had forged a poetic instrument out of the themes of loss and recovery through regression into dream and vision. Death and fear were established as the conventions that rule the dialectic of sense and conscience. This instrument became his means of apprehending the rational problems of his experience also, and lent them the deep sense of crisis that accorded well with the feelings of his class and of his age. The future of art, the nature of society, and the issues of science and religion, take the colours and disposition of his subjective strife. For this reason, the death of Hallam, a personal loss, became a magnet for larger issues. The subjective crisis and its non-rational modes encompass the crisis of Tennyson's culture.

These themes converge in "The Palace of Art," where the Soul feels a conscientious despair that "divided quite The kingdom of her thought." But she does not, like Conscience, destroy the "pleasurable flowers" of her paradise. Although she departs, she promises to return. If the issues of involvement and non-involvement were not to be settled easily, neither were they to be ignored. "The Lady of Shalott" sketches the predicament of a mind trying to free itself from a web of fantasy. When the Lady, moved by desire, looks away from the deep subjective mirror in which she reads the shadows of the world, the mirror cracks from side to side. She accepts her destiny and dies as she drifts down to Camelot. It is the first poem in which Tennyson thoroughly controlled his legendary materials, so that the poem with its symbolic action becomes an image of the mind.

The liberating power of legend works also in "The Lotos-Eaters." Exactly because it is managed as an episode in the return of Ulysses to the responsibilities of Ithaca, Tennyson could follow very far the impulses to "slothful ease" and vague erotic happiness. Yet in escaping so far, upon that island, the frustrations of conscience and the censures of the gods (who do not care), the poem risks the denial of transcendental reality, which was supported in Tennyson's experience by subjective revelations that lay deeper than fantasies of dream and vision. Because the poem is an episode of the wider legend, Tennyson does not have to make amends: the argument for responsibility was implied in the outer reaches of the story.

All these strands twine together in "Œnone," the steadiest and most deftly woven of the poems that Tennyson wrote before the death of Arthur Hallam on September 15, 1833. Œnone's monologue combines day-dream and legend while elaborating the rigid erotic attitudes of "Mariana" and "Fatima." Here Tennyson studies the issues of his poetry. They are expressed in the choice that Paris makes between the gifts proffered by the goddesses: power and fame, wisdom founded on self-restraint, and erotic bliss. Paris's lack of judgment in taking Aphrodite's bribe calls forth Œnone's prophecy of disaster to society through the sins of adultery (as in *Idylls of the King*). Although both the poet and the nymph applaud the ascetic principles of Pallas Athena, the secret of the poem lies in the symbol of Œnone herself, who combines the promise of erotic pleasure with wisdom that leads to power. In the warfare between Sense and Conscience, Tennyson achieves equilibrium, though not stability, for the symbol is genuinely ambivalent. The balance of powers is not guaranteed by any "objective foundations common to all men." That the basis of moral action has been defined is only the triumphant illusion of an art that looks neither far out nor in deep. It is the climate of the idyllic mood.

III

The idyllic mood was shattered, and the mask of age became the lineaments of reality. The strategy of memory and desire "came true." Word of Arthur Hallam's death in Vienna reached Tennyson at Somersby, Lincolnshire, on October 1, 1833. To Henry Alford, another member of the Apostles Club, it seemed "a loud and terrible stroke from the reality of things upon the fairy building of our youth." How much more so to Tennyson, who felt his personal grief re-echoing in every chamber of his being—so closely had he bound his rational doubts to fantasies of loss and death in the strife of Sense and Conscience.

The series of elegiac stanzas that would become *In Memoriam* was begun almost at once. The earliest to appear in J. M. Heath's *Commonplace Book* ("Fair ship, that from the Italian shore") bears the date "Oct. 6 1833." The substance of the poem is Tennyson's life, but the formal biographical structure is artificial. Sections written early are set down in the midst of later ones, and the three Christ-mases and the other anniversaries are formal devices. There is no evidence for supposing that Tennyson actually toiled three years in the cycle of moods through which the poem runs. Nor is the theme of the poem seriously philosophical, as Tennyson was at pains to point out. The "brief lays, of Sorrow born" reflect only the "random influences" of controversy.

The theme of *In Memoriam* is loss and the subjective crisis it provokes. For this reason, the poem recapitulates much of Tennyson's previous development: the moods of frustration and longing, the strategy of the mask of age, the issues of sceptical doubt, the question of the poet's involvement in the world of affairs, and the issues of social disorder and social inertia encountered in the political songs. Tennyson was fully aware that his private grief for Arthur Hallam involved his "passion of the past" and worked its way through all his being:

> Likewise the imaginative woe,
>   That loved to handle spiritual strife,
>   Diffused the shock thro' all my life,
> But in the present broke the blow. (85)

The melancholic temperament upon which Tennyson had boldly erected the structure of his art was now baptized in the experience of real grief. Freud theorized "that melancholia is in some way related to an unconscious loss of love-object, in contradistinction to mourning, in which there is nothing unconscious about the loss." [5] Freud's insight would reveal the nature of Tennyson's fixed response to "the picture and the past," that he idealized in "Tears, Idle Tears" and stated more explicitly, long afterward, in "The Ancient Sage."

>   . . . for oft
> On me, when boy, there came what then I call'd,
> Who knew no books and no philosophies,
> In my boy-phrase, "The Passion of the Past."
> The first gray streak of earliest summer-dawn,
> The last long stripe of waning crimson gloom,
> As if the late and early were but one—
> A height, a broken grange, a grove, a flower

Had murmurs, "Lost and gone, and lost and gone—"
A breath, a whisper—some divine farewell—
Desolate sweetness—far and far away—
What had he loved, what had he lost, the boy?
I know not, and I speak of what has been.

This passage leads at once to a description of such a mystical trance as takes the centre of "Armageddon." If there is a definitive Tennysonian theme, this is it—a reiterated and dreamlike sense of loss that becomes idyllic self-assurance.

If we suppose such a loss or alienation, Arthur Hallam's role in Tennyson's development would be to clarify the motive in Tennyson's remarkably dependent nature that rendered his mind sluggish in freeing itself from supporting ideas and habits and that made him lean heavily upon his friends, his wife, and his son. It is a supposition that lets us see in Arthur, the symbolic figure of *In Memoriam* and of the *Idylls of the King*, the means by which Tennyson gained some conscious control over his divided nature. The conscious loss of Arthur Hallam enables Tennyson to confront the demon of his temperament. If we are to see in Arthur Hallam a possible surrogate for Tennyson's father,[6] we may better understand what the friendship meant to Tennyson and why the loss of Hallam seemed more than the death of a friend. Hallam's death would re-enact the father's death and would arouse again the sense of guilt that springs from the repression of aggressive impulses, "the blindfold sense of wrong" that Tennyson finds alien to his love for Hallam and that yet marks the anniversary of his death "as with some hideous crime." Later, the imaginative reunion with Hallam might also touch some thrilling overtones of reconciliation with the father. To the degree that the unconscious elements of melancholia are not entirely resolved in conscious grief, *In Memoriam* would remain somewhat asymmetrical and strange:

> But there is more than I can see,
>   And what I see I leave unsaid,
>   Nor speak it, knowing Death has made
> His darkness beautiful with thee. (74)

Because the death of Arthur Hallam is both a real and a symbolic loss that radiates from the centre of Tennyson's art, the tone of amatory affection which suffuses *In Memoriam* cannot be read as simple evidence of an erotic relationship in fact between Tennyson and his friend. It is enough that the loss of Hallam touches Tennyson at every nerve and that the demand for reunion is expressed with an energy that will not forgo the connotations of physical bereavement. Hallam himself had emphasized the intimate connection between intense spiritual devotion and erotic expression in his "Remarks on Professor Rossetti's 'Disquisizione sullo spirito antipapale'": "What is the distinguishing character of Hebrew literature, which separates it by so broad a line of demarcation from that of every ancient people? Undoubtedly, the sentiment of *erotic devotion* that pervades it." Whatever we may choose to call the bond between Tennyson and Hallam, the crisis of *In Memoriam* would not have been induced by the rupture of feelings less complex and profound.

The stages and the achievement of *In Memoriam* are in some respects more clearly visible in those other poems that the death of Hallam almost immediately called forth. "The Two Voices" (at first called "Thoughts of a Suicide") bears in the *Poems* of 1842 the significant date "1833." In J. M. Heath's *Commonplace Book* "Ulysses" is dated "Oct: 20 1833," and "Tithonus," which Tennyson called a "pendant" to "Ulysses," was drafted at about the same time, although not published until 1860. "Morte d'Arthur" was in hand before the end of 1833. Considered together, these poems strongly suggest that Tennyson rapidly passed through the stages projected across a longer scheme of time in *In Memoriam*.

The theme of all these poems that cluster together is loss, frustration, and the need to explore,

> How much of act at human hands
> The sense of human will demands
> By which we dare to live or die. (85)

"The Two Voices," a diffuse debate between Self and Soul, turns on the question of whether life can be endured. The affirmative, not easily gained, rests upon "the heat of inward evidence," like that cry of "I have felt," in section 124 of *In Memoriam*. The poet then passes into the vernal woods that symbolize his reborn existence. Characteristically, the impulse toward "suicide" is more fully objectified in the imaginative sympathy that Tennyson shows for the legend of Tithonus. The poem "Tithonus" is an elaborate and beautiful ritual for release from frustration. If love is withheld, death is desired. Tithonus, caught in the web of memory and desire, appeals for a release no less idyllic than the erotic vision of Aurora that motivates his plea.

"There is more about myself in 'Ulysses,'" said Tennyson. "It was more written with the feeling of his loss upon me than many poems in 'In Memoriam.'" As in "The Lotos-Eaters," the Ithaca of responsibilities is renounced, this time explicitly, in favour of a voyage into ever-widening "experience." But this is not mere experience and it is not true that "the margin fades, Forever and forever when I move." Ulysses moves toward a possible reunion, as in the dream-voyage described in *In Memoriam*, section 103, toward the Happy Isles and a meeting with "the great Achilles, whom we knew." In small compass, Tennyson forecasts the dual answer of *In Memoriam*: life and nature are a continuum extending uninterruptedly toward a spiritual climax; yet at some point the "lower" material world passes over into the "higher" spiritual world. The continuum belongs to the world of nature and history; in the subjective vision of reunion with Hallam the poet crosses the bar between two separate spheres.

"Morte d'Arthur" unites the themes of all these poems in Sir Bedivere who must "go forth companionless," and in the death of King Arthur. Defeated in the material world, he voyages without abrupt transition to the happy island-valley of Avilion. A vision of his return and a dream of reunion with him close the lines which frame the epic fragment.

The theme of reunion is the personal core of *In Memoriam*. It develops in a series of fairly distinct approaches that culminate in the trance-vision in section 95 and the dream of the future in section 103. In these two lyrics Tennyson contrives to knit the past to the present and the present to the future. The stages of approach to reunion are most clearly defined in sections 41-7, which discuss death as a barrier to reunion, sections 60-5, which suggest that friendship may cross the barrier, and the series of dreams, sections 67-71. These advance painfully, through imagery recalling the ominous preludes of "Armageddon" and "A Dream of Fair Women," to a sleep, akin "To death and trance And madness," in which there is "forged at last"

> A night-long Present of the Past
> In which we went thro' summer France. (71)

After a pause quickened only by the lyrics of spring (83 and 86), the forward movement begins again with vivid recollections of Hallam's presence at Cambridge and at Somersby (87 and 89).

Sections 90-5 achieve reunion with Hallam in the present. The ritual preparation is fastidious. It begins (90) with a passionate invocation—"Ah dear, but come thou back to me"—that is qualified (91) by a rejection of mere dreams of the past—"Come: not in watches of the night." Sections 92 and 93 refuse to invoke a stage-phantom, "a wind Of memory murmuring the past." Tennyson thus invites the return of a mystical disclosure, and section 94 is symbolic lustration. Then, in the moonlight on the lawn of Somersby (95), in the midst of images from memory,

> The dead man touch'd me from the past,
> And all at once it seem'd at last
> The living soul was flash'd on mine. . . .

> . . . at length my trance
> Was cancell'd, stricken thro' with doubt.

In "the doubtful dusk" of dawn, the breeze that had trembled in "In Deep and Solemn Dreams" shakes sycamore and elms, and dies away at the talismanic hour when

> East and West, without a breath,
> Mixt their dim lights, like life and death. . . .

The lyrics concerning Tennyson's departure from Somersby are crowned by the dream (103) that blends many elements of Tennyson's poetry and merges the present in the future. The Hall with a river flowing past recalls "The Lady of Shalott" and "The Palace of Art." The "summons from the sea" and the poet's voyage with maidens down the river toward the sea have affinities with "Ulysses," "Morte d'Arthur," "Locksley Hall," and "Crossing the Bar." The magic of the dream increases,

> Until the forward-creeping tides
> Began to foam, and we to draw
> From deep to deep, to where we saw
> A great ship lift her shining sides.

> The man we loved was there on deck,
> But thrice as large as man he bent
> To greet us. Up the side I went,
> And fell in silence on his neck. . . .

Although the reunion with Hallam's spirit is imperfect and consequently demands renewal (for example, in section 122), Hallam becomes the symbolic thread that knits Tennyson's world of experience together again. Section 103 is followed at once by the "third Christmas" lyrics (104, 105) that renounce the observance of "an ancient form Thro' which the spirit breathes no more." The New Year song (section 106) celebrates instead "the Christ that is to be"; and section 107 ("It is the day when he was born") establishes the observance of Hallam's nativity. The remaining lyrics of *In Memoriam* are the apotheosis of Hallam as "herald of a higher race" who redeems from doubt and pain the intellectual difficulties that had joined in the train of personal grief.

If the nature of Tennyson's subjective crisis had made him unusually sensitive to the moral implications of the revolution that was occurring in art, in society, in science and in history, the loss of Hallam had quickened that awareness. He perceived the approach of Darwinian materialism and the rising class struggle as outward manifestations of that loss of values which he had suffered in his own life. Unsanctified by tradition and lacking "objective foundations" in common morality, the scientific view of nature and the liberal position in politics resolve the conflict between good and evil into a mere struggle for existence and cast the artist to the mercy of his impressions:

> This round of green, this orb of flame,
>   Fantastic beauty; such as lurks
>   In some wild Poet, when he works
> Without a conscience or an aim. (34)

The full weight of modern knowledge, "Submitting all things to desire," seemed cast into the balance on the side of sense. In the dialectic of his poetry, Tennyson had rendered himself fully responsive to the attractions of materialism and of a monistic ontology, most visibly in "The Lotos-Eaters," to which he could not commit himself. If art, nature, and history are empty of a higher will,

> 'Twere best at once to sink to peace,
>   Like birds the charming serpent draws,
>   To drop head-foremost in the jaws
> Of vacant darkness and to cease. (34)

But when he finds darkness "made beautiful" by reunion with Hallam, that friend becomes the "higher hand" that frees knowledge from the bonds of sense.

Yet as "Ulysses" showed, Tennyson's answer to the intellectual difficulties that he faced is paradoxical. He tries to accept the materialist-monistic continuum of nature and of history as a scale upon which evil is merely historical process. Ends justify the means, and evil is redeemed in the evolutionary faith,

> That all, as in some piece of art,
>   Is toil coöperant to an end. (128)

At some point the material cosmos is to sail smoothly and imperceptibly across into the realm of spirit. The presence of spiritual and "higher" values renders the materialist continuum tolerable, yet at times unendurable. A thoroughly material progress was not the answer to Tennyson's needs, and he spurns a purely evolutionary faith in "the greater ape," whose scheme of values gave no room to the qualities that endeared Arthur Hallam to his friend. The "far-off divine event" could not happen in the Malthusian world of Huxley and Darwin.

The material world must be, at length, defeated; the great result of time must be negated. The Battle in the West and the defeat of Arthur herald his departure into the happy island of Avilion. The way to transcendental values lies through loss, death, and defeat. No accumulation of material advances can leap the transcendental barrier. Tennyson is tossed between the wealthy attractions of materialistic monism and the dualistic demands of his subjective strife and system of values. The world of nature can be sanctified only by another and a higher. At least once, he got the paradox fully stated:

> Dear friend, far off, my lost desire,
>   So far, so near in woe and weal;
>   O loved the most, when most I feel
> There is a lower and a higher;
>
> Known and unknown; human, divine;
>   Sweet human hand and lips and eye;
>   Dear heavenly friend that canst not die,
> Mine, mine, for ever, ever mine;
>
> Strange friend, past, present, and to be;
>   Loved deeplier, darklier understood;
>   Behold, I dream a dream of good,
> And mingle all the world with thee. (129)

The irredeemable flaw of Tennyson's poetry is that he habitually weakens and dulls his perception of this paradox. Because he could sometimes make the transcendental leap in his own experience, he is bemused into regarding it as an objective truth common to all men. Thus he inclines to further in his art the idyllic mood rather than the tragic perspectives that a genuine dualism might have afforded. Nevertheless, the tragic view develops, almost surreptitiously, in the themes of defeat and disaster that dominate *Idylls of the King* and even the plays. Without the constant support of any traditional systems of value, Tennyson contrived to face, and in part to comprehend, the problem of tragedy in modern art. No English poet explored more widely the range of possibilities that had closed.

IV

Tennyson is a modern poet, also, in his attempt to provide the personal themes of *In Memoriam* with a formal structure responsive to both private instinct and the elegiac traditions. His attempt embodies in practical form the question of the artist's involvement or non-involvement in the life of his culture. Tennyson withholds himself from the objective form of the pastoral elegy and at the same time he draws upon its inherent strength. *In Memoriam* was undertaken "for his own relief and private satisfaction," and was anonymously published. Yet it is, of course, an enormously ambitious work, and imbedded in its discursive and informal manner are many of the traditional elegiac conventions. It opens with a formal invocation to a higher power and closes with an epithalamium. It describes the funeral procession (the voyage of the ship returning Hallam's body to England) and the mourning of nature, which is a kind of death. The poet himself represents the mourners. In accordance with the sophisticated tradition of the elegy, Tennyson launches forth on sober and noble themes, both personal and general, concerning the meaning of history, the nature of nature, and his personal destiny as man and as poet. The poem draws to a close with a lengthy apotheosis that dismisses the mood of grief, settles the perplexities, and issues upon a higher plane.

The presence of these traditional elements helps Tennyson in playing out the ritual of his private grief and in giving it objective form. Under the personal theme lie the ancient elegiac conventions, and through them the poem observes a simple, pastoral ritual of the cycle of the year: the death and reawakening of nature. This "natural piety" underlies the comparatively superficial time-scheme of three years and is organically related to the theme of loss and reunion. It is adumbrated rather than announced. The death of nature is symbolized by the autumn and winter imagery dominating the allusions to nature in the poem as far as section 83, by the mournful observances of Christ's nativity (sections 28-30, 78), and by the commemoration (section 72) of the "disastrous day" of Hallam's death. Section 83, a sudden invocation of spring, initiates the series of springtime poems (sections 86, 88, 89, 115, 116) that light the way toward reunion with Hallam and his apotheosis. As the statesman that he might have become, Hallam symbolizes that "life in civic action warm" that may

329

turn society from its wavering course. He also represents that wisdom of a "higher hand" that must control the results of scientific and practical "Knowledge." Hallam's efficacy as a symbol that "touches into leaf" the issues that had been filled with pain and death depends on the subjective experiences which revivified Tennyson's universe of values. The experience of loss itself became endeared as the prelude to reunion:

> That out of distance might ensue
> Desire of nearness doubly sweet,
> And unto meeting, when we meet,
> Delight a hundredfold accrue. . . . (117)

The cycle of nature is completed, and into the future is projected the passion of the past. The marriage-song that finishes the poem can welcome again the imagery of living nature and the conception of a child whose birth is the rebirth of Hallam and of Tennyson.

Beyond this achievement Tennyson could not or did not go. In his individual experience he had not found the objective foundations that he required. This he sometimes recognized and sometimes forgot. When he forgot, he became facile, sentimental, and mechanical, though there are few poems in which the pulse of uncertainty does not stir at all. The history of his career after 1850—indeed, almost from 1833 onwards—is basically a recapitulation of his earlier development. Even *Idylls of the King*, defaced in parts by his delusions of certainty, was a project which he had begun to conceive before the death of Hallam. It is a poem, on the warfare of Sense and Soul, that is wrenched from its idyllic oversimplifications into a study of erotic and mystical motives and the disintegration of an ideal society. The defect and the nature of the poem are manifest in its strange hero, who does not himself embody the conflicting values but shares them with Lancelot.

Because he did not really advance toward "solutions," and because he reached in *In Memoriam* the clearest apprehension of his own nature that he was capable of, Tennyson's later poetry does not break from the pattern of his past. This is why he could revise his early work, as he did for the *Poems* of 1842, with as much grace and tact as if he were still in the midst of writing it for the first time; he had not moved beyond it. With thorough integrity he could publish in his later books some poems written long before and could introduce passages of this early work into poems written a half-century later. The persistence of his motives brings his later poetry back to the inescapable themes: in "The Ancient Sage" he returns to the debate of "The Two Voices," in "Lucretius" to the fierce and open warfare between erotic and conscientious impulses, in "Demeter and Persephone" to the ritual of the death and reawakening of nature, in "Crossing the Bar" to the dream-voyages of "Morte d'Arthur" and "In Memoriam," and in his last book to "The Death of Œnone." Force of habit sometimes dulled, sometimes strengthened, his artistry.

The Tennysonian theme is frustration, and his poetry offers an analysis of its symptoms rather than the cure. What is overcome through the elaborate strategies of dream and vision is not the frustration but the disappointment that follows it. It is a poetry of illusions, some painful, some happy, none of them wearing the ultimate authority of reality. The recurrent pattern is a transition through death, loss, or dream toward ideal moods that dissolve the edges of thought and appetite. Under such illusions, Tennyson sometimes mistakes the sense of relief for the signs of truth. But because the sources of his poetry lay, finally, beyond his control, he could not get free of what is genuine as well as painful.

What saved him, at last, was that he felt his predicament even if he did not thoroughly comprehend it. He saw the crisis of art and society as a war of values, a matter of conscience. He does not theorize about it nor arrive at systematic principles. Yet in viewing the function and origin of conscience, he offers a more complex and subtler insight than T. H. Huxley, who supposed conscience to be merely a social monitor, the inner voice of social obligations. For Tennyson, it is more primitive and more powerful, arising in partly unconscious levels of the mind and presenting to the reason and the will an ambiguous scene of unreconciled motives and values. In Tennyson's anatomy of conscience, our human action upon nature and society meets a crisis of the divided will, which cannot be healed until it frees itself from fantasy and despair. That freedom Tennyson could not really win. His failure accurately represents the continuing crisis of our culture.

Walt Whitman, who liked Tennyson, discerned that "his very doubts, swervings, doublings upon himself, have been typical of our age." The price that Tennyson pays for being a "representative" poet is great. He suffers our disease and our confusion. He triumphs not as a master but as a victim. It is a vicarious role, and upon him we heap our detested sins. If the circumstances of his breeding, his generation, and his temperament had made him a convert to Catholicism, socialism, or theosophy, he might have written more interestingly to us. He might have been admired to the extent that he escaped the general malaise. But he kept to the mid-stream of his culture. As a result, he works out remorselessly the fatal consequences of the romantic tradition, bankrupts its style by his lavish expenditures, and reduces its intellectual ambitions to the accidents of individual perceptions and personal blindness. After him the deluge, the spreading chaos of "modern art." He is one of its makers.

There is no Tennyson tragedy. The themes of frustration can scarcely amount to that, and the tragic order of values is lacking. Besides, the victim himself, though not our father, turns out to be a well-remembered uncle, and no hero. Yet there was in him, as Hawthorne instantly perceived, "the something not to be meddled with," as he moved with the shuffling gait of a man whose injury cannot be healed and who makes of it, by force of will, the secret of his strength.

NOTES

1. R. C. Trench, *Letters and Memorials* (London, 1888), I, 73.

2. Printed among the tantalizing oddments of *Unpublished Early Poems,* edited by the poet's grandson, Sir Charles Tennyson (1932). Rewritten, this poem became the basis for Tennyson's prize poem, *Timbuctoo.* Quotations from *Unpublished Early Poems* are made with the kind permission of the Macmillan Company.

3. This poem parallels in several ways the lyric, "O that 't were possible," which was the nucleus of *Maud:*

> Half the night I waste in sighs
> Half in dreams I sorrow after
> The delight of early skies;
> In a wakeful doze I sorrow
> For the hand, the lips, the eyes,
> For the meeting of the morrow,
> The delight of happy laughter,
> The delight of low replies.

Although the maddened lover is not Tennyson in any simple biographical sense, he wears the characteristic mask of Tennyson's personality. Tennyson does not fully disengage himself.

4. *Tennyson in Egypt,* University of Kansas Humanistic Studies, no. 27 (Lawrence, Kan., 1942).

5. *Collected Papers* (London, 1925), IV, 155.

6. Dr. George Clayton Tennyson died in March, 1831. Paden thinks it probable that the death of Dr. Tennyson rather than that of Hallam is the personal theme of "Morte d'Arthur," because it deals with "the end, not the beginning, of an epoch." Certainly Hallam's death felt to Tennyson like the

end of an epoch. But it is not necessary to make a simple choice between the father and the friend.

Freud's hypothesis would also intimate why *In Memoriam* opens with what may be a covert allusion to the grave of Tennyson's father (section 2) and ends not simply with a marriage-song but with the rebirth of a being like Hallam. And it would clarify the otherwise clouded theme of section 102, in which "Two spirits of a diverse love Contend for loving masterdom" as Tennyson is on the point of leaving the Somersby home. In the face of his father's ambiguous comment, Hallam Tennyson plainly identified the two spirits as Alfred's father and Arthur Hallam (*Alfred Lord Tennyson: A Memoir* (New York, 1897), I, 72).

To see the function of melancholy sensibility in Tennyson's poetry does not require, however, that we disentangle the subtle skein of biography, interesting though it is to try.

CLEANTH BROOKS

———◆———

The Motivation of Tennyson's Weeper

TENNYSON is perhaps the last English poet one would think of associating with the subtleties of paradox and ambiguity. He is not the thoughtless poet, to be sure: he grapples—particularly in his later period—with the "big" questions which were up for his day; and he struggles manfully with them. But the struggle, as Tennyson conducted it, was usually kept out of the grammar and symbolism of the poetry itself. Like his own protagonist in "In Memoriam," Tennyson "fought his doubts"—he does not typically build them into the structure of the poetry itself as enriching ambiguities.

Yet substantially true as this generalization is, Tennyson was not always successful in avoiding the ambiguous and the paradoxical; and indeed, in some of his poems his failure to avoid them becomes a saving grace. The lyric "Tears, Idle Tears" is a very good instance. It is a poem which, from a strictly logical point of view, Tennyson may be thought to have blundered into. But, whether he blundered into it or not, the poem gains from the fact that it finds its unity in a principle of organization higher than that which seems to be operative in many of Tennyson's more "thoughtful" poems.

Any account of the poem may very well begin with a consideration of the nature of the tears. Are they *idle* tears? Or are they not rather the most meaningful of tears? Does not the very fact that they are "idle" (that is, tears occasioned by no immediate grief) become in itself a guarantee of the fact that they spring from a deeper, more universal cause?

It would seem so, and that the poet is thus beginning his poem

---

with a paradox. For the third line of the poem indicates that there is no doubt in the speaker's mind about the origin of the tears in some divine despair. They "rise in the heart"—for all that they have been first announced as "idle."

But the question of whether Tennyson is guilty of (or to be complimented upon) a use of paradox may well wait upon further discussion. At this point in our commentary, it is enough to observe that Tennyson has chosen to open his poem with some dramatic boldness— if not with the bold step of equating "idle" with "from the depth of some divine despair," then at least with a bold and violent reversal of the speaker's first characterization of his tears.

The tears "rise in the heart" as the speaker looks upon a scene of beauty and tranquillity. Does looking on the "happy Autumn-fields" bring to mind the days that are no more? The poet does not say so. The tears rise to the eyes in looking on the "happy Autumn-fields" *and* thinking of the days that are no more. The poet himself does not stand responsible for any closer linkage between these actions, though, as a matter of fact, most of us will want to make a closer linkage here. For, if we change "happy Autumn-fields," say, to "happy April-fields," the two terms tend to draw apart. The fact that the fields are autumn-fields which, though happy, point back to something which is over—which is finished—*does* connect them with the past and therefore properly suggests to the observer thoughts about that past.

To sum up: The first stanza has a unity, but it is not a unity which finds its sanctions in the ordinary logic of language. Its sanctions are to be found in the dramatic context, and, to my mind, there alone. Indeed, the stanza suggests the play of the speaker's mind as the tears unexpectedly start, tears for which there is no apparent occasion, and as he searches for an explanation of them. He calls them "idle," but, even as he says "I know not what they mean," he realizes that they must spring from the depths of his being—is willing, with his very next words, to associate them with "some divine despair." Moreover, the real occasion of the tears, though the speaker himself comes to realize it only as he approaches the end of the stanza, is the thought about the past. It is psychologically and dramatically right, therefore, that the real occasion should be stated explicitly only with the last line of the stanza.

This first stanza, then, recapitulates the surprise and bewilderment in the speaker's own mind, and sets the problem which the succeeding stanzas are to analyze. The dramatic effect may be described as follows: the stanza seems, not a meditated observation, but a speech begun impulsively—a statement which the speaker has begun before he knows how he will end it.

In the second stanza we are not surprised to have the poet characterize the days that are no more as "sad," but there is some shock in hearing him apply to them the adjective "fresh." Again, the speaker does not pause to explain: the word "fresh" actually begins the stanza. Yet the adjective justifies itself.

The past is fresh as with a dawn freshness—as fresh as the first beam glittering on the sail of an incoming ship. The ship is evidently expected: it brings friends, friends "up from the underworld." On the surface, the comparison is innocent: the "underworld" is merely the antipodes, the world which lies below the horizon—an underworld in the sense displayed in old-fashioned geographies with their sketches illustrating the effects of the curvature of the earth. The sails, which catch the light and glitter, will necessarily be the part first seen of any ship which is coming "up" over the curve of the earth.

But the word "underworld" will necessarily suggest the underworld of Greek mythology, the realm of the shades, the abode of the dead. The attempt to characterize the freshness of the days that are no more has, thus, developed, almost imperceptibly, into a further characterization of the days themselves as belonging, not to our daylight world, but to an "underworld." This suggestion is, of course, strengthened in the lines that follow in which the ship metaphor is reversed so as to give us a picture of sadness: evening, the last glint of sunset light on the sail of a ship

> That sinks with all we love below the verge . . .

The conjunction of the qualities of sadness and freshness is reinforced by the fact that the same basic symbol—the light on the sails of a ship hull down—has been employed to suggest both qualities. With the third stanza, the process is carried one stage further: the two qualities (with the variant of "strange" for "fresh") are explicitly linked together:

> Ah, sad and strange as in dark summer dawns . . .

And here the poet is not content to suggest the qualities of sadness and strangeness by means of two different, even if closely related, figures. In this third stanza the special kind of sadness and strangeness is suggested by one and the same figure.

It is a figure developed in some detail. It, too, involves a dawn scene, though ironically so, for the beginning of the new day is to be the beginning of the long night for the dying man. The dying eyes, the poem suggests, have been for some time awake—long enough to have had time to watch the

. . . casement slowly [grow] a glimmering square . . .

The dying man, soon to sleep the lasting sleep, is more fully awake than the "half-awaken'd birds" whose earliest pipings come to his dying ears. We know why these pipings are sad; but why are they *strange?* Because to the person hearing a bird's song for the last time, it will seem that he has never before really heard one. The familiar sound will take on a quality of unreality—of strangeness.

If this poem were merely a gently melancholy reverie on the sweet sadness of the past, Stanzas II and III would have no place in the poem. But the poem is no such reverie: the images from the past rise up with a strange clarity and sharpness that shock the speaker. Their sharpness and freshness account for the sudden tears and for the psychological problem with which the speaker wrestles in the poem. If the past would only remain melancholy but dimmed, sad but worn and familiar, we should have no problem and no poem. At least, we should not have *this* poem; we should certainly not have the intensity of the last stanza.

That intensity, if justified, must grow out of a sense of the apparent nearness and intimate presence of what is irrevocably beyond reach: the days that are no more must be more than the conventional "dear, dead days beyond recall." They must be beyond recall, yet alive—tantalizingly vivid and near. It is only thus that we can feel the speaker justified in calling them

> Dear as remember'd kisses after death,
> And sweet as those by hopeless fancy feign'd
> On lips that are for others. . . .

It is only thus that we can accept the culminating paradox of

O Death in Life, the days that are no more.

We have already observed, in the third stanza, how the speaker compares the strangeness and sadness of the past to the sadness of the birds' piping as it sounds to dying ears. There is a rather brilliant ironic contrast involved in the comparison. The speaker, a living man, in attempting to indicate how sad and strange to him are the days of the past, says that they are as sad and strange as is the natural activity of the awakening world to the man who is dying: the dead past seems to the living man as unfamiliar and fresh in its sadness as the living present seems to the dying man. There is more here, however, than a mere, ironic reversal of roles; in each case there is the sense of being irrevocably barred out from the known world.

This ironic contrast, too, accounts for the sense of desperation which runs through the concluding lines of the poem. The kisses feigned by "hopeless fancy" are the more precious because of the very hopelessness; but memory takes on the quality of fancy. It is equally hopeless —the kisses can as little be renewed as those "feign'd / On lips that are for others" can be obtained. The realized past has become as fabulous as the unrealizable future. The days that are no more are as dear as the one, as sweet as the other, the speaker says; and it does not matter whether we compare them to the one or to the other or to both: it comes to the same thing.

But the days that are no more are not merely "dear" and "sweet"; they are "deep" and "wild." Something has happened to the grammar here. How can the *days* be "deep as love" or "wild with all regret"? And what is the status of the exclamation "O Death in Life"? Is it merely a tortured cry like "O God! the days that are no more"? Or is it a loose appositive: "the days that are no more are a kind of death in life"?

The questions are not asked in a censorious spirit, as if there were no justification for Tennyson's license here. But it is important to see how much license the poem requires, and the terms on which the reader decides to accord it justification. What one finds on closer examination is not muddlement but richness. But it is a richness achieved through principles of organization which many an admirer of the poet has difficulty in allowing to the "obscure" modern poet.

For example, how can the days of the past be *deep?* Here, of course, the problem is not very difficult. The past is buried within one: the days that are no more constitute the deepest level of one's being, and the tears that arise from thinking on them may be said to come from the "depth of some divine despair." But how can the days be "wild with all regret"? The extension demanded here is more ambitious. In matter of fact, it is the speaker, the man, who is made wild with regret by thinking on the days.

One can, of course, justify the adjective as a transferred epithet on the model of Vergil's *maestum timorem;* and perhaps this was Tennyson's own conscious justification (if, indeed, the need to justify it ever occurred to him). But one can make a better case than a mere appeal to the authority of an established literary convention. There is a sense in which the man and the remembered days are one and the same. A man is the sum of his memories. The adjective which applies to the man made wild with regret can apply to those memories which make him wild with regret. For, does the man charge the memories with his own passion, or is it the memories that give the emotion to him? If we pursue the matter far enough, we come to a point where the distinction lapses. Perhaps I should say, more accurately, adopting the metaphor of the poem itself, we *descend* to a depth where the distinction lapses. The days that are no more are *deep* and *wild*, buried but not dead—below the surface and unthought of, yet at the deepest core of being, secretly alive.

The past *should* be tame, fettered, brought to heel; it is not. It is capable of breaking forth and coming to the surface. The word "wild" is bold, therefore, but justified. It reasserts the line of development which has been maintained throughout the earlier stanzas: "fresh," "strange," and now "wild"—all adjectives which suggest passionate, irrational life. The word "wild," thus, not only pulls into focus the earlier paradoxes, but is the final stage in the preparation for the culminating paradox, "O Death in Life."

The last stanza evokes an intense emotional response from the reader. The claim could hardly be made good by the stanza taken in isolation. The stanza leans heavily upon the foregoing stanzas, and the final paradox draws heavily upon the great metaphors in Stanzas II and III. This is as it should be. The justification for emphasizing the fact here is this: the poem, for all its illusion of impassioned speech—with the looseness and *apparent* confusion of unpremeditated speech—is very tightly organized. It represents an organic structure; and the intensity of the total effect is a reflection of the total structure.

The reader, I take it, will hardly be disposed to quarrel with the general statement of the theme of the poem as it is given in the foregoing account; and he will probably find himself in accord with this general estimate of the poem's value. But the reader may well feel that the amount of attention given to the structure of the poem is irrelevant, if not positively bad. In particular, he may find the emphasis on paradox, ambiguity, and ironic contrast displeasing. He has not been taught to expect these in Tennyson, and he has had the general impression that the presence of these qualities represents the intrusion of alien, "unpoetic" matter.

I have no wish to intellectualize the poem—to make conscious and artful what was actually spontaneous and simple. Nevertheless, the qualities of ironic contrast and paradox *do* exist in the poem; and they *do* have a relation to the poem's dramatic power.

Those who still feel that "simple eloquence" is enough might compare "Tears, Idle Tears" with another of Tennyson's poems which has somewhat the same subject matter and hints of the same imagery, the lyric "Break, Break, Break."

> Break, break, break,
>> On thy cold grey stones, O sea!
> And I would that my tongue could utter
>> The thoughts that arise in me.
>
> O, well for the fisherman's boy,
>> That he shouts with his sister at play!
> O well for the sailor lad,
>> That he sings in his boat on the bay!
>
> And the stately ships go on
>> To their haven under the hill;
> But O for the touch of a vanished hand,
>> And the sound of a voice that is still!
>
> Break, break, break,
>> At the foot of thy crags, O sea!
> But the tender grace of a day that is dead
>> Will never come back to me.

It is an easier poem than "Tears," and, in one sense, a less confusing poem. But it is also a much thinner poem, and unless we yield comfortably and easily to the strain of gentle melancholy, actually a coarser and a more confused poem. For example, the ships are said to be "stately," but this observation is idle and finally irrelevant. What relation has their stateliness to the experience of grief? (Perhaps one may argue that the term suggests that they go on to fulfill their missions, unperturbed and with no regard for the speaker's mood. But this interpretation is forced, and even under forcing, the yield of relevance is small.)

Again, consider the status of the past as it appears in this poem: the hand is vanished, the voice is still. It is true, as the poem itself indicates, that there is a sense in which the hand has not vanished and the voice is yet heard; otherwise we should not have the poem at all. But the poet makes no effort to connect this activity, still alive in memory, with its former "actual" life. He is content to keep close to the conventional prose account of such matters. Memory in this poem does not become a kind of life: it is just "memory"—whatever that is— and, in reading the poem, we are not forced beyond the bounds of our conventional thinking on the subject.

In the same way, the elements of the line, "the tender grace of a day that is dead," remain frozen at the conventional prose level. The day is "dead"; the "tender grace" of it will never "come back" to him. We are not encouraged to take the poignance of his present memory of it as a ghost from the tomb. The poet does not recognize that his experience represents such an ironical resurrection; nor does he allow the metaphors buried in "dead" and "come back" to suffer a resurrection into vigorous poetic life. With such phenomena the poet is not concerned.

Of course, the poet *need* not be concerned with them; I should agree that we have no right to demand that this poem should explore the nature of memory as "Tears, Idle Tears" explores it. At moments, men are unaccountably saddened by scenes which are in themselves placid and even happy. The poet is certainly entitled, if he chooses, to let it go at that. Yet, it should be observed that in avoiding the psychological exploration of the experience, the poet risks losing dramatic force.

Mere psychological analysis is, of course, not enough to insure dramatic force; and such analysis, moreover, carries its own risks: the poem may become unnatural and coldly rhetorical. But when the poet is able, as in "Tears, Idle Tears," to analyze his experience, and in the full light of the disparity and even apparent contradiction of the various elements, bring them into a new unity, he secures not only richness and depth but dramatic power as well. Our conventional accounts of poetry which oppose emotion to intellect, "lyric simplicity" to "thoughtful meditation," have done no service to the cause of poetry. The opposition is not merely superficial: it falsifies the real relationships. For the lyric quality, if it be genuine, is not the result of some transparent and "simple" redaction of a theme or a situation which is somehow poetic in itself; it is, rather, the result of an imaginative grasp of diverse materials—but an imaginative grasp so sure that it may show itself to the reader as unstudied and unpredictable without for a moment relaxing its hold on the intricate and complex stuff which it carries.

GORDON N. RAY

Vanity Fair: One Version of the Novelist's Responsibility

My title, I am afraid, has an old-fashioned ring. The novelists of to-day who best know their job believe with André Gide that "the moral issue for the artist is not that he should present an idea that is useful but that he should present an idea well."[1] They have relinquished their ethical role by eliminating themselves, and therefore the question of responsibility to their readers, from their books. Their credo is summed up by Evelyn Waugh in an article on Graham Greene's *The Heart of the Matter.* Greene's style is functional, not at all "specifically literary," he writes. "The words are simply mathematical symbols for his thought. Moreover, no relation is established between writer and reader. The reader has not had a conversation with a third party such as he enjoys with Sterne or Thackeray." There is not even an observer through whose eyes events are seen. The technique employed is that of the cinema, with Greene as director and producer. "It is the modern way of telling a story."[2]

Victorian novelists, on the other hand, cherished the relation of writer to reader and pondered very seriously their moral obligation to their audience. Of them all Thackeray has been most severely reproached by later critics for intruding upon his stories in the character of guide, philosopher and friend. But perhaps it has been too hastily assumed that the advantage in this particular must lie with the modern novelist. At any rate, instead of taking it for granted that Thackeray's penchant for moral commentary is an excrescence, un-

From *Essays by Divers Hands: Being the Transactions of the Royal Society of Literature of the United Kingdom,* New Series, XXV (1950), 87–101. (Read April 27th, 1949.) Reprinted by permission of the Royal Society of Literature and the author.

happily all too common among the naïve and primitive novelists who lived before Henry James, I propose to inquire how he came to entertain his conception of the novelist's responsibility, how his work was altered by it, how it affected his standing with his readers, and how it is related to his intellectual position in his age.

I

When the first monthly number of *Vanity Fair* appeared in January, 1847, Thackeray had for ten years earned his living by his pen; yet what reputation he had achieved hardly extended beyond his fellow-writers and a small audience of discriminating readers. Because they were either anonymous or written over one or another of his various *noms de plume,* his long series of brilliant contributions to *Fraser's Magazine, Punch* and the *Morning Chronicle* had little cumulative effect. The "great stupid public," [3] as he called it, passed him by indifferent. "Mrs. Perkins's [Ball] is a great success—the greatest I have had—very nearly as great as Dickens," he remarked of the first of his Christmas books in December of 1846, "that is Perkins 500, Dickens 25,000—only that difference!" [4]

The reception accorded the yellow-wrappered parts of *Vanity Fair* was at first hardly more encouraging. But gradually they began to be talked about. Friendly paragraphs underlined their excellence in *Fraser's Magazine,* the *Scotsman* and the *North British Review.* In July, after the seventh monthly number had appeared, the *Sun* hailed Thackeray as "the Fielding of the nineteenth century." [5] By September Mrs. Carlyle was convinced that *Vanity Fair* "beats Dickens out of the world." [6] A long panegyric by Abraham Hayward in the *Edinburgh Review* of January, 1848, sealed the success of the novel. "There is no use denying the matter or blinking it now," Thackeray wrote a few days later. "I am become a sort of great man in my way —all but at the top of the tree: indeed there if the truth were known and having a great fight up there with Dickens." [7]

How is one to account for this sudden and splendid elevation to eminence of a writer who had been regarded a year earlier, so Henry Kingsley relates, as "a man known certainly to some extent, but who was thought to have had sufficient trial, and to have found his métier as a clever magazine writer"? [8] What was the element hitherto lacking in Thackeray's books which explains the immense prestige of *Vanity Fair* with Victorian readers? A glance at his career before 1847 may answer these questions.

Connop Thirlwall said of the England of Thackeray's youth: "Society possesses two or three strong, stiff frames, in which all persons of liberal education who need or desire a fixed place and specific designation must consent to be set." [9] Thackeray obstinately sought success outside these frames. Abandoning the university after five terms and the Inns of Court after a few months, he tried his fortune as an artist and as a journalist, both employments then well beyond the social pale. He discovered before long that he could not draw well enough to succeed as a painter; and he later confessed that *what I wrote was bad and poor stuff for many years*." [10] Meanwhile, not wholly by his own fault, he had lost the modest fortune on which he had relied for a competence while he pursued his unconventional path. He was consequently exposed for many years to the distresses and humiliations of shabby gentility. When a happy marriage and recognition as a periodical writer began to promise compensation for earlier misfortunes, his wife became insane. It is not surprising that Thackeray accumulated from these experiences what Taine calls "a treasure of meditated hatred."

His history as a writer was hardly more propitious. Coming to literary maturity in the eighteen-thirties, an age of uncertain taste and uninspiring example, he turned decisively away from prevailing formulas for the novel, which seemed to him either childish or unwholesome. It was his endeavour, he said in a rare statement of purpose, "to work as an artist telling the truth and morbidly perhaps eschewing humbug." [11]

Telling the truth to Thackeray meant describing life as he had seen it during the bitter years since he came of age. "He was created," he told Dr. John Brown, "with a sense of the ugly, of the odd, of the meanly false, of the desperately wicked; he laid them bare: them under all disguises he hunted to death." [12] The first readers of *The Yellowplush Papers, Catherine, Denis Haggarty's Wife,* and *Barry Lyndon* not unnaturally found the themes that Thackeray's experience suggested to him low and sordid.

The second part of his programme, even morbidly to eschew humbug, led him to tell his stories substantially without commentary; for as a young man he was inclined to identify humbug with moralizing. Whenever he could, he adopted a dramatic disguise. The opinions of Yellowplush, George Fitz-Boodle and Barry Lyndon are intended for the most part to characterize those worthies; not to convey Thackeray's judgments. In more than one of his critical essays of the middle eighteen-forties, Thackeray explicitly stated that it is not the novelist's business to teach.

344

If we want instruction, (he wrote of Lever's "St. Patrick's Eve,") we prefer to take it from fact rather than from fiction. We like to hear sermons from his reverence at church; to get our notions of trade, crime, politics and other national statistics from the proper papers and figures; but when suddenly, out of the gilt pages of a pretty picture book, a comic moralist rushes forward, and takes occasion to tell us that society is diseased . . . persons who wish to lead an easy life are inclined to remonstrate against this literary ambuscadoe.[13]

To a public eager for guidance from its literary mentors, this attitude recommended Thackeray hardly more than did his subject matter.

Moreover, the disappointments of Thackeray's life sometimes goaded him to savage and devil-may-care protest. We find him resolving to contribute to *Punch* in 1842, at a time when that magazine was still identified in the public mind with the notorious *Age* and *Satirist* newspapers, because it offered him "a great opportunity for unrestrained laughing, sneering, kicking and gambadoing."[14] He made little effort, indeed, to ensure success by conciliating his audience. *The Book of Snobs* was designed from beginning to end to prick its readers out of their complacency. And none of Thackeray's earlier books lacks many passages in the same vein, of which the following imaginary after-dinner conversation from *The Irish Sketch-Book* may stand as an example:

One word more regarding the Widow Fagan's house. When Peggy brought in coals for the drawing-room fire, she carried them—in what do you think? "In a coal-scuttle, to be sure," says the English reader, down on you as sharp as a needle.

No, you clever Englishman, it wasn't a coal-scuttle.

"Well, then, it was in a fire-shovel," says that brightest of wits, guessing again.

No, it *wasn't* a fire-shovel, you heaven-born genius; and you might guess from this until Mrs. Snooks called you up to coffee, and you would never find out. It was in something which I have already described in Mrs. Fagan's pantry.

"Oh, I have you now, it was the bucket where the potatoes were: the thlatternly wetch!" says Snooks.

Wrong again—Peggy brought up the coals—in a CHINA PLATE! Snooks turns quite white with surprise, and almost chokes himself with his port. "Well," says he, "of all the *wum* countwith that I ever wead of, hang me if Ireland ithn't the *wummetht*. Coalth in a plate! Mawyann, do you hear that? In Ireland they alwayth thend up their coalth in a plate!"[15]

Stung by such taunts as this, it mattered little to the average Englishman that none of Thackeray's works after 1840 was without many touches of profound insight and tenderness. Such mitigations were forgotten, and the reader was left with the prevailing impression of a brilliant but forbidding talent which made him uneasy while it amused him. He regarded Thackeray as a writer for whom he could feel no affection and with whom he could achieve little solidarity.

II

If Thackeray had continued in this vein, he would hardly have written *Vanity Fair*. But late in 1846 he experienced a change of heart, the culmination of a progressive reconciliation to life, which can be compared with John Stuart Mill's awakening from Benthamite Utilitarianism twenty years earlier. Attention is directed to it by a letter which Thackeray wrote to Mark Lemon, the editor of *Punch*, in February of 1847. His subject was the last paragraph of "The Snobs of England": "To laugh at such is Mr. Punch's business. May he laugh honestly, hit no foul blow, and tell the truth when at his very broadest grin—never forgetting that if Fun is good, Truth is still better, and Love is best of all." [16]

> What I mean, [he explained to Lemon], applies to my own case and that of all of us—who set up as Satirical-Moralists—and having such a vast multitude of readers whom we not only amuse but teach. . . . A few years ago I should have sneered at the idea of setting up as a teacher at all, and perhaps at this pompous and pious way of talking about a few papers of jokes in *Punch*—but I have got to believe in the business, and in many other things since then. And our profession seems to me to be as serious as the Parson's own.[17]

What happened to Thackeray in the eighteen-forties affords at least a partial explanation of his altered attitude towards the writer's task. After the break-up of his marriage he fell into a life of Bohemian bachelorhood, living in lodgings and finding his amusement in taverns, clubs, or the homes of his friends. It was a hectic, rootless existence, which he was by no means self-sufficient enough to enjoy. In June of 1845 family circumstances at last made it possible for his mother to bring his two daughters to visit him in London. They stayed only a few days, and after their departure, Thackeray wrote to his mother:

> I wish you had never come that's the truth—for I fancied myself perfectly happy until then—now I see the difference: and what a deal of the best sort of happiness it is God's will that I should lose. Whitebait dinners are all very well but—hang the buts—it is those we are always sighing after.[18]

346

He set his heart on re-establishing his home; and fourteen months later he realized his desire. The society of his daughters, aged nine and six, brought him to an attitude of mind quite different from that which he had displayed among his rough and sometimes raffish "companions . . . over the bottle." [19] He wrote to his mother in December, 1846:

> Now they [his daughters] are with me I am getting so fond of them that I can understand the pangs of the dear old mother who loses them. . . . Continual thoughts of them chase I don't know how many wickednesses out of my mind: Their society makes many of my old amusements seem trivial and shameful. What bounties are there of Providence in the very instincts which God gives us. . . . Remember the children are in their natural place: with their nearest friend working their natural influence: getting and giving the good let us hope, which the Divine Benevolence appointed to result from the union between parents and children. [20]

The revolution that Thackeray's reunion with his family worked in his scale of values radically altered his conception of what fiction ought to be. By good fortune the fragmentary manuscript of the early chapters of *Vanity Fair* survives in the Pierpont Morgan Library to show exactly what happened. It would appear that Thackeray began his novel early in 1845 and soon completed enough for two monthly parts. These eight chapters he wrote in his slanting hand. When Colburn and two or three other publishers refused *Pen and Pencil Sketches of English Society*, as the story was first called, Thackeray laid his manuscript temporarily aside. By March of 1846 Bradbury and Evans had accepted it; but other work intervened, and Thackeray did not return to his novel until the last months of that year. The changes that he made at this time are readily identifiable, for they were entered, perhaps at the printer's request, in his more legible upright hand.

Thackeray's revisions everywhere bear the mark of his new view of fiction. For the noncommittal *Pen and Pencil Sketches of English Society* he substituted the pregnant phrase *Vanity Fair*, in itself a judgment on the life that he was describing. Here and there in his earlier narrative, which was almost as devoid of authorial intrusion as *Barry Lyndon*, he introduced passages of moral commentary. The next to the last chapter of *Pen and Pencil Sketches of English Society*, for example, had originally been devoted entirely to Becky's first letter to Amelia from Queen's Crawley. In his revision Thackeray added six concluding paragraphs which sum up the serious and responsible view that he had come to take of novel-writing.

And, as we bring our characters forward, [he wrote], I will ask leave, as a man and a brother, not only to introduce them, but occasionally to step down from the platform, and talk about them: if they are good and kindly, to love them and shake them by the hand: if they are silly, to laugh at them confidentially in the reader's sleeve: if they are wicked and heartless, to abuse them in the strongest terms which politeness admits of.

Otherwise you might fancy it was I who was sneering at the practice of devotion, which Miss Sharp finds so ridiculous; that it was I who laughed good-humouredly at the reeling old Silenus of a baronet —whereas the laughter comes from one who has no reverence except for prosperity, and no eye for anything beyond success. Such people there are living and flourishing in the world—Faithless, Hopeless, Charityless; let us have at them, dear friends, with might and main. Some there are, and very successful too, mere quacks and fools: and it was to combat and expose such as those, no doubt, that laughter was made.[21]

Similarly, in the chapter following Thackeray inserted after his portraits of old Sir Pitt Crawley and his wife passages underlining the fashion in which each of these characters exemplifies the theme of his novel. Of Sir Pitt he wrote:

Vanity Fair—Vanity Fair! Here was a man, who could not spell, and did not care to read—who had the habits and the cunning of a boor: whose aim in life was pettifogging: who never had a taste, or emotion, or enjoyment, but what was sordid and foul: and was a dignitary of the land, and a pillar of the state. He was high sheriff, and rode in a golden coach. Great ministers and statesmen courted him; and in Vanity Fair he had a higher place than the most brilliant genius or spotless virtue.[22]

As Thackeray went on from the point where his 1845 narrative ended, he was able to avoid the relatively crude and awkward patchwork of these earlier insertions. He moved with increasing ease from narrative to commentary and back again. His theme sufficiently stated, he no longer found it necessary to insist heavily on its explicit formulation. Nevertheless, he did not lose his guiding vision of the world as "Vanity Fair," and all his effects were planned to emphasize it. His letters everywhere reveal his concentration upon the ethical issues raised by the action of his novel. In July of 1847, for example, he told his mother:

Of course you are quite right about Vanity Fair and Amelia, it is mentioned in this very number. My object is not to make a perfect character or anything like it. Don't you see how odious all the people are in the book (with the exception of Dobbin)—behind whom all there lies a dark moral I hope. What I want is to make a set of people living without God in the world (only that is a cant phrase) greedy pompous mean perfectly self-satisfied for the most part and at ease about their superior virtue.[23]

And after his novel was completed, he explained to Robert Bell, who had protested against the "foul atmosphere" of, *Vanity Fair:*

If I had put in more fresh air as you call it my object would have been defeated—It is to indicate, in cheerful terms, that we are for the most part an abominably foolish and selfish people "desperately wicked" and all eager after vanities. . . . I want to leave everybody dissatisfied and unhappy at the end of the story—we ought all to be with our own and all other stories. Good God don't I see (in that may-be cracked and warped looking glass in which I am always looking) my own weaknesses wickednesses lusts follies shortcomings? . . . We must lift up our voices about these and howl to a congregation of fools: so much at least has been my endeavour.[24]

III

Thackeray's contemporaries were profoundly impressed, as we are to-day, by "the generalizing eye, the penetrative humour, and the genial breadth of sympathy"[25] which enabled him to present convincingly the immense panorama of English life that one finds in *Vanity Fair.* No doubt these qualities in themselves suffice to explain his emergence to popularity after ten years of relative neglect. But Thackeray's novel brought him prestige as well as popularity; and this prestige derived from his capacity to judge the social scene as well as to portray it. Indeed, the conception of the novelist's responsibility which informs *Vanity Fair* was the chief factor in establishing Thackeray's contemporary reputation. It freed him from the diffidence and scoffing aloofness that had previously prevented him from giving his talent free play; and it provided him with an organizing idea, about which to arrange the wealth of impressions that he had accumulated.

The proof that Thackeray's novel earned him a position, not merely as one more accomplished entertainer of the calibre of Ainsworth, Disraeli, or Bulwer-Lytton, but as a great moralist, is not far to seek. Charlotte Brontë wrote, in dedicating the second edition of *Jane Eyre* to Thackeray:

There is a man in our own days whose words are not framed for delicate ears; who, to my thinking, comes before the great ones of society, much as the son of Imlah came before the throned Kings of Judah and Israel; and who speaks truth as deep, with a power as prophet-like and as vital. . . . I see in him an intellect profounder and more unique than his contemporaries have yet recognized; because I regard him as the first social regenerator of the day—as the very master of that working corps who would restore to rectitude the warped system of things.[26]

To-day these phrases sound almost ludicrously overstrained. But we are deficient in historical understanding if we dismiss them as merely Miss Brontë's excited way. There is abundant corroborative testimony to the powerful effect of Thackeray's novel upon its first readers, from which I cite the recollections of John Cordy Jeaffreson:

> Men read those much-abused yellow pamphlets that came out month after month; and strong men, men not given to emotion, least of all to religious excitement, laid them down with tearful eyes and full hearts; and they were not a few who prayed earnestly to the Almighty for mercy and help, and rose from their knees with a determination to be men of charity.[27]

The early reviews of *Vanity Fair* everywhere reveal sluggish consciences stirred by the evidence of social corruption that Thackeray had amassed and interpreted. Harriet Martineau left *Vanity Fair* unfinished, unable to go on from "the moral disgust it occasions";[28] Miss Rigby, who persisted, declared in the *Quarterly Review* that it was "one of the most distressing books we have read for many a long year." [29] John Forster in the *Examiner* was appalled by its "exhalations of human folly and wickedness." [30] Robert Bell in *Fraser's Magazine* found it a "revolting reflex of society," which forced its readers "to look into the depths of a loathsome truth." Hogarth's "Gin Lane" did not seem to him a far-fetched comparison.[31] An anonymous reviewer in a magazine published on the continent, where the lessons of the revolutionary year 1848 loomed large for all to read, went further still. Observing that *Vanity Fair* portrays "naked and prosaic actuality which is often hideous of aspect but always true to life," he asked anxiously: "Is it advisable to raise so ruthlessly the veil which hides the rottenness pervading modern society?" [32]

IV

To inquire why Thackeray's contemporaries took *Vanity Fair* and its author so seriously is to ask in effect what was his intellectual position in his age. A modest and unassertive man, Thackeray did not regard himself as a prophet. In the words "I have no head above my eyes,"[33] he once emphatically disclaimed any capacity for abstract thought. But conceivably the very fact that his unsystematic mind found expression in attitudes rather than in theories made his opinions the more acceptable to his Victorian readers. They found in him a teacher who provided a loose but temporarily tenable synthesis of ultimately irreconcilable social standards.

This point can best be illustrated by comparing his view of fashionable society, the epitome of the small class in whose interest England was then organized and governed, with that of two fellow novelists, Disraeli and Dickens. A quarter of a century before *Vanity Fair* was written, members of the upper world hardly troubled to justify their monopoly of privilege. They displayed instead a superb disdain of conflicting interests neatly summed up in Lord Melbourne's remark that he liked the Garter, because "there was no damned merit about it." Consider, for example, Lord Orford's reply to an invitation to become President of the Norwich Bible Society in 1824:

> Sir,—I am surprised and annoyed by the contents of your letter. *Surprised,* because my well-known character should have exempted me from such an application; and *annoyed* because it compels me to have even this communication with you.
>
> I have long been addicted to the gaming table. I have lately taken to the Turf. I fear I frequently blaspheme. But I have never distributed religious tracts. All this was known to you and your society. Notwithstanding which you think me a fit person to be your President. God forgive your hypocrisy.[34]

Disraeli adopted without reserve the aristocratic attitude illustrated in the letter of this Regency grandee. Like Lockhart he thought that there was no greater pleasure than "the calm contemplation of that grand spectacle denominated 'the upper world.' It is infinitely the best of theatres, the acting is incomparably the first, the actresses the prettiest."[35] To him society was opportunity, the embodiment of the career open to the talents.

Disraeli's picture of fashionable society in *Coningsby* is cool and detached, devoid of emotional colouring or moral implications. Here is a characteristic vignette of Lord Monmouth, modelled upon the same Marquess of Hertford whom Thackeray was later to portray as Lord Steyne:

> Lord Monmouth beheld his grandson. His comprehensive and penetrating glance took in every point with a flash. There stood before

him one of the handsomest youths he had ever seen, with a mien as graceful as his countenance was captivating; and his whole air breathing that freshness and ingenuousness which none so much appreciates as the used man of the world. And this was his child; the only one of his blood to whom he had been kind. It would be exaggeration to say that Lord Monmouth's heart was touched; but his good-nature effervesced, and his fine taste was deeply gratified. He perceived in an instant such a relation might be a valuable adherent; an irresistible candidate for future elections: a brilliant tool to work out the Dukedom. All these impressions and ideas, and many more, passed through the quick brain of Lord Monmouth ere the sound of Coningsby's words had seemed to cease, and long before the surrounding guests had recovered from the surprise which they had occasioned them, and which did not diminish, when Lord Monmouth, advancing, placed his arms round Coningsby with a dignity of affection that would have become Louis XIV, and then, in the high manner of the old Court, kissed him on each cheek.[36]

Disraeli is delighted by the scene and by the actors in it. Without illusions as to Monmouth's moral worth, he yet savours all the refinements of his character, and is at pains to communicate them with delicacy. "It would be exaggeration to say that Lord Monmouth's heart was touched; but his good nature effervesced and his fine taste was deeply gratified." The sentence is that of an artist who loves his subject.

In Dickens's *Little Dorrit* we find the reverse of the medal. Dickens's radicalism had been counterbalanced in his early books by a pervasive optimism; as late as *David Copperfield* the edge of his social criticism was blunted by farce. When Mrs. Waterbrook announces over the dinner table that if she has a weakness, it is Blood, Dickens intends us to be amused, not indignant. By the time that he wrote *Little Dorrit*, however, he meant mischief. The book is an attack on "the Society business"[37] as the organizing principle of the Victorian social hierarchy. Dickens shows society bowing and scraping before "the great and wonderful Merdle," a financier whose vast operations have raised him suddenly from obscurity to celebrity. Early in the story Dickens describes a dinner party given by the great man:

There were magnates from the Court and magnates from the City, magnates from the Commons and magnates from the Lords, magnates from the bench and magnates from the bar, Bishop magnates, Treasury magnates, Horse Guard magnates, Admiralty magnates—all the magnates that keep us going, and sometimes trip us up.

"I am told," said Bishop magnate to Horse Guards, "that Mr.

Merdle has made another enormous hit. They say a hundred thousand pounds."

Horse Guards had heard two.

Treasury had heard three.

Bar, handling his persuasive double eye-glass, was by no means clear but that it might be four. It was one of those happy strokes of calculation and combination, the result of which it was difficult to estimate. It was one of those instances of a comprehensive grasp, associated with habitual luck and characteristic boldness, of which an age presented us but few. . . .

Admiralty said Mr. Merdle was a wonderful man. Treasury said he was a new power in the country, and would be able to buy up the whole House of Commons. Bishop said he was glad to think that this wealth flowed into the coffers of a gentleman who was always disposed to maintain the best interests of Society.[38]

Everyone is delighted with Merdle's success, everyone expands in its presence, except the great man himself, who is haunted by an undefined *malaise*, by a complaint for which his physician can find no cure. Not until Merdle has cut his throat in his bath near the end of the novel does Dickens reveal what has troubled this idol of "Society."

The late Mr. Merdle's complaint had been, simply, Forgery and Robbery. He, the uncouth object of such widespread adulation, the sitter at great men's feasts, the roc's egg of great ladies' assemblies, the subduer of exclusiveness, the leveller of pride, the patron of patrons, the bargain driver with a Minister for Lordships of the Circumlocution Office, the recipient of more acknowledgment within some ten or fifteen years, at most, than had been bestowed in England upon all peaceful, public benefactors, and upon all the leaders of all the Arts and Sciences, with all their works to testify for them, during two centuries at least—he, the shining wonder, the new constellation to be followed by the wise men bringing gifts, until it stopped over certain carrion at the bottom of a bath and disappeared—was simply the greatest Forger and the greatest Thief that ever cheated the gallows.[39]

The same society which delighted Disraeli bored and disgusted Dickens. Too impatient to analyse it in detail, to explore its refinements, he summed it up in terms of types and general impressions, judged it and dismissed it.

In *Vanity Fair* Thackeray steers a middle course between two extremes. Equally repugnant to him were Disraeli's amoral acceptance of the *status quo* and Dickens's destructive radicalism. His response to high life was ambivalent, his picture of it oblique. He was fascinated by the aristocratic outlook—no attitude is more often explored in his books—but he could not identify himself with it in the manner of Disraeli, for he recognized that it had become an anachronism in a prevailingly middle-class world. In describing fashionable society he took refuge in irony, which permitted him to convey at once his attraction and his repulsion, or in a professed ignorance of its ways, which made it necessary for him to rely for information on what other persons, not always reliable witnesses, had told him.

The masterly chapter entitled "Gaunt House," for example, is composed chiefly of gossip about Lord Steyne and his family communicated by sardonic old Tom Eaves, "who has no part in this history," says Thackeray, "except that he knew all the great folks in London, and the stories and mysteries of each family." [40] To complete Eaves's revelations we are accommodated with a cross-section of London opinion as to the propriety of attending Lord Steyne's entertainments:

> "Lord Steyne is really too bad," Lady Slingstone said, "but everybody goes, and of course I shall see that my girls come to no harm." "His lordship is a man to whom I owe much, everything in life," said the Right Reverend Doctor Trail, thinking that the archbishop was rather shaky; and Mrs. Trail and the young ladies would as soon have missed going to church as to one of his lordship's parties. "His morals are bad," said little Lord Southdown to his sister, who meekly expostulated, having heard terrific legends from her mamma with respect to the doings at Gaunt House; "but hang it, he's got the best dry sillery in Europe!" And as for Sir Pitt Crawley, Bart.—Sir Pitt that pattern of decorum, Sir Pitt who had led off at missionary meetings,—he never for one moment thought of not going too. "Where you see such persons as the Bishop of Ealing and the Countess of Slingstone, you may be pretty sure, Jane," the baronet would say, "that *we* cannot be wrong. The great rank and station of Lord Steyne put him in a position to command people in our station in life. The Lord Lieutenant of a county, my dear, is a respectable man." [41]

Adopting the guise of "Rumour painted full of tongues," Thackeray presents Lord Steyne and Gaunt House in perspective, with no less wit and delicacy than Disraeli displays in portraying Lord Monmouth, with no more attempt at palliation than Dickens employs in describing Merdle.

The resulting picture of high society was precisely what the intelligent Victorian reader desired. He still had, in Gladstone's phrase, "a sneaking kindness for a lord"; but he had lost his assurance in the essential rightness of the aristocratic system. Thackeray satisfied both his taste and his conscience. "Thackeray's *Vanity Fair* is pathetic in its name, and in his use of the name," Emerson wrote; "an admission it is from a man of fashion in the London of 1850 that poor old Puritan Bunyan was right in his perception of the London of 1650. And yet now in Thackeray is the added wisdom, or skepticism, that, though this be really so, he must yet live in tolerance of, and practically in homage and obedience to, these illusions." [42]

What comment on the validity of Gide's formula that "the moral issue for the artist is not that he should present an idea that is useful but that he should present an idea well" is suggested by the account which I have given of Thackeray's acceptance of moral obligation towards his readers and of the consequences of this acceptance in his career? The hazards latent in Thackeray's conflicting views became only too evident in his later work. In 1908, when Galsworthy published *Fraternity*, Conrad wrote to him of the novel:

> . . . before all it is the work of a moralist . . . a humanitarian moralist. . . . This fact which you cannot help, and which may lead you yet to become the Idol of the Public—if I may so express myself—arises as the greatest danger in the way of your art. It may prevent the concentration of effort in one simple direction—because your art will always be trying to assert itself against the impulse of your moral feelings. [43]

In the eighteen-fifties Thackeray's critics increasingly urged similar counsels upon him, but he was as incapable as Galsworthy of following such advice. And indeed, *The Virginians, Lovel the Widower* and *Philip*—whatever their other merits—oppress the reader by their tired rehearsal of moral commonplaces. In these stories the figure that Thackeray cuts as a moralist almost inclines one to regard Gide's statement as axiomatic.

But a consideration of Thackeray's finer work redresses the balance. To reread *Vanity Fair, Pendennis, Esmond* and *The Newcomes* is to understand why Henry James placed Thackeray among the novelists whom he thought of "primarily as great consciences and great minds," [44] why James Hannay admired in him "the broad sagacity, sharp insight, large and tolerant liberality, which marked him as one who was a sage as well as a story-teller, and whose stories were valuable because he was a sage." [45] In *Vanity Fair* above all Thackeray's acceptance of the novelist's responsibility was a liberating decision that immeasurably deepened his capacity for social judgment. The moral fervour which fills *Vanity Fair* with the urgency of a fresh revelation gives it a unity and intensity attained by few novels of comparable scope. Confronted by the complexity of contemporary life and by general disagreement regarding ethical presuppositions, the modern writer must no doubt leave the task of moral judgment to his readers; but he suffers as a novelist by doing so.

NOTES

1. Quoted by François Mauriac, *God and Mammon* (London, 1936), p. 58.

2. "Felix Culpa," *Commonweal*, XLVIII (July 16th, 1948), p. 323.

3. *Cornhill Magazine*, XIII (January, 1866), 48.

4. *The Letters and Private Papers of William Makepeace Thackeray*, ed. Ray, 4 volumes (Cambridge, Mass., 1945–46), II, 258. Cited hereafter as *Letters*.

5. *Letters*, II, 312n.

6. *Letters and Memorials of Jane Welsh Carlyle*, ed. James Anthony Froude, 3 volumes (London, 1883), II, 3.

7. *Letters*, II, 333.

8. "Thackeray," *Macmillan's Magazine*, IX (February, 1864), 356.

9. *Letters Literary and Theological* (London, 1881), p. 93.

10. Rowland Grey, "Thackeray and France (With an Unpublished Thackeray Letter)," *Englishwoman*, XXXVII (May, 1918), 112–13.

11. *Letters*, II, 316.

12. *Horae Subsecivae, Third Series* (Edinburgh, 1884), p. 180.

13. "Lever's St. Patrick's Eve—Comic Politics," *Morning Chronicle*, April 3rd, 1845.

14. *Letters*, II, 54.

15. *Works*, ed. Saintsbury, 17 volumes (London, 1908), V, 91–92.

16. *Works*, IX, 493.

17. *Letters*, II, 282.

18. *Letters*, II, 197.

19. *Letters*, II, 210.

20. *Letters*, II, 255.

21. *Works*, XI, 96.

22. *Works*, XI, 102–03.

23. *Letters*, II, 309.

24. *Letters*, II, 423–24.

25. H. D. Trail, *The New Fiction and Other Essays on Literary Subjects* (London, 1897), p. 169.

26. Two volumes (Oxford, 1931), I, ix–x.

27. *Novels and Novelists from Elizabeth to Victoria*, 2 volumes (London, 1858), II, 279.

28. *Autobiography*, ed. Maria Webster, 2 volumes (Boston, 1877), II, 60.

29. *Vanity Fair*—and *Jane Eyre*, LXXXIV (December, 1848), 155.

30. *Vanity Fair*, July 22nd, 1848, 468.

31. *Vanity Fair*, XXXVIII (September, 1848), 321–22.

32. Quoted from the *Magazin für die Litteratur des Auslandes* in the Readers' Classics edition of *Vanity Fair* (Bath, 1919), p. 61.

33. Reported by George Curtis, *Harper's Magazine*, VIII (May, 1854), 840.

34. Quoted by Sir Algernon West, *Recollections*, 2 volumes (London, 1899), I, 26–27.

35. Quoted by Andrew Lang, *The Life and Letters of John Gibson Lockhart*, 2 volumes (London, 1897), II, 82–83.

36. Book Four, chapter 6; *Works*, 12 volumes (London, 1927), VIII, 195–96.

37. *Letters of Charles Dickens*, ed. Walter Dexter, 3 volumes (London, 1938), II, 766.

38. Book the First, chapter 21; *Complete Works* (London, 1901–02), XVI, 300–01.

39. Book the Second, chapter 25; *Complete Works*, XVI, 835.

40. *Works*, XI, 90.

41. *Works*, XI, 597.

42. *Journals*, ed. E. W. Emerson and W. E. Forbes, 10 volumes (London, 1913), VIII, 113–14.

43. Quoted by H. V. Marrot, *Life and Letters of John Galsworthy* (London, 1935), p. 229.

44. *French Poets and Novelists* (London, 1878), p. 113.

45. *Brief Memoir of the Late Mr. Thackeray* (Edinburgh, 1864), p. 22.

BRADFORD A. BOOTH

———◆———

Trollope's *Orley Farm:* Artistry *Manqué*

I DO not know that anyone at all sympathetic to the Victorian novel has ever failed to like Trollope's *Orley Farm*. At all events, no unfavorable reaction has been recorded. Trollope thought the plot his best, and when he began to list the well-drawn characters, he could not stop much short of a total roll call. There is not, he says, "a dull page in the book." Such prideful language, so uncommon for Trollope that it is found nowhere else, is almost, if not quite, justified. On this occasion he had, as Henry James saw, an "admirable subject." It is one that not only suited perfectly his own mature temper but gave him a welcome opportunity to skirt certain mid-Victorian clichés and conventions in the design and development of a novel. The result is that *Orley Farm* is one of Trollope's richest and most satisfying books. If, like *The Last Chronicle of Barset*, it fails to attain true greatness, the failure is in large part the measure of his incomplete break with the familiar stereotypes of plotting.

When in 1862 Trollope published *Orley Farm* the Victorian sensation novel was sweeping everything before it. *The Woman in White* had created a taste for melodrama which *Lady Audley's Secret* was currently satisfying. Trollope, of course, cared for neither the premises nor the methods of the sensation novelist, but as a businessman writer, conscious of public demand, he was not above compromises and concessions. These he was able to make very skillfully without abandoning his position as a realist. In *Doctor Thorne* he had indeed come perilously close to giving way to sensationalism in adopting his brother's

From *From Jane Austen to Joseph Conrad,* edited by Robert C. Rathburn and Martin Steinmann, Jr. (pp. 146–59). University of Minnesota Press. Copyright 1958, University of Minnesota. Reprinted by permission of the publisher and the author.

idea of a good plot, but in *Orley Farm* the danger is minimal. Though there is an ample quota of story interest, the novel is essentially a study of character.

Some years later, when he wrote his *Autobiography*, Trollope expressed fear that he had shown his hand too soon, needlessly sacrificing suspense. The plot, he said, "has the fault of declaring itself, and thus coming to an end too early in the book." It is true that we learn of Lady Mason's guilt very quickly, and at least one critic has suggested that the trial is vulnerable to the "charge of anticlimax." But this is quite to misunderstand Trollope's basic intent. A novel whose interest turns on discovering whether or not a forgery has been committed would be thoroughly un-Trollopian. The question of Lady Mason's guilt is not really at issue, any more than is the question whether or not in *The Last Chronicle* Josiah Crawley stole a cheque for £20. These novels do not have their *raison d'être* in the solving of a mystery. In *Lady Audley's Secret*, however, there is no interest whatever beyond that which may be found in discovering at last that George Talboys was pushed down a well by his wife and left for dead.

Early in *Barchester Towers* Trollope invites the reader to turn to the last chapter, confident that such interest as his novel possesses does not rest on twists of plot. He might have made the same statement on behalf of *Orley Farm*, for again he breaks the Victorian stereotype by deliberately foregoing the interest that attaches to surprise. Lady Mason is guilty; indeed she soon avows her guilt to Sir Peregrine Orme. The power of the novel arises not from the shock of the unexpected, but from the skill with which Trollope explores the tenacity of a woman who will dare all for her son and who will break upon the rack of neither conscience nor the public tribunal. Trollope's main plot, secured and sustained by tensions of its own, needed no help from adventitious maneuverings and manipulations.

Unfortunately, however, Trollope's independence of the tradition does not extend beyond the main plot. In *The Last Chronicle*, which should have been one of the triumphs of the novel, the patiently accumulated effects are scattered by the introduction of three separate sub-plots, only one of which has any relevancy or interest. Collectively they tend to disperse the emotion that gathers sympathetically around the figure of Josiah Crawley, the tragic hero whose fatal flaw is pride of self. In *Orley Farm* one's attention is constantly diverted, by a series of minor characters and issues, from the only matter of importance, the wretchedness of Lady Mason, the tragic heroine whose fatal flaw is ambition for her son. It is not germane to the issue that we should be made intimate with the economy of Groby Park, the legal reformations of Von Bauhr, or the marital hesitancies of John Kenneby. All this is egregious make-weight, as are the four chapters describing the Christmas festivities at Harley Street, Noningsby, Groby Park, and Great St. Helens.

A splinter of plot which calls for fuller comment is the episode (and its many ramifications) of Mr. Moulder, Mr Kantwise, and the commercial gentlemen of the Bull Inn. The Victorian stereotype demanded that a somber story be offset by a certain amount of high jinks. Trollope does not always oblige, but here, having pulled pretty heavily on the tragic bow, he let fly a shower of arrows from a lighter weapon. The tyrannical Mr. Moulder, baiting Samuel Dockwrath over the wine bill, and entertaining his dinner guests with affecting recollections of his father's early apoplexy, is a lively sketch, as is Mr. Kantwise, the traveling salesman for the Iron Furniture Co., specializing in designs of the Louis Quatorze pattern. Trollope was pleased with what he had done ("Mr. Moulder carves his turkey admirably, and Mr. Kantwise sells his tables and chairs with spirit"), and indeed Dickensian ghosts are raised in a very substantial form. But the pungent air of warehouse and pub which clings to these amusing vulgarians has offended some delicate critical sensibilities. George Eliot, who thought Trollope "admirable in the presentation of even average life and character," wrote Sara Hennell that she liked *Orley Farm* very much, "with the exception of such parts as I have read about Moulder & Co." She does not much further the cause of realism when she adds, "he [Trollope] is so thoroughly wholesome-minded that one delights in seeing his books lie about to be read."

More important than the clutch of commercial gentlemen and their relatives, who in no way forward any issue of importance, are the Staveleys and the Furnivals. Madeline Staveley, together with her suitors Felix Graham and Peregrine Orme, represents Trollope's reluctant acquiescence in the stereotype of the Victorian love story. There is no doubt a large measure of irony in Trollope's statement that Madeline "shall, to many of my readers, be the most interesting personage in this story." The heroine, he had acknowledged earlier, must "by a certain fixed law be young and marriageable." Lady Mason, of course, could not qualify. Yet in the final chapter, as he bids farewell to Lady Mason, he admits, "as we do so the chief interest of our tale will end." Clearly, therefore, the love story is for those who must have it, not for Anthony Trollope.

The participants in this sentimental drama act out another Victorian cliché. Felix Graham is represented as a brilliant young lawyer who writes for the literary reviews. But his family is unknown, he has no funds, he is ugly, and he has contracted a quixotic engagement with the unimaginative daughter of a sniveling alcoholic. These things mean nothing to Madeline, who, burning with true love, rejects the addresses of Peregrine Orme, a suitable young man and her mother's favorite. Felix is the familiar Trollopian hero who with no other gift than mother wit triumphs over his more favored rival. As for Madeline, she is the apotheosis of the Victorian heroine: demure and self-effacing, yet warm and loyal. Unfortunately, however, she is dull. But the self-seeking Sophia Furnival, set up as foil to Madeline, is lively and amusing. By his allegiance to the formula Trollope very nearly forfeits sympathy for his sweet but rather colorless heroine. Sophia's father, as Lady Mason's chief legal adviser, has his necessary place in the general framework, but his domestic misunderstandings and the intrusions of the officious Miss Biggs are the most obvious filler. In such a novel as *Orley Farm*, which is the story of Lady Mason, nothing should have been permitted to deflect attention from her bitter problem. But Trollope fractioned his plot in deference to the Victorian stereotype of the huge, baggy monster. The inexorable demand for three volumes could not be refused, and the temper and experience of the reading public, still largely feminine and clerical, did not permit the close situational studies through which James imposed order on chaos.

As a realist and anti-sensationalist, Trollope cared so little for details of plotting that he appears to have relied not on design but on the inspiration of the moment to carry him over difficulties. Even in so extraordinary a circumstance as the stealing of the Eustace diamonds there seems to have been no forethought. It is significant that the fragmentary outlines from which Trollope worked when engaged on a novel consist only of thumb-nail sketches of the characters. Once launched, they were expected to create by the expression of their own personalities such movement of the plot as might be required. Uncommitted by necessities of plotting, Trollope was free to let his characters develop naturally, and to bend in response to the pressure of people and events. Indeed, his own attitude toward them remained flexible. One of the most extraordinary confessions in fiction must be Trollope's admission in the last pages of *Orley Farm* that in the telling of his story his concept of his central character had undergone a radical change.

Trollope's concern in *Orley Farm,* and in others of his most thoughtful novels, is not with what happens but with its effect upon the individuals most directly involved. Thus, in *The Warden-Barchester Towers* (it is useful to think of them as a single novel) Trollope interests himself in the analysis of a situation: the effect upon Septimus Harding, a man of impeccable honor, of the suggestion that his tenure of a sinecure is ethically indefensible. In *The Last Chronicle* it is the effect upon the Reverend Josiah Crawley, a man of stern, almost forbidding, rectitude, of the charge that he has stolen a sizable cheque. In *Orley Farm* it is the effect upon Lady Mason, an essentially good, if misguided, woman, of the growing certainty that she has ruined not only her own life but, more importantly, that of her son.

The three characters just named are, in my opinion, the best that Trollope created. By "best" I mean, of course, not the most colorful or most amusing or most ingratiating, but those through whom he got beneath the topsoil of superficial manners to the bedrock of fundamental human emotions. It should be noted that one is an old man and the other two are middle-aged. When Trollope broke through the stereotype love story, he did his most significant writing. It is quite possible, of course, to probe deeply into man's basic responses through the study of young love. We learn much of what is fundamental in human nature by observing Elizabeth Bennet's discovery of her lesser self, Maggie Tulliver's lack of perfect self-discipline, Marty South's unwavering devotion in the face of neglect. But Trollope's young people take us into no new areas of self-knowledge, nor is it through them that he tries to enlarge the boundaries of man's sympathies.

Such sharpened perceptions as Trollope can give us of the dignity and the power of life, of its abnegations and renunciations, its terrors and humiliations, come through characters of mature years. The drama of young love did not move him greatly. His own life in this regard seems to have been singularly equable and serene. There is no evidence that he experienced either the ecstasy or the anguish of love. A realist who neither depreciated nor deified women, he wasted no emotion in Shelleyan longing for the unattainable. He preferred a plain girl of common sense to one of supernal beauty who was, to use his favorite adjective, "strong-minded." However wise such views may be, they do not suggest that the possessor will satisfy the taste for romance which largely determined the nature of the mid-Victorian novel. Trollope's observations of what is significant in life simply did not frame themselves in terms of young love.

It should also be remarked that Trollope came to the novel relatively late, with settled, middle-aged views of the decorum of life and of its ultimate values. *Orley Farm* is an early Trollope novel, but it was written in the author's forty-sixth year. In it there is a passage which beautifully exemplifies the harmony and composure of his life at this time, and emphasizes his conviction that while youth is beset with uncertainties and old age with infirmities, middle-age is ripe and golden.

> There is great doubt as to what may be the most enviable time of life with a man. I am inclined to think that it is at that period when his children have all been born but have not yet begun to go astray or to vex him with disappointment; when his own pecuniary prospects are settled, and he knows pretty well what his tether will allow him; when the appetite is still good and the digestive organs at their full power; when he has ceased to care as to the length of his girdle, and before the doctor warns him against solid breakfasts and port wine after dinner; when his affectations are over and his infirmities have not yet come upon him; while he can still walk his ten miles, and feel some little pride in being able to do so; while he has still nerve to ride his horse to hounds, and can look with some scorn on the ignorance of younger men who have hardly yet learned that noble art. (Ch. LIX)

These are the sentiments of a man who will not put his heart into a recital of the charms of romantic love but who may illuminate sympathetically and understandingly the psychology of maturity.

Lady Mason, in whom is reflected the intensity with which the older characters are perceived, is one of the triumphs of Trollope's art, and one of the most moving characters of Victorian fiction. She is a forger, and has carried the gnawing secret of her guilt for twenty years, yet she is a good woman. The nature of the circumstances under which the crime was committed are such that only the sternest moralist would turn his face from Lady Mason, and only the most bitterly vindictive would pursue her with retributive justice. Sir Joseph Mason cared little for his wife and nothing for his younger son, for whom he refused to make provision in his will. Lady Mason's act, therefore, in protecting the legitimate rights and interests of her child, enforces rather than violates the equities involved. Trollope further establishes sympathy for his embattled heroine by ranging against her a set of despicable antagonists: Joseph Mason of Groby Park, a shallow man without sensibility, sourly nursing his grievances over the years (Trollope calls him "a bad man in that he could never forget and never forgave"); and Samuel Dockwrath, a prideful country lawyer, narrowly self-seeking, repudiating the friendly instincts of his wife in the pursuit of a petty revenge. The lines of antagonism are well drawn here, and the moral issue is an engaging one.

Ultimately, the law declares Lady Mason "Not Guilty." But there are few, even among outsiders, who do not regard the verdict as a Scottish "Not Proved." The bullying of the skillful Chaffanbrass and the eloquence of Mr. Furnival have carried everything before them. As for the wretched victim, she has not escaped, and the laws of compensation have not been abrogated. The devoted but misguided mother, who has risked all for a son who turns out to be a rather objectionable prig, opinionated and willful, suffers on earth the tortures that are promised the erring in hell. Trollope never loses his firm hold upon character and situation, nor does he fail to engage our sympathies powerfully on behalf of his very human protagonist.

The extent to which Trollope succeeds in immersing his readers in Lady Mason's shattered life is measured by the credibility of the love between her and Sir Peregrine Orme. The relationship between the gallant old gentleman (whose characterization owes something to Colonel Newcome?) and the by no means young widow was fraught artistically with the gravest perils. One false word and the whole structure of this pathetic affair would come tumbling down. The word is not given, and the dignity of the episode is preserved. Though Lady Mason recognizes that the unimpeachable honor of Sir Peregrine's name will provide her with the sheet anchor of support she desperately needs, she cannot at last sacrifice the old man. Instead, she sacrifices herself—and all she has fought for—by confessing. It is not simply a theatrical gesture, it is a total relinquishment, placed on the altar of affection and respect by nobility. The moment of her confession is conceived with great art and executed with a sensitiveness and balance that is quite beyond praise.

Two scenes following upon Lady Mason's confession indicate the power that Trollope has when he meets an emotional situation squarely and the depth of his failure when he avoids it or passes it off conventionally. When Lady Mason leaves Sir Peregrine, knowing that she has sealed her future in the blackness of disgrace and irrevocable misery, she retires to her room at his suggestion and sitting on the bed, her teeth chattering both from the bitter midwinter cold and from nervous exhaustion, casts up the self-abasements of a future irredeemably desolate. The many critics, Victorian and modern, who have charged against Trollope the inability to picture tragedy without shrillness or calculated sentiment, have forgotten this terrible scene. Yet after such an artistic triumph Trollope contrives a moment later that Lady Mason should be visited by Edith Orme, who offers a few words of consolation and forgiveness.

> Many will think that she was wrong to do so, and I fear it must be acknowledged that she was not strong minded. By forgiving her I do not mean that she pronounced absolution for the sin of past years, or that she endeavoured to make the sinner think that she was no worse for her sin. Mrs. Orme was a good churchwoman but not strong, individually, in points of doctrine. All that she left mainly to the woman's conscience and her own dealings with her Saviour,—merely saying a word of salutary counsel as to a certain spiritual pastor who might be of aid. (Ch. XLV)

This is disappointing. Trollope has shirked his task, first by giving us through summary a scene that should have been dramatic, and second, by straddling the moral problem. The truth is, of course, that Trollope had no consistent view of his character. Lady Mason was never intended to be evil, but there is an evident change after her guilt is established that cannot be accounted for solely in terms of the deepening of her nature. The change is in Trollope's attitude toward her. Hester Prynne is shown to have become through her sin more thoughtful, more tolerant, more spiritual. Lady Mason's character, however, is relatively constant. Trollope has led us to a kindlier view because he has himself become more sympathetic.

> I may, perhaps, be thought to owe an apology to my readers in that I have asked their sympathy for a woman who had so sinned as to have placed her beyond the general sympathy of the world at large. If so, I tender my apology, and perhaps feel that I should confess a fault. But as I have told her story that sympathy has grown upon myself till I have learned to forgive her, and to feel that I too could have regarded her as a friend. (Ch. LXXIX)

In the middle of the novel, however, he is not sure of Lady Mason. Consequently, he is careful to take the conventional ethical point of view.

It is highly probable that in the climatic scenes of Lady Mason's agony Trollope's mind reverted, consciously or unconsciously, to another notable moment of retribution. Unique among nineteenth-century novelists for his knowledge of the old drama, Trollope was one of England's keenest amateur students of the Elizabethan and Jacobean theater. He had a first-rate collection of the period's best plays, 257 of which he annotated with critical remarks, still unfortunately unpublished. Among plays he read at least twice is Marlowe's

Doctor Faustus, which seems to have cut deeply into his mind. Certainly there are more parallels between *Orley Farm* and *Doctor Faustus* than can be accounted for by mere coincidence. This is especially true of the final scenes of the novel, in which one hears palpable and extended echoes of Faustus's last agony and torment.

Both play and novel bring forward centrally a mature person whose essentially noble ambition is carried to criminal lengths: in Faustus the desire for mastery which comes through knowledge, in Lady Mason the world's recognition for her son. In both play and novel the author resorts to a curiously archaic mode of embodying the evil impulse to crime. Marlowe's tragedy is strongly reminiscent of the morality plays which flourished at least half a century before his time, and the bright figure of his Mephistopheles never quite conceals the standard primitive devil beneath. Trollope maintains a running current of stock devil imagery to express not only the evil of Lady Mason's deed but also the inevitability of its disclosure. Her mind runs to such images as that of "the beast [which] had set its foot upon her," and the archfiend is always appearing to her mind in a visible form:

> The black unwelcome guest . . . had ever been present to her; but she had seen it indistinctly, and now and then the power had been hers to close her eyes. Never again could she close them. Nearer to her, and still nearer, the spectre came; and now it sat upon her pillow, and put its claw upon her plate; it pressed her bosom with its fiendish strength, telling her that all was over for her in this world:—ay, and telling her worse even than that. (Ch. LIII)

Just as the forces of evil find in both works a symbolic expression, so do the forces of good: Lady Mason's staunch friend, Mrs. Orme, not less than Faustus's Good Angel, is an almost disembodied voice which cries, "Repent, repent, and be saved." The parallels extend even to small details. Just as the two greatest scenes of *Doctor Faustus* take place in the darkness of night, so do most of the scenes of Lady Mason's crime and punishment. Just as Faustus's impulse to the crime finds culminating expression in the signing of the bond, so Lady Mason's impulse culminates in the signing of the will, and, as Trollope's plot unfolds, we see that Lady Mason, no less than Faustus himself, had signed with her heart's blood. Again, just as "for vaine pleasure of 24 yeares . . . Faustus lost eternall ioy and felicitee," so the period of Lady Mason's vain pleasure covered the same span: "She had lived in this house for some four-and-twenty years." It is significant that this figure rose to Trollope's mind as he was portraying one of the most horrible moments of Lady Mason's suffering, for he elsewhere makes it clear that actually only twenty years had elapsed between her forgery and the confession to her son.

Faustus's torment reaches its height in his unforgettable last speech, which apparently inspired Trollope in his moving portrayal of Lady Mason's almost unendurable agony.

> There are [says Trollope] periods in the lives of some of us—I trust but of a few—when with the silent inner voice of suffering we call on the mountains to fall and crush us, and on the earth to gape open and take us in. (Ch. XLV)

Just so had Faustus cried:

> Mountaines and hilles, come, come and fall on me,
> And hide me from the heauy wrath of God.
> No, no.
> Then wil I headlong runne into the earth:
> Earth gape. O no, it wil not harbour me.

And Trollope continues:

> When, with an agony of intensity, we wish that our mothers had been barren. In those moments, the poorest and most desolate are objects to us of envy, for their sufferings can be as nothing to our own.

So Faustus:

> This soule should flie from me, and I be changde
> Vnto some brutish beast: al beasts are happy,
> For when they die,
> Their soules are soone dissolud in elements,
> But mine must liue to be plagde in hel:
> Curst be the parents that ingendred me.

(For recognition and development of the *Orley Farm-Doctor Faustus* parallel I am indebted to my colleague Professor Hugh G. Dick of the University of California at Los Angeles.)

The moment toward which the action of *Orley Farm* moves is Lady Mason's trial. Since Trollope shares with Dickens and Wilkie Collins a vital interest in the law, frequently making legal matters of the greatest importance in the resolution of his plots, it may be appropriate here to consider the role of the lawyer in *Orley Farm* and, by way of comparison and contrast, in a few other novels. There are eleven jury trials in Trollope's novels, and, additionally, the interpretation of the law is a basic plot concern in *The Warden, Doctor Thorne, Is He*

Popenjoy?, *Cousin Henry*, and, especially, *Mr. Scarborough's Family*. In none of these do the lawyers carry the burden of the main plot. Either through lack of acquaintance with the legal mind and character (which considering Trollope's experience is not likely) or through a conviction that lawyers do not lend themselves well to the fictional purposes he favored, Trollope does not allow them to become the chief actors in the drama. Unlike his clergymen, they serve, in general, only "to swell a progress, start a scene or two."

One exception to the adjunctive role for the lawyer is the inimitable Mr. Chaffanbrass, who is more sharply conceived than any barrister in Dickens. Much has been written about the transcendent merits of Bardell *v.* Pickwick. To at least one observer the three court appearances of Mr. Chaffanbrass (in *The Three Clerks, Orley Farm*, and *Phineas Redux*) are in another and higher echelon of excellence. Trollope's characterization is here more subtle, his humor more pervasive. Chaffanbrass does not escape completely, perhaps, from the stereotype of the shrewd criminal lawyer whose inquisitorial deftness can break down in cross-examination the testimony of the most confident witness, but he is carefully individualized. The slovenly little figure in a rumpled suit, with wig askew, picking his teeth and taking large quantities of snuff remains a memorable characterization. Trollope satisfied himself with the laconic remark, "I do not think that I have cause to be ashamed of him."

There are a few other lawyers, as well, who escape being typed into familiar patterns: Thomas Furnival, dignified defender of Lady Mason, master of direct severity and concealed sarcasm; Samuel Camperdown, aggressive representative of the Eustace interests; Gregory Masters, devoted guardian of the Morton properties; Thomas Toogood, patient adviser to the exasperating Josiah Crawley; and John Grey, harassed attorney for the violent and unpredictable Mr. Scarborough. It might be difficult, however, to add appreciably to this list, even though the lawyers in Trollope's novels number well over one hundred. The frequency of their appearance indicates the delight which Trollope took in introducing them, but the vast majority shade off from indistinct background figures to mere names. These very names—Mr. Allewinde, John Cheekey, Neversay Die, Mr. Gitemthruit, Sir Abraham Haphazard, George Stickatit, *et al.*—make it clear that many, if not most, of the lawyers are conceived as humour characters, exploited for satiric, ironic, or humorous purposes. But the intense seriousness of the *Orley Farm* trial precludes Pickwickian high jinks of the Serjeant Buzfuz variety.

It is clear from several remarks in *Orley Farm* that Trollope was acutely aware of the chicanery of the law and inclined to emphasize what he thought to be a general opportunism and lack of idealism in the profession. Mr. Furnival is represented as defending Lady Mason with eloquence and apparent sincerity:

> And yet as he sat down he knew that she had been guilty! To his ear her guilt had never been confessed; but yet he knew that it was so, and, knowing that, he had been able to speak as though her innocence were a thing of course. That those witnesses had spoken truth he also knew, and yet he had been able to hold them up to the execration of all around them as though they had committed the worst of crimes from the foulest of motives! And more than this, stranger than this, worse than this,—when the legal world knew—as the legal world soon did know—that all this had been so, the legal world found no fault with Mr. Furnival, conceiving that he had done his duty by his client in a manner becoming an English barrister and an English gentleman. (Ch. LXXII)

Earlier Trollope had observed: "I cannot understand how any gentleman can be willing to use his intellect for the propagation of untruth, and to be paid for so using it." Mr. Furnival was, of course, no shyster, but the legal fraternity, by and large, is not attractively presented by Trollope. The unprincipled Hyacinth Keegan, the unspeakable Moylan, the scheming Samuel Dockwrath, the mean-looking Squercum, the grasping Scruby—these are disagreeable people. If it be objected that it is unfair to assume Trollope's judgment of a group on the basis of its renegades, one must answer that among a hundred lawyers there is not one of such large-souled benevolence that he can be taken to one's heart. In *Orley Farm* only Judge Staveley, who does not appear in his legal capacity, and Felix Graham, who is shown to be a frustrated man of letters, are presented sympathetically.

The issues involved in Lady Mason's trial are so grave, and the scenes are described with such patient care, that critics have taken the legal action very seriously. The early reviews were very hard on Trollope for alleged misunderstanding of judicial procedures, and the substance of these attacks was repeated and developed in *Out of Court* (1925), a volume of essays by the distinguished jurist Sir Francis Newbolt, whose caustic remarks have been faithfully repeated by all subsequent critics. In the last few years, however, two American lawyers have come stoutly to Trollope's defense. Henry S. Drinker in "The Lawyers of Anthony Trollope" says, "Numerous strictures on its legal accuracy to the contrary notwithstanding, *Orley Farm* will be found, on careful examination, to be remarkably free from legal mistakes, except for occasional slips in small matters purely technical, such as would naturally be expected and are readily excusable in a novelist." Clement F. Robinson in "Trollope's Jury Trials" studies the proceedings at length and concludes:

> Looking at the report of Lady Mason's case as a whole, I should say that it is more accurate than the usual newspaper account of a trial. . . . I am impressed with the few errors that Trollope seems to have made in English procedure, and am inclined to believe that the trial might have taken place in the United States just as Trollope reports it, except in a few minor respects.

Two Harvard law professors, the late Zechariah Chafee, Jr. and John M. Maguire, chose *Orley Farm* as one of ninety books to be read by all law students, recommending it as "a will case with a notable cross-examination."

Orley Farm is a characteristic Victorian novel. Its many-faceted plot is kept more rigorously under control than is traditional, and the tensions of the principal action are maintained with what is, for Trollope, unaccustomed tautness. The problem considered is worthy of a serious artist, and its resolution develops expectancy and invokes pity. If, as I believe, *The Last Chronicle* is a more satisfactory performance, the measure of its superiority must be sought in its leading character. *Orley Farm* fails, in part, because there is no greatness in Lady Mason. Her strength, and it is considerable, is exerted in support of a morally indefensible position. Her moment of renunciation is bitter indeed, but the pity she arouses is tempered by a recognition of her palpable weakness. Josiah Crawley, by contrast, though foundering in his social relationships because of grievous personality faults, has a nobility of soul that makes him a genuinely and impressively tragic figure. But the plot of *The Last Chronicle* is flawed beyond redemption. Each of these two novels, then, has what the other lacks; and Trollope, unable to bring all his powers to a focus in a single novel, left no perfect work of art.

Henry James has told us that a superior novel can be produced only by a fine intelligence, and the point is not likely to be disputed. At this level of criticism, perhaps, the case for Trollope breaks down. He was shrewd, observant, humorous, kindly, tolerant, sympathetic—a man of uncommon common sense; but his mind was not subtle or profoundly creative. That inability to make fine distinctions with which some of his contemporaries charged him was part of a nature not gifted philosophically. The highest reaches of the novel were thus denied him. But still open was a middle ground in which his lively imagination could function effectively. Here, as a home base, he pitched his tent firmly; and striking out across green meadows he wandered into Barsetshire. In *Orley Farm*, still avoiding main-traveled roads, he idled happily among some of the most fascinating people in English fiction.

SELECTIVE INDEX